THE BANJO

THE BANJO

America's African Instrument

LAURENT DUBOIS

THE BELKNAP PRESS OF HARVARD UNIVERSITY PRESS

Cambridge, Massachusetts, and London, England

2016

First printing

Library of Congress Cataloging-in-Publication Data

Dubois, Laurent, 1971– author.

  The banjo : America's African instrument / Laurent Dubois.

    pages cm

  Includes bibliographical references and index.

  ISBN 978-0-674-04784-6 (alk. paper)

  1. Banjo—History. 2. Banjo music—History and criticism. 3. African Americans—Music—History and criticism. 4. Music—Social aspects—United States. 5. Music—United States—History and criticism. I. Title.

  ML1015.B3D83 2016

  787.8'81909—dc23

2015031048

FOR ANTON

Contents

THE BANJO

Introduction

The banjo has had many names.

Banza	Banjar	Kitt
Bangier	Banja	Bangil
Bonja	Strum strum	Bonjour
Banjaw	Banjou	African bango
Banjah	Bangoe	Merrywang
Bonjoo	Bandjo	Banjee
Creole bania	Bonjaw	Banjor
Congo banjo	Banza nèg Guinée	

But they all name one sound: the sound of strings humming over skin. That is the sound a banjo makes, the sound that defines it. That sound has accompanied songs and stories, consoled lonely souls, and electrified crowds. It has had many meanings: it is the sound of Africa, the sound of slavery, the sound of blackness, the sound of progress, the sound of protest—the sound of America. But most of all, the banjo has been the sound of solidarity, of gathering in the midst of exile, of being together and in so doing being able to recount the past and imagine a future. This book is about that sound.

When you step back and take a good look, the banjo is a rather strange concoction. A drum on a stick, it might be called. But the stick is a neck. And the neck has that odd peg sticking out of the top to hold a little short string. And the drumhead itself requires elaborate tacks or screws or brackets to hold it together. More often than not, banjos hum and buzz. They get out of tune, it seems, just to cause a hassle. When they are in tune, it isn't always obvious. And people can't quite agree on what "in tune" means on the banjo in any case. How did it end up so strange? And why, even though it is so strange, have so many people persisted in picking it up and playing it? How is it that this awkward kid has ended up one of the great stars of musical life in the Americas?

The banjo's journey—from its African inspirations, to its Caribbean and North American invention, through its humming in a bewildering array of music movements and forms—is our journey. In this curious instrument lives a history of American culture, a culture born out of the layered encounters between Africa, Europe, and the diverse societies of the Americas, from north to south. This is a story about its unexpected appearance in unlikely places, where it turns out to be just what is needed. And so it is befitting to begin our journey through the banjo's history in an unexpected place: not in the Appalachian Mountains or the Piedmont or New Orleans or Philadelphia, but rather on the banks of the Mediterranean, sometime in the 1920s.

Wandering the port town of Marseilles with a ragtag group of men from Senegal, the Caribbean, and the United States, Lincoln Agrippa Daily makes what little money he can by playing the banjo. But the instrument is more than his livelihood; it is his identity. His friends call him "Banjo"; and, caressing the instrument, he declares that he will never part with it: it is more than "a gal, moh than a pal; it's mahself."[1]

Banjo, the eponymous main character of a novel published in 1929 by Claude McKay, is "a child of the Cotton Belt" who has "wandered all over America": his life is "a dream of vagabondage that he was perpetually pursuing and realizing in odd ways, always incomplete but never unsatisfactory." Wanting to go to Europe, he "hit upon the unique plan of getting himself deported." The problem was convincing immigration officials that he was a foreigner. "They had all been thunderstruck when he calmly announced that he was not American. Everything about him— accent, attitude, movement—shouted Dixie." Despite his insistence on his foreign "parentage," he could "never convince any American, especially a Southern-knowing one, that he was no Aframerican." The immigration officials nevertheless helped him find passage on a boat headed across the Atlantic, which dropped him in Marseilles.[2]

McKay, one of the great writers of the Harlem Renaissance, was born in Jamaica and traveled a great deal in Europe and North Africa. In his poetry and novels, he tried to capture the dramas, humor, and struggles of the far-flung African diaspora. In *Banjo,* inspired by his time in Marseille and completed in Morocco, he found a way to use the instrument as the perfect symbol for the history of wanderings and encounters that had connected Africa, the Americas, and Europe. The instrument from which McKay's character got his name has long followed its own "dream of vagabondage," which it has realized in "odd ways," changing shape and sound across time and space. Like the characters in his novel, the instrument is difficult to pin down. It is rooted everywhere and nowhere in particular. Is it American? African? Caribbean? African-American? Is it southern? White? Rural? For all its untethered movement and circulation—or perhaps because of it—it is nevertheless an instrument that *seems* (just like McKay's character) to be fundamentally "America's instrument," which is what its late nineteenth-century boosters called it. Trying to deport it from our culture would be a joke. And yet it is an instrument with no birth certificate. It has seemed fundamentally at home in so many places because it is truly at home nowhere.

This book is a biography of the banjo. Its protagonist is the instrument itself, its plot the story of the complicated and layered meanings that resonated out of the instrument over the centuries. It is the story of an instrument with character, character deeply grounded in a range of contexts, but one that (thankfully) cannot really be pinned down.

McKay understood that the banjo *is* in fact a perfect object through which we can understand the meaning of what is "American," precisely because it has its roots in the institution that was, for hundreds of years, the central pillar of the American economy: slavery. It is so deeply American because, like the slaves who crossed the Atlantic from Africa, it was uprooted. The banjo embodies a story of crossings and exchanges that go far beyond the mainland United States, highlighting the constant connections between the Caribbean and North America in a world shaped by plantation slavery. It is at once African, Caribbean, and North American, its history a cartography that respects no national borders, but rather maps a story of unruly movement and unpredictable encounters. By following the banjo, we get a privileged view of American history as a crossroads, a story defined as much by the intensive exchange between cultures as by a profound, violent, and ongoing set of struggles between the communities that ultimately collaborated in creating its sound.

The history of the banjo begins in Africa, in the long and deep tradition of stringed instruments that were the foundation for instrument. But the instrument's New World origins were the result of the encounter, convergence, and ultimate solidarity among a diverse range of African peoples in exile in the Americas. Through its history, we dwell in the American experience of slavery: the passage of many millions from Africa to the Americas; the lives they lived on the ships and in the towns and plantations of the Americas; and the forms of communal and cultural imagination that were, somewhat miraculously, cultivated within the interstices of that system. The banjo was the first "African" instrument, a result of the need for music that could bring together diverse peoples from different parts of the continent in the midst of exile and oppression. The banjo succeeded in this context by being an African instrument in a general sense without being specifically tied to one or another group.

That a unique instrument would emerge from this experience is, in a sense, not surprising. For this was a unique moment in world history: never before or since have so many people, speaking so many different languages and carrying so many cultures, been forced into the kind of brutal conditions and life as those suffered on the plantations of the Americas. How were those who found themselves in this strange and overwhelming new world to interpret, express, and document their experience? How, in the midst of many languages and points of reference, were they to find a way to share their pain, mourning, struggle, and resistance? The responses to those questions ended up laying the foundation for much of the musical culture of the Americas and, ultimately, the world. And the story of the banjo offers us a powerful illustration and condensation of this broader, transformative process.

The banjo represents the triumph of what the Cuban anthropologist Fernando Ortiz famously termed "transculturation"—a process by which all of the cultures of the Atlantic, whether from Africa, Europe, or the indigenous Americas, shaped one another to create something new.[3] An instrument whose prototypes are African was first built and played by plantation slaves in the Caribbean and the U.S. South. It was taken up by white musicians in the early decades of the nineteenth century and became the foundation for the most popular form of American theater, the minstrel show. It could play this role precisely because it carried with it the history of exchange and encounter that has defined our national experience. But precisely through this process, the banjo also became a central carrier and condenser of images of the plantation, of slavery, and of degradation. As such, it became tied inextricably to a series of deeply racist images. Even this process, however, was full of ambiguity, for the many whites who were taken with the banjo were both attracted to it and repelled by it for precisely the same reason. It was linked to the plantation, to blackness, and to slavery. And, in fact, the instrument remained central to African-American vernacular and theatrical performance throughout the nineteenth and early twentieth centuries, even as it found new roots in rural white communities in the South. Invented at the crossroads, through the experience of diaspora, loss, and survival, the banjo was embraced by many different individuals and communities. It offered itself up as an instrument that provided a sense of rootedness in the midst of displacement.

Starting in the late nineteenth century, some people were eager to unhinge the banjo from its African, Atlantic, and African-American histories. They sought to transform it into the essential "American" instrument by either seeking to forget its origins or relegating them to a prequel to the "real" history of the instrument, which became what it was truly meant to be only once it was in the hands of whites. And so the banjo also carries with it a history of denial, the attempt to erase its roots in Africa and in slavery. But of course the banjo—like American culture—cannot escape its roots in Africa and the Atlantic slave trade and in the African-American experience. Today, many musicians, collectors, and fans understand this and are working to revive an understanding of the instrument's complicated history. This book draws on the insights of the scholars and musicians who are part of this movement.

The banjo has also served as a powerful symbol deployed in larger battles over the morality of slavery in the eighteenth century, the definition of America in the nineteenth, and the role of tradition and the "folk" in the twentieth. Here too, there have been many tides of reinvention and redeployment by those who made, listened to, and marketed its music. It has seen tremendous, near constant, forms of musical innovation that have been tied to a range of broader cultural movements. At the same time, through its many iterations as both instrument and symbol, there has been a striking consistency in at least one aspect of the banjo's meaning. It has repeatedly been presented as something very old, a concentrated form of tradition. Curiously, but perhaps appropriately enough, an instrument defined most of all by its rootlessness has given people a sense of connecting with their own deep pasts.

As I tell these stories, I invite readers to listen to the banjo, to consider and remember what it is that draws people to this instrument, to its symbols, and to its sound. I tell the story of those whose hands made, and played, the banjo in many places and times. As we learn about the communities that created the banjo, we also learn about the communities the banjo created as people gathered, sang, listened, and signified about the instrument.

If this is a story about all of the representations of the banjo, and all the desires and phantasms that it has encompassed, it also argues that there is some reason the instrument has had such a long and successful run as a music maker. That reason is its capacity to condense and crystallize a range of musical traditions, and indeed its ability to condense both rhythm and melody together in one sound. This particularity can help explain how and why it has survived by taking on different forms, and creating diverse communities of players and listeners, over the years. At the heart of its sound, and therefore its power, is the one element that remains consistent across the whole history of the banjo: the use of a skin to cover the body of the instrument. That skin, and the resonance between it and the strings strumming and humming over it, is what identifies a banjo everywhere it goes. It is what makes the space around the banjo change, just a bit, every time it sounds out.

*

Where do instruments come from? How and why do they evolve a certain way? There is an entire scholarly field of study devoted to answering this question: organology. One of the first works of organology was Filippo Buoananni's eighteenth-century publication *Gabinetto Armonico,* which included 152 plates of "antique" instruments, including several African instruments, with reconstructions of how they would have been played. But the field really began to flourish as a result of European colonial expansion into Africa and Asia in the nineteenth century, when a number of European thinkers—particularly in France, Belgium, and Germany—began to gather instruments collected in Africa, the Americas, and Asia and place them side-by-side with European instruments. By gathering, cataloguing, and analyzing musical instruments from all over the world, these thinkers hoped they might gain a better understanding of some of the universal features, and perhaps even the origins, of music in human society, and perhaps even to write a universal history of musical instruments.[4]

Organologists have always confronted a basic problem: musical instruments are fragile. Unless intently preserved and cared for, they tend to vanish. The ancient musical instruments of Egypt, Greece, and Rome can be read about, and images of them can be viewed; but not many of these instruments can be held, or played, or heard. "History," as Andre Schaeffner noted in 1936, "only leaves us 'archives' in the places where it has almost ended. When musicologists say they are dealing with 'history' they are in fact focusing on very late periods, ones in which things are already fixed, where to put it another way *almost nothing is happening anymore.*" Given material limitations, organologists have tended to focus on recent developments and changes in the forms of musical instruments: the changing nature and varied technologies of pegs and strings and resonators or the history of different instrument makers.[5]

Still, the field of organology—and more broadly of musicology and ethnomusicology—has always been haunted by preoccupying questions: How did musical instruments emerge? Why did they take one form rather than another? Along with anthropologists of the nineteenth and early twentieth centuries, scholars working on music often thought they had found an answer not in a method but in a place: Africa. By the nineteenth century, European collections were full of instruments—many of them brought back from colonial expeditions—from the African continent. Scholars hoped that "primitive" objects could help them travel back in time to solve the question of origins. As some scholars saw it, since African societies were more backwards than European ones, African instruments were relics that could help explain the early history of European

instruments. Schaeffner, who was involved in ethnomusicological research in the French colonies in West Africa, noted that working in
Africa allowed scholars to "confront instruments which seem to have, at a
certain moment and for mysterious reasons, stayed 'broken down'." The
assumption was that musical instruments were meant to take a journey
culminating in modern European instruments, but some of them have
ended up stuck along the way, literally wrecked by the side of the road.
"Their apparent 'growth crises,'" continues Schaeffner, "mark the path
that should theoretically have gone from more primitive instruments to
our own." The hope that such "broken down" instruments might illuminate the lost history of Europe's own instruments helped to spur on a
great deal of collecting and scholarship throughout the nineteenth and
twentieth centuries, filling the great musical instrument museums of
Europe with instruments from Africa, Native American groups, and Oce-
ania. More broadly, the vision that the history of musical instruments
was one of evolution from the "primitive" to the "modern" shaped the
attitudes of commentators and instrument makers in the nineteenth century toward the history of the banjo and continues to influence some
discussions of the instrument's history to the present day.[6]

   This approach to the history of music, in which non-European
societies, particularly those of Africa, are seen as essentially "broken down"
on the path to the progress exemplified by Europe, was just one mani-
festation of the broader ways in which anthropological theory developed at the time. Johannes Fabian famously dubbed this approach the
"denial of coevalness," a way of seeing the world in which various contemporary societies were interpreted as literally living in a different
historical epoch. Its interpretive, moral, and political limitations—its
misplaced confidence in progress and its unfounded hubris—are by now
clear to most scholars. But this vision of the world still undergirds a surprising amount work within the field of music.[7]

   That is partly because of the ways in which the core categories of
music theory have, from the first, been imbricated with distinctions between European and non-European music and an evolutionary approach
to the history of music. Going back to the writings of the French philos-
opher Jean-Jacques Rousseau about music, theorists have often differenti-
ated between systems of musical practice that involve what they describe
as an analytic or scientific approach and others in which players and

listeners do not consciously categorize the various components of the music. According to this distinction, various kinds of folk music within Europe and so-called primitive music in other parts of the world lacked the kind of systems and languages of music that European composers of orchestral music, for instance, used and deployed. Rousseau defined this as a contrast between "artifice and theory" on the one hand and "nature and practice" on the other. The different ways of approaching music didn't necessarily have to be placed in a hierarchy; but in practice they often were, with music produced out of "artifice and theory" seen as a higher, more complex accomplishment, the pinnacle of human musical achievement. This, in turn, has led to a kind of self-fulfilling prophecy within musicology, since music theory has almost exclusively been based on the study of a relatively narrow segment of human musical activity: European art music.[8]

Traditionally, music theory revolves around interpretations of a musical trinity: melody, harmony, and rhythm. Each of these categories was infused with meanings and associations: melody is linked to spirit, harmony to soul, and rhythm to body. The music of the African continent, notes Gerhard Kubik, has generally been seen as one driven by rhythm and therefore anchored in natural or bodily responses devoid of the higher level of abstraction represented by harmony. Africans were "described as born with a 'natural rhythm' but lacking higher intellectual development symbolized by 'melody' and 'harmony.'" In the 1920s the German musicologist Hornbostel, for instance, wrote that "rhythm and harmony (as far as it exists) in non-European music show characteristics which are the natural outcome of pure melody." In this typology, the musical forms and achievements of the non-European or non-Western peoples were seen as the result of natural performance rather than the artifice and science that generated European musical achievement. As late as 1967, a French ethnologist could write that "primitive peoples" did not understand harmony. Such distinctions have been taken up by certain African intellectuals, notes Kubik, who have argued that rhythm symbolizes the "core of 'African culture'"—reversing the "negative charge" of European stereotypes without upending the broader models that had generated them. All of this does little to help us understand the incredible variety and complexity of African music itself. The best work in African ethnomusicology has found ways to either skirt or directly confront these distinctions;

but they linger in both popular thought and scholarship, though often articulated through "substitute expressions." But even when deployed with the best of intentions, these distinctions reproduce a certain kind of hierarchy, often along racial and cultural lines. The idea that certain kinds of musical expression are more "natural" was never confined to musicology but influenced popular commentary and therefore musical performance itself. In the United States, this has taken the form of a consistent strand of interpretation—one often repeated during the period of blackface minstrelsy—that described African-Americans as being "naturally" attuned to certain kinds of more "pure" or "primitive" musical expression. Such distinctions continue to shape the ways that both African and African-American music are often discussed.[9]

Our discussions of music, then, are still haunted by ideas of cultural difference and alterity, along with a vision of musical evolution and progress. How do we escape? Schaeffner urges scholars to "avoid, as much as possible, the use of the terms *evolution* and *progress*." The "complexity" of the relationship between different types of instruments, and the fact that there just as often seem to be "leaps" from one construction to another rather than smooth "passages," force us to doubt the possibility of writing a "linear history," and "especially a unilinear one." He notes that no instrument was ever born "in a vacuum" without an intricate relationship to the music that was being played. "From the beginning, something like the collective birth of instruments of different types seems more probable."[10]

Banjo scholarship is still sometimes freighted by the idea that the banjo essentially reached its full potential only at the hands of white instrument makers in the nineteenth century. But the best work in the area has avoided the pitfalls of earlier approaches in organology by offering an increasingly rich portrait of the possible African sources and inspirations for the banjo. Scholars have focused particularly on an exploration of the many resources and examples that West African instruments would have offered to those Atlantic Africans who were at the origin of the banjo in the New World. Cecelia Conway has offered a pioneering study of the African roots of the banjo, and the recent work by Philip Gura and James Bollman builds on an analysis of the early history of the instrument to provide a rich and compelling history of the nineteenth-century instrument, based on a rich material archive of banjos and the written archive surrounding the instrument. Similarly, a series of exhibits on the banjo have illustrated and presented this history to a broader public.[11]

My own sense, which guides the analysis in the following chapters, is that any history of music that is predicated on the notion of progress or development is likely to lead us to a dead end. Although there are of course forms of music and cultural achievement that stand out as particularly powerful and popular in certain contexts, there is no grand narrative of progress in music leading from a primitive past to a fully realized present or future. Instead, we should embrace a history of ebbs and flows, exchanges and crossings, one in which music and society have interacted over the centuries, and one in which ideologies about music have changed over time in different societies. If we do this, we can seek to emancipate ourselves from earlier interpretive constraints. And we can began to tell a different story in which a musical instrument like the banjo reveals our own Atlantic, and global, history in a new way.

To tell the story of the people who invented the banjo, of the artisans and musicians whose hands made it live, is to enter a hall of mirrors where we see only reflections and refractions. We almost never hear their voices. It is a work of cultural archaeology, of piecing together fragments left by chance, taking advantage of the words left by a few observers who happened at one point to take a deeper interest in something disregarded by most others. Still, a mosaic of texts, images, and visual culture allows us to reconstruct the history of the banjo's creation and consolidation in the Americas, showing us how the banjo emerges at the crossroads of a range of West and Central African cultures in the plantations and port towns of the Caribbean and U.S. South.

From the beginning of the colonization of the Americas, African and African-American individuals and communities produced their own forms of interpretation and representation meant to analyze, depict, and survive what they were experiencing. One of the most powerful and consistent of these was music. Through form and content, thought and performance, it offered a way of understanding and confronting the colonial situation. The musical and performance cultures produced by

Afro-Atlantic music represent an alternative archive through which to tell the history of African and African-American individuals and communities in the Americas. This archive has the powerful advantage of being largely the creation of these communities, a space in which and through which they articulated their vision of the past, their experience of the present, and their aspirations for the future. It is extremely rich and diverse, and in its musical forms, instruments, and sung lyrics both condenses and reflects on the experiences of exile, struggle, and emancipation. Developed in critical spheres of social life—religious practice, social dancing, funerary rites, carnival, and other spaces—it provides a record of the visions and ideals cultivated within the interstices of plantation life. Like other forms of music, it offers "glimpses of larger, undocumented worlds."[12]

This archive has to be reconstituted out of bits and pieces of observations by outsiders, visual and material culture, and the music itself. Gathering these widely scattered fragments requires a geographically and chronologically adventurous approach that ranges across regions and periods in the Atlantic world during its formative period of the sixteenth through the eighteenth centuries. If we link diverse imperial histories, with texts, archives, images, and music drawn from multiple sites in the Atlantic, the play of research and interpretation grows exponentially in both material and interpretive terms. Music offers not only accounts and reflections of historical experience and political aspiration but also in many cases the story and meaning of the very cultural processes that produced it. Embedded within the songs and objects of that music are notions of what it has meant to continually reconstitute, often out of fragments, a sense both of rooted history and of an alternative future in the face of spirals of dispossession and refusal. I have taken as my task here to gather shards of evidence relating to the banjo's history, especially during its earliest periods, and to offer up those pieces of evidence to tell a larger story about how this instrument created new communities of sound and meaning. The early musical history is "sonically absent," for we have few ways of capturing what banjo playing in the seventeenth, eighteenth, and early nineteenth century sounded like. This problem, though, is a familiar one for historians studying the experience and perspective of the enslaved. It can be confronted by interpreting and connecting available fragments with precision *and* imagination.[13]

The foundation for most subsequent explorations of slave music in North America is Dena Epstein's *Sinful Tunes and Spirituals,* published in 1977. As she was beginning her research, Epstein found an "almost total lack of any documentation" about music during the colonial period when "Africans were newly arrived in the New World." Then, in 1969, she read Orlando Patterson's *The Sociology of Slavery,* which cited "numerous contemporary descriptions of African music and dancing in Jamaica." She began looking for sources from the Caribbean and found many "contemporary descriptions of African dancing, instruments, and music" that "far exceeded" her "highest hopes." Since these sources "were quite consistent with the fragmentary accounts of the mainland," their use "made it possible to demonstrate from contemporary documents the introduction of African music in the New World, its survival for generations in some areas, and its transformation into something different—Afro-American or Creole music."[14]

It is not surprising that the Caribbean is where we first find traces of the banjo and more developed sources than in North America. The Caribbean, rather than being on the margins as it is often considered to be today, was at the very center of the seventeenth- and eighteenth-century Atlantic imperial world. It is the region in the Americas that consumed the largest number of African slaves over the course of the slave trade, followed closely by Brazil. At the height of the Atlantic plantation system, in the late eighteenth century, North America was on the edge of this system, while the Caribbean was at its center. Epstein's work, as well as a recent book by Christopher Smith, powerfully show how the study of the history of music, and particularly of the banjo, allows us to see the tight cultural connections between the areas and to understand that beyond imperial and national boundaries there was a shared world of circulation, exchange, and influence.[15]

One of the earliest and most powerful reflections on how music emerged from the African-American historical experience is a chapter of *The Souls of Black Folk* in which W. E. B. Du Bois famously turned to what he called "The Sorrow Songs" in African-American music—those "weird old songs in which the soul of the black slave spoke to men." When he first heard these songs, Du Bois wrote, "at once I knew them as of me and of mine." These songs were not just "voices of the past." They were, he argued, "the sole American music": "the most beautiful expression of human experience born this side of the seas . . . the singular spiritual heritage of the nation and the greatest gift of the Negro people." The purest and most important form of American culture, Du Bois insisted, *was* African-American culture. This interpretation of its music was the culmination of his broader argument: just as slavery had laid the foundation for the country's economic development, and the struggle for freedom had expanded and perfected its political culture, it was African-American music that ultimately best voiced and embodied what America should be.[16]

The soaring universalism of Du Bois's claim about music, however, gained its power from the way it was expressed through a much older past in Africa. Contemporary African-American songs, he wrote, were "indeed the siftings of centuries," the music "far more ancient than the words." "My grandfather's grandmother was seized by an evil Dutch trader two centuries ago; and coming to the valleys of the Hudson and Housatonic, black, little, and lithe, she shivered and shrank in the harsh north winds, looked longingly at the hills, and often crooned a heathen melody to the child between her knees. . . . The child sang it to his children and they to their children's children, and so two hundred years it has traveled down to us and we sing it to our children, knowing as little as our fathers what its words may mean, but knowing well the meaning of its music."[17]

Du Bois's attempt to grapple with the power and meaning of music was at the center of his entire project *The Souls of Black Folk*. It was the inspiration for the "polyphonic montage technique" he developed in writing the work: each chapter in *The Souls of Black Folk* begins with a counterpoint between two epigraphs, one drawn from European or American romantic poetry, and the other from a slave song. We might say that Du Bois was trying to find a way to make words speak as powerfully about the African-American experience as the music did. As such, his chapter on "The Sorrow Songs" might be considered the founding text in writing about black music.[18]

Du Bois's thoughts on music embody and illuminate a set of contradictions that have continued to animate and haunt debates about black music. Was black music fundamentally American and therefore a kind of universal heritage, "the singular spiritual experience of the nation"? Or was it something transmitted within community and particular to it, linked fundamentally by a particular social experience? This book builds on the approaches taken by more recent interventions into the history of black music in insisting that ultimately there is no way to separate these two stories, to write any history of America that is not also fundamentally about Africa. One way to say this is that the history of the banjo I offer here is the history of the black banjo, a fundamentally Afro-Atlantic history. But it is also to point out that the term "Black Banjo"—just like "Black Atlantic"—is a redundancy. The banjo, like the Atlantic world in which it emerged, was always fundamentally "Black." That we feel the need to keep repeating this is a sign of how far we remain from accepting our history and incorporating it into how we imagine the present.[19]

A musical instrument is the extension of the musician who plays it. So while our subject is an object, our story is also an ode to those who made it sound. It is a celebration of what they achieved. We know the names of many of them—from Trois-Feuilles and Pompée, two banza players from eighteenth-century Haiti, to Picayune Butler and Joel Sweeney, early pioneers who helped create blackface minstrelsy, and on to Johnny St. Cyr and Pete Seeger. These musicians all found the banjo. Or maybe the banjo found them. They—and all the others whose names we don't know—propelled and changed the instrument, what it meant and what it could mean, each time they struck its chords and made that skin head hum.

But there is a special place in this story for the early musicians, many of whom probably made their own instruments and who remain largely nameless. They were the ones who first experimented with and ultimately consolidated the instrument. They were Africans in exile in the spaces of the Atlantic. The Atlantic was a "catalytic historical space" because "if you went out into it, whether leaving from Africa or Iberia or anywhere else, you had to learn how to deal with an incredible variety of strangers." It was a world of ports and ships, of plantations in which many African languages were spoken. Music made in and for these spaces had to be able to travel, not just in space, but also through different traditions and forms of cultural imagination. It had to be recognizable but also to address the fact that the world had become alien for many trapped within it. Music needed to give people space, to allow people to breathe. And to do that, it needed to sound strong and deep.[20]

Musicians within any community, particularly those who aspire to make (and sometimes succeed in making) money from playing, are exceptional. Though music is often to be widely shared, and many musicians play instruments, those who emerge as regular performers, those who define styles and condense community around them, are able to do so because of their particular and notable talents. That talent is in large part about responsiveness and flexibility, the ability to reach and satisfy an audience, whether they are gathered in a clearing or a barn, sitting in a concert hall, listening to the radio, or buying recordings. That is a challenge anywhere, but it was a particular challenge in the world out of which the banjo emerged: the plantation zones of the Caribbean and North America and the ports that sustained those zones. In time, of course, the banjo found other homes—in rural Appalachia and other parts of the South—far from the heart of the plantation complex. But there, too, the instrument often existed—and helped to articulate—the pivot between the old and the new, the space of anxiety and possibility created by change and migration. If they wanted to be heard, musicians had to speak for and to these contexts.

Any individual musician is part of what André Schaeffner calls a "society of musicians." They are the hub, the crossroads between tradition and immediacy, between past and present, between the abstract and the concrete of musical expression, and between the ideal of music and its sonic production. And when we write from the perspective of musicians, Elijah Wald reminds us, we need to be careful about forcing them into categories they themselves rarely respected. They often saw the "aesthetic categories" of critics and historians as constraining. Being placed in any kind of box—as a "folk" or "bluegrass" musician, even as a "black" or "white" musician—is and was a limitation, one that could undermine their livelihood. Especially in the days before recording, "it was the band's job to play whatever music suited the dancers, rather than vice versa." And most musicians played in a local context in which versatility was the key to regular employment. "A band in Clarksdale, Mississippi, or Montpelier, Vermont, didn't have to be able to play the tango as well as someone in Buenos Aires or the ragtime as well as someone in St. Louis—it just had to play them better than anyone in the same price range in

Clarksdale or Montpelier." In rural areas, meanwhile, bands were often made up of "locals who could scrape a little on fiddle or guitar and who might play one or two songs for the entire night." Wald quotes musician John Jackson, who was from Virginia and played guitar and banjo and put it this way: "You started playing one thing, and if it didn't suit them to dance you'd stop it and start on another one and, if that suited them, that's what they wanted. You sat right there and played that song all night, and when you got tired of playing it, two more people'd move in the corner and go to playing." The history of music is the accumulation of such scenes.[21]

This book is an invitation to listen to the sound of our history and to the remarkable and beautiful ways musicians—and the instrument makers they depended on—have created spaces of solidarity in the midst of life's harshest and most violent conditions. From the beginning, banjo players needed to be in constant motion, and even to embody that motion by making music present: to offer up whatever audiences considered to be their tradition at the same time as they offered innovation in the form of new songs and forms, or simply surprise and delight in the way a song was played. The banjo has, in a remarkable range of sites and contexts, allowed musicians to do that: to embody both the old and the new, to offer nostalgia and forward communal motion all at once. That, in the end, is the secret of its power, and its survival. That is how it has sung its own history.

1

Sounding Africa

WHAT SOUND WILL ACCOMPANY THE END OF DAYS? One tenth-century Spanish artist thought he knew: the music of sixteen lutes played by sixteen saints. Creating an illustration for the Book of Revelation 14:2–5, he depicted elders holding books along with the Lamb of God holding the cross on Mount Zion. The saints surround the Lamb, playing, waiting, and seemingly ready.[1]

In most times and places, the act of creating instruments left no record, either written, visual, or material. There are, however, evocative traces of how this all happened: in text, in paintings, in drawings, and sometimes in a few preserved instruments themselves. Through such images, scattered here and there in the historical archive, the practice of music—and the shape of musical instruments—is passed on to us. Often these traces tell a story that is as much about how and why people found it fitting to write about or paint musical instruments in certain times and places as it is about the musical landscape itself. They have to be interpreted with attention paid to the context in which they were produced and with caution about how much we can really conclude from them. Still, they offer us an outline of a story.

Saint Beatus, Presbyter of Liebana, d. 798, Commentary on the Apocalypse (MS M.644) vol II, fol 174 verso. Courtesy of the Pierpont Morgan Library and Museum.

In illustrating a theological theme, this artist reached for what he observed around him in tenth-century Spain. The music of lutes was widespread and beloved, entertaining kings and courts, and so it was easy to imagine them in the hands of saints confronting the end of one world and the beginning of another. The image is striking for a particular detail about the instruments: their oval bodies are covered with an animal skin. These are not the kinds of lutes—with bodies made entirely of wood, often with a round hole underneath the strings—that would ultimately become standard in Spain and elsewhere in Europe. These sainted instruments would have sounded different as a result: when strings resonate across a drumhead made with an animal skin rather than a wooden body, a different sonic spectrum is created. The sound might be described as an added hum, perhaps a buzz, parts of it easy to perceive and some perhaps barely palpable. The difference would be felt in the ear, but also the bones.

It is a simple, seemingly innocuous distinction. Yet it turns out to be critical for our story. For if there are many ways to define precisely what a banjo is, when all of them are peeled away, what remains is one key, consistent feature: a rounded or oval body covered with an animal skin. This is what makes the sound particular and distinguishes it from other instruments. The repeated decision to make the resonator a kind of drum has remained constant in a history defined by constant flux, change, and experimentation. That is what defines a banjo.

The reason for a particular artisan's or musician's choice of one or another form for his or her instrument is often relatively straightforward: certain materials are available, and certain styles of construction are familiar. There may be constraints placed on what is possible by the climate or by what construction technology is available in a given time and place. Within these limitations, the choice is guided by social or cultural traditions. But it can also be an aesthetic assertion, the result of the exploration, innovation, and dreams of an individual. Out of the accumulation of such choices is made the history of musical instruments.

Scholars of musical instruments use the term "chordophone" to describe the family of instruments that make sound through the use of strings. They broadly categorize them into four groups: lyres, zithers, harps, and lutes. Lyres, mostly associated with the music of ancient Greece, have strings stretched within a frame and are effectively a kind of harp.

Zithers are made up entirely of a resonator with strings stretched across the entire body. The two other groups of instruments are harps and lutes. The key difference between them is that the strings on a harp stretch along a plane perpendicular to the body or neck of the instrument, whereas the strings on a lute run parallel to the body and neck.[2]

European and African musical cultures have influenced each other through a process going back centuries, indeed millennia. The stringed instruments known in Europe during the Renaissance—various types of lutes and guitars—were born out the interaction between Africa and Europe in the Iberian world from the seventh through the fifteenth century. But by the sixteenth century, as the intertwined European contact with Africa and expansion into the Americas accelerated, there was a category of stringed instruments in Africa that was essentially unknown in Europe: lutes and harps whose resonators were covered with animal skins. These instruments, present in societies throughout West and Central Africa, created a particular sound, and they were at the heart of a wide range of musical performance.[3]

There are today—and have long been—an incredible diversity and profusion of both harps and lutes throughout the African continent. Broadly speaking, lutes are more common in West Africa than they are in Central Africa, although there are many kinds of harps in both areas. But there are many parallels between the ways harps and lutes were and are constructed. Both almost always use some kind of resonator to amplify their sound. In many cases these are carved entirely out of wood, the way that the resonators of European guitars and lutes are. But in many other instruments, resonators are made of either wooden frames, or else gourds or calabashes, covered with animal skins. Such resonators are most familiar to international audiences through the structure of the *kora,* one of the most elaborate African harps, which has twenty-one strings. But they are a feature of many other chordophones throughout the continent. These traditions, brought across the Atlantic in the minds and memories of enslaved people, would nourish the creation of the New World banjo. Its form drew on a range of technical and aesthetic traditions from different parts of the African continent. While West African lutes were clearly the most direct inspiration for the banjo, I argue in the following chapters that the instrument's shape, aesthetics, and meaning were influenced by the entire spectrum of stringed instruments on the continent, and that it emerged from a cross-pollination between West and Central African musical cultures. Instrument makers in Africa understood that, on some basic level, to be human meant to have music, and so many of the stringed instruments were constructed in an anthropomorphic style, their bodies and necks shaped and carved to resemble human beings. Some aspects of this aesthetic and symbolic choice also influenced the construction of some early banjos in the Americas.

In this chapter, we journey back to ancient Egypt, medieval North Africa and Spain, and West and Central Africa in order to understand these deep traditions and genealogies out of which the banjo emerged. Unfortunately, there are very few surviving examples of ancient instruments themselves. The wood, gourds, calabashes, and animal skins out of which they were made were "highly perishable." Only in Egypt— thanks to the dry climate and the existence of well-sealed and protected royal tombs—did some specimens of ancient instruments survive, and even there they are relatively few. In more tropical climates, concludes one scholar, there is "little chance—one feels tempted to say no chance— of the survival of a chordophone beyond a few score years. . . . Because chordophones are so fragile, their life span is short, even, or perhaps especially, in the hands of musicians: frequent use, however expert it may be, wears the instrument out. The ever changing tension on the strings eventually affects the string bearer." As a result, the first part of our story is told from bits of texts and image created here and there, collateral pieces generated from political commentary, travel accounts, or religious debate—a series of evanescent though evocative echoes of distant soundings.[4]

Receding from a flood, the Nile left behind the corpses of dead animals, including a tortoise. The flesh inside had decayed, but the creature's nerves were still stretched across the shell. The god Mercury picked it up, and plucked the nerves, creating a sound that resonated within the turtle's body. So it was, according to the German musician Ernst Gottlieb Baron, that the first stringed instrument was born.[5]

Baron was tapping into a long tradition stretching at least back to Homer's poem *Hymn to Hermes,* which describes how Mercury passed on the gift of music to Apollo, who in turn passed it on to his son Orpheus. Renaissance thinkers, notably Ovid, returned to these ancient texts, making them enduring touchstones for European discussions about the origins and magic of music. In 1820, Percy Bysshe Shelley published a modern, adapted translation of Homer's poem, calling it *Hymn to Mercury*. He cast the invention of the original stringed instrument as an act of will by a child possessed by the desire to sing his own song. The infant Mercury exits his cave and, seeing a live tortoise, shouts: "A Treasure!" Having enticed the unsuspected creature into the cave, he tells it: "you will sing sweetly when you are dead." "Then scooping with a chisel of gray steel/He bored the life and soul out of the beast." Shelley offers a richly detailed account of how Mercury then proceeded to make an instrument out of the shell and a piece of leather.

> And through the tortoise's hard stony skin
> At proper distances small holes he made,
> And fastened the cut stems of reeds within,
> And with a piece of leather overlaid
> The open space and fixed the cubits in,
> Fitting the bridge to both, and stretched o'er all
> Symphonious cords of sheep-gut rhythmical.[6]

Such stories are ways of arguing about music itself, about what role it serves and what it should mean. In Shelley's version, it is an innate drive to communicate that ultimately creates instruments. In Baron's version, it is nature that actually inspires human music. Indeed in one version of the tale, preserved in the Persian tradition, it is the wind that whistles through the nerves inside the decaying tortoise shell that first makes the strings hum, inspiring Mercury's construction of an instrument meant to repeat nature's sound.[7]

However they were first invented, lutes were a well-established part of the musical culture of ancient societies. Some of the earliest known depictions of lutes come to us from the archaeological remains of Mesopotamia. A small carving from 3100 BC, now in the British Museum, includes a seated man playing a stringed instrument with a long neck. In Iraq another carving from sometime between 2900 and 2370 BC clearly shows a man playing an instrument with a small resonator held to his chest and a long neck. From Susa in Western Iran comes to us a carving of lutes on a boundary stone and a terracotta sculpture of a naked, bearded man playing a lute, from between the twelfth and seventh century BC.[8]

Were these instruments invented there, or did they come to Mesopotamia and Central Asia or elsewhere? The most detailed history of the lute concludes that it "probably originated in Indian culture in the region that is now Afghanistan," noting that it shows up in various forms of ancient Indian iconography. But other scholars have noted these instruments could just as easily have come from Africa into these areas. It is also very possible that similar instruments were invented in different places in parallel time, as musicians discovered and perfected the possibilities of resonators and strings. Whatever their original source or sources, they ultimately became part of the culture of Egypt, where we find the most detailed early depictions of the instruments. There are pictures of instruments humming and songs being sung on the walls of many Egyptian tombs.[9]

Wall paintings in Thebes from the sixteenth century BC show instruments with round resonators, round necks, and three strings. The musicians in the paintings are often women. In one depiction of a raucous party, painted on a tomb at Thebes, two women with elaborate headdresses and decorated lutes are creating the soundtrack for a range of other activities: beheading and butchering a cow, enjoying bouquets of flowers, various types of fondling, and a fair amount of drinking. In another part of the painting, a male lute player is accompanying a harpist. Several such instruments found in excavations, including one found at Thebes with a relatively large pear-shaped resonator covered with a skin, have been preserved in Egyptian collections.[10]

In time, the lute was adopted into Arab culture and spread all across North Africa and the Middle East, rapidly becoming the most beloved and prominent instrument in the region. A fresco from 728 BC from the Palace of Qasr al-Hayr in Syria depicts a lute being played by a well-dressed woman. A tenth-century text praised the instrument as the "most perfect instrument" produced in the ancient world, and by the fifteenth century it had earned the adulatory nickname "The Sultan of Instruments." There were, in fact, two types of lutes, "one with a wide, rounded body and a wooden top, the other a narrow, club-shaped instrument with either a wooden or a leather belly." The instrument spread into Iberia through Arab conquest: the term lute itself is, in fact, a trans-formation of the Arabic name *al-'ud* into Spanish.[11]

The history of the instrument is interwoven with the history of Islam. There have long been some Muslim theologians who have seen music as a "forbidden pleasure." Since the Koran itself is not explicit about music, these arguments are articulated through subsequent interpretations of cer-tain verses of the Koran or else based on the *hadith,* sayings attributed to Mohammed. Some early Islamic thinkers took particular aim at stringed instruments, which were seen as "signs of the end of the world," and at times they were banned. There has, however, never been unanimity around the question of music; and the courts of the Muslim world were often full of music and dancing, often provided by female slaves acquired and trained for the purpose. One account of an eighth-century Umayyad festival describes "fifty singing girls with lutes behind a curtain," fronted by a famous singer named Jamila. In some quarters, black slaves were seen as possessing a "natural" sense of rhythm and dance. One eleventh-century description of slaves from East Africa claimed: "Dancing and rhythm are instinctive and ingrained in them. Since their utterance is uncouth, they are compensated with song and dance." Such attitudes would have an enduring history in the ideology of Atlantic slavery. They also raise an intriguing question about the ways in which the many slaves from different parts of Africa, many of them musicians in Arab houses and courts, might have shaped the musical culture of this world.[12]

The history of the lute in Europe is inseparable from the story of a man who may well deserve the title of the world's first international rock star: Ziryab. A black slave from the court of Ibrahim al-Mawsili in Baghdad, he made his way to Cordoba, Spain, and became the beloved musician of the Moorish court there. "The story of Ziryab has to be considered something of a myth—true in the way that myths are true," writes Ned Sublette. It comes to us through a labyrinth of mediations: an 1840 translation of an early seventeenth-century Arabic text based on a lost manuscript from the eleventh century. Ziryab's full name was Abu 'l-Hasan 'Ali Ibn Nafi,' and his nickname was Black Songbird, a way of referring to the "sweetness of his singing and his dark complexion."[13]

Ziryab apparently left the court of Baghdad because he surpassed the skills of his teacher—the caliph's son—and needed to escape the jealousy this caused. Via Tunisia, and with the help of a Jewish musician, he made his way to the court of Abd al-Rahman I in Cordoba, the center of Al-Andalus. Ziryab was beloved for his remarkable library of songs— apparently more than a thousand—and his playing style. He is said to have improved the lute by adding a fifth string to the instrument, a "red string" which he "placed in the middle." He replaced the usual wooden plectrum with an eagle feather. His influence didn't stop there: like any self-respecting star, he also reshaped fashion, sporting specialized ward-robes for different seasons, and "is said to have given Cordoba that fun-damental cultural contribution of the singing star: a new hairstyle."[14]

Most importantly, Ziryab founded a music school and created a method for teaching and learning the lute. In so doing, he contributed to a flowering of music that would last for centuries. Though his contri-bution was key, the stories about Ziryab almost certainly do what such myths are generally meant to do: they condense a much larger cultural movement and complex into the figure of one person. Much of what is attributed to him was less an act of pure genius and invention on his part than a result of his ability to transmit what he'd learned in Baghdad as a young man to the musical context of Cordoba. In Spain, many other mu-sicians in his century and those that followed certainly played important roles in the continuation and transformation of styles of lute playing and lute making. Most of their names, and much of what they played, simply can't be recovered; and so Ziryab has come to embody all of them.[15]

Lute music rocked the world of Andalusia for centuries. A grouchy visitor to Malaga in 1015 complained that, while stuck in bed sick, he couldn't get any rest because of the constant humming of instruments: "Around me, the strings of lutes, tunburs, and other instruments vibrated from all directions," along with singing, "which was bad for me, and added to my insomnia and suffering." "I . . . detest such tunes by dispo-sition, so that I wished to find lodgings in which I could hear neither, yet it was impossible for me to do so," he lamented. One can imagine a similar lament on the part of a resident of Cambridge or Greenwich Vil-lage a millennium later.[16]

Andalusia developed a unique musical culture, based on the "con-junction of strings and percussion." Today this is mostly preserved and played within the Maghreb, among Algerian and Tunisian musicians, as Arab-Andalusian music. This musical form represents a clear precedent for the kinds of ongoing, multidirectional, and tangled forms of musical influence and exchange that would take place in the Atlantic world centuries later. If it all began with Arab music coming to Iberia, there it mixed with "pre-existing Romance melodies," going back to the Visigoths. There were other influences as well, from the music of the Gypsies to the transregional cross-fertilization brought about by Ziryab, coming from Baghdad, and certainly by many other traveling musicians as well. As Andalusia became a center of musical creation and innovation, songs and styles composed there flowed outwards, including back to North Africa. The networks of musical exchange were startlingly well-established and rapid: it took just a few months for a hit song to spread from Andalusia to Tunis and Baghdad. The popularity of this style meant that lutes, at first brought to the region from the Arab world, gained an enduring place in European music. Artisans began making the instruments in Iberia itself. Seville became a center for the construction of lutes and exported some back to North Africa. Iberian artisans made a variety of other stringed instruments, including the rabâb, played with a bow, and the kwithra, or kithara—from which the form and the name of the guitar was ultimately derived.[17]

All of this long outlasted the slow Reconquista of Iberia by Christian kings. After King Alfonso established himself in Seville in 1248, having expelled the Muslim court, he nevertheless retained many Moorish musicians. More than half of his son's twenty-seven musicians in 1293 were described as Moors. This continuing musical exchange was documented in the legendary medieval manuscript the Cantigas de Santa Maria, whose illuminations depict instruments and performance in several illustrations. One of these illustrations shows two musicians playing lutes side by side. One of the figures is depicted as Arab, the other a blond European. But their instruments are the same. The image is a powerful vestige of the transcultural musical encounter that shaped Iberian and therefore European culture over centuries.[18]

From its origins in Iberia, the lute spread throughout Europe. Renaissance thinkers celebrated the lute as the greatest of instruments, drawing on Greek and Roman myths and writings surrounding the lyre. This deployment of Greek and Roman myth helped the lute gain a "high status" as a European instrument. For Renaissance and Baroque-era writers, these origin stories were a reminder that music once had truly magical powers that some hoped could be revived. A genealogy that connected the Renaissance-era lute to the Greek lyre also allowed those who played and wrote about music to link themselves to venerable poetic and theoretical traditions that celebrated the importance of their art.[19]

Such writings, however, erased a crucial part of the story: the fact that the lute's origins lay in the Arab world and that the instrument's history in Europe had started through a process of cross-fertilization and exchange between cultures. Part of a broader silencing of the contributions of Arabic science, philosophy, and culture, Renaissance versions of musical history conveniently elided the actual history of many of Europe's instruments, which were born not out of the genius of an ancient God but out of the sedimentation and collective genius of musicians in North Africa and Iberia. What was lost in the process was the recognition of the centuries of transcultural dialogue that had shaped the styles and instruments played on the European continent. One day long ago, a person—or a god—may well have found a tortoise shell lying on the banks of the Nile and created an instrument. But to get from there to the European lutes that hummed in Renaissance courts took a different kind of history, and magic: that of journeys, invasions, migrations, and exchanges that connected Europe and Africa for several centuries.

With the history of musical cross-fertilization in Iberia silenced, Europeans came to look at the cultures of North and West Africa as sharply distinct from their own. The belief in racial and cultural difference was both sustained and reinforced by the new interactions between the continents, which in the late fifteenth century increasingly revolved around the slave trade. European travelers to Africa were primed, in a sense, to see difference. And they were often fascinated in particular to encounter unfamiliar forms of music, dance, and performance.

Among the unknown objects visitors in Africa saw were musical instruments made with resonators of animal skin, a style of construction once present in Iberia but now novel and foreign-looking to Europeans. The distinction between types of resonators on stringed instruments was largely mapped onto the distinction between geographical regions. Europe had few, if any, instruments constructed with skin-covered resonators, while they continued to be made and played throughout North, West, and Central Africa. Enslaved individuals, brought as slaves from Africa to the Americas, were the ones who carried this ancient style of instrument making. And the European settlers who encountered instruments built in this way found them unfamiliar and new. The result was a renewed process of exchange between European and African musical instruments, rooted in a deeper history but taking shape in a new cultural and social context.

Why were drumhead resonators unfamiliar to Europeans by the fifteenth and sixteenth centuries? Although they had been part of the music of Andalusia, they seemed to have vanished from Iberian instrumentation by this time. And, unlike lutes and other stringed instruments that emerged from Arab-Andalusian culture, they never spread to other parts of Europe. There is one probable reason for this, and it has to do with climate. Animal skins expand and contract with the temperature, and in cold weather they tighten. To keep a skin affixed to a piece of wood when it contracts was quite difficult with the type of instrument-building technology that was available in Europe during this period. This didn't include the tension hoop and brackets that would eventually reshape the banjo in the nineteenth-century United States. Although skin heads were used in drums throughout Europe, the problem was less serious for such instruments. Heads could be switched easily on drums if they contracted or wore out; whereas a chordophone built with a skin head included a much more complex construction with a neck, bridge, and strings that would have to be redone. In much of Europe, finding lumber suitable for building instruments was relatively easy. The difficulties surrounding the construction and maintenance of instruments with animal skins, along with other aesthetic and cultural considerations—including perhaps the inclination to differentiate the lutes being constructed during the Renaissance period from those associated with Arab-Andalusian culture—all likely contributed to the solidification of a tradition in which resonators made entirely out of wood became the norm in Europe.[20]

The environment was quite different in both West and Central Africa. There, temperature conditions made it easier to maintain the tightness of a skin over a resonator with tacks or other holding mechanisms. And, importantly, the environment in Africa offered up a gift for the makers of instrument: gourds and calabashes. These fruits could be grown and harvested in different sizes and shapes and then carefully crafted into resonators for instruments. Both gourds and calabashes are relatively fragile, and attaching a neck to the side of one is very difficult. As a result, instrument makers developed the technique of building "spike-neck" lutes and harps, where the stick that makes the neck of the instrument goes all the way through the resonator, providing a strong anchoring for strings that are tied on both ends of the stick and stretch either above the resonator (for harps) or across it (for lutes). This technique allowed artisans to make an instrument that took advantage of the beautiful sound created by strings humming over a drumhead and through the walls of a gourd or calabash. Going back centuries, such instruments were everywhere in Africa, humming and speaking in a variety of different musical tongues.[21]

West African kings understood that music is power. They made sure their official audiences were accompanied by song. They traveled with music, too: when the king of Mali returned from a journey, wrote the fourteenth-century scholar Al-'Umari, "a parasol and a standard are held over his head as he rides," while ahead of him came musicians playing "drums, guitars, and trumpets, which are made out of the horns of the country with a consummate art." The legendary chronicler Ibn Battuta described similarly how when the king of Mali arrived for an audience, "the singers come out in front of him with gold and silver stringed instruments in their hands and behind them about 300 armed slaves." A 1655 account of the court of Askia Mohammed-Gâo, the seat of the Songhay empire, described him surrounded by "instrumentalists who played the guitar" along with other instruments, sitting "under the pasha's tent, behind the dais."[22]

These writers used various Arabic terms to describe the instruments: Al-Umari used *tanbūr* or *tunbūr,* a Persian term for a long-necked instrument, while Ibn Battuta used a term rendered as *kanābir* in the 1922 French edition, *quinburī* in the more recent English one. And the "Kano Chronicle," first published in 1804 on the basis of earlier materials, mentions a stringed instrument called the "Algaita" that was requested by a Kano ruler for his court in 1703. But these writers were using the terms for their own familiar stringed instruments, so we can't assume that this was the name used by the musicians themselves or draw conclusions about the construction of the instruments beyond a general analogy.[23]

There is a fascinating glimpse in a series of metal plaques from the thirteenth-century Kingdom of Benin. These renderings, the earliest visual depictions of West African instruments, include only one figure holding a stringed instrument: a small harp. A gold sculpture from the Akan people of Ghana, however—dated sometime between the fifteenth and seventeenth centuries—shows a musician playing a stringed instrument with a curved neck and a rounded resonator that looks as if made from a calabash.[24]

To understand what the music meant, and how it was intertwined with practices of storytelling, memory, and power, we need to turn to the lessons carried in the music itself. And that means looking to the griots, the "expert hereditary professional musicians" whose practice as makers of instruments and performers of music defined the cultural meaning and uses of stringed instruments in many societies in the region over the past centuries. The history of the griots is a story about the power of music and the attempts made over time to channel that power.[25]

Griot traditions offer a version of their origin story in the legendary Sundiata Epic, which was passed down in Mali within family lineages for generations and legitimizes their social role by anchoring it deep in the region's political history. One of the key characters in the story is griot Balla Fasséké, who plays a vital role in assuring the victory of the epic hero Sundiata Keita, an early king of the empire of Mali. The griots, as the epic explains, serve as "depositories of the knowledge of the past." "Every king wants to have a singer to perpetuate his memory," the epic explains: with their songs, they rescue "the memories of kings from oblivion, as men have short memories." But the role of Fasséké, and by extension of griots in general, is not only to cultivate memory. In the epic, the power he has to recount history enables him to help make it. He helps to prepare Sundiata's forces for battle by calling "to mind the history of old Mali" and spurring them on to their own feats of heroism: "I have told you what future generations will learn about your ancestors. What will we be able to relate to our sons so that your memory will stay alive?" With the final victory assured, Balla Fasséké composes "the great hymn 'Niama' which the griots still sing." At the great celebration, "the musicians of all countries were there," but it was Balla Fasséké who commanded them all. His prize for his loyalty was won not just for himself, but for his descendants: Sundiata Keita declared that the kings who would follow him would always "choose their griot from among your tribe." The role would come with a particular privilege, that of being able to "make jokes about all the tribes, and in particular about the royal tribe of Keita."[26]

The Sundiata Epic can help us understand how and why so many West African societies have cultivated and maintained a system in which music is provided by special "castes," groups—like the griots—whose role is passed on, and guarded, within particular families. That such work became hereditary is of course logical enough: musical skills, instrument building, and the corpus of song in memory could be preserved, protected, and passed on within families. But griots in West Africa also occupied a kind of curious double role. They were respected but also feared, included but also excluded. Within the social and political structures of West Africa, the creation of hereditary groups of musicians was probably a mechanism for containing and channeling the power of music. In some cases, one group that conquered another might absorb its former enemies' musicians, establishing them as a group apart within society in order to capture the power of their music. But in many cases griots became itinerant, moving from place to place, groups to be appropriated or deployed by those in power.[27]

What instruments did the griots play? In the Sundiata Epic, Fasséké plays the bala, or balafon, which creates "sounds of an infinite sweetness, notes clear and as pure as gold dust." But at some point in this history many griot musicians adopted stringed instruments that, in time, would become part of their signature practice. The turn to stringed instruments could have been driven by practical considerations: they are lighter and easier to carry than the bala. The griot became not only the players of these instruments but also their makers. In the long term, the widespread adoption of harps and plucked lutes by griot musicians helped to assure their presence throughout West Africa. In particular, a group of instruments with an oblong wooden body covered with an animal skin resonator—and known variously as the xalam, ngoni, or hoddu (among other names)—were familiar in many different regions. Their use by griots also meant that these instruments were celebrated and understood as vital participants in the transmission of memory and history, as well as accompanying the songs of praise and humor griots offered to communities. These instruments functioned as powerful symbols, condensing history and lineage, their sound connecting the living to generations of their ancestors.[28]

Taken together, Arabic sources, fragments of visual culture, and griot traditions offer a glimpse of the role played by stringed musical instruments in the culture of royal courts. What they don't give us is a sense of the music played by the "subordinate classes" in these African societies. There were other types of traditions of vernacular instrument making and playing, some of which were described by European travelers who began to venture into West and Central Africa during the fifteenth and sixteenth centuries. Such texts are often superficial, drawing vast conclusions based on punctual encounters, and sometimes infused with disdain and racism. But they are among the few written sources available and also very detail-oriented. These travelers often noticed aspects of daily cultural life, notably about the construction of musical instruments, which attracted their attention because they were unfamiliar. Through these observers, we can catch glimpses, and perhaps even a few bits of sound, from the musical worlds that some of the enslaved in the Americas would recall and draw on as they built and played the banjo.[29]

In 1468, the Portuguese traveler Alvise Ca da Mosto visited Cayor, in what is today northern Senegal. He wrote that the people there had "no musical instrument of any kind, save two"; one was a large drum, the other "after the fashion of viol; but it has, however, two strings only, and is played with the fingers, so that it is a simple rough affair and of no account." The "rough" two-stringed instrument was likely a lute made with an animal skin. Portuguese traveler Valentim Fernandes, who sailed along the coast of West Africa in the early 1500s, was struck by the music-making griots. He described them, interestingly, as "judeus,"—"Jews." He used this term not because he saw this group as part of the Jewish religion, but rather because—like Jews in Iberia—they were seen as a group apart, segregated and despised. He translated the local term for this group, meanwhile, as "Gaul," making for an odd pastiche of European ethnic terms projected onto a totally different social reality: "there are *judeus* and they are called *Gaul* and they are black like their countrymen; however they do not have synagogues and do not practice the ceremonies of other Jews." They lived in "separate villages," he went on, and "are often buffoons and play the viol and *cavacos* and are singers." The cavaco was a stringed instrument familiar in Iberia.[30]

In a 1602 account of the "Gold Kingdom of Guinea," in West Africa, Pieter de Marees described a larger series of instruments, including "wooden Drums cut from a hollow Tree, over which a Cabriet's skin is stretched," and "small Lutes, made out of a block, with a neck, like a Harp with 6 strings made of rush, on which they play with both hands." But the most detailed early European account of West African music comes to us from Richard Jobson, who traveled up the Gambia River in 1620 and 1621. "There is, without a doubt," he wrote, "no people on earth more naturally affected to the sound of musicke than these people." Important members of the community considered music "an ornament of their state, so that when we come to see them, their musicke will seldome be wanting." When traders came to the river to meet him, they always had musicians accompanying them and playing. These musicians, Jobson wrote, had "a perfect resemblance to the Irish Rimer sitting in the same maner as they doe upon the ground, somewhat removed from the company," singing songs that recalled the family history of the King, "exalting his ancestry, and recounting over all the worthy and famous acts by him or them hath been achieved." They also often improvised songs to please their audience. Although the music was highly regarded, the musicians were not. When they died, their corpses were set "upright in a hollow tree" rather than buried, because they were considered to have a "familiar conversation" with "their divelle *Ho-re*." To play well, it was believed, musicians needed to consort with evil beings. Some of Jobson's group actually brought their own instruments on the journey. But, he noted, they avoided playing "upon any Lute or Instrument which some of us for our private exercise did carry with us," because to do so would link them to the griots and therefore invite the scorn of their hosts.[31]

The griots, Jobson wrote, had "little variety of instruments," but the most common was "made of a great gourd, and a necke thereunto fastened, resembling, in some sort, our Bandora; but they have no manner of fret, and the strings they are either such as they place yeldes, or their invention can attane to make, being very unapt to yield a sweet and music sound, notwithstanding with pinnes they winde and bring to agree in tunable notes, having not above six strings upon their greatest instrument." Jobson's description is valuable for its details. Though he used a European term for a particular kind of lute with a circular resonator, the bandore, the instrument he described in detail here could have been either a lute or a harp. In either case, it had a gourd resonator and a system of pins, or pegs, used to tune the strings. Jobson suggests the presence of multiple stringed instruments, with the "greatest" having six strings. These instruments were often accompanied by another musician playing a "little drumme" which was held under the left arm of the player, and played with a "crooked stick" by the right hand and the "naked fingers" of the left, who also made a "rude noyse, resembling much the manner and countenance of those kinde of distressed people which among us are called Changelings." For Jobson, the music had something supernatural about it.[32]

Perhaps the first use of the term "griot" in a European text appeared in a 1685 text by a French merchant based in the port town Saint-Louis du Sénégal, Michel Jajolet de la Courbe. He described musicians encountered on his journeys to the regions to the interior. The "guiriots," as he called them, were "marvelous singing praises to me and their master, and they accompany their voice with a small lute with three horsehair strings that is not unpleasant to hear." De la Courbe had the pleasure of having the musicians praise him. The griots, he wrote, sang "martial" songs, "saying that you are of a great race, which they call *grands gens* in corrupt French, that you will overcome your enemies." They also complimented the French visitors for being "generous," before asking them for money in return for the song. During one journey, de la Courbe encountered a group of what he called Moors. Among them was a woman who played for him: "she held a kind of harp, which had a calabash covered with hide that had ten or twelve strings, which she played well enough; she began to sing an Arab song that was melodious but quite languishing, somewhat in the manner of the Spanish or Portuguese, accompanying herself with her harp with much care." De la Courbe was right to link the Moorish harp playing to the music of the Spanish or Portuguese, though of course the direction of influence had, historically, gone the other way around. His observation that the Wolof griots had begun incorporating French into their singing is a telling detail: musicians must be ever aware of their potential audiences and sources of income. By the late seventeenth century, French visitors, merchants, and slave traders were an increasing part of the economic, and therefore cultural, landscape.[33]

A few years later, in 1691, another French traveler, Jean-Jacques Le Maire, stopped off at the expanding slave trading fort on the island of

Gorée and then traveled along the Senegal River. He too wrote about the "guiriotz," who "Sing Panegyricks" for important men in their community, announcing "that they are great Lords, Rich, and as Puissant as White Men, who are great Slaves of a King." The fact that the griots described Europeans in this way gives us a bit of the complex flavor their praises could take. It was ostensibly a kind of compliment—and in other songs they referred to Europeans as "Rich Lords of the Sea"—but in calling them "Slaves" they also hinted that perhaps they weren't so powerful as they might think. Le Maire found such content "foolish," but admitted he was alone in this, as the Africans around him responded with enthusiasm. "I have seen them strip themselves to reward these false and fulsome Flatteries." Failing to pay the musicians brought with it significant hazards: for if they were stiffed of their "expected Fees" they turned their musical skills from praise to libel, spreading "as many base things as they can rip together," and "contradicting whatever they had said good of them." Le Maire described large drums along with a harp that in the right hands was "sufficiently harmonious" made up of a "row of several Strings of several sizes." He also saw an instrument that was played by a single musician: "a kind of Lute made of a piece of hollow Wood, cover'd with Leather, with two or three Strings of Hair, and adorn'd with Iron Plates and Rings." Le Maire, then, left us with another textual photograph of the kind of instrument that would have been familiar to some of those West Africans being captured and sold to European slave traders. He described this lute in particular as being "Proper for the Chamber of a Sick Person," suggesting it was used for solace and perhaps to accompany acts of healing—two reasons it would have been something the enslaved would seek to rebuild across the Atlantic.[34]

Although the early period of the slave trade centered on West Africa, European travelers, traders, and missionaries also journeyed to Central Africa beginning in the sixteenth century. From their accounts we can piece together a similar portrait of the stringed instruments that the enslaved who came from these regions, who in time became a majority, brought to the Americas. In a 1591 account of the Kingdom of the Kongo, the Portuguese merchant Duarte Lopez included a detailed description of "lutes of curious fashion" played in the royal court. "These lutes in the hollow and upper part resemble those used by ourselves, but the flat side, which we make of wood, they cover with skin, as thin as a bladder."

The strings, "made of very strong and bright hairs, drawn from the elephant's tail," as well as from "palm-tree threads," were strung from "the bottom to the top of the handle, each being tied to a separate peg, either shorter or longer, and fixed along the neck of the instrument." Hung from these pegs were "very thin iron and silver plates," which made "various sounds, according as the strings are struck, and are capable of very loud tones." "The players touch the strings of the lute in good time, and very cleverly with the fingers," Lopez wrote, though he added that he did "not know if I should call the sounds they call forth a melody, but merely such as pleases their senses." The musicians, however, had a remarkable and "very wonderful" capacity for communication, indicating through their playing "all that other people would express by words of what is passing in their minds, and by merely touching the strings signify their thoughts."[35]

In a 1637 description of Africa based partly on Lopez's account, Pierre d'Avity similarly described the presence of "lutes" in Central Africa made "in a way different than ours": the instrument wasn't "covered in wood, but with a parchment as thick as a bladder, with a hole cut out as delicately as possible, and the hairs from the tail of an elephant placed above and stretched out or loosened to create a diversity of sounds, with thin strips of iron or metal hanging from them." The musicians, he wrote, "don't play by distinguishing notes and intervals, but touch the strings without distinction, each of them creating a particular tone, creating more of a confused noise than an agreeable harmony. They nevertheless take pleasure in it, and the men and women move to the sound in cadence, lifting their feet and clapping their hands gracefully. They also express their intentions with this instrument, sometimes touching one string, sometimes another, to signify something." D'Avity's evocative passage caught the eye of a writer named Cyrano de Bergerac, who in a humorous fantasy about an alien land published in 1657 described a population who when they were "tired of talking" picked up "a lute or other instrument that they used as well as they could their voices to communicate their thoughts."[36]

The Capuchin missionary Giovanni Antonio Cavazzi spent nearly two decades, between 1654 and 1677, working the region in West Central Africa, notably in the Kingdom of the Kongo. He created a series of striking watercolors documenting life in the region, among the earliest eyewitness artistic depictions of Africa by a European. One of these images depicts three walking musicians. One is blowing into what looks like a calabash or gourd, another playing a balafon-like instrument, and the third plucking a two-chorded harp.[37]

Like the sources from West Africa, those from Central Africa suggest the presence of both lutes and harps of various styles, played both as part of court music and in more informal, vernacular contexts. Central African lutes and harps, as well as the broader musical practice of which they were a part, would be a critical part of the terrain and memory that musicians in the Americas would have to address. On the plantations West and Central Africans would find themselves brought together, forced to find forms of common language, often seeking the sense of solidarity that only music can generate.

✳

Over the centuries of constant exchange of musical practice and culture between West and North Africa, terms circulated just as people and instruments did. The term *ūd,* for instance, became the "etymological root for the Fulani picked, skin covered lute *hoddu.*" But none of these early texts—whether European or Arabic—transcribed the local names given to the instruments. Instead writers used their own terms to describe the instruments they saw, rather than worrying about what those who played them actually called them.[38]

The first Arabic source to name West African stringed instruments in an indigenous language comes in the form of a condemnation of their dangerous and sinful power. A religious text from the late eighteenth century forbade Muslims to play or listen to any stringed instruments, including a wide variety of Arab chordophones, including the ūd and tunbūr. The Fulani scholar Uthman b. Fūdi, a leader of a jihad that led to the creation of the Sokoto empire in the early nineteenth century, took aim at two other instruments that were specifically West African: the "molo" and "goge." These instruments, he complained, drew people away from Islam and toward immoral practices. "Muslims," he wrote in one poem, "refrain from gambling and deceit./Leave off playing the molo and going about with prostitutes." The music might be sweet to them, but in the end they would pay for listening to it.

Some of them, their intention is to go
  where the *goge* is played.
They fail to return to where the drums are
  played.
In the other world they will pay, for
  they will be uprooted.[39]

Religious leaders in North America would sometimes offer similar warnings: that the banjo and fiddle were "devil's music," something to be eschewed by true Christians.

Mungo Park, who wrote a best-selling account of his travels in Africa in the late eighteenth century, documented the indigenous names of three stringed instruments he encountered: the "*koonting,* a sort of guitar with three strings," along with the "*korro,* a large harp with eighteen strings" and the "*simbing,* a small harp with seven strings." He described two classes of musicians, one of them "*singing men*" called "*Jilli kea*"—a version of the term djeli, another name for the griots—who were present in "every town" and sang "extempore songs in honour of their chief men, and any other persons who are willing to give 'solid pudding for empty praise.'" "But a nobler part of their office is to recite the historic events of their country; hence in war, they accompany soldiers to the field, in order by reciting the great actions of their ancestors, to awaken in them a spirit of glorious emulation." The other class of musicians was made up of those of "Mohameden faith, who travel about the country, singing devout hymns, and performing religious ceremonies, to conciliate in favour of the Almighty, either in averting calamity, or in insuring success to any enterprise." Both groups of "itinerant bards," he added, were "much employed and respected by the people," and the beneficiaries of "very liberal contributions" made to reward them for their artistry.[40]

By the late eighteenth century, in part because of the importance given to the differences between "nations" in Africa by slave traders and purchasers of slaves in the Americas, some writers explicitly identified music and instruments with particular ethnic groups. Olaudah Equiano, in his famous late eighteenth-century autobiography, noted that among his people, the Igbo, there were "many musical instruments," including one that resembled a guitar, which was among those "chiefly used by betrothed virgins, who play on them for all grand festivals."[41]

Hugh Clapperton, a Scot who went on a series of journeys along the Niger River in the 1820s, offered extensive details about the stringed instruments and music of the Hausa. At a market near the town of Sansan Birnee in Bornou, he saw musicians playing in "bands . . . composed of drums, flutes, and a kind of guitar, with strings of horsehair, called the Erbale, each after its rude fashion," who were "parading from booth to booth, to attract the attention of customers." At another point in his travels, in the town of Koolfu, he stayed in a house that was filled each night with music until dawn. "Their music consists of the drum, erbab, or guitar of the Arabs, and the Nyffe harp, and the voice. Their songs are mostly extempore, and allude to the company present." He witnessed the celebrations of the end of Ramadan, during which all in the town visited one another, "giving and receiving presents, parading the streets with horns, guitars, and flutes." Equality reigned, he wrote, "parties of men were seen dancing: free men and slave all were alike; not a clouded brow was to be seen in Koolfu." Clapperton found particular solace in the songs played by one Hausa man. "Finding I could not sleep, and hearing the sound of sweet-toned instruments, I sent for the musician, and made him play and sing to me." He asked the musician to return the next day. "I made a sketch of his instrument, which I asked him to sell to me; but he said he had played on it to his father and mother, and they were pleased with it; they were now dead, and he would not part with it." The instrument was clearly more than simply a material object, carrying in it a family history. Though Clapperton's sketch of this instrument wasn't published, an engraving based on a sketch by one of his companions shows several stringed instruments being played as part of a reception for the group of European travelers by the Sultan of Bornou.[42]

Taken together, these sources offer fragments of the mosaic of musical culture in West and Central Africa. We see and hear of different types of stringed instruments—lutes and harps of different styles, with different numbers of strings—as well as of the various settings in which music was played, from the highest courts to street celebrations and individual houses. The presence of griots throughout many parts of West Africa meant that certain instruments, notably the stringed lutes they often played, were well-known throughout the region. But the general impression is one of a great diversity in styles of musical instruments, of a richly layered cartography of both style and function.

Today, researchers and musicians studying the history of the banjo, notably Greg Adams and Shlomo Pestcoe, are doing vital research aimed at cataloguing and documenting the contemporary traditions of lute playing in West Africa in order to give us a fuller picture of the diversity of styles of construction and performance—including the implications of the distinctions between griot practice and other musical forms—in the region. As it continues, such research will increasingly illuminate and expand our understanding of the West African roots of the banjo. But we can also gain an understanding and appreciation for how varied the stringed instruments of Africa are through a remarkable material catalogue: that made up of the collections of materials gathered by European colonial powers in the nineteenth and twentieth centuries.

*

"Nowhere is there a larger variety of harps than in Africa: they are played by people in more than fifty cultures, each with a distinct musical tradition," writes Sue Carole DeVale. The extensive diversity of West and Central African stringed instruments comes across clearly in the collections and studies generated by imperial administrators and travelers to the French and Belgian colonies. In the Congo, for instance, the Belgian colonial regime intently collected musical instruments—along with many other material and natural objects—that became part of the massive Royal Museum of Central Africa, in Tervuren, Belgium. A catalogue devoted specifically to the stringed instruments of the collection includes descriptions and photographs of a total of 427 in all, with an extremely wide range of styles of construction, including gourd and wood resonators, harps of various types, and a number of anthropomorphic instruments that have sculptures of heads, legs, and arms as part of their constructions.[43]

A 1929 French study by Stephen Chauvet entitled *Musique Nègre* contains a detailed chapter on musical instruments, including several different types of chordophones played in the Belgian Congo as well as in the French colonies of Guinée and Gabon. These include one called the konimesin in the French colonial region of Haute-Guinée, played by griots, made with a wooden resonator covered entirely with an animal skin, a long rounded neck, and four strings tuned with leather bands. Two strings were tuned to the lower octaves, two to the higher ones. The griots wore a panther's nail on their index finger to play, sometimes playing simultaneously with index finger and thumb. At the end of the neck was a metal piece with holes in it, which was moved when the strings were strummed, playing the role of an "accompanying drum." The griot often struck the resonator with his palm as he played. A similar instrument, the dounsoukoni, was played by griots who traveled with hunters. In Gabon, meanwhile, an instrument called an ombi—covered with the skin of a snake, a gazelle, or a goat—was played, the strings made out of long, thin roots from a specific tree. The instruments of the Azande people were described by the study as being particularly beautiful sculpturally. Covered with various types of skins—antelopes, buffalo, elephant—the strings were made either from vines or from the tail of a giraffe. Many included detailed carvings of human heads, sometimes with elaborate hair styles, at the end of the necks; while others were sculpted so that the entire instrument was shaped like a human body, with arms pressed along the body of the resonator, and the neck of the instrument shaped like a human neck and head.[44]

The diversity of construction also means a great diversity of sound. Harps as well as lutes can serve as both string instruments and percussion instruments. Many of these instruments have metal devices attached to them that "add a kind of percussive 'buzzing' quality to the harp that lightly veils the sound of the melodies or patterns played on it." These devices are often thin sheets of metal with holes drilled in them and can be decorated with designs. In some cases they are fitted to the top of the neck of the instruments; in other cases they hang from it or are attached to the resonator itself. They can take surprising forms: on one instrument, lizard skins filled with banana leaves are placed below each string; on another small pellet bells are placed on the resonator; and one has a sound hole covered with "spider-egg cocoons." In addition to delivering a buzz that is valued for its aesthetics, these have the advantage of emitting "a sound considerably higher in pitch than the harp strings, one which may carry further than the strings; the sound of these devices can sometimes announce or lure an audience to outdoor performances from a surprising distance away." The instruments can also be directly played as percussion. Sometimes a harpist is accompanied by another musician who taps out a beat on the resonator with sticks, or plays an "asymmetrical counterrhythm." Players of lutes and harps sometimes tap the skin underneath the strings as they play or flick their fingers against the resonator itself. Others knock their instrument against the ground to make a beat. In some cases, the percussion itself becomes the main focus: in one instrument from Guinea played in Dakar, Senegal, a single string stretched out from a large gourd body covered with a drumhead, and the musician flicked the string with his thumbs as he played the drum with his palms.[45]

We can get a startling picture of how diverse the construction of instruments was from one study of the music of the Hausa, one of the largest ethnic groups in West Africa. Members of this group play about fifty different musical instruments, among them a series of lutes. These include the kuntingo, a single-stringed instrument whose neck is made of bamboo, whose resonator is covered with calf skin, and whose string is made of camel hairs. There is also the garaya, a "two-stringed plucked lute" that comes in two sizes: a small wooden instrument made with a wooden resonator, and the babbar garaya, which is larger and has a gourd resonator. This instrument is often decorated with a kurman laya, a "talisman" usually made up of a "written passage from the Koran sewn in a leather pouch," and was traditionally used to accompany songs in praise of hunters. Another two-stringed pluck lute played by the Hausa is the gurmi, which has indigo seeds placed under the bridge to create the "characteristic 'buzzing' sound" of the instrument. Finally, the molo has three strings, a neck made of bamboo, and a short string that is used as a drone. The instrument, traditionally used to accompany songs in praise of famous warriors, is played in such a way that the fingers of the right hand frequently tap the membrane covering the resonator—generally made of the skin of a goat or duiker (antelope)—as they play.[46]

These kinds of instruments are also still played in North Africa. The most commonly used term to describe them is gunbrī or gunībrī, usually rendered in English today as guimbri or ginbri. These are instruments that look a lot like those being played by saints in the tenth-century illustration mentioned at the beginning of this chapter as well as those depicted in the Egyptian tombs. But in the Maghreb today, particularly in Morocco, the guimbri has come to occupy a rather contained and specific role within musical culture, usually, though not exclusively, associated with a group called the Gnawa and their religious ceremonies. The term Gnawa is believed to be derived from the word Guinea and refers to people descended from West African merchants, mercenaries, and slaves who have been part of North African societies for centuries. Their religious ceremonies are announced publicly by the playing of large drums. "Once inside the house," writes Philip Schuyler, "the musicians put down their drums in favor of the ginbri, a three-stringed lute with sliding leather tuning rings and metal sound modifier." A given tune played on the instrument "may be used to summon the saint or spirit who 'owns' that melody; if the music then sends one of the participants into a trance, that is taken as proof that the spirit has responded to the summons."[47]

Although many of those who play lutes and harps throughout the African continent "entertain with stories, recite oral histories and genealogies," and share myths and fables, musicians also often play roles in religious rituals like those of the Gnawa: "their harps may be mediums for communication with the spirits of the ancestors." In fact, harps themselves can be the focus of rituals "tied to their life cycle," with the instruments themselves subject to initiation. And in many cases their "sound can be essential to the efficacy of a ritual for a person, place, or thing other than the harp itself, whether seen or unseen." This is true of lutes as well: as J. H. Kwabena Nketia notes: "The lute player of the Konkomba of Ghana plays his instrument in seclusion when he wishes to commune with his god."[48]

The decorations on some instruments condense their cultural and religious meaning into a set of powerful symbols. One particularly rich example of this is a harp called the ngombi, played in the context of Bwiti religious ceremonies practiced in the regions of Gabon and Cameroon since at least the nineteenth century. The harp's very construction "represents both the microcosmic world of the living and the macrocosmic world of the gods and ancestors." Bwiti emphasizes the "complementarity of female and male," and the harp is built so that "the resonator symbolizes the stomach of the female principle, the source of all life" while the neck is "the symbol of male potency." The "juncture of the neck and resonator" represents "sexual union." The harp is painted half red, to symbolize the blood of menstruation, and half white, to symbolize semen. But the harp also resonates with the imagery of Nyingwan Mbege, the Sister of God, who is central to Bwiti practice: "her features are carved or sculpted on the shelf of the harp; the resonator is her stomach, her womb, her spiritual Source of Life; the neck and the tuning pegs are her spine and ribs; and the strings, her tendons and sinews." The sound holes on the harp are positioned so that the two on the top represent her breasts, and a lower one "the birth hole." When the musician takes up this instrument, Nyingwan Mbege works through him. "The powers of the Sister of God work through the harpist, who is considered to be the guardian of the chapel, and the spirits of ancestor harpists enter the body of the harp, as the rest of the ancestors enter the chapel." The harp is the mechanism of communication between the living and the gods and ancestors: it is "the sound of the music played by the dead in the afterworld" and "transmits their blessings to the living Bwiti," even as it also carries "their prayers" in the other direction. Without the music of the harp, the ceremonies cannot happen: "the *ngombi* serves as the primary path of communication between the world of the living and that of the gods and ancestors, the seen and the unseen."[49]

The construction and meaning of instruments was never static. Sometime in the seventeenth or eighteenth centuries, the kora emerged as part of a group of West African instruments that were the "newest members of the African harp family." The kora has a system of additional stabilizers that make it possible to have two necks to accommodate its twenty-one strings, which enable a broader musical spectrum of more than three octaves. These innovations allowed for a different kind of tuning and a "seven-tone scale" to be used, which opened up new possibilities for melody and vocal accompaniment. The instrument was immortalized in several preserved sculptures, including one made by the Dogon people of Mali. In time, the kora would become a defining instrument for many griot traditions, and some musicians have taken these traditions to the international stage and made them—and the instrument itself—widely recognizable to audiences worldwide.[50]

As recent research by Greg Adams, Shlomo Pestcoe, and Ulf Jagfors has demonstrated, the West African plucked lute that is the closest in construction to the New World banjo is an instrument called the akonting, played today among the Jola in Gambia. It was mentioned in Mungo Park's narrative and in recent years has been brought to the attention of banjo players and researchers through the work of Daniel Jatta, a musician from Mandinary, Gambia. This instrument has a large round resonator made with a gourd covered with an animal skin. It also has a bridge that stands upright on the skin head of the instrument. It is similar to a few other West African instruments, including the Manjak bunchundo, Bijago ngopata, and the Balanta kusundu and kisinta, all still played in Guinea-Bissau. The akonting has three strings, and the top one is shorter than the other two and is played with the thumb, while the other strings are played using a downstroke technique with the top of the fingers—in a way very similar to what is called "clawhammer" style in the United States. Jola societies have not included castes of musicians, as many other West African societies have, and the akonting is not played by particular families. Its construction, playing style, and the fact that it was a popular and vernacular instrument all suggest that it was likely one of the influential examples in the formation of the banjo in the Caribbean.[51]

The regional ancestors of the Jola people, like other agricultural peoples in the coastal regions of West Africa, were particularly vulnerable to slave traders, who, in the seventeenth and eighteenth centuries, transformed life in the region. Boat after boat took people away across the waters, carrying with them the memory of music and instruments, heading into an exile of suffering in which that memory—and the ability to make music anew—would be key to survival. Those who remained behind had to find ways to speak about, and to remember, the disappeared. Several instrument makers seem to have found a way to do so, making what one scholar has called "shiplike" instruments. Four such instruments were collected in the nineteenth century in different parts of West Africa and are now housed in collections in Sweden, Switzerland, Holland, and England; but their precise dates of construction are unknown. Their resonators are carved to look like the hull of a large ship, the kind that would sail across the Atlantic, and two of them have rudders carved at their base. The necks of these instruments are decorated with figures, the way that many harps are but also the way that the front of a ship might be decorated with a symbol or carved sculpture. On two of these the figure is an antelope. But on one of them, collected in Sierra Leone, the short neck is topped with a beautifully and elaborately carved head of a woman. The strings would have stretched from this head and neck to a small peg sticking out of the body of the instrument, almost like a tilted mast. But she faces downwards; if the boatlike instrument were on the ocean, she would be looking under the water.[52]

On the other side of the ocean, those who survived the crossing desperately needed music to survive and make sense of their new reality. Though some musicians were certainly among those who made the crossing, the structures surrounding musical performance and transmission were, like so much else, gone. So, too, were the instruments that had sounded in communities left behind. In a new world, a new instrument would ultimately be born, based on the memories of those from the other side but responding to the need for a music that would cross boundaries and create new solidarities.

2

The First African Instrument

In Derek Walcott's epic poem *Omeros,* the fisherman Achille is carried in his boat from the Caribbean to Africa. Back in his ancestral homeland, he confronts fragmentary images of the ravages of the slave trade and speaks to his departed father. Then, he hears music: "the griot muttering his prophetic song / of sorrow that would be the past." The griot describes Achille's "ashen ancestors / from the Bight of Benin, from the margin of Guinea," and then recounts the story of the Middle Passage: "We were the colour of shadows when we came down / with tinkling leg-irons to join the chains of the sea, / for the silver coins multiplying on the sold horizon."[1]

With the griot's song done, the poem's narrator reflects on what was lost:

> So there went Ashanti one way, the Mandingo another,
> the Ibo another, the Guinea. Now each man was a nation
> in himself, without mother, father, brother. . . .
>
> Yet they felt the sea-wind tying them into one nation
> of eyes and shadows and groans, in the one pain
> that is inconsolable, the loss of one's shore

49

with its crooked footpath. They had wept, not for
their wives only, their fading children, but for strange,
ordinary things. . . .

They cried for the little thing after the big thing.
They cried for a broken gourd.[2]

"But they crossed, they survived," writes Walcott. The "epic" story
he evokes is the history of Afro-Atlantic culture and of the foundations
of American culture. That process—the loss of a shore, and of the institutions and practices of being part of a particular African "nation," and
the experience of survival and reconstitution that followed—has pulled
at generations of writers, scholars, and artists. What did this loss mean
to those who lived it? How did they do the unthinkable and survive?
Walcott identifies the key to that process when he writes of the enslaved
crying "for the little thing after the big thing." The process of survival
was fundamentally about reasserting and reconstituting both the big and
the small. This process was carried out, in no small measure, through the
creation of sounds that conveyed memories, longings, and the assertion
of self and community.

Scholars have developed a term to describe this epic of cultural creation: "creolization." The term is now so elastic and overburdened by
decades of debate that using it is sometimes more trouble than it is worth.
But the core theorizations of creolization—the fertile anthropological
essay by Richard Price and Sidney Mintz, the historical writings of
Edward Kamau Brathwaite, the writings of Edouard Glissant—all in one
way or another seek to understand how the enslaved on Caribbean plantations were able to create vibrant new cultures in the midst of oppression
and exile. They all begin by acknowledging the extreme and relatively
unique historical situation that developed in the seventeenth and eighteenth centuries in the Caribbean. By the end of that period, several
colonial societies—including Jamaica, Suriname, and French Saint-
Domingue—had a population that was about ninety percent enslaved.
Because of high death rates, hovering around fifty percent among those
arriving from the Middle Passage, and the rapacious importation of new
slaves, the majority of the population on these islands was African-born.
The free white population was concentrated in urban centers, so that in

plantation zones the enslaved made up the vast majority of the population. Even in port cities slaves were a majority. Though the enslaved were marginalized from the powerful cultural and religious institutions, they occupied most of the physical space of these colonies, especially its sonic space.[3]

The patterns of the slave trade to the Caribbean rose and fell, shifted and scattered, according to the choices of the Europeans who bought slaves and the Africans who sold them, the economics of shipping, happenstance, weather, and disease. The result was a constant demographic unpredictability in the plantation world. There were generations of arrivals from certain regions, and thus heavier concentrations of slaves from one part of Africa or another in certain places and times. But the pace of cultural encounter and exchange must have been bewildering. On most Caribbean plantations, newcomers were a permanent feature of social life. Often, they did encounter a familiar language or traditions among the enslaved who were already on the plantation. But sometimes they didn't. And in all cases, they had to figure out how to integrate themselves into a world that was brutal, threatening, and in many ways incomprehensible and absurd in the way it was built. "Most would carry," writes Sidney Mintz, "in hand and heart and head, memories of before, skills and songs, and lots of ideas about the proper way to do this and that: to eat, to greet, to court, to pray, to care for children, to make love—even to gesture, to walk, to smile."[4]

In many other places and times, people from different cultures, speaking different languages, have found themselves thrown together. But the intensity and compression of the Caribbean plantation system, in which the diversity of the enslaved was matched by the demand for homogeneity of a totalitarian racial order, created a very specific environment that had never been seen before. There had not previously been societies in the world in which the vast majority of the population was enslaved. Nor had prior slave systems, such as those of ancient Rome, been so intensely racialized or created such an intractable link between skin color and inherited social status. The Caribbean was just one part of a larger plantation complex stretching from Brazil through North America, with different demographics and social structures. The processes that took shape there were not unique, and there were many links with other regions as well. But because of the very early development of plantation societies in the region, and the pivotal role they played in the expansion of the French and British empires in the Americas, the region played a foundational role in the development of practices and culture of both masters and slaves.

Part of what happened in the Americas, notably in the Caribbean, was the invention of something called "Africa." Within the continent itself during the seventeenth and eighteenth century, the term had little meaning. But in the plantation context, it took on a new importance as displaced people from throughout the continent were thrown together and had begun to communicate and survive together. In the midst of a brutal plantation world, within a community made up of peoples from throughout the African continent, they sought out ways to create moments of commonality and coalition. What the enslaved invented, what they in many cases decided they needed, were cultural forms that were welcoming, that could embrace variety, but that were still familiar enough to be recognizable. Most importantly, they had to bring people together, to create new solidarities. Music and dance were particularly powerful ways to create moments of commonality and coalition. They could call up Africa in a way that created links and resonances between enslaved people from widely different cultures. The enslaved generally shared an understanding of the social and ritual necessity of music, of its power to channel memory, and to heal. From their diverse experiences in Africa, they fashioned something new, assembled out of past practices but repurposed in a new environment.

The banjo was the growing of a new gourd in strange lands to replace the broken ones of the old, the crafting of strings to sound out new songs. It became a way to connect with both the past and the present, to build a bridge of memory and recall. It welcomed different styles, generating solidarity and community through its sound. The child of the Middle Passage and the bewildering situation of exile and oppression in the plantation world, it brought together traditions of instrument making from various parts of West and Central Africa. In this way, it offered something vital to those on the plantation: it was recognizably African, an instrument capable of offering familiar melodies and rhythms, but without being clearly derived from the traditions of any single African ethnicity. It was the first African instrument.

The story of how this happened lies in the evanescent traces left by those who made the earliest of banjos in the Caribbean and North America. But it can only be understood as part of a larger story: that of the cultural movements created by the enslaved, that of the gatherings, dance, and song that created spaces in which past lives could be remembered and new ones, beyond the world of slavery, could be imagined.[5]

*

Father Labat was disturbed but resigned. There was a movement afoot, and it couldn't be stopped or contained. The enslaved in the colonies of Martinique and Guadeloupe, where Labat lived between 1694 and 1696, were determined to gather and dance what they called the calenda. It was, he reluctantly admitted, such an enticing dance that not only the slaves but also many Spanish colonists in the New World had taken it up with enthusiasm, performing it "in the same way as the Negroes." He had even seen a group of nuns perform it, at Christmastime, in front of a delighted crowd. This was particularly alarming to him, given that the calenda exuded eroticism.[6]

The dancers formed two lines across from one another, women on one side, men on the other, surrounded by a circle made up of spectators and the drummers. The "most talented" among the group offered up "a song composed on the spot, on whatever subject he chooses, whose refrain, sung by all the spectators, is accompanied by strong hand-clapping." The dancers held their arms in the air "as if they were playing castanets." They jumped and twirled about, moved toward one another and back again, following the beat laid down by the drums. When the drummers changed the beat, they moved close together and began slapping their thighs against one another. This was the part that made the monk Labat most uncomfortable: men thrusting against women, women against men, thighs and stomachs pressed together. The dancers then pulled back and "pirouetted," then pressed together again with "totally lascivious gestures, as many times as the drums called, which was often several times in a row." Sometimes, too, they entwined their arms together, circling around a few times while striking their thighs together and "kissing each other."[7]

The local authorities, Labat noted, had passed several regulations outlawing the calenda dance, both because of the "indecent postures" it entailed and because when too many slaves assembled and got "carried away by joy" the result could be "revolts, uprisings, or groups getting together to go steal." But it was, the monk admitted, essentially impossible to stop the calenda, because "of all their pastimes it is the one that they like the most, and to which they most respond." French masters and authorities had tried a process of substitution, teaching French dances like the minuet. The enslaved took these up quickly, so much so that Labat admitted they were better at them than "many who pride themselves on being good dancers." But learning these dances didn't stop the enslaved from seeking out the calenda whenever they could. "Their passion for this dance is beyond the imagination: the old, the young, even children who can barely stand up" all loved it. "It seems like they danced it in the wombs of their mothers."[8]

The calenda wasn't the only dance Labat has seen during his time in the colonies. There were others performed by groups of slaves from a particular region in Africa. Those from the Congo got in a circle, and staying in one spot, did "nothing but lift their feet in the air, and stomp on the ground in a kind of cadence, holding their bodies half curved over in front of each other, mumbling some story that one member of the group told, to which the dancers replied with a refrain, while the spectators clapped their hand." The Mina danced by moving in a circle, their faces outwards. Those from Cape Verde or Gambia had their own dances as well. "Dance is their favorite passion, and I doubt there is any people on earth more attached to it than they are," he wrote. Labat, who had directly overseen the work of slaves, recommended that masters allow the enslaved to hold dances on their own plantations: if they didn't, he explained, they would simply leave and look elsewhere for them. Even after working in the sugar mills until midnight on a Saturday, he claimed, they would walk several miles to get to "some place where they know there is a dance."[9]

Guadeloupe and Martinique had been settled in the 1630s, and were well-established plantation societies by the time Labat arrived in the 1690s. Their cultures were already somewhat creolized, populated by a few generations of both settlers and enslaved people and their children. But, as the plantation complex expanded, there were increasing numbers of new African arrivals. Labat observed how the members of certain ethnic groups helped one another, setting aside food so that they could offer it to "those of their country" who were in need. He noticed a "kind of dice game" slaves played with "shells that serve as money," and which were tossed on a surface: players won or lost based on how many landed face up or down. He was witnessing the transference of the use of shells—cowrie shells in West Africa—as both money and for play, as well as other uses. The shells he saw used to play a game were also used, in both African and Afro-Atlantic contexts, for divination and other religious purposes.[10]

The calenda dance, Labat wrote, was African in origin: it came from the "Coast of Guinea," and "from all appearances from the Arada Kingdom." The dance and music likely did have West African origins, but by the 1690s it clearly was a phenomenon that brought together enslaved from a variety of different backgrounds. It was a dance of coalition, different from those still identifiable as Congo or Mina, clearly identified as African but in a general sense, and transmitted through continual, effusive participation. Labat doesn't say what language the songs were in, and that may have depended on who was singing: some songs and refrains were probably in African languages, others in the Creole tongue that had emerged on the island. The music for the calenda was provided by two drummers who communicated intricately with the dancers so that they could move from one part of the dance to another. The drums were made out of carved tree trunks covered on one end with "the skin of a hairless goat or sheep, scraped like a parchment." One was known simply as the grand tambour, or "big drum," sometimes as many as four feet long, and a smaller one known as the baboula. They were played with the "flat part of four fingers on each hand." The larger drum was played with "measure and poise," while the baboula was played more quickly and "almost without keeping a beat," according to Labat, making a sound that was "very sharp" and marked neither the cadence nor the "movement of the dancers." In this the normally very observant Labat had clearly missed something, since the interlaced beat of the two drums certainly shaped the dance.[11]

Besides drummers, other musicians played at the gatherings of the enslaved, including some "who play the violin rather well, and make money playing for gatherings and at the celebrations of their marriages."

But, Labat noted, another stringed instrument was much more popular: "Almost all of them play a kind of guitar made of a half of a calabash covered with leather scraped into the shape of parchment, with a rather long neck. On it they place only four strings made of silk, pitre, or dried bird intestines, and prepared with castor oil." (Pitre is a filament taken from the agave plant). Labat continued: "These strings are elevated a good inch above the skin that covers the calabash with a bridge. They play by pinching and beating the strings." Labat complained that the music they played was "not agreeable" and not very melodic but admitted that some considered it as highly as they did the music of "Italian or Spanish peasants, who all have guitars and play very badly."[12]

Labat didn't explain exactly when this "kind of guitar" was played, though he suggested it was fairly ubiquitous among the enslaved. It may have accompanied some of the dances, perhaps the calenda, as well as being played in smaller and more intimate settings, in plantation quarters and houses for instance. His detailed description of how the instrument was constructed suggests that he had seen a number of them in different places, which means that artisans in both Guadeloupe and Martinique were likely making the instrument in similar ways. The technology on display there drew on African traditions: the gourd, the skin head, the bridge. Labat didn't specify the shape of the neck, though his description of the instrument as a "kind of guitar" and the fact that it had four strings suggest that it was probably flat.

Who was making these instruments? And who was playing them? Labat had seen many groups of Africans who were singing and dancing in their own languages. But it is unlikely that there would always have been a musician from each of these groups available in any given community. In the areas of West Africa from which most of the enslaved coming to the Caribbean at the time were from, the music would often have been provided by specialists from particular families, such as the griots. The most prized court musicians, even if captured in war, were unlikely to be sold into Atlantic slavery but rather incorporated into a conquering kingdom's own orchestra. Members of other musical "castes" operating in the region probably were enslaved and sold at times, as were individuals who played music in less formalized and hereditary contexts. Such musicians, however, would most of the time have been most familiar with one tradition of music. And in the Caribbean, they would often have had difficulty finding or building the kind of instruments they had played in Africa. The "kind of guitar" observed by Labat, and the musicians who played them, therefore had to play multiple musical roles for various groups of Africans seeking different songs and rhythms.[13]

The music might not always have been just right, but in time skilled musicians—drawing on past knowledge and learning from others in the new context—would have been able to offer enough. And they would have needed an instrument that gave them the flexibility and latitude to play different kinds of songs within the diverse gatherings of the slaves who met at the cultural crossroads that was the Caribbean. In a sense, this already ubiquitous instrument was like the calenda dance, crossing boundaries and gathering audiences with the musicians busy "pinching and beating the strings" as they sought out the sounds of solidarity.

According to an account written in 1687, life on a Jamaican plantation went like this: at four in the morning, the enslaved were called to work with the sound of a "horn or shell." Until dusk, they worked in the fields, where the whip was used to make sure they didn't "loiter." At the end of the day, "those pore slaves leave off work and repair to their houses, where they gett their suppers, make a great fier, and with a kitt (made of a gourd or calabash and one twine string) play, sing and daunce according to their own countrey fashon, making themselves all mirth, men and women together in a confused manner."[14]

So wrote a man with the unassuming name of John Taylor and the unassuming profession of math teacher. A short and wearing stint in the army, a set of family quarrels, and the need for money had convinced him to embark on the risky venture of seeking his fortune in Britain's newest Caribbean colony: Jamaica. He invested in three convicts as indentured laborers and in late 1686 boarded a ship across the Atlantic. On arrival, Taylor sold these three indentured laborers to raise some money and then promptly got sick and lost most of it. He found paid work trolling the Caribbean for pirates. After a brief stint at this, and in the wake of a devastating earthquake that sent a good portion of Jamaica's capital, Port Royal, tilting into the sea, he returned to the Isle of Wight in England, where he wrote up a manuscript account of what he had seen in the

Caribbean. Though Taylor seems to have planned on publishing the work, he never did so. Luckily for us, however, the manuscript made its way to the Library of Jamaica and is now recognized as one of the key sources for understanding the early history of the Caribbean.[15]

Jamaica was in many ways a frontier society: ceded to the English from the Spanish in 1670, its interior was populated partly by groups of escaped slaves, known as Maroons, who had already consolidated their communities under Spanish rule. Like the French, the British had developed their first colonies in the Eastern Caribbean. The most successful of these was Barbados, which was already so heavily populated by the late seventeenth century that it was hard for new settlers to come by land. New arrivals wanting to get in on the growing industry of sugar production needed other places to go. Some ended up in the southern states of North America, creating colonies in the Carolinas. Others made their way to Jamaica and set up plantations. More than 33,000 enslaved Africans had arrived in Jamaica since 1670, with more than 3,000 arriving in 1687 alone. This was small compared with what was to come: more than 900,000 slaves would be brought to Jamaica by the early nineteenth century, with more than 27,000 arriving per year at the peak of the slave trade in the 1790s.[16]

All of the African-born slaves shared one thing: the experience of exile through the Middle Passage. As Taylor noted, having been sold in Jamaica the enslaved seemed "to grieve and lament the loss of their country freedom, and their now captivity, which they sing or bellow forth in their own language in a mournfull manner." The population on any given plantation might include clusters of enslaved people from a particular African group, sometimes bought together from the same slave ship, who could therefore gather to sing in their "country fashion." But many arrivals found themselves alone amidst unfamiliar languages and practices. Taylor noted how individuals from different plantations sought one another out on Sundays, "goeing to vissit their countrymen in other plantations, where according to their own country fashon they feast, dance, and sing (or rather howle like beasts) in a anticque manner, as if they were all madd." He similarly described the larger celebrations that took place on religious holidays: "they meet with those of one and the same countrye, and feast, sing, and dancce in a confused manner, seeming all mixth men and women together; thus they howle instead of singing, and play on a kitt whilst others drum, or beatt against a hollow tree, or board, and the rest nimbly dance in a strange anticque manner after this their musick, in such sort that they all seem madd." In these dances, Taylor may have actually been witnessing ritual events that included some of the forms of possession that were part of African traditions and would become a cornerstone of Afro-Atlantic religion. Such rituals, reconfigured and reconstituted in a new context, would become a cornerstone of Afro-Caribbean social and religious life. They provided a space of consolation and consolidation, and at times resistance, to the truly mad world of the plantation.[17]

Not long after Taylor left Jamaica, a man named Hans Sloane arrived in the colony. He too, rapidly became fascinated with the cultural and spiritual life of the enslaved. "The *Negroes* from some Countries," Hans Sloane wrote, "think they return to their own Country when they die in *Jamaica,* and therefore regard death but little, imagining they shall change their condition, by that means from servile to free, and so for this reason often cut their own Throats." Whether they committed suicide or died "naturally," he went on, "their Country people make great lamentations, mournings, and howlings about them expiring, and at their Funeral throw in Rum and Victuals into their Graves, to serve them in the other world. Sometimes they bury it in gourds, at other times spill it on the Graves."[18]

Hans Sloane's ancestors had been colonizers too. He was part of an aristocratic family from Scotland that was part of the English colonization of Northern Ireland. By the time Sloane was born, his family was relatively poor; and like many others who had fallen on hard times in seventeenth-century England and Ireland, Sloane looked to reinvent himself by journeying to the New World. He traveled as the physician in the service of the Duke of Albemarle, who was named governor of Jamaica in 1687. His employer died within the year from disease, which was common in Jamaica and elsewhere in the Caribbean for new arrivals. But Sloane remained in Jamaica in service of the Duke's family, as a guest on the governor's estate. And he embarked on the work that would ultimately become his life calling: that of an observer and collector of the natural world, as well as the human one.[19]

Sloane had studied in France and absorbed some of the developing approaches and methods of scientific observation, collection, and analysis of nature. In Jamaica he set about studying the environment of the island, hoping to produce a catalogue of the plants and animals of the Americas. He soon realized that the best way to learn about the flora and fauna was to tap into the rich knowledge on the part of the indigenous people and the enslaved of Jamaica. As he worked with them, he became as interested in the artifacts and practices of the humans in Jamaica as he was in its plants and animals.

Sloane later described his journey to Jamaica as a pilgrimage, and he returned from it transformed. In the Caribbean he had encountered a truly new set of sedimented histories and cultures—indigenous, Spanish, African, emergent Creole—and as a result, his practice of collecting became "diverse, multifaced and eclectic." The encounters and dialogues he had with people on the island expanded what had begun as a focused botanical project into something that aimed at documenting and exploring cultural and social practices. Sloane's vision was ambitious, if not utopian: his goal became nothing short of "aiming to archive every thing in the world, each a specimen of truly infinite variety." His influence transformed the scientific club of which he was a part, the Royal Society, from a "gathering of a few English gentlemen" interested in observing the natural world to "a global institution which received, and actively sought," objects, accounts, and interpretations from throughout the expanding British empire. The Caribbean world had incited and inspired in Sloane a new intellectual project with far-reaching consequences.[20]

Sloane became the hub of a new world of collecting. Building on the foundation of what he had gathered in Jamaica, he expanded what was effectively a personal museum and library with objects that were either donated to him or acquired from travelers and administrators returning from journeys within and beyond the growing British Empire. It was such a diverse and rich collection that it ultimately became the foundation for the new British Museum, founded in 1753. One of its most remarkable holdings was three hundred bound volumes of dried plant specimens. The most famous was one of cacao that Sloane had brought back from Jamaica in 1689; for among Sloane's accomplishments, perhaps the most enduring was his creation and marketing of a drink called hot chocolate. But perhaps the richest and strangest part of his collection was the group of two thousand items ultimately catalogued as "miscellaneous things." A portion of this collection was devoted to slavery: "a bullet that had allegedly belonged to one of Jamaica's free black maroons," clothing, weapons, whips, and—in a startling condensation of the brutality of the plantation world and the imbrication of elite intellectual culture with it—a gift sent to Sloane as a "token of friendship and esteem" by a Virginia planter, "some tissue he had removed from the vagina of a slave girl."[21]

In fact Sloane's intellectual work was built, quite literally, on the bodies and minds of Africans, both enslaved and free. His collecting projects were made possible financially by his strategic marriage to the widow of a Jamaican planter, Elizabeth Langley, who inherited a third of the income from plantations totaling 3,000 acres in Jamaica. It was Langley's money that enabled Sloane to buy many of his items as well as to acquire the Manor of Chelsea in 1712. But Sloane's collection was also intellectually dependent on the knowledge of Africans, both in the Caribbean and on the continent. In his *Voyage to Jamaica,* he acknowledged his debt to the local "Europeans, Indians, or Blacks" that he consulted with in Jamaica. He clearly spent a lot of time talking to people of African descent, both slave and free, about what they grew in their gardens, "wherein they took care to preserve and propagate such Vegetables as grew in their own countries," that is, in their places of origin in Africa. Such gardens—which were also maintained among the enslaved on plantations in Jamaica—brought together the flora of three continents, Europe, Africa, and the Americas, along with multiple traditions of cultivation, harvesting, and use. Sloane gathered this information and offered it in rich detail in his work.[22]

Sloane's consultation with enslaved Jamaicans about their use of plants was only the beginning of a long series of work with such informants. One of his later collaborators was Job Ben Solomon, a Muslim man from Senegal who was sold into slavery in Maryland and who Sloane helped emancipate in the 1730s. Solomon collected arrows and pipes in the Gambia for Sloane and also translated Arabic texts for him. Because of his prominence and high social rank, Solomon was known and named as a collaborator; but in fact throughout Sloane's life—in his own work and that of agents and collectors who brought him materials—the knowledge of Africans on both sides of the Atlantic sustained and infused his work. Their contributions, though largely obfuscated, are the main reason that Sloane's collection offers us such rich traces of the cultural lives of the enslaved. His method of collecting, with its "universalism" and "a breathtaking aim of comprehensiveness," meant that he gathered materials that some of his colleagues saw as worthless. But, in the end, "some of the items in his possession for which contemporaries mocked him are those which in retrospect are most highly prized."[23]

Sloane stands out among early chroniclers of the Caribbean for the detailed attention he gave to music. In Jamaica, Sloane found himself in the midst of a key moment of cultural invention and transformation. He was smart enough to realize this and also to understand he needed help in documenting it: during "one of their Festivals, when a great many of the Negro Musicians were gathered together," he asked one "Mr. *Baptiste,* the best Musician there to take the Words they sing and set them to Musick, which follows." Based on Baptiste's work, he published musical notation for three songs, the earliest such documents of Afro-Atlantic music in existence.

Sloane's introduction to these pieces of music is vague and elliptical. Where did he hear these songs? What role did the musicians themselves play in creating the notation? Might these in fact be more of a composition by Baptiste than a transcription of songs he heard? And who exactly was this Mr. Baptiste? Though historians have assumed that "Mr. Baptiste" was a Frenchman, it is also very possible that he was in fact a free person of African descent. In the Caribbean during the eighteenth century, many blacks, both free and enslaved, worked as professional musicians, including in contexts where they would have had to read music, such as the theatre. Baptiste's name suggests he made have originally come from one of the French colonies, perhaps nearby Saint-Domingue, where there was an extremely active and rich musical and theatrical life that involved many people of African descent. And although these songs could have been played and heard on a plantation, they also just as easily could have been performed in some kind of urban setting. Wherever the performance took place, it did clearly involve crosscurrents of musical influence, offering up fascinating insights about the nature of cultural encounter and creolization in late seventeenth-century Jamaica. It was, as historian Richard Rath writes, a "remarkable scene: several languages—pidgin, English, French, at least (and probably more) unrelated African tongues—three discrete musical styles being recorded by someone versed in a fourth, participants ranging from slaves to gentry, with connections to three continents, all thrown together for a moment in time."[24]

Those who came together to play in the gathering Sloane witnessed clearly were from a variety of different regions within Africa. That meant that their very relationship to sound was culturally diverse. "A culture's music," Rath writes, "has a phonology of aesthetically permissible notes, a vocabulary of acceptable scales and rhythms, and a syntax of customs and rules that govern the largely unconscious ways people represent themselves through these notes, scales, and rhythms to produce what they recognize as music." This collection of habits, which Rath calls "soundways," are established and passed on in different ways in different contexts through a mix of "tradition and adaptation." In the plantation world, Rath argues, an intensive process of negotiation between different soundways had to take place in a situation conditioned by exile, intrusive oversight, and the confrontation with an extremely oppressive slave system. In that context, the production of music that would serve the needs of the community was both particularly vital and particularly challenging.[25]

The titles of the three songs offered by Baptiste each point toward a particular African ethnic group. "Koromanti," often spelled Coromantee, was a term used to describe enslaved people brought from the Akan region of Africa (in modern-day Ghana), who were a prominent and much discussed group in Jamaica. Akan had played leading roles in early slave revolts in Jamaica and would continue to do so in subsequent years as well as in other parts of the Caribbean. The second song, titled "Angola," used a designation to describe enslaved peoples imported from the coast of Central Africa, who could be drawn from a wide range of cultures in the interior. Finally, a short piece titled "Papa" was, in Rath's interpretation, probably referring to a group of enslaved people known as the "Popo" from the Bight of Benin, who were imported into Jamaica during this period as well.[26]

Each of these categories, however, was complex and shifting, just as the music written down by Baptiste was. What was documented, argues Rath, was a very specific moment in which "Koromantis, Papas, and Angolans" were "using instrument sounds and their voices to forge identities as Africans under the bonds of slavery in a harsh new world." The project would have been to "craft sonic spaces that in some ways existed not in reference to slavery but to their own interests," with instrumental music serving as a "powerful tool in delimiting a covert set of knowledge." Slave masters clearly knew and understood that Africans "had ways of communicating through music, but they did not know how to stop them." The law books of the early Caribbean and North America include numerous ordinances banning or limiting the use of music among the enslaved. Planters were particularly worried about drums and horns, which they rightly understood—from experience—could be used to call the enslaved to revolt as well as inspire and organize them as they fought. These instruments were first banned in Jamaica in 1688, with masters encouraged to search slave quarters and confiscate and burn any instruments they found. But the constant repetition and expansion of such ordinances—along with the many accounts describing the constant presence of dance and music on the plantations and in the port towns—make clear planters never achieved their goal of silence. Still, although music was never fully suppressed, the criminalization of certain types of music must have shaped the cultural practices of the enslaved. "They banned loud instruments, ignoring quieter ones in their laws," failing to understand that these other instruments could still be "powerful tools" for the articulation of the agenda and hopes of the enslaved without drawing as much attention. "Drum patterns might be carried on in the rhythms of the stringed instruments or on smaller percussion instruments. Lutes and harps could easily be made." An oppressive legal order that saw certain types of sound as a threat, then, shaped the contours of musical practice. And getting around the rules, notably by finding ways to express resistance that eluded detection, became part of what musicians needed to be able to do.[27]

This process took place both in larger dances and in countless smaller musical gatherings, like the one that Sloane and Baptiste documented. Unfortunately the account of these songs doesn't include an indication of what instruments were used to play them. But elsewhere in his *Voyage,* Sloane offered a detailed description of a series of instruments, some of which were likely in the hands of one of the musicians there that night. Despite their "hard-wrought" lives, Sloane wrote, the enslaved "will at nights, or on Feast days Dance and Sing; their Songs are all bawdy, and leading that way."

> They have several sorts of Instruments in imitation of Lutes, made of small Gourds fitted with Necks, strung with Horse hairs, or the peeled stalks of climbing Plants or Withs. These instruments are sometimes made of hollow'd Timber covered with Parchment or other Skin wetted, having a Bow for its Neck, the Strings ty'd longer or shorter, as they would alter their sounds. . . . They have likewise in their Dances Rattles ty'd to their Legs and Wrists, and in their Hands, with which they make a noise, keeping time with one who makes a sound answering on the mouth of an empty gourd or Jar with his Hand. Their Dances consist of great activity and strength of body, and keeping time, if it can be. They very often tie Cow's Tails to their Rumps, and add such other odd things to their Bodies in several places, as gives them a very extraordinary appearance.[28]

During his time in Jamaica, Sloane acquired at least three musical instruments. There is no record of how he got them: he may have purchased them from an instrument maker or musician, either free or enslaved, or he may have collected them (perhaps forcibly) on a plantation with the aid of a slave master or overseer. He brought these back to England, where they became part of his extended collection of "miscellanies." His hand-written catalogue of these objects includes these entries: a "Jamaica strum strum or musicall instrument, made of an oblong—hollowed piece of wood with a cross in the side, strings of a scendent herbs caulis"; "The same made of cucurbita lagenaria covered wt. skin—holed in the side" (curcubita lagenaria is a kind of bottle gourd); and "One of another form wt. a bell on it."[29]

In August of 1701, Everhardus Kickius, then Sloane's chief botanical illustrator, made a sketch of three musical instruments and titled it "American and African guitars." Two of these instruments are recognizable as early versions of the banjo: they have gourd resonators, skin heads, and flat engraved necks with strings of different lengths, held by pegs.

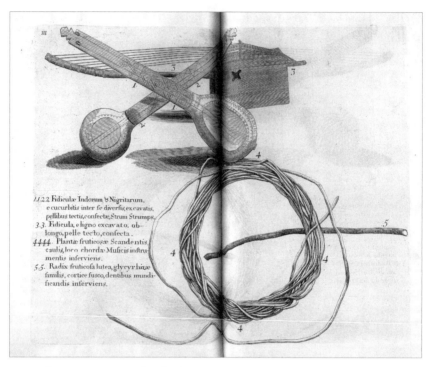

Hans Sloane, *A voyage to the islands Madera, Barbados, Nieves, . . . and islands of America* (London, 1707), vol. 1, Plate III.

Photo courtesy of David M. Rubenstein Rare Book and Manuscript Library, Duke University.

The third is of a different form: a harp with a box resonator, likely made of wood, and eight strings.[30]

Kickius's sketch was the basis for another image of the three instruments, which was published in Sloane's *Voyage*. This engraving is far better known than the original sketch and has often been reproduced and has shaped discussions of the early banjo. The relevant captions, in Latin, describing the instruments can be translated as follows: "1.1.2.2. 'Strum Strumps,' lutes of the Indians & Blacks, made of different hollowed-out gourds covered with animal hides. 3.3. Lute [with] an oblong [body] made of hollowed-out wood and covered with an animal hide." In addition to the instruments in Kickius's original sketch, there are two other objects: some plant fiber described as the kind that was used to make the strings for the instrument along with, somewhat out of place perhaps, a whittled tree branch used for cleaning teeth.[31]

There is an intriguing shift between the terminology used in the original sketch and that used in the engraving. The instruments go from being "American and African guitars" to being "lutes of the Indians & Blacks." Scholars have long puzzled over the illustration and its different captions, with some suggesting that the instrument in the foreground may actually be East Indian or else made by indigenous peoples in the Caribbean. While in Jamaica, Sloane did note the presence of enslaved indigenous people from the "Mosquitos" of Central America and Florida, owned by the English. These indigenous slaves and enslaved Africans lived together, wore similar clothing, ate similar food, and could easily have shared other aspects of their cultural life. Sloane had also encountered the groups of "Blacks and Indians" who had lived in Jamaica under Spanish rule and remained on the island after the English conquest. So he understood there were many longstanding avenues of cultural exchange between surviving indigenous individuals and communities and newly arrived Africans and perhaps concluded that the instruments he had collected had been influenced by indigenous practices. There is an intriguing possibility that the crosshatching decorations on the necks of the instruments in front could have indeed been influenced by indigenous aesthetics. Some who have studied the *vévé* in Haitian Vodou—ritual drawings made with meal on the floors before ceremonies—have argued for possible Taino influence on these aesthetics, and something similar could be at work in these early banjos.[32]

There is one area where there may have been a particularly intriguing cross-fertilization between the practices of indigenous peoples in the Caribbean and African arrivals: in the uses of gourds and calabashes. Although the terms have often been—and still are—used somewhat interchangeably and loosely, even in botanical works, gourds and calabashes are actually two different species. Gourds grow on vines, and calabashes grow on trees. Though both can be dried, scraped clean, and used in similar ways—including as resonators for instruments—there are nevertheless some differences between them. The inside of a calabash, for instance, is smoother and therefore easier to decorate. Starting with Columbus himself, Europeans in the Caribbean described the widespread use of calabashes among indigenous groups, including for the construction of rattles. Calabashes also grew in Africa, but they seem to have been used less often than gourds for making instruments. Though tracking this process is extremely difficult, it does seem that Africans in the Americas probably absorbed indigenous traditions surrounding the cultivation and use of calabashes, transferring some of what they had usually done with gourds to this new, common plant. Within this story of two species of plants seems to reside, though carefully hidden, traces of the cultural encounters between indigenous American and African worlds in the early history of the Caribbean. These encounters happened far from the eyes of European observers, however, so that it is difficult to identify what influences were indigenous and what were African, notably in the realm of music.[33]

Sloane's engraving offers up another mystery: the origin of the third instrument, the harp with a box-shaped resonator. Based on the evidence from the engraving, the sketch, and the descriptions from the catalogue, we can conclude that the two instruments in the foreground were collected by Sloane in Jamaica. But there remain two possibilities about the trajectory of the third instrument. The first is that this was the third instrument listed in the catalogue, of "another form," collected in Jamaica. If this was the case, it would mean that such harps were being made and played in seventeenth-century Jamaica, alongside the "strum-strum." The other possibility, however, is that this was in fact part of Sloane's collection of African objects, included here for comparison. That would explain Kickius's use of the title "American and African guitars" in his original sketch. If that is the case, then Sloane and / or Kickius subsumed the "African" of the original sketch into the "Black" of the caption of the later engraving. In so doing, and in the positioning of the instruments in the image, they were perhaps also making an argument: that the New World banjo was the child of African parents. If so, the first visual depiction of the banjo also involved the first, correct, assertion of the story of its lineage.[34]

One final detail, from both the sketch and the engraving, stands out: the cross-shaped sound hole on the body of the harp in the background. This style of functional decoration was to reappear on other New World banjos a century later, and it was very likely a choice made with a particular reason. Such crosses were quite common in aesthetic practice of the Afro-Atlantic world, serving as cosmograms linked to the intertwined aesthetic and spiritual practices of the Kongo region. Whether the instrument and the cross itself were made in Africa or in the Caribbean, the symbol almost certainly had ritual significance.[35]

The combination of descriptive text, musical transcription, and images makes Sloane's work one of the most crucial sources on the early history of Afro-Atlantic music. Though it is fragmentary, it at least gives us several points of entry and analysis into the musical culture he witnessed. And it offers us a trace of one of the fundamental technical transformations in the creation of the New World banjo: the use of a flat neck. In West and Central Africa, necks were rounded sticks or rods, on both lutes and harps. In late seventeenth-century Jamaica, enslaved people were building instruments that used the same technique of growing a gourd for the resonator, covering it with an animal skin, and putting a neck through that gourd. But that neck was a flat board, as Labat's description suggests it may have been at the time in Guadeloupe and Martinique as well. Why? The reason could be a basic one of using what was easily accessible and at hand. Some of the enslaved in a plantation society like Jamaica worked as carpenters, putting together buildings, carriages, and also the many barrels that were used to ship sugar and molasses out of the colony. Artisans making instruments would have had an easy time finding a flat boards, and the tools to saw or carve them, on almost any plantation. They may, too, of course, have found inspiration for doing so in the shape of European instruments with flat necks: a lute, a guitar, indeed a concert violin, all would have provided a kind of invitation and demonstration of the usefulness of flat necks and peg tuners. However this decision came about, and whatever incited this innovation, it was ultimately to become relatively standardized, although instruments constructed with rounded necks seem to have persisted at least through the late eighteenth century.

Although these instruments were carefully collected, drawn, engraved, and showcased as part of Sloane's major work in the seventeenth century, they did not get handed down to us. At some point in the process of the transformation of Sloane's collections into those of the British museum, they disappeared, leaving just their traces in images and text. As much as we might strain to hear the particular tones of those instruments, or to truly hear the songs sung that evening on the late seventeenth-century plantation, the sound vanishes from us. Yet the images are enough for today's banjo makers, working in the tradition of unknown and unnamed ancestors, to reproduce a version of the instruments collected by Sloane.

Based on the musical notation and the images of the instruments from Jamaica, Richard Rath has reconstructed the songs with what he sees as the most likely instrumentation, offering us the chance to hear an echo of that long-ago gathering in Jamaica. He argues that each of these songs, though their names cited particular ethnic groups and regions in Africa, was already shaped by various kinds of cross-pollination and influence. "Angola," he suggests, included different musical styles: "Both musicians were using their own particular cultural knowledge to produce a suitable musical expression. In all likelihood, neither the musicians nor their companions found the results fully satisfactory."[36]

Over time, in gathering after gathering, as musicians came and went, expanding and then winnowing their repertoire, figuring out what made those around them dance, sing, pray, or listen in reflective silence, the results ultimately became satisfactory, even revelatory. New music and dance was created, providing solace and force. And the musicians operating in this world seem to have increasingly opted to play instruments constructed according to a consistent pattern: gourd, animal skin, flat neck. This had happened around the same time in at least three Caribbean colonies—Jamaica, Guadeloupe, and Martinique—that were part of different empires. The small amount that is known about this process is thanks to the presence of unusual observers there—Taylor and Sloane in Jamaica and Labat in Martinique—who stood apart from most of their contemporary European travelers in their particular fascination with the culture of the enslaved. But the lucky accident of their observation hints that, had others similar to them visited places like Barbados or New Orleans or South Carolina, they might have seen something similar.

Did the development of this instrument take place in parallel time, or did patterns of influence and movement tie one area to another? The Caribbean was relatively well connected and also tightly linked to North America by constant trade and by ships often manned by enslaved sailors. Music and musical instruments would have traveled easily along these routes, just as news, political projects, and other cultural forms did. Martinique and Jamaica, however, were not particularly well connected in the late seventeenth century—getting from one to another was, in fact, relatively complicated given the currents, not to mention the winds of imperial rivalry, within the Caribbean. The early history of the banjo suggests that what was happening in various islands was probably the result of parallel contexts producing parallel results. In similar conditions, with similar points of reference, artisans and musicians seem to have gravitated toward a common solution, that of having one style of instrument serve different performance goals. But in time, an understanding of the instrument—and some instruments themselves—would increasingly have circulated between islands and regions. The instruments seen by Taylor, Sloane, and Labat were dispersed cousins, but in time they would meet and recognize one another.[37]

The banjo's first appearance in writing in North America comes to us in the form of an enigma, from a place called Utopia. In March of 1736, a letter signed simply, and mysteriously, by "The Spy" was published in the *New York Weekly Journal,* which advertised itself as containing "the freshest Advices, Foreign and Domestick." It was introduced by an equally mysterious note signed simply "F. C." requesting that the letter be inserted into the newspaper. Such practices of presenting "letters" of mysterious origin were, in fact, relatively common in eighteenth-century publications, though the double anonymity here is unusual. Who wrote the letter, and why did the writer call himself The Spy? Was this nothing more than a set of fake tropes used to present something written by an editor as a truthful dispatch?[38]

The Spy dated his letter from "Utopia," somewhere outside of New York City. He proceeded to describe what—given the date of April 10th, 1736, for the letter—was probably a Pinkster celebration. This festival, which began the Monday after Pentecost, was of Dutch origin. But in the Americas it became "almost an entirely African-American event." It reached its "apogee" during the 1790s and 1800s in Albany, New York. At the edge of the town, on "Pinkster Hill," hundreds gathered for a weekly event overseen by one "King Charles," an African-born slave "whose authority is absolute, and whose will is law." Decades later, a man named James Eight described his vivid childhood memories of Charles, who had "been brought from Angola, in the Guinea gulf" as a boy.

"Never, if our memory serves us, shall we forget the mingled sensations of awe and grandeur that were impressed on our youthful minds, when first we beheld his stately form and dignified aspect, slowly moving before us and moving to the centre of the ring." Charles wore the outfit of a "British brigadier of the old time," that was "gayly ornamented everywhere with broad tracings of bright golden lace," and a "tri-cornered cocked hat trimmed also with lace of gold." Eight recalled the music, particularly that of a drummer named Jackey Quackenboss, who sat astride a wooden drum made with a "cleanly dressed sheep skin."[39]

The Pinkster celebrations continued during the early nineteenth century. In 1845, James Fenimore Cooper memorably depicted one in his novel *Satanstoe*. The protagonist, Jason, finds himself "confounded with the noises, dances, music, and games that were going on." He saw "nine-tenths of the blacks of the city" who were "collected in thousands in those fields, beating banjoes, singing African songs." The distinguishing features of the "Pinkster frolic," Cooper wrote, were "of African origin." Though few enslaved "of African birth" were left, he went on, "the traditions and usages of their original country were so far preserved as to produce a marked difference between this festival, and one of European origin."[40]

What struck visitors over the decades most about Pinkster was "the visual and sonic strangeness of this black gathering." This was already true of The Spy in 1736, who presented one of the first depictions of the festival. Aiming to dismay, and also perhaps to amuse, the readers of the *New York Weekly Journal,* The Spy offered his notes on a "Days Ramble" through a striking Afro-Atlantic cultural landscape. "It was no small Amusement to me, to see the Plain partly covered with Booths, and well crowded with Whites, the Negroes divided into Companies according to their different Nations, some dancing to the hollow sound of a Drum, made of the trunk of a hollow Tree, others to the grating rattling Noise of Pebbles or Shells in a small Basket, others plied the Banger, and some knew how to joyn the Voice to it." Alongside the music there was plenty of (often drunken) fighting, with cudgels, "small sticks in imitation of a short Pike," and presumably fists, at times accompanied by "cursing and swearing" in a "Christian dialect." His further rambles in search of "refreshment" confronted him with various shocking spectacles, "mixt Company" in which the "Gentleman was the Mechanic," a purportedly

Christian family man consorting with a "Hagg," and one or two couples locked in a "Close Hugg." He ended up watching a cockfight where the audience was a "mixt Multitude" from "Gentlemen" to "Day Labourers" all happily cheering together. "You can't imagine how irksome it is to me who have been used to a regular Life" our Spy opined, "to hear the Impieties, and see the Outrages daily committed in the common Streets, not only by the Blacks or the poorer Whites, but even by the genteeler Sort; and all this too often with Impunity." This celebration of the holiday was shocking, he concluded.[41]

The day's amusements had been announced, according to The Spy, with this encounter: "This morning I heard my Landlord's black Fellow very busy at tuning of his Banger, as he call'd it, and playing some of his Tunes; I, who am always delighted with Music, be it never so rustic, under a Pretence of Washing came into the Kitchen, and at last asked, what the Meaning was of his being so merry? He started up and with a blithsom Countenance answered, *Massa, to day Holiday; Backerah no work; Ningar no work; me no savy play Banger; go yander, you see Ningar play Banger for true, dance too; you see Sport to day for true.*"[42]

There is always, of course, a disjuncture between textual traces and musical reality. Banjos almost certainly had been built and played in North America before 1736. Indeed, the familiarity with which this source describes the instrument—the name is simply offered up, with no explanation of what the instrument looks or sounds like—suggests the writer assumed readers would have already heard the term. What is striking about this description, however, is the familiarity of the context. As in the Caribbean, the instrument found its home in New York in the midst of a festival that was an assembly in exile, a gathering of Africans and their descendants around music and dance that recalled and channeled specific nations even as it collected them in recognition of the realities and necessities of a new cultural world.

The banjo also seems to have been part of a different kind of African-American festival, the "election days" practiced in some New England towns during the mid-eighteenth century. During these events, which often took place at the same time as an official election, local African-Americans elected a "governor" to represent their community. The practice brought together African political traditions with colonial American practice. One such election took place in 1756 in Newport, Rhode

Island. All African-American male residents voted; and once the governor was elected, they gathered under a "large, spreading tree" to celebrate. As an account written decades later described it, "every voice upon its highest key, in all the various languages of Africa, mixed with broken and ludicrous English, filled the air, accompanied with the music of the fiddle, the tambourine, the banjo, drum, etc." Such celebrations were often banned by authorities—such as those of Salem, Massachusetts, in 1758—who saw them as a public, and indeed a political, threat.[43]

We find other traces of this process of cultural invention during the same period in the form of runaway banjos. Throughout the Americas, when an enslaved person escaped the plantation, masters placed advertisements in local newspapers offering rewards for the capture of their property. These advertisements were tools of power; and as written texts, they could be reproduced and travel in many directions at once. In their narratives of escape, many former slaves described the "uncanny feeling of being overtaken by the transmitted news of their own fugitive status." For masters who composed these advertisements, the important thing was to share the maximum amount of information about the individual in order to recapture their property. The irony was that in order to do so, they produced the most detailed—and even human—description of slaves that we ever get from masters. Indeed, they offer us remarkable capsule biographies of enslaved individuals.[44]

Many advertisements mention musical skills. Those who had such skills, in fact, were perhaps more likely to try and escape, since they could use these to make a living in the city and to pass as a free person. Such runaways often left both with instruments and with multiple sets of good clothing, both of which would serve them well if they were planning to perform. An 1800 advertisement in Virginia described a man named Jack, who had "a down look, speaks slowly and wore his hair cued" and fled wearing "a brown hat, faced underneath with green." The master added that he "was told" that Jack "was seen making for Alexandria, with the intention of taking the stage thither: he is artful and can both read and write and is a good fiddler." Another Virginia advertisement from 1790 mentioned a man named Francis, who "plays on the fife extremely well" and left with "6 good linen shirts, a fine new brown broad cloth coat, a green shaggy jacket, breeches of several kinds, with shoe-boots and shoes."[45]

The most common instrument mentioned in such advertisements is the violin, which many enslaved played both for themselves and for their masters. It was easy to carry as well as to use to get work playing in a variety of musical contexts. Some advertisements mention enslaved individuals who were skilled at playing drums. But there were also a few banjo players among the runaways. In 1749, when a slave named Scipio ran away from his master and headed for Philadelphia, his master tried to track him with an advertisement that fingered Scipio as a man who "played the banjo" and "can sing." Scipio perhaps tried to make a living with his skill; and if so, perhaps it was that detail in the runaway advertisement that got him caught, as he soon was. But twice in the next decade, he ran away from slavery again. After his third escape—perhaps one that led him to freedom for good—his master paid him a sort of compliment, describing him in a new advertisement as someone who "plays well on the banjou." A few years later, in 1754, another banjo-playing slave in Maryland escaped from his master. According to an advertisement placed in the *Maryland Gazette* by his master, the man was "a dark Mulatto" named Prince, and he had gone off "in company with a white servant man" named John. Prince, the master noted, was "a pert lively Fellow and plays well on the Banjer." He was wearing "a country Linnen shirt, short Linnen breeches, and an old Felt Hat" when he left. A reward was offered to any who brought him back. These two advertisements suggest that some masters were beginning to be familiar with the instrument called the "banjer," and even to enjoy its music. And they suggest that, at least in some places and some communities, playing the banjo could get you places—even, perhaps, a little closer to freedom.[46]

The banjo playing practiced by slaves also exercised an attraction for the members of some master's families. In 1773 and 1774, a young student named Philip Vickers Fithian traveled to a Virginia plantation in order to serve as a tutor to the children of the household of a local planter, Robert Carter. The Carter family had been entrenched in the Tidewater region since the mid-seventeenth century; and at one point Robert Carter owned 500 slaves, an extremely large number for North America. Among the ten children entrusted to Fithian's care was Carter's eldest son, Benjamin, who was eighteen, and a relative named Harry Willis. One Sunday evening in January 1774, Fithian noted in his journal, the "Negroes collected themselves in the School-Room, & began to play the *Fiddle, &*

dance." When he went to see what was going on, he found that "*Ben, &*
Harry were of the company" and "Harry was dancing with his Coat off."
"I dispersed them however immediately," wrote Fithian. But at the end
of the next week, on Friday night, the scene repeated itself, this time with
a different instrument: "This Evening, in the School-Room, which is
below my Chamber, several Negroes & *Ben, & Harry* are playing on a
Banjo & dancing!" This time, Fithian didn't write that he had dispersed
the group. Did he stay for a while and enjoy the music?[47]

*

By the second half of the eighteenth century, the banjo was very much
at home in many parts of the Caribbean and North America. The instrument was common enough that slave owners seeking runaways, newspapers writing articles about unusual street celebrations, and young tutors
on assignment all generally knew how to name it. They used one of a
set of similar terms—banjo, bangier, banza—and they expected readers
to know what they meant.

The first use of the term in writing seems to be in a 1708 work about
Barbados written by John Oldmixon, who described the instrument as a
"bangil, not much unlike our Lute in any thing, but the Musick." Within
a few decades, various forms of this term were in relatively widespread
use throughout the Caribbean and North America. The German traveler Johann David Schoepf, who visited North America and the Caribbean in the early 1780s, described the banjah as a "musical instrument of
the true negro." "Over a hollow calabash . . . is stretched a sheep-skin,
the instrument lengthened with a neck, strung with 4 strings, and made
accordant." "It gives out a rude sound," he wrote, and was accompanied
by "the drum, or an iron pan, or empty cast, whatever may be at hand."
"In America and on the islands they make use of this instrument greatly
for dance," he added. At times the term was used to describe other types
of instruments. In the early 1770s, for instance, an Englishman named
James Barclay who had worked on a rice plantation in Charleston, South
Carolina, wrote: "Their instrument of musick is called a Bangier, made
of a Calabash." But he then described something that did not have strings
and was played like a drum: "One negroe sits down, and takes it between
his feet, upon which he beats artfully with two sticks, as we do on a drum,

and all the rest dance pair and pair in their own way, hallowing, shrieking, and making an intolerable noise." Still, the instrument's name was established enough by this period that the French author Jean Benjamin Laborde listed it among the stringed instruments in his encyclopedic essay on music. The banza, he wrote, was the "instrument of the negroes of America," and "a kind of guitar with four strings." More than other names—the strum strum mentioned by Sloane or the kitt mentioned by Taylor—it was the various versions of the word banjo or banza that ultimately took root to describe the instrument, resonating for enough people over time and space to establish it as a familiar term.[48]

Where did the term come from? One possible source for the word is the European term bandore, which named a kind of lute with a rounded body. Richard Jobson, who traveled to Africa in the early seventeenth century, made a connection between the European "bandore," a lute-like instrument, and African gourd instruments he saw. But there are also many African terms that could have inspired the name. One theory, sustained by Lopez's description of banjo-like instruments in Central Africa, is that the term "banza" was a reference to the region of Mbanza, in the Kongo. Douglas Chambers, meanwhile, writes that the term banjo "signifies" in the Igbo language, "as in ba-njo (being bad)," and notes that in Jamaican Creole the term banja means "to play the fool," suggesting a connection between the two significations. There are several other possible etymologies in African languages.[49]

Creolization is partly about convergence. If the term "banjo" ultimately gained traction, it is probably precisely because it resonated with possible meanings in different languages spoken by different groups. These varied meanings might have co-existed for a time, but they ultimately combined to give the term a particular, shared, material and social meaning. Precisely because the term could signify in different languages, and evoke different contexts, it made for a good name for an instrument that was doing the same thing. Like the instrument itself, the word ultimately probably worked because it made sense to many who heard and spoke it in the different languages in circulation in the Atlantic space.

The history of the term in Dutch Suriname offers us a density of intriguing linguistic information that can help us understand how the word banjo—and its many variations—might have emerged. Scholars have posited a link between the term banya or bandya and terms for dance used in the colony: the Dutch word baaljaaren (of a common root with the Spanish and Portuguese terms bailar), which was in use to describe slave dances as early as the late seventeenth century. One man who spent more than a decade in Suriname between 1695 and 1706 later wrote: "On Sundays, the slaves of the city of Paramaribo go to the waterfront or walk to the Savana to *Baljaaren,* being a certain kind of Dancing known as such to them, but this is forbidden, because they were able to communicate too much, and singing about their business, which each wanted to know of the other, they could uncover things, sometimes also by whistling at the mouth." No instruments are mentioned, though it is likely that some stringed instruments and drums provided the music for such dances." Baljaaren, in addition to being a general term for dance, also came to name a specific dance as well among Surinamese slaves.[50]

The term banja first seems to have appeared in Surinamese written documents to describe a musical instrument in 1750, when an ordinance was passed seeking to limit the gatherings of slaves. The ban, like many others in the Atlantic world, was far-reaching and draconian, limiting not only the right to "congregate with others in numbers" but also to "stand together talking with three or more." The enslaved were enjoined essentially to public silence, to "neither making the least murmur, clamor, whistling noise, or anything comparable, but on the contrary going quietly along the streets." Specifically, they were banned from "playing so-called *banjas*" as well as other instruments, "neither on the street nor in houses nor in any other place." Two other late eighteenth-century sources about Suriname mention the instrument. A 1770 work notes of the enslaved: "They play the instrument which they call Bagna in their language, grievously and flailingly, regarding it as a kind of fiddle." Another, from 1787, is more positive and richer in its description both of the instrument and its sound: "They have yet another way of playing, with the so-called Banja, being a round calabash cut in the middle, with the open side covered with a sheep skin, with a stick through it and four strings on this, playing on it in the manner of a zither; giving this a very languid sound, very softly singing and dancing to it."[51]

The 1770 source describes the term bagna as being "in their language." But what was the language of the enslaved in Suriname? That itself is a complex question, since this could have meant either an African or some kind of Creole language. Among all the New World colonies, it was Suriname that had probably the largest and best-established communities of Maroons, who escaped from the plantations and created villages in the interior of the colony starting in the early seventeenth century. In 1760 and 1762 the two largest Maroon communities, the Djuka and the Saramaka, signed treaties with the Dutch authorities. The fact that they were able to secure their autonomy and establish independent communities has also meant that a series of Maroon languages, rooted in African languages, developed and took root. Among these Saramaccan, Matawai, and Kwinti languages, all have a term for dance: baya, banya, and bandya.[52]

The Maroon struggle with Dutch authorities stretched throughout the eighteenth century. The treaties signed in the early 1760s were meant to put an end to new escapes from the plantations—the Djuka and Saramaka agreed not to accept new runaways into their communities—but there were always new Maroons, and small bands emerged between the regions controlled by the Djuka and Saramaka. In 1773 a Scottish officer named John Gabriel Stedman arrived in Suriname and during the next five years fought against various Maroon groups. He eventually returned home and wrote a detailed manuscript about his experience, completed in 1790 and published in 1796 with a series of engravings by William Blake. It was widely read and cited at the time and has been a constant reference point for historians of slave society since.[53]

Suriname's slave population had an extremely high ratio of Africans compared to Creoles born in the colony: 25:1 in the colony as a whole, and sometimes 65:1 in plantation districts. By comparison, Jamaica in 1780 had a ratio of 10:1 Africans to Creoles. In many other regions of the Americas, notably North America, the ratios were far smaller during the eighteenth century. The large number of West and Central Africans, a number of whom rapidly joined Maroon communities, created a particularly rich cultural context in the colony, notably in the realm of music and dance. Stedman's narrative includes valuable details about the musical culture that he encountered and which fascinated him.[54]

In 1774 Stedman watched as a group of recent African arrivals on one estate danced. He described them as "Loango-Negroes," and noted that their performance of "Loango-Dancing" was limited to their group, and was not performed by "by any others." Stedman was rather shocked by the dance, which he wrote "consists from first to last in such a Scene of Wanton, and Lascivious gestures, as nothing but a heated imagination, and Constant Practice could enable them to perform; these Dances which are to the sound of a Drum, and to which they strike time by Clapping of hands, are more like a play, divided into so many Acts, which lasts hours together, and during which Pantomime, the Actors in place of being fatigued, become more and more Active and Animated, til they are bathed in a lather like Post Horses, and their Passions wound up to such a degree, that Nature being overcome they are ready to drop into Convulsions." Stedman was disturbed not just by the dance but also by the fact that white men and women watched these "indelicate" performances "without the least reserve." They laughed in pleasure as they watched; although neither they nor Stedman, it is fair to say, probably had a clear idea what the stories and dances being told and performed by these recent survivors of the Middle Passage, making their way through the brutal world of Surinamese plantation society, really were saying, remembering, and envisioning.[55]

Two years later, Stedman had seen enough dances to write generally about them and to offer a more positive account that emphasized them as a space of sharing and community: "No People Can more Esteem or have a Great Friendship for one another than the negro Slaves who enjoy each others Company With an unbounded Pleasure," he wrote, notably during dances "Such as *Soesa,* which Consists in Dancing Opposite each other and Clapping With Their Hands on their Sides to keep in time, When each with Pleasure throws out one Foot." This competitive dance could get dangerous and, "the Violent Exercise having kill'd Some of the Negroes," the local authorities had forbidden it. Such bans, of course, didn't seem to have much effect: the same ordinances that attempted to stop dancing had been on the books since at least 1750.[56]

Intrigued by the dances, Stedman also became fascinated with the musical instruments of the enslaved. Though he had focused at first on the Loango dancing, he ultimately turned his attention to the instruments of "the other nations in General." These "Instruments of Sound," he admitted, were "not a Little in Genious" and were "All made by themselves." Stedman described and named several of these instruments, and his book was accompanied by an engraving that provided images of all of them under the title "Musical Instruments of the African Negroes." It

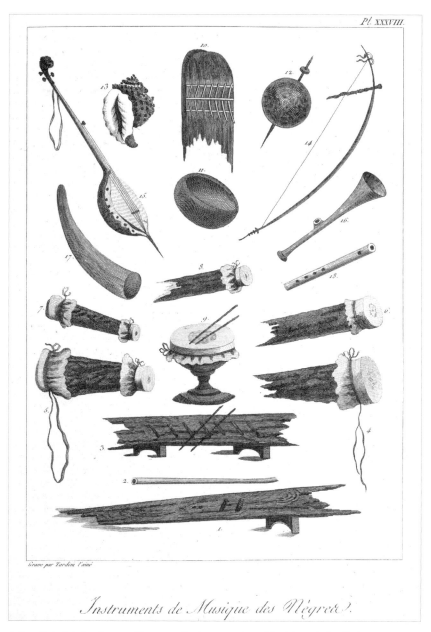

John Gabriel Stedman, *Voyage a Surinam, et dans l'intérieur de la Guiane,* translated by P. F. Henry (Paris: Buisson, 1798), plate XXXVIII.

Photo courtesy of the David M. Rubenstein Rare Book and Manuscript Library, Duke University.

is an extremely rich archive of information, offering up images and de-scriptions of a variety of Afro-Atlantic instruments greater than any other document from the eighteenth century.[57]

Among these instruments, three were named with some variation of the term bania. There was an Ansokko bania (number 3 in the engraving) a "Hard board supported on both Sides like a low Seat, on which are placed Small blocks of Different Sises, which being struck with two Small Sticks like a Dulcimar gives different Sounds that are not at All disagree-able." This description and the engraving show an instrument similar to a balafon, or bala—a xylophone-like instrument made with wooden slats, of the kind celebrated as the original griot instrument in the Sundiata epic. In this version of the instrument, the wooden pieces stretched long-wise along the frame and were seemingly carved with a cross-hatching pattern to create a series of squares to be struck by the sticks. There was another instrument, called a Loango bania (number 10 in the engraving), which Stedman found "exceedingly curious": it was a "Dry board on which are Laced, & kept Closs by a Transverse Bar, a different Sized Ela-stick Slinders of the Palm tree, in Such a manner that both ends are ele-vated by other Transverse Bars that are Fix'd under them," all of it placed over "a large *empty* Gourd to promote the Sound." It was played like this: "the extremities of the Splinders are snapt by the Fingers, Something in the manner of piano Forto & have the same effect." The description and illustration show an instrument that is essentially the mbira, or thumb piano, which is still built in a similar way in both recreational and ritual contexts in Central Africa and often played within a gourd resonator. In the Shona culture, this instrument has "the power to comfort and protect its players, with deep associations to the ancestral spirits"—qualities that would have made it particularly useful in the midst of plantation Suriname.[58]

The final instrument (number 15 in the engraving) whose name in-cluded bania was simply called the Creole bania. It was "like a Mandoline or Guitar, being made of a Gourd Covered With a Sheep-Skin, to Which is Fixed a Verry Long Neck or Handle." The instrument, he added, "has but 4 strings, 3 Long, and one Short. Which is thick and Serves for bace; it is play'd by the Fingers, and has a Verry Agreeable Sound more so when Accompanied with a Song." Stedman was clearly taken with the instru-ment and brought one of them back from Suriname, along with a few other instruments. Over the course of the nineteenth and twentieth centuries, the object made its way through various collections and ultimately to the Rijksmuseum in Amsterdam. In the 1970s, the anthropologists Richard and Sally Price were able to track down this instrument, though it was miscataloged and placed in the Asian wing. Though the instrument has some damage on its neck, it is still in strikingly good condition. Stedman's Creole bania, probably built some eighty years after the instrument collected by Sloane in Jamaica, is, as Richard and Sally Price noted at the time of their find, "(to our knowledge) the oldest Afro-American banjo still in existence anywhere, and serves as a fine example of the four-stringed instruments that were made and used from the 17th century by Afro-Americans throughout the Hemisphere."[59]

The actual instrument itself looks different than the one portrayed in the engraving, which has five strings going to just four pegs and a gourd that is more oblong than rounded. Still, the basic structure is there: the instrument is constructed with a gourd resonator, is covered with a skin head, and has a spike neck that goes through the gourd to which the strings are attached on both ends. Both the collected instrument and the engraving, importantly, show the detail of one short string on the top of the neck. This short string would remain a defining feature of most banjos until the present day. It allows and invites a style of playing similar to that used by musicians playing West African lutes like the akonting and ngoni, where the thumb plucks that string—usually tuned to a higher note than the other strings—to create a complex rhythmic pattern interwoven with the other notes.

As interesting as the instrument's construction is its name, which speaks volumes: Creole bania. The term bania was, in Suriname at least, flexible enough to be applied to extremely different instruments, such as the Ansokko bania and the Loango bania. This suggests that on some level that term simply meant "musical instrument" or perhaps "an instrument to which we dance." But the other two instruments were associated, through their names, with particular African ethnicities. The stringed instrument was set apart by the use of the term Creole.

The word Creole was also applied to other instruments observed by Stedman, including a "Great *Creole Drum*" made of a "Hollow Tree open at one end and Covered on the Other with a Sheep Skin, on Which they Sit Astride & So beat time with the palm of their Hands" in combination with other percussion instruments. In this case, though, the term was used by itself, presumably in the classic sense of Creole as in "born in the Americas," rather than African. The Creole bania, though, had a double name, pointing in two directions at once. It marked the instrument as part of a family of bania that included very different instruments with clear, deep links to West and Central African musical traditions. But it was tagged with a slight difference: it was related to its African family, but it was born in America. The name suggests the instrument is a Creole child born of African parents, one that maintains links with its parents but acknowledges its New World roots at the same time.[60]

We can catch a glimpse of the kind of musical encounters that probably gave rise to this naming practice in a document produced a few decades later in the same area. By 1828 Dutch Suriname had become the British colony of Berbice, and the colonial administration had become particularly involved in disputes on plantations and issues surrounding the treatment of slaves. One administrator visited a Berbice plantation on July 4th of that year and heard a complaint from one of the managers. The manager explained that a slave named Hero, whose job it was to watch over the irrigation works at night to prevent an overflow, had left his post one night. While he was gone, the water rose because of an unexpected rise in the tide; and as a result, the plantation ended up "under water through his neglect." When questioned, Hero offered this explanation: he had gotten hungry, and with nothing to eat with him, he "came home to the Negro houses and put plantains in the fire to roast." The cooking took a little time, and "in order not to fall asleep at the fireside," he decided to play some music and took out his "bandja." (The administrator hearing the case added in parenthesis that this was a "Congo instrument.") On it, he "played his country tunes"—songs from his African homeland. Though it was the middle of the night—two in the morning, the report specified—he soon had company. "The Creoles being charmed by the music, got up and danced." Hero said that he had "not the least intention of making a dance or any illegal noise in the negro yard." But, he suggested, once things got started he really didn't have a choice but to offer music to those around him on the plantation. His story convinced the administrator. The plantation manager, furthermore, vouched that Hero had an "excellent character." He received no punishment for his "transgression," unlike several other slaves investigated at the same time, who were whipped for various infractions described in the same report. But he did get a warning: he should "never again disturb the gang at such unreasonable hours with his music."[61]

In this scene, as in many others that must have been repeated on plantations throughout the region from the seventeenth through the nineteenth centuries, the bandja serves as an instrument of coalition. The Creoles are drawn to the music played by an African-born man. That the result is a disaster for the plantation—assigned work ignored, the fields flooded—can stand as a kind of metaphor for the ways in which these moments of respite and solidarity could be seen as, and at times could be, a threat to the slave system itself.

The emergence of the banjo was the result of the accumulation of such choices. By the late eighteenth century, those choices were consistent enough across time and space, and known enough, that they could be condensed both in the instrument itself—in its shape, construction, and sound—and in a name that, by accumulation rather than by any decree, had come to be accepted. Though spelled differently in different places and languages, it probably sounded similar when spoken: bandja, banza, banjo. What it meant could not be easily summarized or condensed. Still, the meaning was increasingly clear to those who spoke the name, heard it said, and gathered to hear the instrument sound out.

By the late eighteenth century, the term banjo was common enough to be used by three British travelers to Sierra Leone, in West Africa, to describe instruments they saw there. John Matthews wrote that while the drum was the "principal instrument," he also knew of "two kinds of string instruments": "one is a sort of guitar, and is the same as the bangou in the West Indies; the other is in the form of a Welsh harp, but not above two feet long: the strings are made of the fibres of a plant and the hair of an elephant's tail." Alexander Falconbridge, writing from Granville Town in June 1791 noted: "Sometimes I have seen an instrument resembling our guitar, the country name of which is bangeon." Similarly, in an account of the "native Africans" of Sierra Leone written in the late 1790s, Thomas Winterbottom noted the presence of the "banja or merrywang, as it is called in the West Indies" as one of the instruments played by the residents of the area. These observers might simply have been giving an American name to an African instrument. But it is also possible that the name or even the instrument itself, in its new form, had already begun its journey back to Africa. The powers and the meaning it had gained out of the experience of exile would, in time, allow it to bring solace to many others whose experience resonated with the strange, humming instrument from across the waters.[62]

By the late eighteenth century, the banjo also found its way into literary works. It was the British traveler John Davis, who spent four years traveling in the young United States between 1798 and 1802, who seems to have been the first to make the banjo a character in a story. In his "Memoir of My Life in the Woods of Virginia," which he dedicated to Thomas Jefferson, he included the story of "Dick the Negro." Though presented in unassuming form as part of this memoir, it is in effect a short story. Davis's work was in many ways a satire meant to play with and respond to previous travel accounts about the United States and about slavery. (He introduced his work by listing the differences between his writing and those of other travel writers: he made "no mention of his dinner, whether it was fish or flesh, boiled or roasted, hot or cold"; never complained about his bed or filled "the imagination of the reader with mosquitoes, fleas, bugs, and other nocturnal pests"; and included no drawings of "old castles, old churches," and other structures which had been "abandoned by their possessors.") But his account of the life of Dick—which he claims he heard directly from the slave in question and places in quotation marks—was an early example of a new and long-lived trope in which the condition of the slave was depicted through an evocation of the banjo and its music.[63]

As Dick explained it: "My young master was a mighty one for music, and he made me learn to play the Banger." (The instrument, Davis explained in a note, was "a kind of rude guitar.") "I could soon tune it sweetly, and of a moonlight night he would set me to play, and the wenches to dance. My young master himself could shake a desperate foot at the fiddle," Dick added, and indeed "there was nobody that could face him at a *Congo Minuet*." This musical master was killed, but the slave used his banjo playing to woo a young woman on the plantation: "By the moonlight I used to play my banger under her window, and sing a *Guinea* Lovesong that my mother had taught me."[64]

With all its fanciful elements, Davis's "autobiography" of the slave Dick hints a great deal about the place of the banjo in late eighteenth-century North America. One way to read the story is as a slightly romanced, but still relatively accurate, transmission of what Dick in fact told John Davis about his life. If this is the case, then there are a number of important details about the account. First, there is the interest of a white master in having a slave learn to play the banjo. Why didn't the master just learn to play himself? He was clearly musical enough, being able to hold his own on the fiddle, even playing a style known as the *Congo Minuet.* Songs labeled "Congo" in fact seem to have been a regular feature of balls in Virginia by the end of the eighteenth century. Samuel Mordecai, for instance, recalled the playing of an enslaved man named Simon or Cyrus Gilliat, who was "the leading violinist" at the dancing parties of the aristocracy of Virginia. "All sorts of capers were cut" to his music, including a dance called a "Congo." The master in the story as well as other slave owners in Virginia at the time were clearly open to—even particularly intrigued by—new forms of music that combined African and European elements. At the same time, they seemed to see the banjo in particular as an instrument best played by a slave rather than himself, a view that would shape ideas about the banjo throughout the early nineteenth century.[65]

From Davis's story, as well as other sources, it is clear that exchange and cross-fertilization were taking place among white and black musicians at this point in the late eighteenth and early nineteenth centuries. But Dick's description of how he played a "*Guinea* Lovesong" that he learned from his mother on the banjo also suggests the instrument continued to be used to play songs that were understood as being distinctly African in origin and orientation. Though we don't hear more—was Dick's mother African born? Was the song sung in an African language?—the reference is important.

There is, however, another way to read Davis's account, and that is as primarily a work of fantasy. In this sense, the presence of the banjo in the story would mark something quite different: a reflection of an *expectation* among readers that a slave tale, especially one involving music and love, would include some banjo playing. If this is the case then the text can be seen as a very early example of the forms of representation and storytelling that became the foundation for blackface minstrelsy a few decades later. Ultimately, Davis's text is probably best read as some combination of a refracted reality of a particular slave's life and a series of literary forms that influenced the shape the story took in the text. It is, like many of the sources that would be produced about the banjo in subsequent years, simultaneously a window onto the history of the instrument and a piece in the history of its representation.

*

The banjo's consolidation was certainly not a simple, one-way process. Yet there are striking consistencies between the instruments described by Labat, Sloane, and Stedman, notably the presence of four strings on the neck. And all, importantly, had resonators covered with animal skins—a connection to the long and deep tradition going back to the ancient world. That core sound, the hum and buzz of strings vibrating through skin, would have been familiar, probably comforting, to many of the Africans who heard it. And, through that sound, the instruments offered something more intangible—a link, a reminder, a way back to the old country. That sound could—at least for a moment—stand in for an absent Africa, a place that existed as a very specific individual origin and, increasingly, as a broader and more collective point of reference.

To write the history of the cumulative meaning of the banjo—meaning constituted through the repeated practice of performance, and through sound itself—is a particularly difficult, even quixotic, task. But we can find a guide to understanding how this process might have unfolded in a later musical story: that of another instrument invented in the Caribbean, which ultimately found its true home in Africa: the gumbe drum. Kenneth Bilby has pieced together and analyzed the history of this instrument, which he dubs "Africa's Creole Drum." This story is "a transatlantic story of displacement, cultural reinvention, and creolization." It is, in a way, the story of the banjo, but in reverse. It is the story of how a Caribbean instrument with a very particular structure and sound, developed by the Maroons of Jamaica, journeyed back to Africa and there, in time, became a popular and widespread instrument throughout much of the continent.[66]

In October of 1800, approximately six hundred Maroons from Jamaica arrived on the shores of Sierra Leone on a British ship. They had been deported from their home island after participating in a revolt in 1796 and were first settled in Nova Scotia. After four years there, during which they vociferously protested their situation and demanded another home, they were ultimately brought to the nascent British colony, which had been set up in 1787 as a home for free people of African descent from England. They brought a set of cultural practices developed over several generations, since their ancestors had escaped slavery and established free communities in the mountains of Jamaica in the late seventeenth century, forcing the colonial government to acknowledge their liberty. "Among the things they carried with them," writes Bilby, was the knowledge of a distinctive type of musical instrument—an unusual square frame drum with four legs."[67]

The earliest traces of the instrument go back only to the late eighteenth century. As with the banjo, the precise process through which the gumbe was developed and the precise sources of inspiration that the Maroons who created it drew on are difficult to document. But the result was a very particular kind of drum: it resembled "a stool with four legs," and featured a drum skin attached with "an unusual tuning mechanism, consisting of an inner frame driven by wedges against skin stretched over an outer frame." The drum was played within the Maroon communities of Jamaic, but also featured in the "John Canoe" or "Junkanoo" celebrations: one of them, for instance, was captured in an 1837 image made by the artist Belisario in Jamaica.[68]

Bilby sees the story of the gumbe as a way of understanding the process of creolization as both a "fluid social process" and "a cultural phenomenon that, in order to be meaningful, always entails some degree of continuity with multiple pasts." The gumbe traveled successfully in Africa in part because it encountered circumstances there in the early nineteenth century that were very similar to those which had taken shape in the plantation Caribbean beginning in the seventeenth and eighteenth centuries. The British abolished the slave trade in 1808, and their navy ships were patrolling the waters off West Africa and captured slaving vessels. Those on board, known as "liberated Africans," were often resettled in Sierra Leone. A German missionary documented 160 languages and 40 dialects in the early 1850s among these communities. They had come from all over Africa and as far away as Mozambique. In this new "crucible of creolizing culture," music once again became a way of creating connection and solidarity in the midst of tremendous cultural diversity.[69]

What the gumbe offered in this context was both musical and symbolic. Its development within the Maroon culture of Jamaica enabled it to be African in a general sense without being tied specifically to any particular African ethnic musical culture. Music that was "closely identified" with one or another ethnicity, argues Bilby, would have been "divisive" and possibly served to highlight "linguistic and musical differences" and maintain boundaries between groups. But because the gumbe wasn't perceived as belonging to any particular group, "it excluded no one." At the same time, the drum and the beats it offered "remained identifiably and palpably 'African' in a broad aesthetic sense." People from all the varied ethnic groups brought together in Sierra Leone would have "heard and felt" something familiar in the music. This made it appealing among "an uprooted, displaced African population" of "bewildering ethnic and linguistic diversity."[70]

What the gumbe drum did in West Africa the banjo had already done for at least a century in the Caribbean. The musicians who played it needed to respond to the dislocation and constant movement posed by the experience of the slave trade and plantation life. To be able to join into or lead performances for enslaved audiences, musicians circulating in Jamaica, Martinique, or Suriname needed something that could travel, something recognizable across the cultural boundaries that constituted the Caribbean plantation world. Over time, they found that in the banjo. We catch glimpses of a few of these musicians—those heard by Taylor and Sloane in Jamaica, by Labat in Martinique in the seventeenth century. Every once in a while, we catch their names, such as that of Hero in early nineteenth-century Suriname. These few who left traces in the written archive have to stand in for many, many more whose accumulated talent and imagination ultimately came to reside in the banjo and its music.

The banjo offered a deep, sonic experience—the hum of strings over the drumhead—that would have felt familiar to many African-born listeners. At the same time, the presence of a flat neck and four strings offered some flexibility, the ability to hit and pinch and strum strings, to tune them and play them in different scales and rhythms, so that a musician could absorb, adapt, and offer what was needed in certain circumstances. That combination of a rooted and familiar hum with a flexible range gave the instrument its power, one that was felt and acknowledged by an ever-accelerating and growing community of musicians and audiences.

There must have been many failures in the process: musicians who played a song no one recognized, a dance that began but faltered. There must have been instruments built that didn't sound right, two players sitting together who couldn't figure out how to tune their strings so that melody rather than dissonance would emerge. There must have been many experiments, frustrations, but also bits of laughter too. And then, here and there, the sound must have come together. The strings and the hum of the resonator, a song—a familiar one, or perhaps a new one—all just right, as if it had always been there, taking off, to the sound of an instrument that had built itself a home. There, at the crossroads, the banjo was both old and new, African and American, taking the listeners back and propelling them forward.

That is why the banjo was the first truly "African" instrument. Before its appearance in the Caribbean, there had never been any instrument that connected so many different African musical traditions, stretching from West to Central Africa. It was in the Americas, in the midst of exile, that people came to need a collective concept of Africa and a sound to accompany and consolidate that concept. In time, Caribbean populations explicitly recognized the banjo as African. An 1844 description of post-emancipation Antigua noted that although many ex-slaves enjoyed dancing to "quadrilles" as well as to "country dances and reels," Africans were "content with their own native music of the *Bangoe* and *Tum-Tum*." And when Lafcadio Hearn traveled to Martinique in the late nineteenth century, he recalled Jean-Baptiste Labat's description of the banza in the seventeenth century and added: "The tradition of this African instrument is said to survive in the modern '*banza*' *(banza nèg Guinée)*"—"the banjo of the blacks from Africa."[71]

3

Three Leaves

APPROACHING THE EDGE of New Orleans, his back to the Mississippi, Henry Latrobe heard noise. Or was it music?

Latrobe was a British architect who had moved to the United States in 1796. He designed and oversaw the construction of the U.S. Capitol and then, after his countrymen burned it in 1812, spent several years rebuilding it. When he traveled to New Orleans in 1819, the city had been part of the United States for sixteen years. But he was struck by the continuing presence of French culture: the local boats flying the Republican tricolor flag, as well as the books in French and English for sale along the levee alongside a mouthwatering assortment of "wild ducks, oysters . . . bananas, piles of oranges, sugar cane, sweet & Irish potatoes" and "some excellent & large fish." He strolled one Sunday to a spot known for its music and dance. "In going up St. Peters Street & approaching the Common," he wrote in his diary, "I heard a most extraordinary noise, which I supposed to proceed from some horse mill, the horses tramping on a wooden floor. I found, however, on emerging from the houses onto the Common, that it proceeded from a crowd of 5 or 600 persons assembled in an open space or public square."[1]

I went to the spot & crowded near enough to see the performance. All those who were engaged in the business seemed to be *blacks*. I did not observe a dozen yellow faces. They were formed into circular groupes [*sic*] in the midst of four of which, which I examined (but there were more of them), was a ring, the largest not 10 feet in diameter. In the first were two women dancing. They held each a coarse handkerchief extended by the corners in their hands, & *set* to each other in a miserably dull & slow figure, hardly moving their feet or their bodies. The music consisted of two drums and a stringed instrument. An old man sat astride of a cylindrical drum about a foot in diameter, & beat it with incredible quickness with the edge of his hand & fingers. The other drum was an open staved thing held between the knees & beaten in the same manner. They made an incredible noise.[2]

The experience of "stumbling upon the assembly of negroes" left Latrobe disgusted: "I have never seen anything more brutally savage, and at the same time dull & stupid, than this whole exhibition." He described how a man sung "an uncouth song to the dancing which I suppose was in some African language, for it was not French, & the women screamed a detestable burthen on one single note." It all made his ears hurt: he could still hear the "noise," he complained, a mile away, though after asking around he was at least reassured to learn "that these weekly meetings of the negroes" had never "produced any mischief."[3]

The dances Latrobe saw had been going on for a long time in New Orleans, though he was among the first to write in some detail about them. That was partly because for many earlier travelers, who arrived in the city from the Caribbean, such dances would have been so familiar that there was no reason to make special note of them. Congo Square itself was originally the site of a French fort built in 1758 and rebuilt in 1792 by the Spanish as part of the ramparts meant to protect the town from English invasion. In the end it wasn't the English but the Americans who came, and in 1805 they removed most of the fort. In 1812, the site was made a "public common," dubbed simply "Place Publique" on maps. Around 1816 a Cuban entrepreneur named Signore Gaetana set up a "Congo Circus" on the site, featuring an exhibit of African animals, including a giraffe. It was from that, rather than the African dances performed there, that the site probably first got its unofficial name.[4]

In time Congo Square became famous, indeed sacralized: it is sometimes described as the birthplace of jazz, and even of American dance. Its importance as a symbol has to do in part with the fact that, unlike many other dispersed sites where music was cultivated—"the countless black-town kitchens, garages, backyards, barrooms, and nightclubs in New Orleans, St. Louis, Kansas City, Chicago and Harlem"—Congo Square has a long, deep, and relatively documentable history as a public space. It was never laid out as a formal public square, but rather took its shape as a cultural space "gradually and informally out of particularly New Orleanian circumstances." That history, like those of the Afro-Atlantic spaces of gathering, represents a kind of triumph, the story of how the informal, the disallowed and even outlawed, the misunderstood and maligned, all came to find and occupy its own sonic space. As Ned Sublette notes, this was a place of "sonic marronage: the drums were a way slaves could escape, if only for a few hours."[5]

The day when Latrobe visited, a peculiar object in the crowd caught his eye: a "most curious instrument." He was struck by its construction and decoration: "On top of the fingerboard was the rude figure of a man in a sitting posture, & two pegs behind him to which the strings were fastened. The body was a calabash." It was in the hands of "a very little old man, apparently 80 or 90 years old." As he documented his visit to Congo Square, Latrobe was moved to pick up his pen and make a sketch.[6]

There at the crossroads, on the edge of New Orleans, Latrobe had come across a version of an American instrument that had hummed and strummed throughout the Caribbean and North America for over a century: the banjo. But the instrument struck him as mysterious and unfamiliar. He described it as "a stringed instrument which no doubt was imported from Africa," viewing it not so much as part of America but rather as a strange and disturbing relic within its midst. But what Latrobe saw as a strange import was, in fact, already well-known and widespread within Afro-Atlantic communities, an instrument with more than a century of history in the Caribbean. Though it was built in many places and by many different hands, and still went under various names, it was an established, unique, and recognizable instrument, quite at home there at the square in New Orleans.

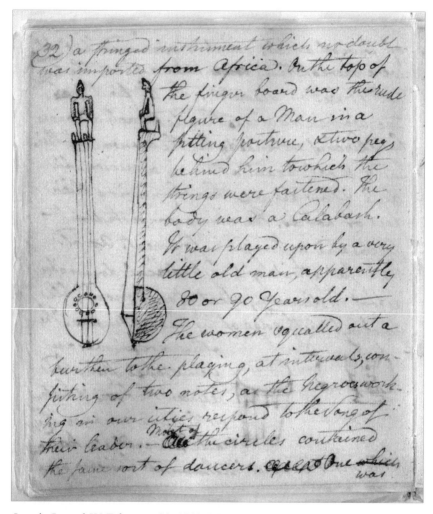

Latrobe Journal IV, February 21, 1819. Manuscript.

Benjamin Latrobe Collection. Courtesy of the Maryland Historical Society.

Banjos themselves, drawn, painted, and in one slightly miraculous case, actually preserved for centuries, can tell their own stories and those of the enslaved people who made and played them. From these fragments in visual art and observers' accounts, we can construct the outlines of a mosaic that reveals the banjo as a way not just for the enslaved to gather with one another, across ethnic lines, but also to connect with ancestors and gods. As the first African instrument, its role was not just sonic but also spiritual. Its sound accompanied funerary rites and wakes, and the musicians who played it occupied roles not just as performers but as individuals who convoked and channeled spiritual power. The instrument, sometimes decorated with the symbol of a cross, was a crossroads between the living and the dead, and between Africa and America.

✳

In 1841, the French abolitionist Victor Schoelcher disembarked in Haiti. He wanted to see for himself how the country, which had won its independence from France in 1804, was building a new society and culture on the ashes of a brutal slave system. He traveled through the countryside, seeing how a place once covered with profitable plantations was now full of small farms held by ex-slaves and their children. He met with a young activist trying to create a cooperative for local farmers. He met many citizens who were very angry with the central government in Port-au-Prince, then led by the authoritarian president Boyer, who two years later would be overthrown by a mass protest movement. And, at one point, he must have met at least one musician. Though he wrote nothing about the encounter, when he left Haiti he was carrying with him an instrument he had acquired there: a beautifully made, delicately carved banza.[7]

A few decades later, Schoelcher donated the instrument to the recently founded Museum of the French Music Conservatory. This institution, a project born of the French Revolution, was to be both an archive and a source of information for instrument makers: the objects in the museum could "through their perfection serve as models." The project had enthusiastic boosters—one dreamed of a museum that, alongside those celebrating the sciences and arts, would celebrate the "sublime riches" of the art of music—and a founding collection of 316 instruments. The priority, however, was given to the development of a music conservatory, and most of the instruments were later sold to pay music teachers. In 1816, twenty harpsichords, deemed "debris," were burned to keep students warm during their classes.[8]

Only in the nineteenth century was the original vision of the museum finally realized, thanks to the composer Louis Clapisson. Over his lifetime, he had painstakingly gathered a collection of 230 musical instruments, which the French government bought from him as the basis for the museum. Clapisson was named the museum's first director: as his successor Gustave Chouquet put it, Clapisson was therefore spared "the pain" of no longer seeing his much-cherished objects. Clapisson's collection was made up almost entirely of European instruments; but Chouquet, who directed the museum from 1871 to 1886, globalized the collection thanks to large donations from two individuals: the celebrated Indian musician Sourindro Mohun Tagore and world traveler Victor Schoelcher.[9]

Schoelcher's eclectic and expansive collection of musical instruments from different parts of the world was, as one contemporary wrote, an extension of his political passions. The man was a consistent "defender of the black race" who held "inflexible principles of honor and liberty." "At once a democrat and an aristocrat," he "dined on a plate of carrots, but on a silver plate." His commitment to abolitionism and racial equality led him to see value and interest in objects others might have overlooked. During his travels in the 1840s and 1850s to the Caribbean, where he visited the French colonies of Martinique and Guadeloupe as well as Haiti, he collected not just the banza but a number of other musical instruments. He also gathered instruments when he traveled to West Africa. In 1871 he donated all these objects, along with others from Egypt, Mexico, and Turkey, to the museum, following up later with instruments from Algeria and Cambodia. One supercilious contemporary described the collection as "a very interesting collection of savage instruments." But Schoelcher was proud of what he had gathered, noting that the instruments were notable for their "rarity," most of them "having never been seen before in Europe." His gift became an inspiration for others who had collections of instruments, including many from outside Europe. In the next decades, instruments from many private collections found a permanent home in the museum, where they received care from specialists who repaired cracks and broken bows.[10]

Chouquet and other scholars of musical history at the time worked according to a clearly civilizational typology: they considered European musical instruments to be the most advanced and sophisticated in the world. "In this Museum," Chouquet wrote in 1884, "we have reserved the place of honor for instruments that are the highest expression of modern art, and relegated those instruments of uncivilized nations or those that are foreign to our musical system to the background." So the instruments donated by Schoelcher, and by the Indian musician Tagore, were relegated within the collection to a kind of generalized category of the "non-European." In this context, the banza from Haiti posed a bit of an interpretive difficulty. Was it African, or American? Someone— perhaps Schoelcher, or perhaps Chouquet, finessed the problem by writing an inscription on the animal skin stretched over the gourd body of the instrument: the banza was an "imitation of an African instrument" that was played by the "black people of Haiti."[11]

More information about the banza was included in a museum catalog produced in 1874. Under the title "Banza d'Haïti," it read: "This type of guitar, mounted with four strings and with a very picturesque form, is in general use among the negroes of Saint-Domingue." As was common in texts of the time, there was a slippage between the name "Saint-Domingue"—that of the old French colony—and "Haiti," the name for the independent country born in 1804. But the observation, presumably gathered from Schoelcher, that this instrument was in "general use" is a precious one. The banza was common enough in Haiti that Schoelcher, who was there for only a brief time, had quickly come across it and collected it because he saw it as a popular indigenous instrument. We can surmise that numerous artisans in different parts of Haiti were making such instruments in the 1840s, and therefore that musicians were playing it throughout the country.[12]

In time, the museum foundered and closed its doors. The banza— along with most of the collection of non-European instruments—was boxed up and put in storage. At some point in the process, it was taken apart into two pieces: the gourd resonator ended in one box, the neck of the instrument in another. So it sat until 1997, when a French curator named Philippe Bruguière working at the newly created Museum of Music inherited the dusty boxes of instruments from the old Museum of the Music Conservatory. The same civilizational typology that had reigned in the nineteenth century was alive and well at the new Museum of Music, which primarily showcases European musical instruments and traditions. Visitors must travel through lots of rooms of violins, trumpets, flutes, and bassoons before they end up, just before the exit, in front of a few displays of Asian and African instruments. Bruguière, a specialist on

South Asian music, was given the task of going through extensive collections he inherited and picking a few specimens to fill this one room. As he did so, he came across a gourd with an animal skin tacked onto it. He made out, written on the skin, the inscription describing the instrument as a banza. He took some notes about the curious inscribed gourd and then continued sifting through the collection.[13]

A few months later, in a different box of instruments from the old conservatory museum, Bruguière came across the neck of a stringed instrument. It was flat, like a guitar neck, but it had pegs for just four strings. Three of them were at the carved top of the instrument. But the fourth peg, for the top string, was up further on the neck, placed to accommodate a much shorter string. Finely carved, the neck also included a decoration, lightly dug into the wood. It looked a little bit like a face, staring up from the instrument. Bruguière went to his shelves, found the gourd he had found months earlier, and realized it had a carved opening— precisely the size of the neck. When he reunited the two pieces, he held in his hand an early nineteenth-century Haitian banza. Though he didn't know it yet, it was a major discovery, one that offers precious details about the history and meaning of the banjo.

In Brussels, at one of the world's greatest musical instrument museums, a curator named Saskia Willaert was then putting together an exhibit on the banjo. She heard about the find and put the banza on display for the first time since the nineteenth century. Soon news about the discovery began circulating among the small, obsessive, and tight-knit community of those pursuing research into the early history of the banjo. One of the visitors to the exhibit was an independent researcher named Ulf Jagfors, a retired Swedish telecommunications executive who had been working with West African musicians to better understand the origins of the banjo. Alerted to the find by Jagfors, musician and banjo historian Bob Carlin, and a banjo maker named Pete Ross traveled to Europe to see the instrument and began making exact replicas for museums and private collections in the United States. In March 2005 Jagfors and Ross presented the history of the banza—along with a replica made by Ross—at the Black Banjo Gathering held at Appalachian State University. Since then, Bruguière has welcomed a small stream of pilgrims wishing to see in material form what they had long been forced to imagine by scrutinizing texts and images.[14]

Haitian Banza, reproduction by Pete Ross. Photograph by Kristina Gaddy.

The discovery of the banza in Paris highlighted the curious fact that no historical gourd banjos have ever surfaced in the United States, despite much searching by a very active and large group of banjo collectors. This is perhaps not surprising: these were handcrafted and built around fragile gourds, and in contexts of slavery it is difficult to preserve such materials from generation to generation. The lack of physical relics posed a serious limitation for scholars of music: an image, after all, doesn't really communicate the precise construction of an instrument, its hidden interior structure, or its sound.

Seeing the Haitian banza is a powerful thing: on its neck is a face carved by one of the artisans who, across the Caribbean and North America, created a musical legacy. It is a testament to the work of those who grew gourds, dried animal skins, collected wood and vines, and put them together to make instruments. To hold in one's hands an example of what they had made is to reconnect with—and therefore to render homage to—the unnamed and unnameable inventors of the banjo. In the banza we have a concrete legacy, passed on to us. And the instrument carries a message, that the banza was not just a source of sound and music but also healing and remembrance.

By the middle of the eighteenth century, with the entire economy and political structure of the Atlantic world based on slavery, questions about its profits, costs, and morality were posed with increasing persistence and ferocity. The problem of slavery—whether it was morally justified, whether it was economically viable, the dangers it might pose to the very social order it enabled—suffused Atlantic culture. Observers increasingly sought to depict and capture the lives of the enslaved, in essays and travel writing as well as in works of literature and theater. Enlightenment philosophers and Caribbean planters offered written accounts of plantation life, many of which included reflections on the musical culture of the enslaved and what it said about their condition and perspective. Describing plantation music, including the banjo itself, became a way of representing what it meant to be a slave.

The lives of Caribbean planters and plantation managers were literally built on the principle that human beings could be bought and sold as objects, and that economic calculations justified a plantation system in which slaves were worked to death and replaced rather than being treated in a way that helped them survive. Music, however, is perhaps the most human of expressions. Those authors who recognized and listened to the songs of the enslaved were forced, in a sense, to confront the deep contradictions of slavery. And though depictions of song and dance were sometimes used to buttress arguments of racial superiority and difference, very often even openly racist and hostile observers who encountered music left behind rounded and complex portraits of what they saw and heard.

In a lengthy 1764 poem written about sugarcane—a kind of agricultural manual in verse—Thomas Grainger, who had left England in 1759 to become the manager of a plantation in St. Christopher, recommended that slaves be allowed to enjoy the music of the banjo. "On festal days; or when their work is done; / Permit the slaves to lead the choral dance, / To the wild banshaw's melancholy sound." In one of the many footnotes that accompanied his poem, he explained that the banshaw was "A sort of rude guitar, invented by the Negroes" that "produces a wild pleasing melancholy sound." He described the intricate dancing that would accompany the music of the banjo: "Responsive to the sound, head, feet, and frame / Move awkwardly harmonious. . . . A thousand tuneful intricacies weave, / Shaking their sable limbs." He suggested the banjo was safer than other instruments. "But let not thou the drum their mirth inspire," he warned slave masters, "nor vinous spirits," or they might be "to madness fir'd, / (What will not bacchanalian frenzy dare?) / Fell acts of blood, and vengeance they pursue." For Grainger, the banjo's pleasing sounds allowed release; the drum, accompanied by alcohol, incited revolt.[15]

William Beckford was born in Jamaica into a well-established family of planters. He was educated in England but in 1774 returned to the island and began to manage several plantations. "They are extremely fond of music and dancing," he wrote of the slaves, complimenting them for having "good ears" and preserving "the most perfect tune and time." He nevertheless reserved plenty of disdain for them: when he began his list of their "musical instruments," he quickly added a caveat: "if such they may be called." He listed "a kind of Spanish guitar," that he claimed was called a "bonjour." Providing yet another explanation for the origin of the name "banjo," he suggested it might have been "originally taken" from "a French word, as many have found their way by corruption among the negroes." It was accompanied by other instruments, including "a gomba, which they strike with their hands; a drum; a box filled with pebbles, which they shake with their wrists; and, to close the account, the jaw-bone of an animal, from which is produced a harsh and disagreeable sound." Beckford was not a fan of the result, and assumed his readers would share his distaste: "It may be easily be imagined, when these all together join in a chorus, and are accompanied by a number of voices, what kind of music must assail, and fill the ear."[16]

One of the occasions during which such music was played, Beckford noted, was after slave burials, which he described as their "principal festivals." After an elaborate burial, during which the body was accompanied to the grave "with a song," mourning was set aside, and "the face of sorrow becomes at once the emblem of joy." "The instruments resound, the dancers are prepared; the day sets in cheerfulness, and the night resounds with the chorus of contentment." Beckford's account of slave life had one major intent: to make it seem that slavery was not all that bad. And so his descriptions of the "joy" and "contentment" of the slaves are certainly overdrawn. But his identification of the instruments, and of the important role they played in accompanying the passage between life and death, suggests the important spiritual role that such instruments, including the banjo, played in many slave communities.[17]

Other observers of life in the British West Indies writing in the same period also noted the presence of the banjo, usually with a similar intent. One visitor described a ring dance on a plantation he visited. As with many other white observers, his account combined a certain sympathy with a heavy dose of disdain. "The music of these poor creatures has a wildness that finds its way to the heart," he wrote. Though "none of their rude instruments could produce any very pleasing effect, without the assistance of their voices," when they were supported by singing, "the Banjaw, the Goombay, the Jawbone, inspire mirth and alacrity."[18]

Opponents of slavery, however, found a weapon in music. In his legendary 1788 attack on slavery and the slave trade, Thomas Clarkson condemned the increasingly common idea that the music and dancing of the enslaved demonstrated that they were in fact quite content with their condition. Proslavery writers, he noted, argued that the enslaved were happier than English peasants, pointing to their moments of leisure during "holy-days" and "dances" to argue that their life was "a scene of festivity and mirth" in which they were much happier than they had been in Africa. Such claims, Clarkson insisted, were absurd. The small plots of land ceded to them by their masters were not, as defenders of slavery seemed to imagine, "made for *flowers*" or "places of *amusement* in which they can spend their time in botanical researches and delights." They were a place where, after having spent long days working in the fields, the enslaved struggled to produce food for themselves because of the "deficiency" of the provisions supplied by masters. The "holy days" during which they were allowed to rest, seethed Clarkson, meant only that they had one out of fifty-two weeks of the year away from the fields, while even a horse in England was given Sundays off, and therefore had "*one* day in *seven* to refresh his limbs."[19]

"With respect to their dances, on which such a particular stress has been generally laid," Clarkson went on, people had once again been "shamefully deceived." Proslavery writers made it sound as if the enslaved were generously given "certain hours allowed them for the purpose of joining the dance" and were given "every comfort and convenience" in order to do so. In fact, of course, the only time left for dances was "the time allotted to them for sleep." And the dances were not the sign of "any uncommon degree of happiness," but rather of "an uncommon depression of the spirits," which drove the slaves to "even sacrifice their rest, for the sake of experiencing for a moment a more joyful oblivion of their cares." That the enslaved danced after grueling days of work was, for Clarkson, just proof of their desperate desire to escape the brutality of the slavery.[20]

The next year Gilbert Francklyn, presenting himself as a "gentleman in Jamaica," sought to refute Clarkson. He remarked that if the enslaved really suffered from "insupportable fatigue" caused by overwork, it would be impossible for them to "travel several miles, after their work, to a dance," then "dancing all night, and (which they must do) traveling the same number of miles back again, by six o'clock in the morning." Clearly, Francklyn suggested, they couldn't be *that* tired. Clarkson, furthermore, offered no actual proof that they did want to return to their native land—and if they did, he wrote, it was only so that they could "dance there for ever, without interruption" and "live without any other labour than this."[21]

Writings about the United States during the same period also sought to use the banjo to interpret the condition and attitudes of the enslaved. A 1784 account by a British man included details about the difficult life of the "poor negro slaves." After a grueling day of labor, the author wrote, "instead of retiring to rest, as naturally might be concluded he would be glad to do, he generally sets out from home, and walks six or seven miles in the night, be the weather ever so sultry, to a negroe dance." There, he "performs with astonishing agility, and the most vigorous exertions, keeping time and cadence, most exactly, with the music of a banjor (a large hollow instrument with three strings), and a quaqua (somewhat resembling a drum)," and barely had time to return home before it was time to work again the next morning. More laconically, the Philadelphia merchant William Attmore, in a journal of a 1787 trip to North Carolina, noted that one night after dinner he "saw a dance of Negroes to the Banjo in his Yard."[22]

Journeying north from his home in Virginia a decade later, Thomas Fairfax stopped in Richmond for the night. "After going to bed I was entertained with an agreeable serenade, by a black man who had taken his stand near the Tavern, and for the amusement of those of his colour, sung and played in the Bangoe." Fairfax listened with pleasure to music meant for another audience and appreciated the musician's skill: "He appeared to be quite an adept on this African instrument, which tho it may not bear a comparison with the Guitar, Is certainly Capable of Conveying much pleasure to a musical ear." Still, he couldn't help situating the sound he enjoyed in some kind of hierarchy: "Its wild notes of melody seem to Correspond with the state of Civilization of the Country where this species of music originated."[23]

Some writers began to present the banjo not only as a link to Africa but, simultaneously, as a symbol of America's uncivilized and rough culture. One evening in 1806, the British traveler Thomas Ashe found himself at a noisy inn in Virginia. He entered the "ball-room," which was "filled with persons at cards, drinking, smoaking [*sic*], dancing, &c." "The *music*," he wrote—insisting on putting the word in italics to suggest it didn't sound much like real music to him—"consisted of two bangies, played by negroes nearly in a state of nudity, and a flute, through which a Chickesaw breathed with much occasional exertion and violent gesticulations." It was hard to hear the "music of Ethiopia," though, because of the "clamor of the card tables." Pretending a tolerance he belied little elsewhere in his text, Ashe declared: "A man should never judge of the principles of the entertainment of others, by his individual conceptions." And he admitted that, though he considered the "ball" nothing more than "a violent vulgar uproar," it "afforded the utmost delight to the assembly, and possibly would have concluded with infinite joy and satisfaction at an early hour next day," if it had not been for an "unlucky" politician in the crowd who started a fight. Seizing "a friend by the throat," he "threatened to annihilate him, if he did not drink 'Damnation to Thomas Jefferson." Within a few minutes, the entire inn was cleared out save one sleeping drunk on the floor.[24]

Ashe's description of the event, and its music, was part of a series of passages that made fun of American "vulgarity," and his description of nearly naked black banjo players accompanied by a Chickasaw flute player may have been partly fantasy. The account, though, suggests that there may have been some exchange and encounter in performance styles between African-American and Native American, at least in certain regions. Whether rooted in fact or fiction, it signals the emergence of the banjo itself as a broader sign of a process—one that could be both vilified and celebrated—of unexpected crossings and exchanges in a land that was increasingly defining itself as "American." The banjo also appeared as a sign of the curious and wild life of the frontiers of North America. In a description of "the young town of Knoxville" in 1798, for instance, one traveler described a place "confused with a promiscuous throng of every denomination," that included blacks playing banjos to the delight of the surrounding crowd.[25]

In a series of "letters from the South," the self-described "Northern man" James Paulding assuaged his initial concern about the condition of the slaves by focusing on their music. The blacks, he wrote, were a "gay, harmless, and unthinking race." They were also "by far the most musical of any portion of the inhabitants of the United States, and in the evening I have seen them reclining in their boats on the canal at Richmond, playing on the banjo, and singing in a style—I dare say, equal to a Venetian gondolier." Their laughter was "the very echo of thoughtless hilarity." Paulding went on to wonder whether, while this admission would "mortify the pride of the white man," the slaves were in fact *happier* than their masters. They were, he claimed, freed from the burdens of worries for the future and able to fully enjoy their leisure because it was such a relief from their hard work. Paulding was careful to note that he was not "an advocate of slavery." But he found himself reassured that as they drank "the bitter draught of slavery," the slaves had music and dance to console them.[26]

These accounts were all refracted through the lens of debates about slavery. Writers clearly picked out the details that fit with their varied positions. But precisely because of the fact that they come from such a range of perspectives, taken together they can give us a sense of the social and ritual uses the banjo had taken on by the late eighteenth century. It gathered people together so that they could, for a time, find a space constituted out of different kinds of relationships with each other and the world around them. During funerary rites, the banjo accompanied the journey into the next world, one often perceived in Afro-Atlantic contexts as a journey home across the waters to family and ancestors in Africa. There and in other contexts, the banjo offered solace and a kind of mourning for lost places and lost lives. It also accompanied commentary on life in slavery, in the process sustaining a vision of what life might be beyond or outside of it.

While some writers debated whether the dancing of the enslaved signified happiness or desperation, others looked to music to answer a different question: are Africans culturally inferior? It is in the texts that take up this question that we find the most details about musical practice and the construction of musical instruments. Some writers celebrated the musical abilities of Africans, using accounts of music to directly challenge the ideas of racial superiority that buttressed and infused slavery. For William Dickson, writing in 1784 in order to prove "the natural equality of the Africans to the Europeans," the musical skill of the enslaved, even if it did not "demonstrate their rationality," at the very least helped to prove their "humanity." Dickson, who had lived in Barbados, compared the "banjay" along with other instruments from the island to "several ancient musical instruments" he found descriptions of in a contemporary history of music. He argued that the banjay would "lose nothing" in the comparison with these venerable ancient instruments.[27]

One of Dickson's contemporaries in North America, Thomas Jefferson, also brought up the banjo as he reflected on the question of the musical capacities of blacks. In his *Notes on the State of Virginia,* first published in 1782, Thomas Jefferson grudgingly admitted that blacks, who he otherwise described as quite inferior, were "more generally gifted than the whites" in music, having "accurate ears for tune and time." They had, he went on "been found capable of imagining a small catch," that is a short piece of music. To this sentence he added a footnote: "The instrument proper to them is the Banjer, which they brought hither from Africa, and which is the original of the guitar, its chords being precisely the four lower chords of the guitar." Jefferson had little confidence in the broader musical talent of blacks: "Whether they will be equal to the composition of a more extensive run of melody, or of complicated harmony, is yet to be proved," he wrote. At the same time, he seemed ready to concede that the banjo was in fact the "original," presumably the ancestor, of the guitar. And so, in the midst of a run of commentaries that were mostly denigrating of the capacities of people of African descent, he allowed for an African origin for a modern European instrument, though one he perhaps also regarded with little respect.[28]

"Negroes are very fond of the discordant notes of the banjar," John Luffman wrote in a 1789 account of the British colony of Antigua. The instrument was "somewhat similar" to a guitar, but the bottom was formed of "one half of a large calabash, to which is prefixed a wooden neck, and it is strung with cat and gut wire." Echoing Thomas Jefferson's comments, he noted: "This instrument is the invention of, and was brought here by the African negroes, who are most expert in the performances thereon." These were, he added, "principally their own country tunes"—that is, songs from Africa—and he "did not remember ever to have heard any thing like European numbers from its touch." The music was commonly played on Sunday afternoon, after the "great market" in town was over. To the music of the banjo, accompanied by the toombah, a drum with "gingles of tin or shells," one could see "a hundred or more dancing at a time," with gestures that while "not altogether graceful" were of "astonishing" agility and might even be "well received" back home—at least, he specified, if they were introduced by "French or Italian dancers." Luffman called what the banjo created music, but not without adding witheringly, "if it deserves the name." And he explained the skill of the enslaved in dancing by attributing it to "their being habituated to a warm climate, where elasticity is more general than in colder latitudes." In an idealized 1800 description of the functioning of a plantation in the British Caribbean, meanwhile, Charles McPherson wrote: "The dance and the song went hand in hand with the labour; the sound of the tom tom and the bangah was nightly heard on the estate." Here—as it had been earlier in Thomas Grainger's poem—the sound of the banjo was taken as a sign of the good order of slave life, a counterpoint to the day's labor that justified the way it was extracted.[29]

Bryan Edwards, a British-born planter in Jamaica who produced an influential history of the British Caribbean colonies, first published in 1793, was harsher in his evaluation of the music of the enslaved. "An opinion prevails in Europe," he wrote, "that they possess organs peculiarly adapted to the science of musick [sic]; but this I believe is an ill-founded idea." They were poor singers, he claimed, and while "as practical musicians," there were some who "by great labor and careful instruction, become sufficiently expert to bear an under-part in a publick concert," he could not recall ever having "seen or heard of a Negro who could truly be called a fine performer on any capital instrument." "In general they prefer a loud and long-continued noise to the finest harmony, and frequently consume the whole night *in beating on a board with a stick*." This was, "in fact one of their chief musical instruments." Among the others, he wrote, was "the *Banja* or *Merrywang*" which was "an imperfect kind of violincello; except that it is played on by the finger like the guitar; producing a dismal monotony of four notes." Where Jefferson had described the banjo as the "original of the guitar," here it is described as a kind of degraded version of a European instrument. "From such instruments," Edwards concluded, "nothing like a regular tune can be expected, nor is it attempted." He did note that during their "merry meetings, and midnight festivals," the instrument accompanied ballads where they gave "full scope to a talent for ridicule and derision, which is exercised not only against each other, but also, not unfrequently, at the expence of their owner or employer."[30]

Edward's description would be repeatedly recopied by other writers purporting to describe the music of the slaves of Jamaica. "Like all rude nations, they are fond of noisy music and dancing," Robert Renny wrote in an 1807 description of the "negroes" of Jamaica. He borrowed Edward's words directly in describing "the banja, or merriwang," which was of "African origin." Edwards had described the music of the slaves as "melancholy," and Renny expanded on this, writing that it was "impossible to hear this music, and remain unaffected with the dismal melody produced by the Negro, who, sitting in the door of his cabin, enjoying the coolness, and delighting in the stillness of the evening, accompanies it with a melancholy song, expressive of his feelings." Indeed the music was such that it drew "tears from the affectionate, the melancholy, or the contemplative" and was, Renny acknowledged, "often extremely affecting."[31]

Renny described the wide range of music styles and circumstances in which the banjo was played. At their "merry meetings," the songs allowed the slaves of Jamaica to "give a full scope to their talent for ridicule." They amused themselves at the expense of the new arrivals in the colony, whether the "awkward *new-come* Negro," or the *"buckra"* (whites), and portrayed the "follies or foibles of their masters and mistresses." There were also "funeral songs of a heroic nature, considering death as a wholesome release from the calamities of life, and as a passport to the delightful and never-to-be-forgotten, scenes of their nativity; an event, which, while it frees them from bondage, restores them to the society of their dear, long-lost relatives of Africa." In Renny's account, we see the banjo accompanying melancholy songs, social satire, and the passage of the dead from this world to the next and from the new world to the old.[32]

In an account of the celebration of the abolition of slavery in British Caribbean on August 1, 1834, Nicholas Madden—who was in Montego Bay, Jamaica, serving as a "stipendiary magistrate" helping to oversee the process of emancipation—described how a well-known quadrille "was done great justice to on a bonjoo and a gombah, the violoncello and kettle-drum of the negro orchestra." The "Abolition bill," he went on, seemed to have "made the limbs of the dark-complexioned ladies and gentlemen as their ears; and there was no end to the pleasure and perspiration of the evening, till the head of the gombah was fairly beaten in, and the last string of the bonjoo was scraped to pieces."[33]

In a letter published from Barbados in 1816, the physician George Pinckard offered a more appreciative description of the banjo. The instruments of the enslaved, he wrote, were "a drum, a kind of rattle, and" what he described as "the ever-delighting banjo," which was "a coarse and rough kind of guitar." As if catching himself being too positive, Pinckard did add a series of caveats: the music and dance were "of a savage nature" with "very simple" songs that were "harsh and devoid of melody." But he went on to describe how the musician "strikes the banjo," accompanied by a rattle and by a third musician who, "sitting across the body of the drum, as it lies lengthwise along the ground, beats and kicks the sheep-skin at the end," while another musician struck the body of the drum with sticks. These were accompanied by singing, and "on great occasions," were augmented by many more "drums, rattles and voices," and formed the foundation for a range of dances over the course of the day. Among those who participated were not only slaves but at least one white soldier who pushed his way into the circle, and a Scottish soldier's wife who looked on, though with "features marked with surprise and dissatisfaction."[34]

Frederick Bayley, who spent several years in the British colonies of the Eastern Caribbean in the late 1820s, described the "wonderful variety" of music played by slaves he encountered there. Their instruments included an "empty barrel" covered by a "large piece of parchment," along with a "kettledrum, a tambourine, a pipe, a *gumbay* or *bonja*," accompanied by "vocal efforts." The result was "sounds of most terrific merriment." The slaves, he wrote, could not be accused of the "crime" of creating "inharmonious and nonaccordant" music. "On the contrary," they had "generally a good ear for music, they sing or whistle with wonderful correctness any tune they may have heard, they dance in excellent time, and are altogether very intelligent persons in any thing connected with music."[35]

The banjo was also popular in the Danish colony of Saint-Croix, notably at Christmas celebrations. It was "customary," wrote the American traveler Sylvester Hovey, "for slaves on the different plantations, attired in their choicest dress, to go in a body to the house of their master, and to receive admission to his best apartments; where they set up the music of the banjo and commence dancing." This symbolic admission to the house of the master was also an invitation to the master's family to participate: "The family made it a point to be present, and not unfrequently join in the dance." But the event was also about showcasing the generosity and paternalism of masters: "This is the occasion, when presents are distributed among them of provisions, clothing, or even of money."

"The feelings of the slaves towards their master," Hovey noted, "depend very much on the treatment they receive at these times."[36]

These textual descriptions of music offer us refracted details of moments of performance, conviviality, mourning, and perhaps solace among the enslaved. The banjo played a key role at the interface of relationships between slaves and masters. The instrument enlivened and supported enslaved commentary, critique, and parody of masters. Slave owners understood this and sought to channel and contain—and at times appropriate—the music it provided by bringing the celebrations to the plantation houses. Whatever they saw was always just one side of the music: the same song sung in different contexts had different meaning and content. But what also comes through in these depictions is that at least some whites found themselves—sometimes despite themselves—drawn to the sound of this unfamiliar but electrifying instrument.[37]

In the 1790s, for the first time, the banjo appeared on canvas, painted by two very different artists. One of them, Samuel Jennings, a Philadelphia native living in London, inserted the banjo into an abolitionist allegory celebrating the gifts of liberty. The other, John Rose, was a southern plantation owner, himself a master of slaves, who nevertheless produced one of the most important and enduring visual artifacts of the cultural life of the enslaved in North America.

In 1790, Jennings heard that one of the major cultural institutions of his home city, the Library Company of Philadelphia, was moving into a new building. Founded in 1731 by Benjamin Franklin, the library housed the most important collection of books in Philadelphia and became a hub of intellectual activity frequented in particular by a number of Quaker abolitionists. On hearing of its imminent move, Jennings wrote to the directors of the institution offering to paint them an image—which he hoped would be prominently displayed in the new reading room—that celebrated learning and wisdom. He offered three possibilities: "Clio—Goddess of History, and Heroic Poetry. Calliope—Goddess of Harmony, Rhetoric and Heroic Poetry. Minerva—Goddess of Wisdom, & all the Arts." The latter, it seemed to him, would be best, because Minerva wore

Samuel Jennings, Liberty
Displaying the Arts &
Sciences (Or the Genius
of America), 1792.

Courtesy of the Library Company
of Philadelphia.

the best clothes: "The Dress of Minerva is grand, and would make a better picture than either of the others."[38]

The directors of the Library Company liked the idea of the painting but decided Jennings needed a bit more direction. They suggested a different female figure as its main focus: "the figure of Liberty (with her Cap and property Insignia) displaying the arts of some of the most striking Symbols of Painting, Architecture, Mechanics, Astronomy & ca., whilst She appears in the attitude of placing on top of a Pedestal, a pile of books, lettered with Agriculture, Commerce, Philosophy & Catalogue of Philadelphia Library." And they added another request, aimed at making the painting a clear statement in favor of the abolition of slavery: "A Broken Chain under her feet, and in the distant back Ground a Groupe of Negroes sitting on the Earth, or in some attitude expressive of Ease & Joy." Jennings obliged, offering up a painting in which Liberty is blond, smiling gently, and clad in a white gown. All around her are the tools of learning and research—scientific instruments, a sheet of calculations, palettes and brushes, and a scattering of books including Homer, Virgil, Milton, and Shakespeare, and the catalogue of the Library Company, which Liberty is picking up as a kind of offering. Yet every one of the recipients of all this knowledge—a total of fourteen figures, including men, women, children, and one baby—are African-American. Jennings fulfilled the request of the directors by depicting a group outside the library having a picnic, at which a group dances around a "Liberty Pole." Jennings went further, however, adding another "Groupe of Negroes" kneeling in the foreground of the painting who, he explained, "are paying Homage to Liberty, for the boundless blessings they receive through her."[39]

The image refers to Africa in several places. A bust in the foreground portrays Henry Thornton, an English abolitionist who was the chairman of the Sierra Leone Company. Founded in 1791, as Jennings was painting, the goal of this company—which was soon fulfilled—was to create a settlement of freed slaves on the coast of West Africa. The painting includes a globe turned to show the viewer the Atlantic world—on the top left are North and Central America, in the center the Caribbean and the northern coast of South America, on the bottom Brazil, and to the right is Africa. Europe, interestingly, is not visible on the globe. Leaning against the globe is a Lyre, and stretched in front of it, as if the instrument is reading the music, is a bit of the Handel air "Come, Ever-smiling Liberty."[40]

The composition of the painting centers around a banjo player. Though he is small in the painting, the viewer is drawn to him. Jennings explained that he had intentionally composed his painting so that the eye would be "conducted" from the foreground "to the Negroes paying homage to Liberty" and then to the "Shipping, & Sky" in the background. The banjo player is right there, at the crossroads of the land, the river, the mountains, and the sky above. No one is looking at him in the painting except an admiring boy standing behind him—and us. He is well-dressed, in a blue jacket, red vest, and white pants. The colors are no accident, and one might in fact see him as America itself. He is the only figure in the painting wearing all three of these colors together. But, strikingly, the instrument he is playing is a very African one: it is made of an oblong gourd, and the neck of the instrument is not flat but a rounded pole. His hand is balled up in a fist, his fingers seemingly striking downward against the strings. Though the instrument contrasts with those instruments surrounding Liberty—instruments of classical culture like the lyre, a telescope, maps—it is depicted, as is the musician, with dignity and agency.[41]

Jennings's 1792 depiction of the instrument is strikingly detailed and specific and can't easily be traced to other visual representations of the banjo in circulation at the time, since there were so few of them. Jennings could have seen Hans Sloane's engraving of the banjos in Jamaica, but his looks different from them: it has an oblong gourd and seems to have a stick neck rather than a flat neck. It is most likely that Jennings had in fact seen such a banjo someplace, perhaps when he was growing up in Philadelphia, perhaps even in London. Such a memory could explain why he was inspired to offer up banjo music to animate the dance in celebration of the figure of Liberty he had been asked to portray. And it would mean that the instrument was painted from life, or at least from remembered life. A celebration of a library, and of liberty, ended up offering an enduring document of America's musical history as well.

During the same period, but far away both geographically and ideologically from the hub of Quaker abolitionism in Philadelphia, John Rose was also painting a banjo he saw in South Carolina. The image he produced, now known by the title *The Old Plantation,* is powerful and unique

The Old Plantation, attributed to John Rose, Beaufort County, South Carolina, Probably 1785–1790, watercolor on laid paper.

Accession #1935.301.3, image #T1995–1. The Colonial Williamsburg Foundation. Abby Aldrich Rockefeller Folk Art Museum. Gift of Abby Aldrich Rockefeller.

for its careful depiction of a moment of sound and performance among the enslaved. Rose was born in the early 1750s, and he owned land and slaves first outside of Beaufort, South Carolina, and later in Dorchester county, about twenty miles from Charleston along the Ashley River. He knew how to read music and sang and played the organ in his local church. By the 1790s, when he painted *The Old Plantation,* he owned forty-nine slaves, some of whom he depicted in the watercolor.[42]

Rose's painting is roughly contemporary with *Liberty Displaying the Sciences and Arts.* But, unlike that abolitionist allegory, it seems to have been painted essentially from life and without any intention of critiquing slavery. It is, instead, a plantation scene, but one observed with a remarkable—indeed unique—level of care and precision. Rose's work is a striking reflection of the contradictory ways in which slave masters, even as they bought, sold, and exploited the enslaved, also at times related to them in other ways. Before painting *The Old Plantation,* Rose had painted a portrait of one of his slaves, Breme Jones, on the back of which he had quoted a few lines from Milton: "Grave in her steps / Heaven in her eye's / And all her movement / Dignity and Love."[43]

The Old Plantation captures a moment of music and dance among a group of twelve enslaved men and women, all from one plantation, many of them likely related. Each of them is painted with care, and they are very well-dressed. The colors of the clothes, notably the red and the blue of the man dancing in the center of the painting, stand out. There is a lot going on: A couple is standing behind the musicians; and there is a rather complicated, physical triangle on the left. Across the river is a plantation, along with smaller slave cabins lined up on the hill. This visual perspective is a striking reversal, since many plantations were traditionally set up so that the slave quarters could be observed from the great house. Given that Rose almost certainly painted this scene based on observing his own slaves in their quarters, we can conclude that the banjo player was one of several men owned by Rose: Ansell, Cain, Dick, Isaac, Mingo, Peter, Solomon, Tom, Young Tom, or Tybee—the last of them tried for burglary and hung for the offence in 1807.[44]

At the center of the painting are three dancers, one holding a stick and two women playing an instrument known in contemporary Africa as a shegureh, a "rattle made of a gourd enclosed in a net of variable length into which hard objects have been woven." As they danced, the women would have shaken the shegureh. The beat of this instrument would have combined with the beat of the drum played beside the dancers. And both would have interwoven with the music coming from the strings of the banjo.[45]

The banjo is rendered with tremendous, even loving, detail. We see the drumhead mounted into the calabash resonator; and the instrument clearly has four strings, one of them shorter than the others, on a flat neck with peg tuners. It is a spike neck, with the strings attached to the piece sticking out of the bottom of the gourd, and a bridge holding up the strings. The technique of the banjo player is also carefully rendered: we can see his thumb and first finger plucking the strings, while the rest of his fingers are ready to strum downwards. And Rose captured a critical detail about the instrument: the sound holes carved into the side of the resonator are both functional and symbolic. One is in the form of a star with six spokes. But at least two others are in the shape of square crosses. Like the cross on the harp depicted in Sloane's late seventeenth-century

engraving, and like other crosses found in a wide range of artistic production in the Afro-Atlantic world, these are probably cosmograms
depicting the crossroads between the spirit and human worlds.[46]

In the Kongo context the cross represents both the cycle of a person's life and the site of the ritual encounter between the world of the
living and the world of the dead. Through the symbol, the border between the two worlds is both recognized and overcome: one part of the
cross is the boundary, the other the path across it. A drawing of a cross
creates "a map of the path from here to there, linking this world and the
other." By the seventeenth century in the Atlantic world, the cross was
also a many-layered symbol, in some contexts bringing together meanings rooted in African tradition with those of the cross of Catholicism,
which was a crucial part of the religious culture of the Kongo starting in
the sixteenth century. In its multiple and transcultural forms, it was consistently a sign of the crossroads between the living and the dead, between descendants and ancestors, and between humans and gods. Carved
into the gourd in this Carolina banjo, the symbol likely served as a reminder of the spiritual crossings incited and accompanied by music.[47]

John Rose clearly witnessed a gathering on his plantation, observing
it long enough to glean these types of material details, down to the technical and aesthetic construction of the banjo. But what, precisely, is going
on? Interpreters of the image have offered different answers. Some—
familiar with the African-American tradition of leaping over a broom-
stick to celebrate a marriage—have argued that it is a wedding ceremony
of some kind, perhaps bonding the male dancer with one of the women
dancing across from him. Others see a recreational dance, with the stick
as an accessory, in the way that it is in different carnival and performance
traditions in the Americas, such as the carnival marching music of rara
in Haiti—or the North American baton twirling that evolved from these
traditions. Rose's painting depicts a sexual encounter, as the woman on the
right has two male admirers, one of them with his hand on her breast. All
of this suggests that Rose's intention was to depict what he saw as a relatively common, social event among the enslaved on his plantation, with
music, dance, flirting, and drinking from the jugs on hand at the feet of
the musicians.[48]

But another painting, clearly inspired by *The Old Plantation,* offers a
rather different, and powerful, interpretation of what was afoot. The work

of an unknown artist, it has never been clearly dated though it was likely done in the early to mid-twentieth century. We can think of it usefully as a kind of painted analysis and interpretation of the earlier painting, one that offers one explanation for what was going on beneath what Rose saw and depicted.[49]

This painting is clearly a copy of the earlier one. Some of the figures were drawn in pencil and then filled in, and the artist clearly either had seen, or was actually looking at, *The Old Plantation* when the second painting was composed. The male and female dancers in the foreground are in roughly the same position as the two figures in the earlier painting, their clothes the same color, though the man holds a cloth rather than a stick. Two of the other standing figures are also copied relatively closely. The musicians are both there, though now they are separated, balanced on both sides of the image, surrounding the central dancers. And the background and buildings, including the river in the background, are preserved, though the boat on the water in the original has disappeared and there are fewer slave quarters on the opposite bank: three rather than the seven in the original.

There are also fewer figures in all; and the sexual overtones of the earlier painting are gone, along with the three figures on the left. There are no couples except the central dancing pair. The crowded, social sense of the earlier picture is gone: all attention is on the dance and the music. The man on the left is depicted essentially the same as in the earlier painting, with a white collared shirt, but the painter has added a detail to the clothes of the woman standing on the right: her collar is decorated with a stripe of red. In the original painting, the color of and quality of the clothes are carefully documented, but they become part of a larger, jovial scene. In the sparser landscape of the later painting, it is easier to see the colors of the clothes themselves as having significance. In Afro-Atlantic religious ritual contexts, each of these colors—the white clothes of several participants and the striking blue and red of the male dancer— is a way of connecting with particular spirits.[50]

The later painting clearly articulates the dance, and the space in which it takes place, as one saturated with spiritual significance. Five objects are placed sharply and obviously within the visual field that were not there in the earlier painting. The most imposing is the prominent frog in the foreground, positioned directly between the dancers and looking

Plantation Scene, circa late 19th–early 20th century. Unknown American Artist.
Watercolor on laid paper.
Gift of Mr. and Mrs. Donald Upchurch. 1985.83.1. Collection of the Mint Museum, Charlotte, North Carolina

up at them. The frog has a strong spiritual significance in a range of Central African contexts, as well as in Afro-American spirituality, because "as an amphibious creature" it "moves between the world of the living on earth and the dead on the other side of the water." In the painting, it is "unusually large and featured prominently": clearly the artist wanted to make sure it was among the first things a viewer noticed.[51]

But this is only one of a collection of objects that stand out in the painting. On the door right behind the banjo player is an eye. The enslaved were used to being observed by masters, just as the subjects of John Rose's original painting were. This symbol, however, reverses the gaze: out from the door to a slave cabin, an eye is keeping watch. This symbol, along with others in the painting, is most likely part of what Marie Franklin describes as practices of "protective symbolism." These were meant to protect both individuals and community members from "physical and spiritual 'invasion.'" Linked to broader practices of ritual communication with spirits and ancestors, as well as with practices of healing, such symbols created boundaries and altered physical spaces in an attempt to create a zone of safety in the midst of a plantation world of violence and uncertainty. The particular composition of this eye, specifically its placement within a blue diamond, may connect it to Kongo cosmology: similar blue diamonds are painted on gravesites in New Orleans.[52]

On the doorframe next to the eye is another richly symbolic figure. It looks very like the pakèt kongo that are a key part of Vodou practice in Haiti. These anthropomorphic figures are usually made of cloth filled with medicinal herbs and other materials with spiritual power. They are also often topped with feathers, as the object in the painting seems to be. The arms here make what could be seen as the shape of a snake. The figure includes some of the symbols that are associated with the *lwa,* or god, of Grand-Bwa in Haiti. In the context of South Carolina, it could be a representation of another number of spirits. Its placement alongside the door, however, suggests that it was meant to serve, along with the eye on the door, as a form of protection. That function is even more likely given the third spiritual symbol in that area: the open book held by the woman standing next to the door. This open book was part of a tradition of using texts—usually the Bible—in this way to "confuse" evil spirits, who would be forced to stop and read the text and so prevented from going further with ill aims. Alternatively, it may function here in a different way, emphasizing the spiritual knowledge and literacy of the woman.[53]

Across the way, on the other door in the painting, is a final figure: a human-shaped one, half blue and half red, like the man dancing in the center. The figure has a small cross over its chest. This last detail is particularly important, as the banjo itself no longer has decorations on it; but at least one of the crosses originally on the instrument is still in the painting, now over the heart of a human form. So the cosmogram in the original painting, tied to the instrument, has found its way into a different space.

We don't know who painted this image, or why. Yet the painting itself does offer us a few clues. Clearly the artist had a relatively intricate knowledge of patterns of ritual symbolism within the African-American community. The artist, too, was interested in interpreting and saying something about *The Old Plantation* image, which was both copied and altered in such compelling ways. The message seems relatively clear: the original painting captured the scene only partially, blind to some of the deeper ritual significance of what was underway. The later painting restores that symbolism to the scene. It takes the ritual signs that are present in the original only around the banjo's resonator and multiplies and scatters them, creating a landscape rich with religious power and meaning. And it suggests that the music and the dance are something much more than recreation: rather, they are part of an attempt to communicate to other worlds, perhaps to cross the water symbolized here by the river in the background. The broader message of the image, then, is that this music is also about something beyond this world, that it was part of communicating with ancestors and gods. It is the same message that we get when we turn to the sources surrounding Haiti's banza.

*

In 1772 an enslaved man named Pompée escaped his master and headed for the sea. A month later an advertisement placed in the *Affiches Americaines,* the largest newspaper in Saint-Domingue, described him in this way: he had a brand "with the letters NGDP," was "aged approximately 30 years," and was "5 feet 4 inches tall, with a rather pretty face, a scar on top of his forehead, quite corpulent, swinging his hips a little when he walks." He had escaped by boarding "a passenger ship in Fort-Dauphin" and had "since been seen in Ouanaminthe," a town on the border of Spanish Santo Domingo. "It is believed," the advertisement went on, "he might claim he is free." And then it offered one final detail: "The said *Nègre* plays an instrument called the *Banza* very well."[54]

When enslaved individuals ran away from very large plantations of Saint-Domingue—some of which had hundreds of slaves—masters likely often didn't know much about them. The escape itself forced them to gather information about them from other slaves, probably depending on the enslaved drivers who oversaw much activity on the plantations. In the process, as did masters in North America who were faced with the same problem, they pieced together fragmentary information, creating traces of lives that otherwise would have remained invisible. Among the ten thousand or so advertisements for runaways—known under the

French term *marrons* in Saint-Domingue—in the *Affiches Americaines,* for instance, more than two hundred African ethnic groups are named. Such details were important, because they were destined not only for other masters but also probably for enslaved people and free people of African descent who could also collect a reward for turning in a maroon. For Pompée, as for many other maroons, music was probably an aid in flight, giving him an entry into certain urban communities and also a possible source of livelihood. But identifying these skills was also a good way of tracking him down.

Twelve years later, another banza player was listed in the runaway advertisements of the *Affiches Américaines.* His name was Cahouet; he lived in the economic capital of the colony, Le Cap and he worked as a coachman. He was between twenty-four and twenty-six and was five feet one inch tall, with a "large face, stocky and bow-legged." Cahouet was described as "a great *bansa* player" and "songster" who frequented "all the dances of the plantations that once belonged to Mr. Roquefort." Identified as a particularly good musician, he seems to have had a particular zone—a particular set of interconnected plantations—in which he worked. These plantations had once been owned by a particular plantation owner, but no longer were. But the advertisement suggested they still constituted a cultural community tied together by Cahouet's performances. What exactly were these performances? Cahouet was described not just as a songster, but also as an "enjoleur" of the blacks. This term is relatively uncommon—it is in fact misspelled in the advertisement—but at the time it referred to someone who is a charmer or seducer. His songs, the advertisement hinted through the use of this term, had the power to pull the enslaved away from their plantations, toward other spaces. There is a strong suggestion here that Cahouet was not just a musician but also a spiritual figure of some kind, attracting the enslaved to events of sound *and* spirit. After all, the "dances" on plantations were often in fact religious ceremonies, and the music of the banza could well have been linked to the music of drums and song aimed at accessing other planes of existence than that of the sugar plantation-covered Plaine du Cap—those of the *lwa* of the emerging Vodou religion and of the mythical Guinée called up within it.[55]

We learn the name of another banjo player from Saint-Domingue from an intriguing document from 1802. In prison in Havana, Cuba, at the time was a man named Lorenzo, who sought passage back home on a French ship that came into port. The reasons for his imprisonment are unclear, but he had a skill that he perhaps plied in the streets of Havana: he "played a kind of guitar made from a gourd with a very long neck" and "sang in French though always the same melody." His songs may actually have been in Creole, and the instrument he played was clearly a banza. An older man, probably once a slave, he likely had learned to play his instrument—and perhaps built the one he had in Cuba—in the plantations of Saint-Domingue.[56]

We only know Pompée's and Cahouet's names because they ran away, and their masters were determined to force them back into slavery. And we learn of Lorenzo's musical abilities, too, because he had journeyed to another island and found himself imprisoned. Ironically, too, the most detailed description of the artistry involved in building the banzas these two musicians played comes to us from the pen of someone who hated the instrument almost as much as he hated the people who built it.

In 1808 the abolitionist French priest Henri Grégoire published a work called *De la littérature des nègres.* In it, following in the footsteps of Thomas Clarkson, he sought to refute the idea that blacks were intellectually inferior by offering a wide-ranging survey of their cultural and literary achievements. He emphasized their musical skill as one of their qualities, approvingly citing Stedman's description of the "poetical and musical genius" of the enslaved, and his cataloguing of eighteen handmade stringed and wind instruments. Grégoire added that Stedman hadn't even counted the "famous balafou"—balafone—which he wrote "sounds like a little organ." The French priest also cited Thomas Grainger's 1764 poem for its description of "a kind of guitar invented by the *nègres,* on which they play songs that exude a soft and sentimental melancholy." What the slaves sang, Grégoire wrote, was "the music of wounded hearts." He was quick to add, aware that some pointed to the singing of the slaves as a sign of their contentment: "The passion of the *nègres* for music does not prove they are happy."[57]

Defenders of slavery were incensed by Grégoire's book, as they had earlier been by Clarkson's work, and one of them—an ex-planter from Saint-Domingue named Richard de Tussac—wrote a lengthy tome meant to refute all the priest's claims about the qualities of blacks, one by one. He offered this description, presumably based on observation made by him or other planters in the colonies, of how they built one particularly "savage" musical instrument:

> As for the guitars, which the *nègres* call *banza,* this is what they consist of: They cut a calabash (the fruit of a tree we call the *callebassier*) down the middle and longwise. This fruit is sometimes eight inches or more in diameter. They extend over it a goat skin, which they attach around the side with little nails. They put two or three holes on this surface, and then a board or piece of wood that has been rudely flattened, to make the neck of the guitar. They stretch three strings made of *pitre* (a filament taken from the agave plant, known colloquially as *pitre*), and the instrument is built. On it they play songs composed of two or three notes, which they repeat endlessly. That is what the Abbé Grégoire calls 'sentimental and melancholic music," and what we call the music of savages.[58]

In his richly detailed account of life in eighteenth-century Saint-Domingue, Moreau de Saint-Méry noted the importance of the *banza* in the dances of the enslaved. Writing in 1796, the Martinique-born lawyer sounded very much like Labat had a century earlier. All *nègres,* Saint-Méry announced—whether "America was their cradle" or they had "seen the day in Africa"—loved to dance. They would travel great distances, sometimes travelling all night long, to "satisfy this passion." "*Nègre* dance came to Saint-Domingue with those from Africa," he wrote. He noted that it was this fact that made it particularly attractive to the Creole slaves: "For this reason it is common to those born in the colony, who sometimes practice it from the day they are born." The most popular dance carried the same name as it had in Martinique in the late seventeenth century: calenda. It was propelled by the music of drums made, ideally, from a single piece of hollow wood covered with the skin of a goat or sheep. Shorter drums were made of bamboo and so called the bamboula. Accompanying this "monotonous and deafening sound" was another, made by "small calabashes half-filled with stones or grains of corn" attached to handles and tapped against the hands. Around the musicians, a circle of women danced and clapped and improvised songs.

But sometimes, another sound joined the percussion: "When they want to make the orchestra more complete they associate with it a *Banza,* a kind of rude violin with four strings that are plucked."[59]

Saint-Méry wrote at some length about the musical abilities of the enslaved, many of whom played for white audiences in homes as well as in the thriving theatrical life of Saint-Domingue. They preferred the violin, he wrote, which they usually learned to play by ear or from other black musicians who had learned the same way. But this didn't prevent them from mastering the instrument's tones, he admitted. They also played an instrument that he described in detail, a kind of mbira, made with a plank of wood onto which were placed thin pieces of metal, and underneath them bamboo or another material, and played with the thumbs. And, he repeated, at the larger dances they also "exercised" their musical abilities on the banza. Saint-Méry described a context in which this instrument was both quite common and well-integrated into the broader continuum of music and dance that he saw around him in Saint-Domingue. His account enables us to understand the vital role played by musicians like Pompée and Cahouet. The sound of their instruments was both produced by and a producer of social worlds. As it did in other parts of the Caribbean and North America, in Saint-Domingue the banza was an object that created moments of connection, remembrance, solidarity, and imagination as it spurred on motion through dance, the recalling and composition of melodies and song.[60]

The naturalist Michel-Etienne Descourtilz, who traveled to Haiti in the late 1790s, offered similar details about the instrument in several of his works. In an account of his time in Haiti published in 1803, he included a short scene written for the theater. Called "Dialogue créole," it tells the story of Evahim and Aza, two slaves from West Africa. They were engaged to be married in their home in Guinée, but both were captured and sold to European slavers. By miracle, they find one another again on the other side of the Atlantic, on a plantation in Saint-Domingue. Aza, who has been there longer, has already learned Creole and teaches it to his beloved Evahim. In the "enchanted calm of the night," Aza sings the "beloved words of lovers," while "accompanied by his *banza*." He then gathers the words together into phrases to make a song. In the scene, the banza helps to renew a relationship broken by the slave trade and also serves quite literally as the vehicle for teaching and learning the Creole language and therefore a way for Aza and Evahim to find their way in the New World.[61]

Decades later, Descourtilz included a detailed description of the instrument as part of his examination of a type of calabash he called the "courge calebasse" in his work *Flore pittoresque des Antilles*. From these calabashes, he notes, the "Creoles and Blacks" of the Caribbean created "bowls, goblets, and *banzas, a nègre* instrument that the Blacks prepare by sawing one of these calabashes or a large gourd longwise, to which they adjust a neck and sonorous strings made out of fibres of aloe plants." Descourtilz recognized the banjo's cultural importance, in a passage that likely drew on the writings of Saint-Méry: "Though it is not very harmonious, this instrument pleases the Blacks, who make out of it a kind of mandolin that they use to charm their worries by accompanying their voices during the peace of night, or by making their comrades dance during joyous parties, or at the more lugubrious *calendas*, funeral ceremonies followed by celebrations. It is the custom to combine the sound of the *banza* with the louder one of the *bamboula*, a kind of drum that they make resonate with their fingers and fists, sitting astride it. This drum is made with a piece of bamboo covered over at both ends with a skin."[62]

There is one tantalizing visual trace of how the Haitian banza got people moving in an engraving that was part of a series of landscapes made by Nicolas Ponce to accompany Moreau de Saint-Méry's 1796 work. The focus of the image is the planned town of Bombardopolis, in the north of the colony.

But on the right edge of the engraving, far on the outskirts of town, a group is dancing. They are being watched by two whites. And they are being driven in their motion by two barely visible, seated musicians. At least one of them, his back turned to us, seems to be playing a stringed instrument with a neck, perhaps—probably—a Haitian banza.

Many gatherings of the enslaved, like the one pictured here, were likely very small, part of a process of finding openings and moments away from the daily routines of slavery. Occasionally, however, there were large events held on the plantations. Years after the French were expelled from the colony, one former resident named Gaspard-Théodore Mollien wrote a manuscript that was part history and part memoir. It included many details about the lives of the vanished planter class of Saint-Domingue.

"Bombardopolis ou Bombarde dans l'île de St Domingue," 1789, drawn by
Alexis Nicolas Perignon, engraved by Jacquies Louis Copia.

Private collection, Chatillon Marcel (Chatillon Collection). Photo by Lysiane Gauthier and J. M. Arnaud.
© Musée Acquitaine.

In it Mollien briefly describes a rather remarkable party that took place in the years before the Revolution: "We even saw a slave of the Lefeuve plantation, the mistress of the plantation manager, host a dinner on the feast of Saint-Louis, with 400 settings, served on plates and enlivened by the singing of two public singers, Trois-Feuilles and Grand Simone, whose *banzas* (guitars) were garnished with doubloons."[63]

Packed into this one sentence are scintillating details. There is a clue about the banza itself, "garnished" with "doubloons" whose role could have been decorative but also sonic, creating a metallic buzz such as that prized in African chordophones. The designation of the musicians as "public singers" suggests—like the advertisement for Cahouet—the existence of a kind of profession of enslaved musicians who were paid to play not for masters but for other slaves. But the most important detail of all is the name of one of the musicians: Trois-Feuilles. For in that simple detail resides a world of potential implications. Trois-Feuilles translates as Three Leaves, an expression that signifies a great deal in Haiti, symbolizing the role of herbal knowledge within the system of physical and spiritual healing that is Haitian Vodou.

Within the vast corpus of Vodou song, which makes up a rich archive, there is a very well-known song called Twa Fey, Three Leaves. Sung in ritual contexts, it has also been interpreted by popular music groups and is a kind of key anthem within Haitian music. Its core lyrics, as sung by the contemporary Haitian group Ti-Coca, are as follows,

Twa fey	*Three leaves*
Twa rasin	*Three roots*
Jeté blyé	*If I throw down I forget*
ranmassé songé	*If I gather them I remember*
Mwen gen basin lwa	*I've got a basin lwa*
Mwen twa fey tonbé ladan'n	*My three leaves fell in it*

The song, in a few short words and images, captures the power and necessity of connection and memory. The "three leaves" are the knowledge of medicine cultivated in Haitian Vodou but also more broadly the spiritual practice and tradition that are maintained if they are gathered as people collect around them. The song is an injunction of sorts: don't forget the knowledge. Hold onto it. As Ti-Coca explained to me when I asked

"Sick Slaves," 1822, Engraving, Chamberlain and G. Hunt.
Private collection, Chatillon Marcel (Chatillon Collection). Photo by Lysiane Gauthier and J. M. Arnaud.
© Musée Acquitaine.

him about the song, the leaves and roots are gathered when they are needed for healing. After they've been boiled to make the medicine, they are thrown out and may even be forgotten. But they'll be needed again, the next time someone is sick, so the roots and leaves must be remembered so that they can be returned to in time. More broadly, the song is also a metaphor, telling listeners to remember that the knowledge comes from the *lwa,* the gods, who are a link to the past, to the world of spirits that lives under the waters, and to a mythical Africa known as Guinée within Haitian Vodou.[64]

Just as the banjo players depicted in the two versions of *The Old Plantation* were participants in a broader religious landscape, the eighteenth-century musician who called himself Trois-Feuilles was almost certainly signaling his link to ritual practice and healing by using this name. Given the traditional role played by musicians in religious life in various parts of Africa, this role would have been clearly understood by many within the community of the enslaved. It is a role, in fact, clearly documented in a remarkable engraving from Suriname, from the 1820s, depicting a group of sick slaves.[65]

While they are being inspected by some kind of official, off to the side are two figures who clearly are offering a kind of healing. Both are musicians, one playing a bowed stringed instrument with a calabash resonator. To his right is a musician carrying a harp. On his head, he carries a massive basket of leaves, most likely to make herbal remedies. He could simply have been selling these herbs, perhaps announcing their properties with his music. But the musician himself may also have been a healer, offering a medicine that brought together music and herbs, the spiritual and the physical.

The type of harp depicted here resembles those from any number of parts of West and Central Africa. Often such harps were decorated with anthropomorphic engravings or sculptures. This tradition of decoration, interestingly, seems to have been less common on the stringed lutes from West Africa whose construction more closely resembles that of the New World banjo. But the artisan who made the banza collected by Schoelcher tapped into this tradition by carving what looks like a representation of face onto the neck of the instrument. This artistry was itself a kind of adaptation of tradition: on a Central African harp, the rounded neck wouldn't allow for a carving of this size; and instead a head might, or a figure might, be sculpted on top of the neck—as was done on the banjo seen by Henry Latrobe in Congo Square in New Orleans in 1819.

An instrument collected in 1850 in Suriname, now preserved in the Ethnology Museum of the Staatliche Museen in Berlin, has a similar carving on the end of the neck. It was collected by a Moravian missionary working in a plantation area at the time and was catalogued as a "Panja"— probably just an erroneous transcription of "Banja." It is very similar in construction to the instrument collected by Stedman in the same area decades earlier, in the 1770s. It has a gourd resonator, carved in the same way as the Stedman banjo, and a narrow flat neck with four strings, one shorter than the other. It also, however, has a feature not on the Stedman banjo: a carved animal head, probably a ram, on the top of the neck. The figure perhaps had a spiritual significance: the description of the object notes that it is an instrument that was used to accompany a song called

Haitian Banza, Reproduction by Pete Ross, Detail of Neck.
Photograph by Kristina Gaddy.

Ananhitori, which was part of funerary rites among Africans on these plantations.[66]

The Haitian banza, along with those in New Orleans and Suriname, did not have a figure carved on the top of the neck. Instead, the artisan who built it took advantage of the width of the flat neck to create an image staring out at those who listened to the instrument. The engraving looks like a face, or a mask. But it also can easily be read as a particular kind of face: one constructed out of Trois-Feuilles, or Three Leaves. Perhaps there was even a direct connection between this banza and the musician who took this name. Perhaps it was even his banjo, or at least a way of evoking his legacy as a musician. Even if this was not the case, though, both the maker of the banza and the musician Trois-Feuilles seem to have been tapping into a similar well of symbolism surrounding the instrument.

Through these fragments we get a deeper sense of how the banjo tapped into and helped to generate spiritual power. The versions of the instrument that incorporated anthropomorphic symbols of one kind or another were drawing on instrument-making traditions that were common, especially in Central Africa. This was a powerful condensation, and coalition, of different traditions of instrument making from the African continent. It was perhaps a way of signaling to enslaved people from those regions—who were a majority in Haiti—that this was their instrument too. But it also served the same purpose such decorations did in Central Africa, which was to remind musicians and listeners alike that the instrument was sacred, channeling a sacred sound and making it possible to communicate with the dead. The fact that one Haitian banza player called himself Trois-Feuilles, and that a symbol likely representing three leaves is found on an instrument from Haiti, makes clear that the instrument and its music were being linked to the symbolism surrounding memory and healing, and memory *as* healing.

Like the banjo in *The Old Plantation,* the Haitian banza has a sound hole in the shape of a cross, carved into the gourd. In the Haitian context, as elsewhere in the Afro-Atlantic context, this symbolizes the meeting of the world of the spirits with that of the living, the crossroads at the center of much religious practice on both sides of the Atlantic. The cross, more specifically, is also the symbol of Vodou *lwa* Gédé. And, as a

Haitian *oungan* (Vodou priest) named Erol Josué has related to me, there is at least one Vodou song in which Gédé requests that the instrument be played for him. The name of the musician who accompanied Trois-Feuilles hints at another connection between the music and Vodou: Grand Simone may have been the name of one of the thousands of *lwa* in the religious landscape of the early nineteenth-century in Haiti. This layering of symbols makes clear the banza was seen as part of the crossroads between the living and the dead, humans and the *lwa* of Vodou, the here and the beyond.

Today, the banjo is still a common instrument in Haiti, particularly in Twoubado, or Troubadour, music. The most respected and celebrated interpreter of this style today is Ti-Coca, whose version of "Twa Fèy" is also the best-known modern recording of the song. The music remains popular in rural Haiti and is occasionally performed during more recreational portions of Vodou ceremonies as well as rural festivals. Individual banjo players also frequently perform on the streets, notably in towns like Jacmel in the South and Le Cap in the North. The banjo is fundamental to the sound of Twoubado music: as Richard Hector, who has played the banjo in Ti-Coca's group for the past three decades, put it, the instrument "holds the system" of the music together. He plays in a style that combines rhythmic, hard strumming with meandering but pulsing melodic lines. And, as he plays those lines, he thumps out the bass drum line on the banjo head itself. The banjo is the guide and center, allowing the soaring vocal exploration, sometimes languages, sometimes sound, offered by Ti-Coca. Hector plays a Fender five-string banjo with the short, top string removed. The tradition of making banjos locally seems to have died out in Haiti, and musicians play U.S.-made instruments. In fact the term banza itself is rarely used for the instrument, replaced by the English term banjo. But the playing style kept alive in Twoubado music likely keeps alive some older traditions, even as it has been inspired by more recent banjo playing traditions.[67]

The music of Ti-Coca and the banjo playing of Richard Hector embody the crossings between the spiritual and music worlds that have long shaped the history of the instrument. For enslaved Africans in the Americas, crossing the boundary between the living and the dead also meant crossing the boundary between here and there, between the

Americas and Africa. It was that crossing that the symbols in the later version of *The Old Plantation,* including the frog, were meant to symbolize. In this sense, the spiritual meaning of the banjo was about the enactment of an impossible return, about refusing the kind of exile from one's natal community, and oneself, that the slave system demanded. The human figures and crosses that decorated these instruments in Haiti, Louisiana, and South Carolina were a way of saying: this instrument is our link, the part of the cross that takes us back, an insistence on connection and survival. Because it did so also as a way of bringing together people from different parts of the continent, it was also inventing Africa again and again as it sounded, creating a new place that felt like—but could never quite be—the old place.

All of these choices—technical, sonic, aesthetic—would ultimately have been made in order to serve the purpose of making an instrument that could be welcoming, that could be a call to gathering. For a musician like Trois-Feuilles, the key would have been to make sure that all within the diverse world of the enslaved in Saint-Domingue would have found something familiar in the sound of his playing. The banjo had to be heard and understood by the collective of exiles before him, speaking different musical languages, harboring many different spiritual traditions. It had to do a great deal of cultural, sonic, and aesthetic work all at once. Its creation was not a linear tale, and other styles of construction—like the harp depicted in the Suriname engraving, or the banjo with a rounded neck depicted in the 1792 *Liberty Displaying the Sciences and Arts*—persisted alongside the more common construction we see in images like *The Old Plantation* and in the Haitian banza. But, over time, the particular structure we see in the images from Jamaica, South Carolina, Haiti, and Louisiana seems gradually to have been adopted and embraced by musicians as the form that could most successfully offer what they needed. That form was the result of an accumulation of choices, of needs and hopes, that were ultimately condensed in the structure of the banjo. By the end of the eighteenth century, the instrument was consolidated and present far and wide across the Caribbean and North America.

The first stage of its history was complete. The banjo had been made to connect and to travel, to bring together different musical languages and traditions, to sound at once old and new, traditional and welcoming at the same time. Through the dramatic transformations of the nineteenth century, it would find itself in new places, in new hands. But it would carry forward, as a fundamental if sometimes obscured legacy, the essential function that it was created to fulfill: that of creating the sound of gathering and solidarity.

The power of the banza to bring worlds together is captured in one Haitian folktale about a man who uses music to transform his world. The main character, Malice (often called Ti-Malice), is a fixture of many Haitian stories, a trickster whose ruses enable him to turn the tables on the powerful. In a version of the tale collected and published by Mimi Barthelemy, Malice is described as the descendent of Boton, the African hare, and Goupil, the European fox. As a result of this mixing, he plays the banza. The instrument accompanies him in his sad life—barefoot, poor, a pit of hunger in his stomach. But he dreams of something different and one day seizes an opportunity. The king and queen of the land have four daughters, whose names have been kept secret from everyone in their kingdom. The king has offered his fortune and one of his daughter's hands in marriage to any subject who can figure out their four names. But there is a price: any who try and fail will be executed.[68]

Malice is not just a trickster, but a very lucky one. One day Malice wanders down to the river, where there is a beautiful papaw tree full of fruit. He picks a papaw to eat, and just as he is about to crunch into it, he hears laughter and talking. It is the four princesses, bathing in the river. Trembling with excitement as he watches them undress, he drops his apple into the water. The four princesses begin to argue over who will eat it, and in the process one says to the other "Makakofi, it's not yours! It's mine!" Malice realizes that this is how he can learn all their names and proceeds to throw three more apples into the water, learning each of the princesses' names in turn. When he gets home, he composes a song for his banza that recites the four princesses' names and then approaches the palace at night, so that the King won't see he is dressed in rags, and sings it under the window. The King, stunned, asks him to sing the song again. After having him bathed and dressed up, the King, true to his word, offers Malice half his fortune and allows him to choose one of his daughters to marry. He takes the money, spends a night with the princess he has chosen, sneaks into the cellar and drinks all the alcohol, and then leaves to go home. As do many Haitian folktales, the story ends with another twist: the narrator, hiding and watching the story unfold, gets discovered by Malice. "He invited me to follow him, and offered me a banza concert that charmed me so deeply that I listened to him for sixty years, and have only now arrived in order to tell you this story."[69]

4

The Sound of Freedom

IT WAS "A SINGULAR SPECTACLE," wrote the British traveler George Featherstonhaugh in 1844: on the banks of the New River in Virginia, several hundred slaves were being marched toward the auction blocks of Natchez, Mississippi. A few enslaved women and "a great many little black children" were sitting on logs, "warming themselves on the fires of the bivouac." "In front of them, and all prepared for the march, stood, in double files, about two hundred male slaves, *manacled and chained to each other*." The slave traders, white men with "broad-brimmed white hats" were "standing near, laughing and smoking cigars." Disgusted, Featherstonhaugh declared that the scene resembled "those coffles of slaves spoken of by Mungo Park" in West Africa. But instead of African slaves being carried to the sea, these were American slaves being torn from their communities in Virginia. "Black men in fetters, torn from the lands where they were born, from the ties they had formed . . . driven by white men, with liberty and equality in their mouths, to a distant and unhealthy country, to perish in the sugar-mills of Louisiana!"[1]

Throughout the early nineteenth century in North America, the sight of such slave coffles was common across the South. With the transatlantic slave trade to the United States was outlawed, plantation owners seeking slaves for the plantations in the new territories opened up through the Louisiana Purchase had one main source: the slave communities of Virginia and other parts of the East Coast. The defining and traumatic event in African-American life during the first half of the nineteenth century, this process brought the same kind of slave coffles that had traversed West and Central Africa for centuries to the North American continent, to its towns and rural areas, and to its roads and crossroads. It demolished established communities of the enslaved and separated families, often established over several generations, from places like Virginia and the Carolinas.[2]

When the enslaved were still relatively close to home, they looked for opportunities to escape and head back to their families. One of those opportunities had come the morning Featherstonhaugh had happened upon the group: the coffle had to ford a large river. "This was one of the situations," he noted, "where the gangs—always watchful to obtain their liberty—often show a disposition to mutiny, knowing that if one or two of them could wrench their manacles off, they could soon free the rest." The slave traders had developed techniques to try and quell the possibility of such revolt. One of these was to hire entertainers, "other negroes trained by the slave-dealers to drive the rest, whom they amused by lively stories, boasting of the fine warm climate they are going to, and of the oranges and sugar which are there to be had for nothing." As part of their arsenal, these men were told to play the banjo, urging the men in chains to be merry and sing along to the song "Old Virginia Never Tire."[3]

The banjo had, by the 1840s, long been rooted in many of the communities of the enslaved in North America. On the plantations, often combined with the fiddle, it drove dances and celebrations on the plantations and outside them. In holiday festivals, such as Junkanoo in Jamaica and the Carolinas, it was part of a larger, explosive sonic assault. Just as it had in the Caribbean from the earliest days of its invention, the banjo offered a space for solidarity, to sound out the possibility of a world of freedom.

It was, then, particularly sadistic and cynical for the slave traders Featherstonhaugh saw to use the sound of the banjo—a sound that probably sounded like home to many of the enslaved being torn from their communities—as the soundtrack to sale, separation, and dispersal. But the gesture was an extension of what was happening elsewhere in the country, where the banjo was being brought onto the stage as a symbol of slave life. The white musicians who began performing banjo music during this period presented themselves as expert interpreters of the plantation music of the enslaved. They created the form that became known as blackface minstrelsy, the most popular entertainment of the nineteenth century. These performances rapidly became a screen through which the experience of slaves themselves was interpreted, helping to create an image of slaves as ignorant, funny, but largely content with their lot. In the late 1840s, the traveler Alex Mackay wrote of the "light-heartedness" of the slaves, who "make the present as merry as possible." The banjo, he wrote, was the "chief Instrumental accompaniment" to the joyful songs sung at the end of their workdays. The slave traders Featherstonhaugh saw in 1841 were, in a sense, trying to transform real life into a minstrel show, imagining that hearing "Old Virginia Never Tire" would somehow placate enslaved people about their forced expulsion from their home in Virginia.[4]

Minstrelsy brought together a deeply-rooted Afro-American performance tradition—one that had long grappled with and communicated the experiences of enslavement—with a need on the part of audiences to both confront and set aside the terrors of slavery itself. The banjo was central to minstrelsy, which incorporated the social and symbolic meanings already carried by the banjo and put them to new uses. As a result the sound of the banjo, built at the crossroads of the cultures of various African groups in the New World, now became a popular symbol of slave life and slave culture. Minstrelsy was, like the banjo itself, many things at once: a practice, a sound, dance and theatre, and a layering of symbols and meanings that clashed and interlocked with one another to both represent and transform the social order. Its cultural impact runs so deep that its legacies are sometimes difficult to track and enumerate. Indeed, blackface performance never really ended as a central part of our cultural life. The form shaped the literature of the nineteenth century, notably the novels of Mark Twain and Herman Melville. And it had a profound cultural and ideological impact on the ways in which people at the time—and since—understood the link between slavery, race, and music. As a result, to write the history of the banjo during this period is to enter hall of mirrors in which performance and literature intermingle with, and sometimes become indistinguishable from, social and cultural reality.

We can see the collision at work in a disturbing account of one slave's experience on the auction block. Slave traders sometimes used banjo music as part of the presentation of slaves for sale, to the point that the auction block itself was sometimes referred to as the "banjo table." Several former slaves interviewed in the 1930s remembered this vividly. Sam Mitchell, interviewed in South Carolina—who described slavery as nothing but "a murdering" of people—explained that though he had never seen a slave sale himself, he had heard "tell of the banjo table." The former slave Lucretia Heyward, meanwhile, had seen slaves put on "the banjo table" and sold like "chicken." Sam Polite, of Beaufort County South Carolina, also recounted seeing "plenty" of people sold on the "banjo table." He recalled how his uncle was placed on the platform, bringing in a hundred dollars for his owner.[5]

The most detailed account of such an event comes in a 1931 book called *Old Massa's People,* by Orlando Kay Armstrong, which presents accounts of slavery gleaned from more than 200 ex-slaves interviewed during the 1920s. Armstrong's text, like those of the WPA narratives during the same period, attempts to capture the black vernacular speech of those interviewed. It does so, however, in a way that exaggerates the difference of this language. In fact, the construction of black dialect in this and other works was shaped by the broader context of minstrelsy, which for decades had promoted a certain idea, a vocabulary, that supposedly captured black vernacular speech. Nevertheless, these texts give us rare and valuable access to the memories individuals had of slavery, decades on. Armstrong recounts how the ex-slave "Jolly old Uncle Buck" recalled "an incident of the banjo table." Startlingly, she added that he "chuckles all the way through his account of it." When the estate on which he lived was broken up, he was put in a warehouse "chained to four other boys." "One had a banjo—and how that buck could play it! Had to make him hush up so the rest could sleep. Next morning all the people gathered to bid on the niggers. First boy up was Fred. 'Get on de table, Fred,' de bossman say." Fred stood on the table, but the auctioneer wasn't quite ready to begin, needed to fill out some papers. "So Fred jus' stan' on de table."

> By-'m-by-Plunk, plunk, plunkety plunk! Dat nigger wid de
> banjo settin' on the bench waitin' to be sold, he plunk his

banjo. Den he rattle inter a real chune. Hi-yo! Fred 'gin ter shuffle roun' on his big feet, an' fine'ly he cain't stan' it no longer. He gotta dance. He slap his big feet on de banjo table, an we all pat wid de banjo music. White men laugh an' clap dey han's. Make him dance some mo'. Wouldn't let de auctioneer start till Fred dance de buck-an'-wing. Yo-ho! It sho'ly was funny! De white man what bought Fred say he done paid hundrert dollars mo' fo' dat nigger cause he could dance like dat![6]

There is something uncanny about the whole story and the fact that it was delivered with laughter. It is not the volition of an auctioneer or a buyer that makes Fred dance, but rather the brilliant playing of another man, himself chained and ready to be sold. In fact, Buck's telling of the story may have itself been shaped by performance practices of the late nineteenth century: in 1892, one African-American touring musical troupe performed an "auction scene" that included "banjo playing, laughing songs, negro dancing and patting" in 1892, and others in the country may have offered something similar. Through all these layers of recounting and interpretation, we can only wonder what the original scene really looked like, and try and imagine how the musician depicted understood the situation, and wonder what song he played, and why. But in this story, the joyful sound of the banjo fuses with the most brutal aspects of slavery, inviting us to dwell on the disturbing collusion between the two.[7]

The history of the banjo in African-American life is full of such painful and perhaps inscrutable texts. Saidiya Hartman wonders "whether the origin of American theatre is to be found in a no-longer-remembered primal scene of torture, and whether song bears the trace of punishment." How do we untangle the fantasy of the plantation, as presented in minstrelsy, from the actual culture of the enslaved? How are we to understand the link between the terror and uprooting of nineteenth-century slavery and its presence, in the form of exuberant music and comedy, on the minstrel stage? Hartman argues that minstrelsy was in fact a continuation of various kinds of longstanding plantation "amusements" in which masters watched their slaves perform. "What was demanded by the master was simulated by the enslaved," she notes, but they also used performance as "acts of defiance conducted under the cover of nonsense, indirection, and seeming acquiescence." The intricate tactics deployed within these performances turned them against the aims of masters. This created a rich and complex set of strategies of song and performance to deal with an ambiguous and ever-shifting situation in which performance served contradictory roles simultaneously. What for masters was a display of power for the enslaved was an opportunity for layers of response and sometimes resistance. The cycle of imitation and parody and caricature that would be the key to the minstrel show was, then, in fact born much earlier. The minstrel shows' claim to be channeling an "authentic" plantation culture was, in a sense, true: but all that meant was that a sedimentation of practices of imitation and mirroring was being carried on in a new setting.[8]

This deep, troubling, and unavoidable imbrication of forms is crystallized in the song that became one of the most popular and enduring pop hits the United States has ever produced: "Oh! Susanna." Written by Stephen Foster in 1847, it was popularized by the Christy Minstrels and in time became probably the most popular work of music in America during the nineteenth century, spreading throughout the world and still kept alive as one of the most familiar and recognizable of our country's airs. Its chorus: "Oh! Susanna, do not cry for me; I come from Alabama, Wid a banjo on my knee" is perhaps the most familiar line in American music.

Foster was born in 1826 and spent his first years in Pittsburgh. When he was a very young child, his family had a servant named Olivia Pise, later described by his brother Morrison as a "mulatto bound-girl." She was the daughter of a "West India Frenchman," probably a refugee from Saint-Domingue, who taught dance in Pittsburgh in the early 1800s. According to Morrison, when Stephen was just a few years old Pise took him to services at "a church of shouting colored people," where he enjoyed "singing and boisterous devotions" and gained a taste for "negro melody" that he later channeled into his music. As a boy Stephen developed his love of music and began performing in his family's carriage house for local audiences. His repertoire drew on that of a blackface performer named T. D. Rice, notably his hit song "Jim Crow." When he was twenty-one, Foster composed "Susanna," a song calibrated to join the minstrel repertoire. The black narrator of the song sings in dialect, telling of his search for his love Susanna, whom he hopes to find in New Orleans.

When he finds her, he says "I'll fall upon de ground. . . . But if I do not find her, Dis darkey'll surely die, / And when I'm dead and buried, Susanna don't you cry."[9]

There is something odd about the song: the black narrator's free-wheeling and comic journey in search of Susanna from Alabama to Louisiana would in fact have been impossible in the late 1840s, and audiences would have known that. At the time, however, the one very obvious way that black men were traveling toward Louisiana was in slave coffles, or else traveling with white masters who were heading to the state to try and make their fortunes in the sugar economy. It is that experience that was told in a "slave ballad" that may have been an influence on Foster's lyrics. The lyrics were printed in 1835 in the published journal of an abolitionist who had toured the United States and had heard the song sung in Philadelphia. It was a comic lament about being forced to go to Louisiana with a slave master: "I born in Sout Calina, fine country ebber seen / I guine from Sout Calina, I guine to New Orlean." The "boss" was "discontentum," and so took his "mare, black Fanny" and set her on the path to "Lousy-Anny." He pushed on to Alabama, where "de hear de cotton grow: But he spirit still contrary, And he must fudder go." The master felt the same way in Mississippi, and pushed on to Louisiana, to the chagrin of his slave. For, as the last line of the song puts it: "Old debble, Lousy-Anny, dat scarecrow for poor nigger, / Where de sugar-cane grow to pine-tree, and de pine-tree turn to sugar."[10]

Foster could have read these lyrics in the abolitionist publication, or—given that the song was sung in Philadelphia in the 1830s—even heard a version of it somewhere in Pennsylvania during his years growing up. The structure of the story, and of at least part of the journey, is quite similar. Foster may turned a song clearly sung from the perspective of a slave being forced to Louisiana into a comic story of lovelorn wandering. The slave brought away from his home in South Carolina in the earlier song would have likely left behind family. Instead of looking for a loved one in Louisiana, he would have been mourning the fact that he had been torn away from them. Foster's song, then, may be haunted by a plea to a loved one, sent by a slave sold away to Louisiana. And if that was the case, then somewhere hidden in this joyful comic song is a song of mourning, a farewell to a family, by a victim of a slave system whose meanings were as hidden but as persistent as the sound of the banjo itself.

We can glimpse what may have been the underside of "Oh! Susanna" in a story told by the abolitionist Josiah Henson in his autobiography. Henson, who was the inspiration for Harriet Beecher Stowe's character Uncle Tom, began his story with the silencing of song. Henson was born in 1789 on a plantation in Nanjemoy, Maryland, where his father was a beloved banjo player. But he never heard his father sing. In fact his only memory of his father was of seeing him with his "head bloody and his back lacerated" after he had been whipped and mutilated. As he later learned, his father had come upon a white overseer trying to rape his wife in an isolated area of the plantation and had "sprung on the man like a tiger." Only the mother's entreaties, Henson wrote, prevented his father from killing the overseer. He fled into the woods to avoid punishment but was eventually found. The slaves of his plantation and those nearby were summoned to watch "for their moral improvement" as he was given a hundred lashes of the whip, at the end of which his right ear was nailed to a post and sliced off. After the beating, his father was never the same. He had once "been a good-humored and light-hearted man, the ring-leader of all fun at corn-huskings and Christmas buffoonery. His banjo was the life of the farm, and all night long at merry-making would he play on it while the other negroes dance." Now, he was "utterly changed." "Sullen, morose and dogged, nothing could be done with him." Even the threat of being sold West had no effect, and eventually the master did sell him. He disappeared to Alabama, and neither Henson nor his mother ever heard news of him again.[11]

In August of 1839, a tense crowd gathered in the courthouse of Marion County, Ohio. A group of outsiders, white men from the South, brandished pistols and knives in the center of the courtroom. They had come to carry away a man known in the town as Black Bill, whom they claimed was an escaped slave. But many of the residents of the town, including a few Quaker abolitionists, weren't having it: they believed he was a free man being targeted by unscrupulous slave traders. If Black Bill had so many allies, it was partly because in his year living in the area he had made himself "indispensable," working as a barber and a butcher, frequently hired in local houses to cut and cure meat and known in particular for his "Virginny sausage." He was also a musician known for his "ability to play the fiddle and banjo."[12]

The court sided with Black Bill. But as he tried to leave the courtroom, one of the white Virginians grabbed him by the throat, and a melee broke out. Bill's attackers were well-armed and managed to beat and drag Bill out of the courthouse and down the street toward the police station. Unfortunately for them, the town's main street was under construction and had just been covered with a layer of small broken stones: the perfect projectiles. Local residents began pelting the Virginians with rocks, and when they barricaded themselves in the police station, the infuriated crowd demanded access to the local police arsenal. The riot ended when a judge entered the police station and demanded the release of Black Bill, who was able to leave the prison. With the help of several locals, he managed to escape town and was hidden by sympathetic members of the Underground Railroad and soon spirited to Canada. His case became a flashpoint of controversy beyond Ohio, a part of the increasingly hostile national conflict over fugitive slaves in the decades before the Civil War. Despite Black Bill's relatively short residency in the area, music had made him visible. The fiddle and the banjo had, in his hands, ultimately been a critical weapon in his own struggle for freedom, helping to set up a public and quite violent conflict that pitted a community against outsiders claiming the right to kidnap.[13]

But in one famous case, music led to a free man's capture. His name was Solomon Northrop, and in 1841 he was tricked by two men who presented themselves as agents ready to hire him to play, then sold him into slavery. The result was a twelve-year ordeal, one he wrote about in what was to become one of the most famous of the slave narratives of the nineteenth century: *Twelve Years a Slave,* published in 1853. As he recounted, playing the violin was "the ruling passion of my youth." It became a source of his livelihood and after he was sold into slavery, "the source of consolation" both to those around him and to himself. His account is particularly precious for the descriptions it offers us of music on the plantations written by an enslaved musician.[14]

"The African race is a music-loving one, proverbially," wrote Northrop, adding that "many there were among my fellow-bondsmen whose organs of tune were strikingly developed, and who could thumb the banjo with dexterity." The violin, Northrop explained, had enabled him to survive. Without it "I scarcely can conceive how I would have endured the long years of bondage." Northrop offered up a moving tribute to the way a musical instrument could be a form of escape at once concrete—through the opportunities for work away from the field it afforded—and abstract, through the reminder of other worlds and other possibilities:

> It introduced me to great houses—relieved me of many days' labor in the field—applied me with conveniences for my cabin—with pipes and tobacco, and extra pairs of shoes, and oftentimes led me away from the presence of a hard master, to witness scenes of jollity and mirth. It was my companion—the friend of my bosom—triumphing loudly when I was joyful, uttering its soft, melodious consolations when I was sad. Often, at midnight, when sleep had fled affrighted from the cabin, and my soul was disturbed and troubled by the contemplation of my fate, it would sing me a song of peace. On holy Sabbath days, when an hour or two of leisure was allowed, it would accompany me to some quiet place on the bayou bank and, lifting up its voice, discourse kindly and pleasantly indeed. It heralded my name around the country—made me friends, who, otherwise would not have noticed me—gave me an honored seat at the yearly feasts, and secured the loudest and heartiest welcome of them at all the Christmas dance![15]

Northrop described the particular "genuine happiness, rampant and unrestrained," he saw during Christmas dances. That holiday, he wrote, was "a day of *liberty* among the children of Slavery." The enslaved developed forms of sound and motion that expressed and channeled that evanescent freedom. The Christmastime Junkanoo celebrations that stretched from the Caribbean to the Carolinas, for instance, often started on the plantations but soon spilled outside them, creating sounds and gestures that were disruptive and disturbing, difficult to categorize, but also impossible for many to turn away from. One man who saw them in 1797 in Kingston, Jamaica, described them as a sonic assault: "The confusion occasioned by the rattling of chains and slings from the wharves, the mock-driving of hoops by the coopers, winding the postmens horns, beating militia and negroe drums, the sound of pipe and tabor, negroe flutes, gombas and jaw-bones, scraping of the violin, and singing of men and women." Performers made everything into an instrument, redeploying the tools of work and war, taking over public space and using the holiday as an occasion for pleasure, experimentation, and communication. The banjo was one part of this broader orchestration of swirling sound. Jamaica resident Matthew Smith recalled how on New Year's Day 1816 he heard "sudden sounds of the drum and banjee" announcing a procession. "There was no resisting John Canoe," and so he spent an afternoon in the "broiling sun" following and listening. A visitor to the island in 1826 witnessed the slaves gathering in front of the master's house the evening of Christmas Day "with their gombays, bonjaws, and an ebo drum, made of a hollow tree, with a piece of sheepskin stretched over it. Some of the women carried small calabashes with pebbles in them, stuck on short sticks, which they rattled in time to the songs, or rather howls of the musicians." The Baptist Minister James Phillippo, who arrived in Jamaica in the early 1820s, recalled seeing John Canoe, carrying a "wooden sword," accompanied by musicians, "beating banjas and tomtoms, blowing cow horns, shaking a hard round black seed, called Indian shot, in a calabash, and scraping bones of animals together, which, added to the vociferations of the crowd, filled the air with the most discordant sounds."[16]

Junkanoo was celebrated in Jamaica as early as the mid-eighteenth century and was first documented in the writings of the planter Edward Long. During the Christmas holidays, he wrote, enslaved men paraded through the streets in "grotesque habits" with "ox-horns on their heads, sprouting from the top of a horrid sort of vizor, or mask, which about the mouth is rendered very terrific with large boar-husks." Followed by a crowd of "drunken women who refresh him frequently with a sup of aniseed water," these costumed men would dance in front of each door shouting "John Connu!" and dancing. The shout, Long theorized, was in honor of a man named John Conny, a "celebrated" chief from Axim on the Guinea Coast. One linguist suggests instead that the term "John Conoe" came from a term in the West African Ewe language used to describe a sorcerer. The performance tradition continues to this day in Jamaica and other parts of the Caribbean.[17]

One of the defining features of Junkanoo became elaborate head-dresses, wooden sculptures that depicted ships and houses and some-times offered a remarkable condensation, and analysis, of the social order of slavery. Matthew Lewis saw a "Merry-Andrew dressed in a striped doublet, and bearing upon his head a kind of pasteboard house-boat, filed with puppets, representing, some sailors, others soldiers, others again slaves on the plantation." The three groups depicted in the boat—sailors, soldiers, and slaves—were those whose lives and labor kept "the wheels of Atlantic colonial and commercial systems turning," as one historian notes. John Canoe literally carried on his head those who carried the Atlantic economy through their work.[18]

Junkanoo and similar celebrations were an elaborate form of theatre, drawing on performance traditions of both Africa and Europe. A resident of Jamaica named Mary Nugent described their relentless, unending quality: "Nothing but bonjoes, drums, and tom-toms, going all night, and dancing and singing and madness, all the morning." Some participants, she noted, were "superbly dressed" with "gold and silver fringe, spangles, beads." One party of "dancing men and women" who "had a sort of leader or superior at their head, who sang a sort of recitative, and seemed to regular all their proceedings." They were accompanied by a "rude sort of drum, made of bark leaves," on which "they beat time with their feet." There was a party of actors, and "a little child was introduced, who was supposed to be a king, who stabbed all the rest." One man was dressed as "Henry 4th of France." "After the tragedy" was acted out, they "all began dancing with the greatest glee." Such theatrical performances were observed again in 1825, when a man described being visited by a group of slaves "considering of musicians, and a couple of personages fantastically dressed to represent kinds or warriors; one of them wore a white mask on his face, and part of the representation had evidently some reference to the play of Richard the Third; for the man in the white mask exclaimed, 'A horse, a horse, my kingdom for a horse!' "[19]

The celebration was also practiced among North Carolina slaves, who called it "John Koonering," and it took place on Christmas. "The *leading* character," one doctor who visited a plantation in 1829 wrote, "is a rag-man whose 'get-up' consists in a costume of rags, so arranged that one end of each hangs loose and dangles." He wore an elaborate headdress: "Two great ox horns, attached to the skin of a raccoon," with just holes for his eyes and mouth. It was also a musical instrument: it was adorned with "several cow or sheep bells or strings of dried goat's horns" that "jingle at every moment." There were six musicians "arrayed fantastically in ribbons rags and feathers" and playing "gumba boxes"—like those played by Jamaican maroons that became popular in West Africa during the same period—made of "wooden frames covered over with tanned sheep-skins." The dancers demanded change from the residents of the "great house," and jingled it for a while in the cup while dancing. Though it was brief, Junkanoo offered a reversal of roles: for a few hours the enslaved occupied the master's house, dancing and playing drums, demanding money. In some versions of the celebration documented in Jamaica, the enslaved explicitly became white for a day. An 1833 account from Jamaica described performers in a "white false-face or mask," and sometimes they wore white gloves as well. "With white masks and powdered faces," writes one historian, "black laborers turned plantation society into a world in which nothing was at it seemed—a world of uncertainty, confusion, and unlimited potential."[20]

In her autobiography, ex-slave Harriet Jacobs recalls the joys of what she called "Johnkannaus." It took place on the plantation on Christmas morning, and the performers were the "greatest attraction" of the day for the children. "Two athletic men, in calico wrappers, have a net thrown over them, covered with all manner of bright colored stripes. Cow's tails are fastened to their backs, and their heads are decorated with horns." Drummers played a "box, covered with sheepskin, called a gumbo box" and others played "triangles and jawbones." At the center of the celebration were songs carefully composed during the previous months, sung as the performers demanded money and rum from the white masters and overseers. The rum was carried back home to whet a continuation of the celebration within the slave quarters themselves, away from the master's eyes. All the whites gave money, for if they didn't they would be ridiculed in song: "Poor massa, so dey say; down on his heels, so dey say; Got no money, so dey say; Not one shillin, so dey say; God A'mighty bress you, so dey say."[21]

Junkanoo celebrations were among the most visible manifestations of a matrix of cultural and ritual activity with enslaved communities. Other practices were less visible to outside observers. In 1838, a Virginia resident named William Smith published an account in the local *Farmer's*

Register of one such smaller gathering, focused around the wondrous offerings of the persimmon tree. Residents of Virginia found treasures in this tree, making shoes and bedposts with its lumber and medicine with its bark. From its leaves and fruit they made ink, vinegar, sugar, brandy, pie and pudding, and most marvelously a kind of beer that, though nonalcoholic, became intoxicating when combined with the music of the banjo. As Smith wrote: "Although I am of the opinion that persimmon beer is not intoxicating, I have witnessed great glee, and highly pleasurable sensation produced in our slaves, over a jug-gourd of beer; but I ascribe this reverie or pleasurable hilarity to the wild notes of the "banjor," which gives zest to the beer."[22]

Smith was driven to his own reverie about the banjo, seeking an explanation for what it was about the instrument that made it so wonderful to listen to. "There is indescribable something in the tones of this rude instrument, that strikes the most delicate and refined here with pleasing emotion; the uninterrupted twang or vibration of its strings, produces a sound as it dies away, that borders on the sublime." Smith caught something here about the attractive hum of the instrument, though he also seemed a little disturbed at how much he—an educated man, with cultivated musical tastes—liked it. As he sought an explanation, he offered another insight into the banjo's sonic achievement: "I never could account for its wonderful effect on a well-organized ear, capable of distinguishing and appreciating agreeable sounds; unless it be admitted, that concord and discord are so completely blended as to produce perfect harmony."[23]

The concord and discord produced by the sound of the banjo in this case was also a key part of a larger social ritual, whose contours Smith only partially perceived. He'd stopped by the plantation because he'd heard the "tones of the banjor," and was told by the master that the slaves had brewed a barrel of persimmon beer and had requested—and been granted—the "privilege" of having a "beer dance." The event opened "with great ceremony" with a song called "Who-zen-John, who-za"—perhaps a reference to John Canoe. This was the opening for dancing and socializing, to songs about love and songs about family. Inside, meanwhile, was another center of celebration, more focused around the persimmon beer itself. The "banjor-man" was sitting in a chair on top of the barrel of beer. "A long white cowtail, queued with a red ribbon, ornamented his head, and hung gracefully down his back; over this he wore a three-cocked hat, decorated with peacock feathers, a rose cockade, a bunch of ripe persimmons," all of it topped with "red pepper as a top knot." Each of these objects was likely chosen carefully and for a reason tied to the celebration of the tree and what it had offered: a man served up the beer to all those present, while two women put persimmon dough in the fire to make bread. The banjo player's music drove the movement of two men who were dancing "Juber," slapping palms against their bodies and stomping heels on the floor "in perfect unison with the notes of the banjor." The song they sang offered a counterpoint between the "double trouble" of plantation labor—"Hoe corn, hill tobacco" and what came from the seed of the persimmon tree. From its fruit came bounty, and a kind of independence, something the banjo's sound—and the ritual attire of the player—helped to capture and sustain.[24]

Enslaved musicians played complex and multiple roles on plantations. Instruments were sought after on the plantation, as the Canadian writer John Finch, who traveled to the United States in the 1830s, observed. He mentioned the "bandjo" as an instrument that "field negroes" were fond of, though he added that "the supreme ambition of every negro is to procure a real violin." They gathered together the money by saving "a few pence which are given them, selling chickens, and robbing a little, if necessary." "An instrument of music," he concluded, "seems necessary to their existence."[25]

The 1832 novel *Swallow Barn,* set on a plantation in Virginia along the banks of the James River, depicts the vital role a musician could play in plantation life. It includes a character named Carey, who played a "banjoe": "he sings the inspiration of his own muse, weaving into song past and present annals of the family. He is considered as a seer amongst the negroes on the estate." As one historian has written, Carey is represented in the novel as fulfilling a role not unlike that of a West African griot, composing "historical songs about his patrons"—who were also, however, his owners. But his recounting of the "annals of the family" could well have offered one version to white audiences and quite a different one to African-American listeners. And if the musician was a "seer," it meant that he was able to connect past and present in ways that probably evoked a very different set of realities both within and beyond this world.[26]

For one African-American novelist of the period, meanwhile, the sound of the banjo was the sound of revolt. In the late 1850s Martin R.

Delany wrote *Blake; Or the Huts of America,* the story of a Caribbean-born slave who seeks to start a slave revolution. He tours throughout the U.S. South trying to organize the enslaved, but it is finally in Cuba that he is able to launch an insurrection and become its leader. In a remarkable scene, Delany connects the project of revolution with the project of reconnecting with African roots through the banjo. At a great celebration in Cuba for the novel's hero, Henry Blake, "the Leader of the Army of Emancipation and the originator of the scheme to redeem them from slavery," a character named Pino Golias, a "black surgeon," proves himself "master of the favorite instrument of his father land, the African bango." Others play the instrument as well at the gathering, including a woman named Ambrosina Cordora. The instrument surpasses what had been the most popular one before: the Spanish guitar, which proves to be "a secondary instrument when compared with the touching melodies of the pathetic bango in the hands of this Negro artiste."[27]

Martin Delany was born in 1812 in western Virginia. His father was a slave, but his mother was free; and according to the law of slavery, the child inherited the mother's status. Both Delany's grandparents were African born, and they traced their ancestry to West African chieftains. Delany wrote *Blake* while living in the town of Marshall, Canada, a gathering place for many who had escaped southern slavery through the Underground Railroad. During his life, he must have encountered the music of the banjo, seeing how it created spaces of sociability and escape on the plantation. On this basis, he took another step, imagining banjo music as a rebel sound that could ultimately upend the landscape of the plantation, a space usually dominated by rhythms and sound of labor.

Blake was originally published serially between 1859 and 1862 in the *Anglo-African Magazine* and the *Weekly Anglo-African.* But the volume in which the final chapters of the book were published in May 1862 has been lost, so we don't know how he ended the novel. Did Blake's revolution ultimately begin, and succeed? As it is, we're left with a perpetual promise of what is to come, of a redemption foretold and planned but not realized. But Delany's description of the banjo holds a clue about how the story ended. In his description of the performance of the "African bango" in honor of Blake, he flashes forward to the way the incident is remembered later. Having been "heretofore neglected and despised by the better class among them" in favor of European instruments, the

"bango" in time became "the choice" for musical performance. Tied together through "associations and remembrances" with the evening of
the "great gathering" that had coalesced the project of antislavery revolution, the "Nigriton bango could thenceforth be seen in the parlors and
drawing rooms of all of the best families of this class of the inhabitants."
In these lines, we get a glimpse of the future Delany had in mind: one in
which, having secured their freedom, people of African descent—of all
classes—would also embrace their connection to Africa through the sound
of the banjo.[28]

In the 1930s, the Works Progress Administration oversaw a project in
which hundreds of ex-slaves were interviewed about their experiences.
Many of them recalled the sense of liberty they had gained from music
and dance. In contrast to both theatrical representations and Northrop's
more positive rendering of the place of music within slavery, however,
these ex-slaves often emphasized the sense of danger, surveillance, and
constraint that surrounded their attempts to find a space for musical
gatherings. Throughout the south, whites formed "slave patrols" who
traveled the roads looking for slaves away from their plantations. The
enslaved, in turn, cultivated a knowledge of sound as a weapon. In the
nineteenth-century agricultural landscape of the South, sound traveled
far. The sound of horses' hooves on the road signaled to those who were
running away that a slave patrol was nearing. In prairies and on roads,
horses gave an advantage to whites; but this was neutralized in the woods
and swamps, spaces defined "by the precedence of the ear over the
eye." The tromping of the horses offered runaways an "early-warning
system that they could use to track the slaveholders who were trying to
track them." Sound, too, was often "a more useful sense than sight for
coordinating collective action over distance." Escapees used it to find
one another in the woods, planning their next move. And when the
enslaved gathered for dances, they also had to keep constant watch for
those who were trying to keep constant watch over them.[29]

Many ex-slaves interviewed mentioned musical instruments, most
often the fiddle, which had a total of 205 mentions. The second most popular instrument was the banjo, with 106 mentions. And the most

common combination of instruments was banjo and fiddle. Percussion instruments of various kinds were ranked third in the number of mentions. The narratives make clear, then, that during the decades before the Civil War the banjo was well-anchored in rural communities of the enslaved throughout the South, from Virginia to Georgia and west to Arkansas and Mississippi. And they also offer rich details about the banjo's role in the lives of the enslaved.[30]

In a few of these accounts it was the master who played the banjo. Cordelia Anderson Jackson, interviewed in Spartanburg, South Carolina, in 1937, remembered her master taking out his banjo and playing it so that she would sing a song with him: "Oh, Bob white, is your wheat ripe? No. no, not quite." And Georgia-born Isaiah Greene recalled how whites would hire slaves to play music at their own gatherings. "In those days there were many Negro musicians who were always ready to furnish music from their banjo and fiddle for the frolics. If a white family was entertaining, and needed a musician but didn't own one, they would hire a slave from another plantation to play for them." And in Virginia, the ex-slave Robert Williams recalled, some "po' whites"—who he recalled were treated quite badly by wealthier whites, forced to come to the back door of the house and living "just like stray goats"—came to the dances held by the slaves. Local white masters tried to stop them from doing so, and they "would have to steal in to see de dance."[31]

Many ex-slaves vividly recalled the way the banjo animated smaller gatherings on their plantations as well as larger events that brought together individuals from several different plantations. Looking back from nearly a century later, ex-slaves evoked the sense of joyous conviviality and solidarity at these gatherings. In Florida, Louis Napoleon remembered that in the evenings on the plantation where he and his parents lived, people gathered in front of one of their cabins and "would sing and dance to the tunes of a fife, banjo or fiddle played by one of their number." In Virginia, Pierce Cody recalled, after marriages between slaves—officiated by the master himself—there was a long night of celebration: "the guests danced far into the night by music from the fiddle and banjo." Cora Gillam, born in Mississippi, recalled: "On our place, the slaves had a regular band: fiddler, banjo player, tamborine player. They played any kind of song. They would play for the dances." Harve Osborne, born a slave on a plantation near Asheville, North Carolina, around

1825, delighted to tell of "dancing to the music of the banjo" during his youth on the plantation where he lived.[32]

Marriah Hines, born in Virginia in 1835, described how evenings on the plantation were spent quilting, making clothes, telling jokes, and singing "in the moonlight by the tune of an old banjo picker." Another woman who was a slave in Norfolk described how in the evenings "slaves were allowed to visit each other," and sometimes danced "by the tune of an old banjo." She also described Sunday services at a small log cabin, where they would "pray and sing in our own feelings and expressions," singing songs that sounded out across the hills. These small moments of freedom of expression, however, were always watched. She tellingly described the white preacher who attended their services as an "overseer." As soon as the service was done, they all had to rush home to begin cooking the "white folks' dinner." Masters feared that anytime the enslaved gathered in groups "for conversations," they might actually be plotting to escape or "to cause trouble of some kind." Those who were caught at night without a pass, Hines recalled, were "stripped and beaten" where they were caught, and some never recovered from the "severe" whippings. Although the masters sought to contain and limit the musical gatherings of the enslaved, they also took advantage of their talents, bringing those who they thought could sing and dance well to the "big house" to entertain their guests.[33]

A Virginian ex-slave named Baily Cunningham, whose grandfather was a German migrant and whose grandmother and mother were Virginia slaves, was nearly a century old when he was interviewed in 1938. He remembered hearing the banjo often as a child. "They had big dances at night, sometimes. Somebody would play the fiddles and some the banjo and sometimes had a drum. We did the 'buck dance.' A boy and girl would hold hands and jump up and down and swing around keeping time with the music." They drank "coffee, corn whisky or apple brandy," and sometimes ended up drunk. "We would dance and play all night but had to be ready for work the next day," he added. But there was never any full escape from the eyes of masters. "We had to get a pass from our master or misses to go to the dance, as we were afraid that the 'Patty Rolers'"—the slave patrols—"would get us." "The master would have eight or ten men on horses watching and any one caught without a pass was taken up and punished, sometimes whipped." Whatever sense of liberty these events granted was always circumscribed, shadowed by the threat that a dance might lead to a whipping.[34]

Slaves often tried to keep their dances secret and developed a code for telling one another when the patrols had found out about a secret dance. "There's bugs in the wheat," or "weevils in the wheat," they would say. One woman, born just at the end of the Civil War, recalled how her mother, a housemaid, had once planned to go to a "big dance." But on the day of the event, the plantation's footman came to see her and, right in front of their mistress, asked her if she knew there were "bugs in the wheat." The mistress asked the footman what he was talking about, and he replied: "Nothin.'" But the message had been passed on: the "bugs in the wheat" were the patrollers, who had found out about the dance. "Mother said she wouldn't go to the dance," and was glad she didn't, since she'd heard the patrollers had broken up the dance and whipped several of the slaves there. Other slaves, though, said that all those at the dance had escaped by jumping out of the windows or else by hiding behind a door that the patrollers were "too dumb" to look behind. Such stories of escaping and tricking masters, in fact, were sung at the dances themselves. Harriet Robinson, born in 1842 in Texas, remembered fiddlers singing: "I fooled Ole Mastah 7 years / Fooled the overseer three / Hand me down my banjo / And I'll tickle your bel-lee."[35]

One man named James Davis described how banjo playing had been important to him throughout his life. When he was interviewed at the age of 96, he was cotton farmer in Arkansas, but he'd been born in Raleigh, North Carolina, on Christmas morning of 1840. "I went to work when I was seven pullin' worms off tobacco," he recalled, "and I been workin' ever since." But he'd also learned to play the banjo. "I used to be one of the best banjo pickers. I was good." He played for "white folks" at their dances. "We had parties and corn shuckin's, oh lord, yes." "I'll sing you a song," he continued: "'Oh lousy nigger / Oh grand-mammy / Knock me down with the old fence rider / Ask that pretty gal let me court her / Young gal, come blow the coal.'" At the age of twenty-one, Davis was "sold the speculator and sold to Texas"—he sharply re-membered his exact selling price, and the currency it was paid in—but ran away immediately and made his way back to North Carolina, run-ning across Sherman's troops and accompanying them back to his home. To protect the musical gatherings where he played both during slavery and after, Davis developed another skill beyond banjo playing. "I've seen them Ku Klux in slavery times and I've cut a many a grapevine. We'd be in the place dancin' and playin' the banjo and the grapevine strung across the road and the Ku Klux come ridin' along and run right into it and throw the horses down." Davis here combines two historical periods—that of slavery and that of Reconstruction and the era of the Ku Klux Klan, capturing the continuity between the two eras, both in terms of the music that was played and the ways African-Americans could sometimes defeat threats that surrounded them. Other ex-slaves recalled similar scenes, including the Virginian Cecelia Turner, who remembered how both patrollers and their horses ended up sprawled on the ground, while the slaves who had set the trap watched from the woods, laughing. As Saidiya Hartman writes, through such narratives these rural slave gatherings "appear like small-scale battles with owners, local whites, and the law."[36]

Musicians wrote songs about the constant threat of the slave patrols. Robert Williams, born in 1843, remembered Saturday night dances that took place in a "big barn" on the plantation. There was patting and "dancin' for life," driven by a banjo player. The chorus of one of his songs went like this: "Run nigger run, run nigger run / Don't let de paddle rollers catch you / Run nigger run." Williams noted that the master was probably listening, for he sat on his porch not far away, and the music could be heard "for half a mile." The song was well-known throughout the South, though the words varied. Mississippi-born Austin Pen Parnell recalled his father telling stories about the slave patrols and singing a version of the song "Run, Nigger, Run" to him: "'Run, nigger, run / The pateroles'll get you" the chorus rang. "That nigger run / That nigger flew / That nigger bust / His Sunday shoe." Parnell couldn't remember the rest of the song, but he remembered hearing "the boys . . . pick it out on the banjo and the guitar." Henry Turner, also born into slavery in Mississippi, remembered another verse for the song: "Run nigger run, it's almost day / That nigger run, that nigger flow / That nigger tore his shirt into." And Cresa Mack, born a slave in Arkansas, remembered the song sung during the Civil War about patrols who would beat slaves "almost to death" if they were caught without a pass.[37]

Despite the slave patrols, the dances clearly were memorable events. The former slave Nancy Williams, born in 1847, described joyously how every "gal had a beau" at the dances, and recalled bands with two fiddles, two tambourines, two banjos, and two sets of bones—the latter made by "devilish boys" who gathered the bones from out in the woods where cows had gone to die. Williams had since given up dancing for religious reasons but recalled with enthusiasm how she had danced with her friend Jennie—and the "devil"—carrying a glass of water on her head without ever spilling a drop, wearing a yellow dress and yellow shoes she had painted with stolen paint so they would match her dress, shoes that hurt her, though that didn't stop her from dancing.[38]

Mississippi-born Lewis Brown, interviewed in 1938, recalled that although the "grown folks didn't have much amusement in slavery times," they did have the "banjo, fiddle," and other instruments. "They danced the cotillions and the waltzes and breakdown steps, all such as that," he remembered. "Pick banjo," he recalled, adding an "U-umph," maybe attempting to recapture the sound as he remembered it. Ninety-eight-year-old Arkansas resident Jim Davis also brought the sound of song with him. "I used to be a banjo picker in Civil War times," he explained to his interviewer. "I could pick a church song just as good as I could a reel," he added, emphasizing his own versatility as a musician as well as that of the banjo as an instrument. "Used to pick one went like this," he said, and launched into a forelorn love ballad: "Farewell, farewell, sweet Mary / I'm ruined forever / By lovin' of you / Your parents don't like me / That I do know." "I could pick anything," he went on, and offered a verse of "Amazing Grace." "I used to talk that on my banjo just like I talked it there," he concluded, suggesting that his banjo had been, in a way, his voice.[39]

Ex-slaves considered this music precious and made sure to pass it on to the next generation. An Arkansas preacher named James Reeves, born in 1870, remembered his parents and grandparents talking about the "breakdown dances with fiddle and banjo music" they had in "slave time." "Far after slavery," he explained, "they had them." A father in Arkansas was determined to make sure the music he had grown up with was passed on to his children. As Kate Arbery remembered it, he would pull out his fiddle and call to them: "You little devils, come up here and dance" and have them "marchin'." Together, the family had an ensemble that brought together fiddle and banjo with other instruments—quills, played like a flute, and an innovative percussion instrument called a "pack-five in a row," made up of fishing canes tied together "just like my fingers." "Anybody that knowed how could sure make music on 'em."[40]

Betty Curlett recalled in detail how slaves showed similar creativity in building their own banjos. "The only musical instrument we had was a banjo. Some made their banjos. Take a bucket or pan a long strip of wood. 3 horse hairs twisted made the base string. 2 horsehairs twisted made the second string. 1 horse hair twisted made the fourth and the fifth string was the fine one, it was not twisted at all but drawn tight." The strings, she added, were greased with beeswax. On the Georgia Sea Islands, drums and banjos were both made using raccoon skins that were tacked to the side of a house until they were dried and smooth. They were then stretched over a tree trunk to make drums. A woman named Hettie recalled how the music for dances held to celebrate a "good crop" came from what she called "guitah" made with "coon hides stretched over hoops."[41]

Ex-slaves in other parts of Georgia vividly recalled hearing the banjo on their plantations. Henry Bland, born in 1851, recalled how on the Fourth of July and Christmas, the slaves on the plantation celebrated with song and dance, something they also did "after the crops had been gathered," with music "furnished by violin, banjo and clapping of hands." Bland himself sometimes played, with a violin given to him by his master. Susan Castle recalled Christmas parties on her plantation, where there was always someone "ready to pick up the banjo." Berry Clay, born after emancipation, had heard from her parents about plantation "frolics at which square dances were the chief form of entertainment," driven by the music of "banjo or fiddle."[42]

Marshal Butler, in an interview peppered with songs about love, feasting, and a stubborn mule, recalled how people "frolicked" on Saturday nights to "swell music." He remembered an instrument that was almost "like a banjo," made of strings attached to a tin can. One man "beat his hand" on the can, while another "beat the strings" with "broom straws." They sang "Little Liza Jane" and "Green Grows the Willow Tree," until two in the morning, then scattered to head home. Ex-slave Carrie Hudson also recalled how, on Saturday nights, the "young folks" stayed up far past midnight and "picked the banjo." Easter Huff similarly recalled Saturday nights animated by musicians who played banjo and "knocked on tin pans for music to dance by." Another ex-slave, Sarah

Byrd, talked of Saturday-night "frolics," held "anytime the slaves chose to have them." Musicians played banjo, bones, and quills, and the dancing went on so long that as the sun rose on Sunday morning everyone was laying around or sitting on the floor. Emmaline Heard, born a few years before emancipation, also described plantation "frolics" that included dancing and banjo playing and sometimes drew slaves from nearby plantations. "A prize was given to the person who could 'buck dance' the steadiest with a tumbler of water balanced on the head. A cake or a quilt was often given as the prize." Elisha Doc Garey recalled his childhood on a Georgia plantation as a time where he and other children worked "like horses" but also sometimes had dances where musicians played the banjo and quills, creating "stomp down good times."[43]

Music had sustained communities through decades of slavery, and it also accompanied the celebration of the day freedom finally came. Violet Shaw of Arkansas remembered her aunt describing how, one day, they were working in the field when "a great big white man come, jumped up on a log and shouted, 'Freedom! Freedom!' . . . He told them they was free." They stopped working and gathered at the house. "Some got down and prayed, some sung. They had a time that day. They got the banjo and fiddle and set out playing. Some got in the big road just walking."[44]

On the eve of the Civil War, the painter William Eastman Johnson created one of the most enduring images of the place of the banjo in African-American life. He was taken by something he witnessed not on a plantation, but rather in an alley in Washington, DC. In the painting he produced, a banjo player performs for mothers and children, for a couple courting, and for a white woman lurking behind a fence, listening in. In time, Johnson's painting—under the title *Negro Life at the South*—became both his most famous work and "the best-known painted image of American slaves." It was rapidly unhinged from its original context, taken by many to depict the indolent and slow-paced life of blacks in the South. Indeed, it long circulated under the title *Old Kentucky Home,* patently resituating its location, presumably because *In an Alley in Washington, DC,* would not have endowed the painting with the desired sense of distance and nostalgia. But although its long journey through American visual racial ideology is important, more vital here is that it serves as a visual archive of a particular place, time, and sound.[45]

Eastman Johnson, *Negro Life at the South,* 1859.
Robert L. Stuart Collection. Courtesy of the New York Historical Society.

Johnson lived in Washington, DC, beginning in 1855, and began looking for local subjects to paint in the following years. He found some on the block where he lived, on F Street. When Pierre L'Enfant had designed the city in the late eighteenth century, he had created large blocks, which led to the creation of large alleys behind houses. These spaces behind the houses became the areas where slaves worked, lived, and gathered. Outside his back windows, Johnson would have observed these spaces. And he would have been quite aware of the ongoing, and often intense, controversies surrounding slavery in the nation's capital. His neighborhood was a fashionable area that was home to many proslavery southern senators as well as to Massachusetts antislavery senator Charles Sumner—who once found the severed finger of a slave left on his doorstep as a warning against his political activities.[46]

The center of Johnson's painting is the banjo, played by an older man. It is this "node" of sound that "generates the rest of the painting's activity": the music is what "sets the narrative of the painting in motion." There is a couple flirting and an older woman dancing with a child, perhaps her daughter. From a window, another woman holds a small child slightly precariously outside the window, perhaps to take in the sound. From around a wall separating this yard from a neighboring one comes a white woman, well-dressed, curious, and looking in, interpolated by a girl in a blue dress. But she is on the outskirts of the scene, affecting it only slightly, curious but not welcome. The image captures a social and cultural world that stands against the "dehumanizing system" of slavery: "all generations are represented here, children are nurtured by adults of both sexes, and time has been found for communal cultural activities." One gets a portrait of the "inner strengths present in the antebellum African American community."[47]

There is a particular strength and solidity, as well as dignity, to the banjo player himself. His strong hand looks like it has just struck down on the strings with the back of his fingers, and he is about to pick the top string. His banjo looks relatively new and taken care of: this is something the banjo player bought, rather than something he made. Along with his clothes, this suggests that he may be making a living from his music. Johnson was clearly fascinated by this particular image of musical creation: he repainted this part of the image twice afterwards, entitling one version of it *Confidence and Admiration*. Those were the feelings he saw in the young boy standing next to the musician, looking up and watching: the next generation, taking in the music.[48]

One night in the early 1830s, an African-American banjo player named Ben drove a night of dancing in a Tennessee tavern. "He was seated in the corner on his stool, holding his instrument, which he called Sal," wrote Colonel David Crockett in his remembrance of the affair. A white woman shouted out to him "Uncle Ben, strike up!" and she and another began dancing to his song. "Soon the whole house was up, knocking it off—while old Ben thrummed his banjo, beat time with his feet, and sung." The song told the story of an ill-fated journey—"I started off from Tennessee / My old horse wouldn't pull for me / He began to fret an' slip, / An I begin to cus an' whip / Walk jawbone from Tennessee." The "old horse died" the song went on, and Ben inherited only "his jawbone." Interspersed with the verses, Ben offered instructions on how to dance: "Now, back step an' hell an toe" or "Now, weed corn, kiver taters, an' double shuffle." "The dance was all life," Crockett wrote. Dancers called out for more songs—one asked for the song "Jim Crow," and Ben complimented one of them for being "limber" on the dance floor.[49]

Whites could hear the banjo at other sites of public performance. African-American boatmen working on the James River, for instance, often played the banjo "while their bateaux were lying at the landing on the river at Lynchburg," where passersby could listen in. And Virginia also had at least one banjo player who made a career performing banjo tunes for largely white audiences. His name was Titus, and a newspaper profile published in 1818 described him as a regular performer at the Richmond Racetrack. "With an old slouched hat—a coat considerably worse for wear—shoes which had not often known the value of a good polishing—banjo under arm and stick in hand—he marched over the hill to Fairfield . . . to him the great day—of the races." His songs offered the crowd an improvised musical version of what they had just witnessed: "He usually waited until the race was over before he commenced, and then he sang the incidents of the struggle for victory." "Every circumstance was brought in" to Titus's music. He named "every gentleman who owned a horse" and made him a "hero." Searching for a comparison, the author of the newspaper article reached for that of Pindar—the Ancient Greek poet who "immortalized those who triumphed at the Olympic games." Titus sang one appropriate ballad, "which he evidently stole, it being nothing more nor less than the old English ballad, which describes the race between the 'Bonny Gray Mare,' and the 'Noble Skewball.'" But Titus sang about more than horse races. One of his songs offered "an elaborate narrative of the acts and deeds of a certain individual who would otherwise have been lost to history, whom he designates as 'Archie Mullen,' whose story he commences by telling us that 'he shot the devil.'"[50]

The most remarkable piece of Titus's repertoire, however, was about an event that would have been vividly remembered in Richmond. He played, and perhaps had composed, "an entire piece, giving a true and graphic account of the capture of the 'nigger general,' as he calls him,

Gabriel." Eighteen years after one of the most important slave conspiracies in the history of the United States, which was organized at the time of the Haitian Revolution and led to the public trial and hanging of the main organizer, Gabriel, Titus was telling his story. It was a bold move: the threat of an insurrection of the enslaved was a constant fear in the South, and Gabriel's vision—which was based on the idea that an alliance between radical white artisans and enslaved people could overthrow slavery and create a new Republican order—was a serious threat to the social order in Virginia at the time.[51]

Unfortunately the words of Titus's version were not noted by the author of the 1818 article. A few decades later, however, various versions of a song called "Uncle Gabriel" appeared in the minstrel repertoire. Many of them made no reference whatsoever to the events of 1800 in Richmond. One 1848 version performed by the Ethiopian Minstrels, for instance, had a chorus that asked "What will Uncle Gabriel say," recounting the story of a comical hunt for a "coon" and its happy consumption at a plantation frolic: "De niggers de come all around / and kick up a debil of a splutter; Dey eat the coon and clar the ground, to dance the chicken flutter, Dey dance all night till de broke of day, to a tune on de old banjo."[52]

But at least one minstrel act performed a version of "Uncle Gabriel" which, like Titus's version, focused on Gabriel's rebellion: the Christy Minstrels. They published sheet music to the song in 1848. The words include a startling level of detail about the conspiracy of 1800, which, there is reason to believe, may have even come from Titus's version. "Oh my boys I'm bound to tell you," the song began: announcing a kind of necessity on the part of the singer to recount the story. The chorus sang "Hard times in Old Virginy," and from the focus and tone of the rest of the song, the "hard times" were those of the enslaved and of Gabriel himself. The verses of the song were as follows:[53]

> Oh don't' you know Old Uncle Gabriel,
> Oh! Oh!
> He war the Chief of de Insurgents,
> Way down in Southampton
>
> It war a little boy betrayed him,
> Oh! Oh!

A little boy by the name of Daniel
Oh! Oh!
Betrayed him at the Norfolk landing,
Oh! Boys I'm getting done.

The whites dey fought him and dey caught him
Oh! Oh!
To Richmond Court House dey did brought him
Oh! Oh!
Twelve men sot up on de jury;
Oh! Boys I'm most done.
Hard times in Old Virginy

Dey took him down to de Gallows
Oh! Oh!
Dey drove him down, wid four grey horses,
Oh! Oh!
Brice's Ben, he drove de wagon,
Oh! Boys, I'm most done.
Hard Times in Old Virginy.

And dare dey hung him an dey swung him,
Oh! Oh!
And dey swung him and dey hung him,
Oh! Oh!
And that war the last of the Niger General,
Oh! Boys I'm just done.
Hard times in Old Virginy.

The song is far from critical of Gabriel's actions: it is more than any-thing a lament, with the guilty parties—even the four grey horses who pulled the cart to the gallows—named, almost as if on trial. Gabriel had made the headlines in 1800 by dreaming of a Virginia without slavery. In the song, he was brought back to life long enough for his story to be remembered and the names of others involved spoken. The lyrics them-selves suggest whoever wrote the song understood it might be a bit hard for people to hear—"Boys I'm most done," he repeats, almost from the beginning, until in the last moments he announces "Boys I'm just done."

One verse in the printed song adds a few details about the boy who "betrayed" Gabriel—and provides a possible link to Titus. The boy, the verse recounts, "Says how he de do my Uncle Gabriel," to which Gabriel—threatened with being unmasked—responds "My name it is Jim McCullen, / Some dey calls me Archey Mullin." It is a curious detail, somewhat at odds with the rest of the verses. But Titus, according the 1818 newspaper account, also sang an "elaborate narrative" of the acts of one Archey Mullin. Perhaps at times he combined the two songs, or perhaps someone who heard him play combined them in this version. Though it is obviously impossible to prove for sure, it seems very possible that there is some filiation between the 1818 performance by Titus and the Christy Minstrel version from 1848. That evanescent trace hints at a much larger filiation: that between African-American banjo players and the white musicians who founded the minstrel genre in the 1830s.

Writing of his childhood in Lynchburg, Virginia, a white man named Norman Eubanks recalled how he had learned to play the banjo from slaves on the plantation where he grew up. He remembered that his father—born in 1777—had often told him that the banjo was "a well-known instrument with the Negroes in the country." "My father had an old Negro, Davey, who was an expert banjo player," he recalled. "The Negroes used horsehair for strings. . . . When I was a boy, Henry, a Negro boy and myself, watched every horse that came by my father's home, and if he had a long tail we got a supply of strings." One can imagine that the horses of the area might well have feared passing by that particular house. Eubanks himself imitated the slaves and built his own banjo in the 1830s.[54]

Eubanks never took to the stage. But in the same area around the same time, another young boy was learning to play the banjo, with far-reaching consequences. His name was Joel Walker Sweeney, and he was born into a farming family in the tobacco country between Lynchburg and Richmond, today Appomattox County. At the time there were about 10,000 blacks in the county and 7400 whites. Most of the latter owned small tobacco farms, but there were a few larger plantations as well. The Sweeney family had been in Virginia since the time of the American Revolution—the grandfather Moses fought in the conflict—and the musician's father was a wheelwright. Several of his siblings also played music, as did some of his local cousins. As a boy, Sweeney learned to play the violin. He was so good, as one local resident named P. C. Sutphin recalled much later, that he played as the "chief violinist at a special dance party of some of the 'elite' of Lynchburg." But his attention turned to another instrument, wrote Sutphin: he "took a fancy to the banjo, which, before that, had only been in the hands of the negro." Sweeney was, in Sutphin's estimation, "the first white person to play on it and introduce it to the society of the whites." By the age of twelve, another resident recalled, Sweeney was already "quite proficient on the banjo and violin."[55]

Who were Sweeney's banjo teachers? Sweeney's father, John, was a small farmer and probably owned a few slaves when Sweeney was a child—an 1850 census listed him as owning two. Next door to their small plot, however, was a larger plantation owned by Major Henry Flood and his son, Joel Walker Flood. They owned twenty slaves in 1820, and 121 by 1850. The two families were close: John Sweeney gave his son the two first names of his neighbor. According to one researcher, the younger Sweeney got to know the coachman on the plantation and learned to play the banjo and "the music of the African" from him.[56]

If this is indeed how Joel Walker Sweeney learned to play, he probably learned techniques and songs by drawing on other sources— including, perhaps, the singing of Titus himself. Sweeney began his public musical career "by wandering through central Virginia, playing and singing for crowds during county court sessions." That was probably where Judge Pore, who in 1895 published his recollections of the boy, first heard him sing. "He was a one-man show, singing the doggeral [*sic*] he had learned from Negroes or had improvised from their tunes, dancing, reciting, and crowing, braying and roaring in imitation of animals. He not only played the banjo; he was equally accomplished on the violin." Around this time, presumably influenced by other acts circulating at the time—particularly those of a performer named T. D. Rice— Sweeney "began blacking his face for these performances." In addition to performing at the courthouse, he almost certainly performed for dances in local homes as well as in the local Sunnyside Tavern. In 1836, he had his first performance on a concert stage when he joined a blackface singer named James Sanford to present "Negro Extravaganzas" at Richmond's

Terpsichore Hall. In the next years Sweeney found a few other gigs in theatres but also performed in circuses and—in 1837 and 1838—at the Lynchburg racetrack. Within a few years, he would go on to New York, where he would bring the banjo to the urban stage for the first time.[57]

Norman Eubanks recalled hearing Sweeney perform a song called "The Coaling Ground" at the Lynchburg racetrack. It was written by another resident named Billy Moon and recounted an ill-fated journey. His cart was "broke in the coaling ground," though in the end the help of various strangers allowed him to go on. He was even plied with rum and cake at a friendly tavern. The song was an intimate one—mentioning names of wheelwrights and tavern keepers and celebrating the fact of people helping one another out. But it also described the travails of working people in a landscape in transformation: Eubanks recalled that the area had been "denuded of all timber to make charcoal" for the local iron works. Though much distinguished, the racetrack songs of Titus and Sweeney, sung decades apart, both spoke of local events and names and places, using music to voice a specific experience.[58]

Titus, however, was ultimately largely forgotten, the sound of his banjo left only in one fleeting textual trace in a Richmond newspaper. Sweeney, meanwhile, became what historian Bob Carlin calls "the Elvis Presley of his time, a white man who could sing like a black man." Because he was white, he was able to do what Titus and other African-American performers could not: bring the banjo to the mainstream stages of North America. "At a time when African American music and musicians were unacceptable or inaccessible to main street America," writes Carlin, musicians like Sweeney "provided an acceptable version of black music for most listeners." "In the process, Joe Sweeney brought African Americans' songs and tunes, as well as their instrument, into American popular music."[59]

In her pioneering study of the African-American banjo, Cece Conway argues that several minstrels truly did begin as "apprentices" who learned to play the banjo from enslaved people on plantations. There was, she points out, no way to learn how to play the instrument at the time except "through oral transmission and imitation." They had to "absorb tradition" from African-American banjo players by listening to them and playing with them. Sweeney is the most obvious example, but other minstrels also learned to play directly from black musicians. Ben Cotton, for instance, explained in an interview late in his life that while he was working on Mississippi riverboats as a young man he would visit slaves and "sit with them in front of their cabins and we would start the banjo twanging, and their voices would ring out in the quiet night air in their weird melodies." "They did not quite understand me," he went on. "I was the first white man they had seen who sang as they did; but we were brothers for the time being and were perfectly happy." The style of syncopation present in early minstrel songs, as recorded in "methods" offered to aspiring banjo players, indicates that they had learned from African-American players. In time minstrels helped to create a body of musical notation meant to transmit the plantation music tradition, a fact that adds another layer of deep irony to the story: the minstrel tradition is in fact one of the few ways we have to access the soundscapes of the plantation and therefore of recovering a crucial piece of African-American musical history.[60]

Minstrels depended on the claim that they had learned their music from blacks: this was a key part of the way they marketed their performances. They were interpreters—or, as they sometimes called themselves, delineators—bringing the black music of the plantations to white audiences in a form they could enjoy and absorb. Though they acknowledged this apprenticeship, and even debt, this never led to an incorporation of black musicians into their acts or any public musical collaboration. Though some minstrels might have wished to play alongside black performers, perhaps even invite their mentors on the stage, this seems to have been a cultural impossibility in the antebellum theatre. The fact that blacks were excluded from the stage gave white minstrels a tremendous opportunity, one they took advantage of. They negotiated the broader racial landscape by simultaneously transmitting certain aspects of African-American tradition and obscuring and transforming some of its key elements. Minstrelsy was an inherently unstable, contradictory, and shifting form. It became both a conduit for, and ultimately a transformation of, earlier forms of music, offering a layered and contradictory pattern of incorporation, appropriation, and parody. On the minstrel stage a song like "Run, Nigger, Run!"—developed as a form of critique, memory, and resistance within the plantation—would become a form of comic relief. And over time, the more overtly racist and insulting aspects of minstrelsy became more dominant. In his pioneering and influential study of blackface minstrelsy, Eric Lott described the contradiction of the form as being the combination of "love and theft": an attraction and even respect for a musical tradition that was ultimately expressed and activated on the basis of racist exclusion. For that reason, minstrels have often been seen as cynical cultural appropriators, and the accusation of "minstrelsy" in contemporary popular culture continues to carry a highly negative charge.[61]

The banjo was, from the beginning, at the heart of the minstrel show. Its sound, and the symbolism surrounding it, made possible the strange transmogrification that sustained blackface minstrelsy. By the 1830s, audiences had come to see this instrument as deeply tied to African-American life. Sweeney was among the first who saw that this created an opportunity, that carrying the instrument onto the stage would provide kind of a badge of authenticity, a visible and material link to the black musical tradition. But for audiences to accept that a white man could play the banjo, he and other performers first made themselves black, tapping into a long theatre performance tradition. It was the encounter between the tradition of blackface and the sound of the banjo that made minstrelsy possible and in turn sent the banjo into a dramatically new chapter in its winding story.

5

The Banjo Meets Blackface

Maybe it was Queen Anne who started it all the day she decided to paint herself black. At her 1589 wedding, a group of four naked "Negroes"—whites in black makeup—danced in the snow. She was perhaps remembering this when, in 1605, she asked the author Ben Jonson to write a play in which she and her court ladies could perform as "black Moors." He offered *The Masque of Blackness,* which features King Niger and his twelve daughters, African "nymphs." They are told that because they are black, they are not beautiful, though redemption beckons: if they find their way to Britannia, they will become white. Niger protests, declaring that in fact they are "beautiful as well as black": they were the "first form'd dames of earth . . . in whose sparkling and refulgent eyes / The glorious sun did still delight to rise . . . in their black the perfect'st beauty grows." In the end, though, the play celebrates the idea that the British crown, expanding into a global empire, will absorb and control black outsiders. Despite the comforting plot, however, there was something provocative and troubling about the spectacle. The Queen of England, six months pregnant at the time, appeared in public with "her face and arms coated with black grease." Everyone watching knew that the African nymph was actually the Queen. But what, exactly—with England beginning its long colonial expansion—was she doing?[1]

European theater long included "black" characters: the *buffon*, or clown, in Italian Commedia dell'arte and various black devils in medieval drama and vernacular performance. The actors playing these roles, however, usually wore black masks. The Queen and her court ladies did something different: they covered their faces and parts of their bodies in black grease, which had to be painstakingly washed off. It was, on one level, an act of rebellion. Indeed, here and elsewhere in their lives, these women were rebels "who resisted patriarchal standards of female decorum." There was Penelope Rich, the mistress of a prominent English publisher and mother of four illegitimate children; Lady Arabella Stuart, who was secretly married to a Lord, a transgression for which she was eventually sent to the Tower of London; one Lady who would go on to poison her husband; and another who in 1621 would be exiled from the court after publishing a romance novel. Queen Anne and the court ladies probably wanted to shock and disturb by commissioning and performing in a play as black nymphs. And what was probably most remembered by those who watched was not so much the satisfying plot celebrating British greatness but the pure and surprising spectacle of the country's leading ladies transformed, for a day, into Africans.[2]

Queen Anne's performance was unusual for its time. But it represented the beginning of a tradition of blackface performance that would slowly expand and root itself in English theater over the course of the sixteenth and early seventeenth centuries. On stage, white actors increasingly painted themselves black in order to depict African characters. Though the trope of "blackness" was applied to many groups—including Native Americans and the Irish—it ultimately coalesced around the "idea of African difference." It was both a reification and a reining in of that difference, an attempt to deal with the meaning of the cultural encounters that were part of England's increasing involvement in the slave trade. From the first, blackface was a concatenation of symbols, a combination of transgression and exoticism, of racism and desire to be someone else. Blackface performance was perpetually unruly, leaving audiences uneasy and destabilized. Despite that—or perhaps because of it—it became increasingly popular, even institutionalized, as part of the landscape of performance not only in England but throughout the Atlantic world.

Understanding the long and complex history of this form beyond the borders of the United States is critical to grasping how and why it became the most important theatrical form in nineteenth-century North America.[3]

It was during the late 1580s and 1590s that a few white actors in England began trying out the full-fledged "*impersonation* of black characters," particularly those from "the exotic and dangerous regions of sub-Saharan Africa." Playwrights found inspiration for such roles in travel narratives about Africa as well as through encounters with African slaves in London. There were also high-profile visitors, such as the ambassador of the Moroccan king Muly Hamet, who was sent to London to negotiate an alliance with Elizabeth I and was the subject of much fascination and commentary. The first such speaking character appeared in the *The Battle of Alcazar:* a violent and tragic "Negro Moor" who sees his blackness as a curse inherited from his mother. But it was Shakespeare's *Titus Andronicus* that, during the same period, most forcefully established a set of long-standing racial tropes. The character of Aaron is a villainous "Black Moor," who "was not black because he was evil, but evil because he was black." The character declares: "Aaron will have his soul black like his face." Aaron was performed by a white actor with a painted face: in the only contemporary sketch of a Shakespearean play, he is set apart both in his color and his body language. The character is an adulterer who has sex with a white woman, making him "the first in a long line of black male heroes (crafted by white authors) who flaunt their sexuality as a quality inherent in their blackness." The most legendary and influential example of this, of course, was the depiction of a "Moor" in Shakespeare's *Othello,* a play performed consistently for the ensuing centuries both in England and North America and eventually rewritten as part of the nineteenth-century U.S. blackface theater.[4]

By the early seventeenth century black figures in plays were often "bedtricksters," central players in romantic romps that involved people unsuspectingly getting in bed with people other than those they intended to. These comical intrigues about adultery and lust frequently depended on the additional charge of planned or unplanned white-black sexual encounters. As one stage direction put it, a key turning point would be "*A bed discovered with a Blackamoor in it."* The theater played with, though then usually dispelled, the specter of white men having sex with black women, bringing everyone back into the racial and marital fold. But these plays were an oblique way of dealing with a reality that was increasingly well-known, if somewhat repressed, in English culture: that in the Caribbean and North America, many white men were having sexual relations with their black female slaves, and children of mixed European and African ancestry were becoming a part of the colonial social world.[5]

At the end of the seventeenth century, Thomas Southern's hit play *Oronooko* offered a very different kind of blackface role. The work was based on Aphra Behn's 1688 novel, which told the story of an African king who was sold into slavery and ended up in Suriname. Southern's play was first performed in 1695, and both it and the novel were popular throughout the eighteenth century. The play was a romance, and *Oronooko* was depicted as a dignified and tragic figure. Along with ongoing performances of *Othello* and Edward Young's play *The Revenge,* whose main character is a villainous slave named Zanga, these works of theater anchored and popularized blackface performance as a mainstay of the English stage.[6]

Curiously, although wearing blackface could earn performers applause in the theater, it could get them thrown in jail if they did so off stage. Some outlaw groups in England used blackface to disguise themselves, notably a group of poachers called the "Waltham and Windsor Blacks," as part of protests against the enclosure of land by the upper class. In 1723 a law called the Black Act made it a capital crime to "black" one's face as a way of trying to stamp out such behavior. The act remained on the books into the nineteenth century. In both Europe and North America, throughout this period, popular street celebrations—part of a long-standing tradition of "charivari" in which social roles were reversed in public spaces—involved participants wearing blackface. In early nine-teenth- century New York and Philadelphia, for instance, callithumpian bands of young men wandered the streets around New Years, "often masked in chimney soot and grease" playing "drums, whistles, horns, pots, pans, and kettles, taunting both their social superiors and inferiors" by demanding money from passersby and residents, pelting "houses and persons with lime, flour, and other white powders" and getting in fights. The realm of the vernacular use of blackface shaped theatrical practice too: the idea that blackness represented a kind of subversion and rebellion—at times an attractive, raffish one—became a critical part of the popularity of blackface.[7]

During the eighteenth century, a few pioneers began to push the boundaries of blackface performance by presenting themselves as "authentic" interpreters of the culture of enslaved blacks in the Americas. These actors donned blackface but also claimed to channel and reproduce black ways of moving, speaking, and singing. The most prominent of these was Charles Dibdin, who first made a name for himself by playing the role of a black slave in the 1768 hit comic opera *The Padlock*. The opera was based on a story by Cervantes about an old miser who keeps his beautiful young bride locked up. The miser's guitar-playing slave, Luys, however, helps a young man sneak in to make love to the imprisoned wife. In *The Padlock* Luys became Mungo, a West Indian slave whose lines were written to reproduce the dialect and speech patterns of the Caribbean. English audiences loved Dibdin's interpretation of the role. They liked the idea that they were hearing black vernacular on the stage, and they absorbed what they heard and repeated lines outside the theater. "Mungo here, Mungo dere, / Mungo everwhere," Dibdin sang in one part of the play, and the phrase became a common saying for describing someone scurrying about. The role helped launch Dibdin's career as a solo performer and impresario whose songs celebrated English sailors and offered burlesques of Irishmen, Italians, and Jews. But it was his imitation of blacks that made him famous and successful. By 1796 he had done so well that he opened his own theater in London, calling it "Sans Souci."[8]

Dibdin drew on accounts of plantation life in the Caribbean and sought to portray aspects of the social and cultural life of the enslaved, including the conflicts between African-born and Creole slaves. And he was perhaps the first white performer to attempt to present black music on stage. In a composition from 1795 called "Kickaraboo," a rough equivalent of the modern phrase "kicking the bucket," Dibdin played the role of a slave reflecting on the death of another slave. He sang in what he presented as black dialect, accompanied by a hybrid instrument he had built "combining the properties of the pianoforte and the chamber organ," to which he added "a set of bells, a side drum, a tambourine, and a gong." There is a comic tinge to the song that makes the whole thing seem like a bit of a joke, but shards of something else come through in the confusion: a sense of the absence of a future and the idea that death erases racial difference: "Black and white be one colour a hundred years hence." The song looks forward to the day when the master finally dies and the enslaved can celebrate: they'll "dance and then sing and a banjer thrum thrum." Dibdin didn't himself play the instrument he invoked—the banjo—on stage. But in time some of those who followed in his footsteps would do just that.[9]

England's blackface theater crossed the Atlantic, and this style of performance thrived in North America as well. Between 1751 and 1843 there were approximately 5,000 performances in which whites blackened themselves to play various roles on stage. Urban audiences had plenty of such performances to choose from, sometimes more than one on the same evening, and they attended them in large numbers. Until the 1820s these were almost entirely plays, operas, or pantomimes brought from England. The most popular of all was *Othello,* first presented in 1751 in North America. *The Padlock* was first performed in 1769 and was also featured regularly on North American stages. Mungo was likely seen by most audiences as African-American, rather than West Indian, making him essentially the first fleshed-out black character in the history of North American performance. By the 1790s there were several new blackface plays being performed, including *The Happy African,* which featured Cubba, who assured the audience she was happy to be a slave. Some black characters, including a musician named Sambo in the play *Laugh When You Can,* pushed against racial stereotypes by being more moral than parodied white characters. All of these roles—from Mungo to Cubba and Sambo—were critical precursors of the various black characters who, in the early nineteenth century, would increasingly take over the stages of North America. Blackface was popular enough that one play, the 1777 *Polly,* starred a main character who paints himself black and becomes a pirate: "I diguis'd myself as a black," he explains, and so became "dead to all the world."[10]

Most histories of blackface performance focus on the English and North American stages. But there was also a thriving tradition of blackface performance in the Caribbean colony of French Saint-Domingue, which may have had an equal influence on the later development of blackface minstrelsy in North America. In 1758 a play called *Jeannot et Thérèse* premiered in the theater of Le Cap, the economic capital of the colony. The play's author, a well-known performer and director named Clément, took Rousseau's French blockbuster opera *Le Devin du Village* and transferred it to a Caribbean plantation. He referred to the resulting play as a "Negro-Dramati-Lyrique opus," and newspapers described it as a "Creole opera." It included dances described as "pas d'esclaves" ("slave dance steps") and "pas *nègres*" ("black dance steps"). Perhaps most strikingly, it was written entirely in the Creole language. This was not the kind of timid incorporation of "dialect" represented in a play like *The Padlock*. Someone who didn't really understand Creole couldn't follow the play. It was, in fact, one of the first attempts to create an orthography for the language, and the earliest existing literary work in Creole.[11]

Jeannot et Thérèse is a romantic comedy that focuses on the characters' jealous conflict and eventual reconciliation. In Rousseau's opera the main female character seeks out a "magician" in her village to get her errant lover back. In *Jeannot et Thérèse* the village becomes a plantation, complete with a "provision grounds" and a slave "hut" depicted on stage. And the "magician" becomes an African-born religious specialist named Papa Simon. Thérèse asks him for an *ouanga,* using a term from Vodou practice for an object that condenses spiritual power. When he offers it to her, Papa Simon sings a song that evokes his home in "Dahomé." Including such religious practices in the play was fairly bold: the play was first performed in 1758, the same year that the famous slave rebel Makandal, who terrorized whites with poison and was credited with having spiritual powers, was burned to death in the central plaza of Le Cap. But white planter audiences loved the play, and the character of Papa Simon seems to have been one of the central attractions of the work. Unlike the later plantation scenes in blackface minstrelsy, which were largely developed and performed in the urban centers of the North, far from actual plantations, *Jeannot et Thérèse* was written and performed at the epicenter of the plantation world in the eighteenth century. Planters got in the carriages on their plantations, driven by an enslaved driver, and headed into town to see a plantation not unlike their own depicted on stage.

Unlike eighteenth-century England and North America, Saint-Domingue had a few actors of African descent. A woman of color named Lise—the sister of well-known actress and singer Minette—once performed the role of Thérèse. Most of the actors, however, were white and performed these plays in blackface. An advertisement for a 1781 performance of *Jeannot et Thérèse* in Port-au-Prince explained that an "amateur" would perform the role of Papa Simon in the "real costume and color of the *nègre.*" In a 1785 advertisement for another local play, an actor playing the role of a black character was described as "being known for perfectly imitating the gestures and language of the *Nègres.*" And a 1788 advertisement for a different play by Clément provided perhaps one of the most striking definitions of the power and oddness of blackface performance. The whites on stage, it noted, would perform, *"a visage noir pour prêter d'avantage à l'illusion de se rapprocher du naturel"*—"in black face in order to add to the illusion of approaching the natural."[12]

The audiences in Saint-Domingue were quite diverse. There were wealthy planters and local authorities, along with sailors and soldiers based in the port towns. But there were also significant audiences of African descent. Though initially they had to struggle to get access to the theater, by the late eighteenth century they had access to significant reserved seating in all the many theaters in the colony. Though seating was segregated, socializing was not. Not only the hallways but the theater itself were often noisy with conversation, as "young people" spoke to the women of color sitting above in conversations that could "offend the ears, even those difficult to harm." During intermissions theatergoers mingled outside or at nearby cafés such as "chez Yoyo," run by Jean-Baptiste dit Yoyo, a black man who had come to the colony from France and advertised the special sauces and desserts he had learned to make in Paris. Some whites were not pleased, and in 1784 a performance was cancelled because of the bad behavior of "*nègres* sitting in the first boxes." In fact the audience likely included some paying urban slaves as well as domestics accompanying their masters. In New Orleans in 1809, just after the arrival of thousands of refugees from Saint-Domingue in the city, one local theater posted an announcement explaining that henceforth masters would have to buy tickets for their slaves, which suggests that prior to this most assumed they could just bring them along for free. People of African descent were more present in the theaters of Saint-Domingue than in most of North America. But the audiences for performances in cities like Philadelphia and New York were also quite diverse, with wealthier patrons in boxes, the orchestra occupied by regular paying customers, and the galleries offering the least-expensive seats and hosting poorer patrons, including African-Americans.[13]

The blackface performances of the late eighteenth century, whether in England or the Americas, were rich with contradiction. They were a way for audiences to grapple with, and sometimes also to deflect, the increasingly intense debates about the abolition of slavery. The Age of Revolution, and particularly the Haitian Revolution and the expanding fear of slave revolt, reshaped the representation of blacks on stage. It also created new patterns of cultural circulation. A mass migration from Saint-Domingue to Louisiana in the early nineteenth century doubled the population of New Orleans and profoundly reshaped the culture of the city. Part of what was carried was Clément's *Jeannot et Thérèse,* which was performed under the title *Papa Simon, ou Les Amours de Thérèse et Jeannot,* emphasizing its African-born character. Advertised as a "Vaudeville créole" it was part of a fund-raising performance, which suggests that it was considered a surefire attraction for audience members. Though this is just one small trace of possible transfer from the Caribbean, it is likely that the eighteenth-century theatrical culture of Saint-Domingue shaped nineteenth-century blackface performance in North America in unacknowledged ways. Where a play like *The Padlock* featured one black character, nearly all the characters in *Jeannot et Thérèse* were people of African descent. The advertisements and content of the play suggest that the attempt to incorporate the gestures, music, intonations, and language of the enslaved went quite a bit further than even in the work of someone like Charles Dibdin. The Saint-Domingue theatrical tradition was in many ways more similar to the early nineteenth-century minstrel tradition than any of the Anglo-American precedents.[14]

In the early 1800s a slave rebel took to the stage in England and North America, occupying it for decades. His name was Jack, and he was the main character in a work called *Obi, or Three-Fingered Jack.* It was based on the true story of a Jamaican slave who between 1779 and 1781 became a "bandit" threatening both whites and blacks. The story was first told at length in a 1799 book about Jamaica, *The Treatise on Sugar,* which was the inspiration for both novels and plays about the character, who become one of the mainstays of the Atlantic stage in the coming decades. Premiering in London in 1800 and in New York in 1801, the play was a curious object. At the height of the age of revolution, a few years after the 1791 slave insurrection in Saint-Domingue and soon after Gabriel's Revolt in Virginia, a play foregrounding a maroon played to packed houses of largely white audiences. That is partly because the plot evokes the specter of slave revolt but then rapidly tames it: the play makes no mention of established maroon communities, or of Haiti for that matter, and enslaved people (who are depicted as victims of Jack along with whites) delight when Jack is caught and killed. The play begins with happy slaves singing about how great their "Massa" is: "When Buckra be kind, then Negro heart Merry." Still, the character of Jack is foregrounded and, in a subterranean and infiltrating way, also celebrated. He never speaks. Instead, he pantomimes and sings. His actions often happen offstage and through sound: at one point, the stage directions say simply "A Noise by Jack is heard." In fact his name itself is uttered only in a whisper, accompanied by "hisses, gestures and poses." His presence onstage is itself almost supernatural and magical. He lives in an "Obi Woman's Cave" and appears and disappears, through paths in caverns and tunnels, with a kind of magical ability. His three fingers—two were cut off, according to the historical account of Jack's life, in a struggle with a Maroon who was trying to capture him—became a kind of trademark for the character, a mark of both mutilation and survival.[15]

Like Jack himself, the play ended up traveling and popping up everywhere, echoing the "bandit's dangerous mobility." It was performed on stages in England and North America for decades, in the midst of a culture that was fascinated with and terrified of black revolt. Jack was, in a sense, a proxy—he was Makandal, he was Gabriel, he was perhaps even Toussaint Louverture—a character who could be displayed, observed, even briefly admired, before being dispensed with and the slave order returned to its regularity. Oddly, reviewers and audiences seem to almost never have directly made a connection—at least not openly—to Haiti or to other revolts. But, in time, the play became a vehicle for African-American performers. It was performed in 1823 in New York City at William Brown's "African Theater," which was black-owned and catered to black audiences in the city. Later, in England, it was performed with the African-American actor Ira Aldridge in the lead role. Jack gained speaking parts, and the play carried a powerful abolitionist message, re-calling the terror of the slave raid that captured him in West Africa and calling for liberation and "due revenge."[16]

The play *Three-Fingered Jack* was perhaps most significant for the fact that it openly incorporated Caribbean vernacular performance into the plot. At the end of the first act, a scene called "Rejoicings of the Slaves" includes a character named Junkanoo, clearly drawn from the much-observed character popular in Jamaica and North America during Christmastime festivities. This represented a kind of breach, one already visible in the Creole-language performance culture of Saint-Domingue, in which the culture and characters of the street and plantation found themselves onstage. Through "vernacular infiltration," forms of public performance and theater visible on the streets and plantations of the Caribbean and North America became part of Anglo-American theater.[17]

But even in works like *Jeannot et Thérèse* and *Obi,* which made a gesture to performing black vernacular music, the instrumentation remained essentially that of European theater. That was the case even in Saint-Domingue, where many, indeed most, of the musicians playing in the theater were of African descent, including enslaved musicians. In the theater, they played scores rooted in French eighteenth-century theatrical music. The simulacra of black people were on stage, but there was relatively little attempt at imitating black music. In a way, blackface was still looking for its soundtrack. It would ultimately find it outside the theater—on the streets, along the wharves, and farther afield on the plantation itself. The great innovation to come in the early nineteenth century would be the bridging of the theatrical culture that included blackface performance with the vernacular musical cultures that existed outside the theater walls. That bridging was the work of a few performers who realized that absorption, appropriation, and impersonation could be the root of a new world of performance.

Music, after all, was everywhere. In Saint-Domingue, the white audiences could not have avoided the sounds of drums, and probably *banzas* in the world in which they lived. And many of those of African descent who enjoyed their time in the theater, including the musicians themselves, almost certainly participated in other cultures of performance in the streets or plantations of Saint-Domingue. There were occasional onslaughts and outbreaks of sound in Pinkster celebrations in the Northeast and Junkanoo celebrations and Kingston and North Carolina. But in fact, all year long, the ports and wharves of the Atlantic world also hummed with music, played in front of diverse audiences.

W. T. Lhamon Jr. has analyzed one remarkable trace of the ongoing encounters around music and dance: an engraving entitled "Dancing for Eels 1820 Catherine Market," on Long Island on the shore of the East River. The image centers on three black figures—a man dancing, another drumming, and a third clapping. To the side are three engaged white onlookers, leaning in and clearly wanting to join in. Behind them is a crowd of onlookers, white and black, taking in the dance. Behind the onlookers we can see the masts of flags of many ships, and beyond that—undrawn—the river and, further, the Atlantic. The engraving is a rare photograph of one moment among a multitude of such moments, of street performers who took advantage of the bustling crossroads of wharves to create styles of performance that drew diverse audiences together. Lhamon Jr. argues these were effectively already spaces of "street culture as theater," and indeed the dancer in the engraving is already performing on boards—of the pier—a short step away from the boards of a theater. In such spaces, where white and black gazes and practices, visions, and desires crossed regularly through a space of labor and trade, an Atlantic performance culture was cultivated.[18]

Using a series of striking portraits of musicians created by the painter William Sidney Mount in the early nineteenth century, Henry Christopher Smith similarly emphasized the importance of a performance culture rooted in practice in sites "along the Caribbean coasts, the U.S. Atlantic coast, and the U.S. inland waterways." "Tunes, dances, and other cultural memes," he notes, "traveled by water" to communities along the rivers and oceans. In these spaces developed, over the long term, "the creole sounds, practices, and procedures" that were ultimately brought to the stage. Over the decades, as new theatrical and musical forms developed, there was "extensive, day-to-day, creative interplay between the street performances and the stage performance." And part of what drew audiences to forms like minstrelsy was the "frisson," "the shock of recognition," felt by a working-class audiences seeing " 'their' performance idiom, the music and dance they knew from the streets, wharves, decks and canals" performed on stage.[19]

The interface between vernacular performance and the theater was taken up early on in a popular work of theater that emerged in the 1820s called *Tom and Jerry, or Life in London*. It rapidly crossed the Atlantic and became a staple in U.S. theaters, spawning imitations and adaptations—

Life in New York, Life in Philadelphia, Life in New Orleans. The original version is the story of three white upper-class men—with the delightful names Corinthian Tom, Jerry Hawthorn, and, best of all, Bob Logic—who go into town to do a little slumming. Tom and Hawthorn are "rakes" from a country estate, and Logic is their sidekick and guide. He brings them to a dive called "All-Max," whose name is a play on the upper-crust social club "Almack's." In the bar, a duo called African Sal and Dusty Bob perform a blackface number, described in one 1823 advertisement as a "Pas de Deux by African Sal and Dusty Bob." The upper-class visitors demand a "double shuffle" from the two performers. In one particularly layered moment, Bob Logic asks the fiddler to play a "danceable" tune, urging him on with some "gin and snuff." To encourage him, he walks over and "begrimes his face." On stage, Logic applies blackface to a white actor already in blackface. Theatergoers who attended the play were invited in a sense to watch themselves both enjoying and laughing at their own fascination with vernacular culture while getting to see that vernacular culture performed through a series of comforting mediations.[20]

Tom and Jerry openly sought to incorporate vernacular street music into theater. In one of the early scenes, the three protagonists enter a "Beggar's Hall" where a banquet populated with "low characters" is underway. One of these is a fiddler named Billy Walters. The character was based on a real musician: a black busker Billy Walters who in the late eighteenth century frequently played for small change outside London's Adelphi Theater. Walters was a sailor who had fought during the American Revolution then made his way to London, where he began to play the Strand for the tips of theatergoers. Some of those watching *Tom and Jerry* in England perhaps remembered the real Walters. And though the musician was dead by the time the play premiered, one white actor who filled the role in the play delighted at the news that some actually thought it was Walters himself performing on stage.[21]

In 1837 a version of *Tom and Jerry* was performed in New Orleans, and it went a step further by actually featuring a live black musician on the stage. His name was Corn Meal, and he had made his reputation as a vendor who sang as he drove his cart, selling cornmeal, through the streets of the city. In time he developed an extensive repertoire, performing in front of large crowds in the public spaces of the city. A visiting English diplomat in New Orleans, Francis Sheridan, who heard

Corn Meal sing in 1840, was enraptured by his remarkable vocal range: "He sings in a manner as perfectly novel as it is inimitable, beginning in a deep bass & at every other 3 or 4 words of his song, jumping into a falsetto of power." One admiring reviewer of one of Corn Meal's performances effused about the "great compass of voice." Others found it easier to describe him as having several "voices" rather than just one. His repertoire included his signature song, "Fresh Corn Meal," the well-known song "Rosin' in the Bow," and his own take on the "Star-Spangled Banner." There were clearly other types of songs as well: a few of his topics were deemed unsuitable to reprint in the newspaper.[22]

With *Life in New Orleans,* Corn Meal got an opportunity that other African-American musicians before him, and even of his generation, rarely if ever got: to perform on a major stage in a major North American city. That this happened in New Orleans was no accident: the city's social makeup and performance culture created an opening that did not exist in other settings. Nevertheless, the limits around Corn Meal's performance were clear: he remained essentially a cherished and celebrated curiosity, contained within a particular kind of role. He appeared on stage with his cart and horse to remind audiences of his true status. In a microcosm of minstrelsy writ large, the event harnessed the popularity of a vernacular street performer in order to bring paying customers into the theater. But the performance was such a success the first night that a second one was organized, and the potential audience reassured by the newspaper that "the celebrated Corn Meal will come out with a new effusion of his comic Extravaganzas." The reviews were largely positive. When some time elapsed between his performances, writers worried: "Where is old Corn Meal? . . . We miss the music of his Ethiopian melodies." He kept performing on stage until his death in 1842, and "fame outran his actual range," with his obituary appearing in New England newspapers.[23]

We don't know what Corn Meal was paid for these performances, though he himself did pay a price: on the second night of his debut in 1837, his horse—spooked by the odd circumstances—fell off the stage and was killed. It was, ultimately, others who profited most from his music, which a series of later performers drew on and adapted for the stage. Corn Meal appears in an early history of minstrelsy only as someone who "furnished" one early minstrel performer with "many airs," which the white performer "turned to account." Corn Meal himself had not been able to turn his talents "to account" for many reasons. Outside New Orleans he would likely not have been allowed on stage at all. Even within the city, his access to the capital and institutions that would have perhaps allowed him to take further control of his work, to create a troop and go on tour for instance, was simply not there. And so, while he was lauded in the New Orleans press of the time, his place in the broader history of American music is that of a curious, local talent whose work required appropriation by others to truly take flight.[24]

Corn Meal's brief sojourn on the New Orleans stage is a ghostly reminder of what might have been: a tradition of African-American performance brought to the stage by African-American performers. That, however, is not what happened. Instead, the racial order of the country ultimately produced a remarkable and curious configuration: one in which white performers, tapping into the long tradition of blackface theater, created an extremely popular genre of music and dance entirely based on a bold attempt to be black and white at the same time. Blackface was reassuring in that it kept the stage as a space for white actors only. But it was troubling, since it made clear that the stage was ultimately made to be a place for black music and dance. In order for this strange balancing act to work, it needed a particular kind of sound, and a symbol. It found it in the banjo.

> About some twenty years ago
> Old Butler reigned with his old Banjo,
>   Ah, ah,
> Twas a gourd, three-string'd, and an old pine stick,
> But when he hit it he made it speak.
> Ah, ah.
> Picayune Butler's comin, comin . . .

Decades after he performed in the streets and on the stages of New Orleans, Picayune Butler was still famous and his memory kept alive. A popular song about him was published in the 1858 *Phil Rice's Method for the Banjo: With or Without a Master,* whose goal was to allow the aspiring banjo player to learn even if there was no "master" musician to be found to teach him. It is fitting that Butler would, within its pages, get his due: for he and other musicians like him were the often-forgotten founders of the tradition of minstrelsy that became America's most important popular and influential form of entertainment in the mid-nineteenth century. The song about Butler had a long and flourishing career: it became a campaign song for a political campaign; inspired a series of white men, including Civil War generals and later musicians, to take on Picayune Butler as a nickname; and was featured in the first minstrel performance in Japan in 1854. In the 1850s, a white banjo player sought to channel the legacy of the song and the musician by taking on the same stage name and debuting a new Picayune Butler.[25]

Beyond the song, we know almost nothing about Butler. But his evanescent presence in the written history of the banjo and of minstrelsy highlights the critical place New Orleans plays in this story. The city had a unique cultural cartography at the crossroads of North America, the Gulf Coast, and the Caribbean; and it was there that some of the critical encounters and collusions that lay the foundations for minstrelsy took place. The 1858 song hinted at the ways his spirit hovers over American history.

> Picayune Butler gwine to rise,
> And meet his friends up in de skies
> Some thing else am mighty true
> De Banjo gwine to be dar too,
> Ah, ah.
>   . . .
> Now ladies all I'll hab you know,
> Dar is no music like de old Banjo
> Ah, ah,
> And when you want to hear it ring,
> Just watch dese fingers on de string.[26]

Music in New Orleans was shaped and sustained by the cultural world of the surrounding Louisiana plantations. Théodore Pavie, who traveled to the territory from France, described seeing a dance on a plantation, part of the "second, nocturnal life" the slaves had after a long day of working in the fields. "When everything was ready for the dance," Pavie wrote, "one of them tuned a rude guitar, mounted on a calabash with

cat gut, and began warming up as if he was playing a Moorish mandolin."
Another turned over a copper tub and drummed a beat. Then, "with the
signal of the guitar player," the dance began. "The songs varied according
to the inspiration of the musicians." They included "melancholy songs
upon which African slaves like to sigh for liberty," and when "the young
négresses" repeated the words, a "monotone murmur" rose up from the
circle of elders, accompanying "this sad and plaintive melody from another hemisphere." "'Dance the dance of the Congos for me!,' ordered
the overseer as he approached the group of slaves, who were resting for
an instant, and they obeyed": "Three elderly *nègres* tuned their *banjas*,"
and others took up their drums. The dance, wrote Pavie, was made up
of moves that were "almost military," and the men threw themselves into
it. Pavie's account seems to suggest a distinction between two such instruments, the first a "rude guitar" made of a calabash, and the second
the "banja," taken out specifically for the "Congo dance" demanded by
the white overseer. If these were indeed distinct instruments, then this
suggests that there may have been a range of construction styles in use at
the time, including differences in how necks were built and in how many
strings the instruments had.[27]

Within New Orleans, the banjo continued to sound in Congo Square.
Like Latrobe, later visitors to New Orleans often made a trip to see the
increasingly well-known space of gathering. Visiting New Orleans in the
early 1830s, the self-styled "Yankee" Joseph Holt Ingraham described
seeing a particular instrument there: "Congo *banjo*." Three decades later,
another visitor described seeing banjos there: "Groups of fifties and
hundreds may be seen in different sections of the square, with banjos,
tom-toms, violins, jawbones, triangles, and various other instruments
from which harsh or dulcet sounds may be extracted." Dancers dressed
with "fringes, ribbons, little bells, and shells and balls," their "jingling
and flirting" adding to the music. When dancers grew tired, they sank
"down gracefully on the grass," were fanned, and were offered a drink,
while others jumped up to take their places.[28]

These varied musical and performance traditions found a home in
the thriving Mardi Gras tradition, the result of the "collision, coordina-
tion, and precipitation" of various cultural elements present in Louisiana,
including plantation festivities (like those of Junkanoo), African practices
among the enslaved, the influence of Caribbean traditions, the impact of

Anglo-American practices, and finally the pressures of the commercialization and theatricalization of leisure. These came together in late eighteenth- and early nineteenth-century New Orleans, condensing and institutionalizing an array of cultural practices that were at once African and European, American and Afro-Atlantic, and deeply Creole in all the senses of the word.[29]

We get a different perspective on what the banjo might have meant in Louisiana from a Creole song first published by George Washington Cable in *Century Magazine* in 1886 and later arranged by folklorist Maud Cuney-Hare, who explained that it had been sung "on a plantation in St. Charles Parish." She called it "Gardé Piti Mulet Là"—"Look at That Little Mulatto"—adding a subtitle "Musieu Bainjo," or "Mister Banjo." Though there are texts of a few different versions of the song, they all use the banjo as a way of offering a satirical portrait of a man who is "insolent" or puts on a "saucy air." In a Creole version published in 1887, the song calls out "Gardé piti milate, ti banjo! Badine dan lamain, ti banjo! Chapo en ho côté, ti banjo"—"Look at that little mulatto, little banjo! A cane in his hand, little banjo! His hat cocked to the side, little banjo!" His boots, the song goes on, are so new they go "crin-crin." The 1921 version offered by Cuney-Hare is similar, making fun of a man with a "saucy air," with his hat "cock'd o one side," shoes so new they go "cric-crac" as he walks, a "kerchief in his vest," and a cane in his hand. Though it was collected in the 1880s, it is difficult to know how old the song was by then. If it was composed in the latter half of the nineteenth century, it probably registers a moment when the banjo had become enough of an urban phenomenon, and a symbol of aspiring to a higher social status, that it could allow for rural people to make fun of the citified dandy. Whatever its moment of origin, however, it offers another marker of the way the instrument was evoked and deployed in Louisiana song.[30]

It was out of this sonic landscape of New Orleans and its surroundings that Picayune Butler emerged as a tentative pioneer who bridged the vernacular culture and sound of the streets and plazas with the more confined space of the theater. His imprint in the archive is light: there are two fragments of written information about Butler. The first is a critical review published in the 1830 *Louisiana Advertiser* about a performer who had appeared on stage. The critic, hoping that the performer would not appear again to perform "Juba," recommended that if he did: "we would recommend him to borrow old Butler's banjow, as an admirable accompaniment." The reference must have been to Picayune Butler, which suggests that New Orleans readers would have been familiar with his playing. That could have been simply from having seen him play on the street, although there is also a chance that Butler had appeared on stage at some point—which would make him probably the first performer in North America to bring the instrument onto the stage. Decades later, a writer named T. Allston Brown gave Picayune Butler a small place in his tale of "The Origins of Minstrelsy." According to Brown, it was Picayune Butler who inspired an early white minstrel named George Nichols to develop his act, centered on a character known as "Jim Crow." "Nichols first sang 'Jim Crow' as a clown," Brown writes, "afterwards as a negro. He first conceived the idea from a French darkie, a banjo player, known from New Orleans to Cincinnati as Picayune Butler—a copper-colored gentleman, who gathered many a picayune by singing 'Picayune Butler is Going Away,' accompanying himself on his four-stringed banjo."[31]

Butler seems to have influenced another early performer, one who ultimately had much more of an impact than Nichols. His name was Thomas Dartmouth Rice, and he brilliantly and enduringly understood that the African-American vernacular culture he saw around him could be effectively translated, codified, and turned to theatrical practice—and profit. Drawing on these Atlantic forms of performance, he created a new form of blackface performance in the 1820s, centered around the character of Jim Crow. In time the stage character became so popular and central in U.S. culture that it became the name of the system of southern segregation. The character's name came from a song Rice had heard played by African-American performers, notably Picayune Butler. Rice explicitly indicated his debt to the New Orleans banjo player in his first recorded performance of the figure of Jim Crow in 1830. One of the songs he performed was "Jim Crow's Trip to New Orleans," with words by Picayune Butler. His entire performance career was based on his claim that he was successfully copying black gesture and dance, channeling deeply rooted forms of vernacular performance in crafting a new form of theater. His appearance in blackface was at once a signal of his authenticity and an act of self-transformation.[32]

For two decades starting in the 1830s, Rice became the most popular actor of his time, traveling throughout the United States and Britain, by "blacking up and imitating black men." By the 1840s he was the highest-paid actor in both Europe and America. Rice has long perplexed historians: some have considered him an "anomaly" who should be ignored, while others have felt that the only appropriate approach is to condemn him for having appropriated black performance in enabling a long tradition of racist caricature. But his cultural imprint was undeniably profound, for he managed to bridge two styles of performance: vernacular and high culture. He was a crucial pioneer in the enduring history of American's cultural industries, which have thrived by bringing the performance styles of the ports and streets to the stage, often to great profit. What Rice did in the 1830s has "recurred in cycles ever since." "Imitating perceived blackness," writes W. T. Lhamon Jr., "is arguably the central metaphor for what it is to be American."[33]

White actors and audiences were drawn to performing blackness in part because they were experiencing shattering economic and social upheaval, as changes in trade, transportation, and industry disrupted and disentangled communities. Many poorer urban whites were experiencing forms of marginalization and dislocation that blacks had long experienced in a much deeper and wider scale. Immigrants from different European cultures were thrown together in extremely diverse neighborhoods, trying to make do in the midst of a confusion of cultures and languages. In "black" identities, which had been built precisely to bridge and bring together a diversity of West and Central African cultural forms, they found a preexisting map for navigating their own confusing and shifting landscape. The diverse strategies developed over centuries in the spaces of the Afro-Atlantic world were "good guides" for whites buffeted by the changes of the nineteenth century.[34]

Jim Crow would have a curious life, winding his way from sites of vernacular performance to the stage, thanks to Rice. From there, he would build a life as an endlessly repeated theatrical icon; and his name would be adopted to refer to a post-emancipation legal system that was aimed in part to prevent the very currents of transmission, sharing, and influence that had been embodied in his figure in the first place. Rice's Jim Crow character was in fact exceedingly complex and not easily summarized as a pure racial stereotype. He represented the opposite of what the term signifies today, in that the character emphasized the deep and unstoppable mixing of African-American and European-American culture and potential alliances between poorer blacks and whites. He was a symbol of the potential of "demotic brotherhood" between these groups. The lower-class urban audiences who made up much of Rice's audience lived in far less segregated spaces than did elites, many of whom sharply criticized his performances. Through Rice's plays, Jim Crow came to wander not just across regions but "across oceans," passing from "commoner to royalty and back again," a troubling figure of "African royalty in rags." "Dressed like a ragamuffin, Jim Crow behaved like a sovereign." He and other black characters took center stage, where they pursued and achieved their own ends by their own means and won support for doing so from the audiences that thronged to see such performances.[35]

At the core of the Jim Crow repertoire was a song, endlessly adaptable, called "Jump Jim Crow," for which Rice wrote hundreds of verses. The chorus was simple: "I wheel about an'turn about / And do jis' so / And ebry time I wheel about, / I jump Jim Crow." In a version published in 1832, some of the verses were frankly political, and oppositional. One verse invoked the possibility that conflict between whites might create an opportunity for blacks: "Should dey get to fighting / Perhaps de blacks will rise, / For deir wish for freedom, / Is shining in deir eyes." Another announced: "I'm for freedom, / An for Union altogether, / Aldough I'm a black man, / De white is call'd my broder." Such lines could be heard as farce or provocation. But they could also transmit antislavery sentiment. In a play performed by Rice in the late 1830s called *Flight to America,* Jim Crow escapes slavery on a Virginia plantation and makes his way to New York, where—before catching a boat to England—he gives a speech celebrating freedom. The last scene of the play has Jim Crow and other characters dancing to celebrate onrushing freedom: "Strike de bango dance and play / Freedom reigns o'er the plains / Bobolition for de nigger / Beat big drum, tamborine thrum / On dis happy day."[36]

Rice's transgressive politics were most clearly on display in his rewriting of *Othello,* performed for the first time in 1844. By this time, *Othello* was often cited by elites as confirmation of the dangers of interracial relationships. John Quincy Adams wrote in 1833 with disgust of Desdemona's "unnatural passion" for a "sooty-bosomed" and "thick-lipped wool-headed Moor." The marriage of the two was the "cause of all the tragic incidents in the play." Rice titled his riposte and rejection of this vision "Otello: Burlesque Opera." There had already been other reworkings of Shakespeare's play, including an 1833 version in which Othello came from Haiti. Rice took this a step further: his Otello was a runaway from a southern plantation who had settled in New York's notorious Five Points district. Rice transforms the tragic impossibility of the interracial relationship offered by Shakespeare into full conceivable romantic reality. In his version, Otello and Desdemona get together. Not only that, they have a child who is presented with a face painted white on one side and black on the other, to the acclamation of the chorus and the audience. The stage direction commanded the "whole house" to dance together to celebrate at the final applause.[37]

Rice's career left behind an unending and unmovable cultural complex that remains with us to this day. It was, however, largely constructed around him as a star performer who condensed all the impossible collusions embodied in the Jim Crow figure. Even as he was performing his provocative *Otello* in New York City, another movement was afoot, seeking to build on his success. A new group of performers would take what he had built and appropriate it to create a new form of theater and music. They would do so by bringing to the stage an instrument that embodied history and its contradictions as richly as Jim Crow did: the banjo. Building on the performance tradition of musicians like Titus and Picayune Butler, these pioneers put the banjo front and center and turned it from an unusual instrument into a necessary mainstay of cultural performance in America. They did so not in New Orleans, or elsewhere in the South, but in the heart of New York City. It was in the Bowery that the banjo finally met blackface.

The instrument came to the stage in the hands of the Virginian Joel Walker Sweeney. In 1839, after years of performing around his home in Virginia, he traveled farther afield and joined a circus in Charleston, South Carolina, in February of that year, appearing in a T. D. Rice production. The circus traveled north, carrying Sweeney to New York in April 1839. The city was a gathering place for musicians: it was where summer traveling circuses assembled before heading out and also where traveling troupes wintered. A lot of talent was gathered there much of the year, and it served as an incubator for many minstrel groups. Despite the competition, Sweeney arrived and quickly got a gig at the Old Italian Opera House near Broadway, playing banjo in between acts by "plate spinners, polka dancers," and "magicians." He caught the eye and ear of audiences, and one reviewer from *The New York Herald* wrote that the "great feature" of Sweeney's act was his "playing upon the 'banjo' which is exceedingly well done and gave general satisfaction." He joined forces with a white dancer from New York named John Diamond, who was advertised as "the Prince of the Darkies!" He was confident enough in his growing reputation that he turned down an offer from P. T. Barnum for a two-week gig in Philadelphia, preferring to stay in New York and hone his solo act. But in the spring of 1840, Sweeney set out with Broadway Circus on a tour of New England, "banjoizing" as one newspaper put it.[38]

"Early minstrelsy's music (or, its noise)," writes Dale Cockrell, "jangled the nervous system of those who believed in music that was proper, respectable, polished, and harmonic, with recognizable melodies." But the banjo seemed a little scary even for the minstrels, at least at first. In the mid-1830s, one performer offered a song called "the Louisiana Banjou Style," but performed it on a violin, which he played in "the true banjo style." One 1840 playbill warned audiences that if they came to the show they would hear "dat terror to all Pianos, Harps, and Organs, de BANJO." Underlying the concern, of course, was the clear understanding that this was an African-American instrument, straight from the plantation.[39]

Promoters of minstrel music quickly sought to domesticate the banjo and reassure their audiences that the instrument was not *too* wild. By 1841 advertisements for Sweeney's concerts celebrated the "scientific touches" of his banjo playing and presented him as the instrument's redeemer: only those who heard him play would truly "know what music there is in a banjo." His playing inspired an effusive praise poem—"magic music thrills those cords of thine / Thou master of the Banjo-string"—and compared it favorably to "Orpheus' famed lyre" and the music of Paganini. "More witching sweetness and melodious fire / Breathes softly from thy Banjo-string."[40]

Sweeney, like many a successful musician, was a great self-promoter and claimed for himself the honor of having improved the banjo by adding a fifth string to it. This has led to long-running confusion regarding the extent of Sweeney's influence on the construction of the instrument: some have gone so far as calling him the "inventor" of the banjo. Sweeney had in no way invented the instrument, of course, and he also did not—as some believed—add the short drone string on top of the banjo, which was also present from its earliest iterations in the Caribbean and North America. By the time he was eighteen, still playing in Virginia, he had however added a lower bass string to the instrument, just above the short string, making a five-stringed banjo. Whether he had come up with this himself or had gotten the idea from somewhere else is hard to say. But he definitely popularized the new construction. The five-string banjo offered a larger melodic range to the instrument and therefore opened new possibilities for different kinds of chords and songs. It became the standard during the nineteenth century.[41]

Sweeney's riveting performances helped transform the banjo from a relative stranger and anomaly on the stage to a near-necessity. Over the next few years, a new style of performance was codified by minstrel acts. What had before been made up of a series of diverse musical and theatrical acts now morphed into a concert-like presentation by an ensemble band with the banjo at its literal center. The major authors of that transformation were the Virginia Minstrels, who came together in New York in 1843. At the core of the ensemble was a man named Dan Emmett, who came from Mount Vernon, Ohio. After a stint in the army, Emmett joined a circus and in 1838 authored what he later described as his "first negro song," about a black man named Bill Crowder who disembarks in Cincinnati. The song was a hybrid, drawing on the example of the already popular Jim Crow and Gumbo Chaff characters for Bill Crowder but incorporating a stereotypical Jewish stock character more common in English theater.[42]

Emmett's foray into songwriting inspired him to learn to play the banjo. While his group was in the western part of Virginia in the spring of 1840, they came across a banjo player named Archibald Ferguson, who as Emmett later put it, "was very ignorant and 'nigger all over' except in color." Emmett, taken by his playing, pushed the circus to hire him. Ferguson accepted a salary of ten dollars a month and was told to "jump on the wagon." He turned out to be "the greatest card we ever had," drawing crowds and becoming the "talk of the town" wherever the circus landed. Emmett set about learning the banjo from Ferguson. Once he got good he returned the favor, in classic showbiz fashion, by replacing the West Virginia man. He then teamed up with an established blackface performer

named Frank Brower, who was from Baltimore. Brower had helped pioneer the use of bones to add percussion to minstrel performances. In their
performances, Emmett and Brower brought together banjo and bones, a
combination that would become central to minstrelsy.[43]

Emmet and Brower brought their act to New York City in the fall
of 1842, where they teamed up with a third performer, a dancer. The
Midwesterner Emmett was praised in *The New York Herald* as "the great
Southern Banjo Melodist," while the Baltimorean Brower became "the
perfect representation of the Southern Negro characters." Emmett
appeared for a week at a Bowery theater offering "an exhibition" of
"enlivening Banjo melodies and Negro dances," including one called
"Ethiopian Serenade." In January of 1843 he performed with Brower
in a performance called "Negro Holiday Sports in Carolina and Virginia."
Though neither of them was a southerner, they understood that this was
what they needed to become and that the best way to do that was to
become black. Both had probably performed in blackface during their
circus days, but New York gave them an opportunity to bring this together with the sound of their music in a new way.[44]

In New York Emmett and Brower got to know another banjo player
and singer named William Whitlock. Traveling in 1837 or 1838 through
the South as part of a circus company, Whitlock had met Joel Sweeney
in Virginia and took a few banjo lessons from him. He later claimed he'd
also learned from watching Virginia slaves play: "Every night during his
journey south, when he was not playing, he would quietly steal off to
some negro hut to hear the darkeys sing and see them dance, taking with
him a jug of whiskey to make them all the merrier." Whitlock impressed
audiences with his banjo playing: an 1842 review described him as "quite
equal if not superior to Sweeney." P. T. Barnum was so impressed that
he offered to manage him, and Whitlock was soon performing regularly
in New York, where he was known for his dancing as well as his skillful
banjo playing, described in one newspaper article as "combustious." In
one of his standard routines, Whitlock played the role of "Sambo Squash,"
who played the banjo in the hopes of seducing "Dear Fanny."[45]

One night Whitlock and Brower were hanging out at the Bowery
boarding house where Emmett was staying. "The banjo, bones, violin
and tambourine, lying around loose, as if by accident, each one picked
up his tools and joined in a chorus of 'Old Dan Tucker,' while Emmett

was playing and singing. It went well, and they repeated it without saying a word. Each did his best, and such a rattling of the principal and original instruments in a minstrel band was never heard before." Another musician, Pelham, stopped by and joined in with the tambourine. "Charmed to the soul" by the music, buoyed and enthused about how well they fell in together, they sauntered to a nearby Bowery theater—probably a little drunk—and, "without a ghost of the idea of what was to follow," demanded a gig from the owner. They calculated that "he would succumb in preference to standing the horrible noise" they were making as they played together. They played their first engagement later that evening in the nearby hotel and soon after at the Bowery Theater.[46]

One of their first performances was prophetically advertised as a moment of transformation. "First Night of the novel, grotesque, original and surprisingly melodious Ethiopian band, entitled Virginia Minstrels, being an exclusively musical entertainment combining the banjo, violin, bone castanets, and tambourine, and entirely exempt from the vulgarities and other objectionable features which have hitherto characterized the negro extravaganzas." Their performance was presented as "musical entertainment" and also as a kind of elevation over prior blackface entertainment, more "melodious" and structured. They offered scenes, such as "Dan Tucker on Horseback," as well as comic interludes, but it was music that structured the evening. The program of an "Ethiopian Concert" performed in Boston in March 1843 was essentially a list of songs—interrupted by "A Negro Lecture on Locomotives," a story told by Whitlock. The songs included "Uncle Gabriel" and concluded with one called "Fine Old Colored Gemman," billed as "a Parody, written by Old Dan Emmet, who will, on this occasion, accompany himself on the BANJO, in a manner that will make all guitar players turn pale with delight." The group quickly released sheet music, including an 1843 collection of "Original Banjo Melodies." The cover shows several black figures dancing and singing, and three of them are carrying banjo. The instrument seems to be in danger: a large goat, head-butting a tree, has his tail wrapped around one of them, while an alligator is trying to chomp down on the body of his banjo.[47]

What exactly was this invitation into a world full of banjos? The use of the term "minstrel" in the name was itself an interesting signal of what was afoot. Before then, some troupes calling themselves "minstrels" had performed in the United States, but these were European singing groups—and their imitators—such as the Tyrolese Minstrels and the German Minstrels who catered to white, middle-class audiences. What the Virginian Minstrels sought to do was to take a medium that had been crafted for rowdy, popular theaters—blackface performance—and give it the cast of something that could be performed in a concert hall. Using the name "minstrel" was a way of doing that. It was on one level a kind of burlesque, making fun of the more respectable genre. But it also signaled "the possibility of accommodation."[48]

Having created this "novel ensemble," the musicians rapidly "turned an experiment into a new medium—the jazz band of the nineteenth century." At its center was Whitlock, who "played his banjo with complete abandon, roughly striking the strings with the nail of his forefinger." All the early minstrels used this same style—what is known today as "frailing" or "clawhammer," striking the strings downward and rhythmically with the backs of the fingers. The Virginia Minstrels announced on their playbills that their "instruments were manufactured by themselves." These banjos had a "mellower, fuller, more resonant sound" than the more bright and metallic one we imagine today, and their gut strings were tuned lower than the modern tuning.[49]

Whitlock called his instrument a "Congo banjo." It had a "long, thin neck" and—unlike Sweeney's banjo—only four strings. He didn't play chords. Instead, the banjo drove the melody for the songs, forming the key accompaniment to the singing, the lead instrument of the ensemble. It also varied the main melody by "inserting into it the open tones of his two highest strings." The motion of the song was "intensified by omitting tones on accented beats," creating a syncopated sound. Sometimes Whitlock added a beat by tapping or stomping his foot on the ground. The show consisted of songs played by the ensemble, bringing together the banjo with other instruments to create a sound that was "scratchy, tinkling, cackling, and humorously incongruous." In between were interludes played on just banjo and bones, like those Emmett and Ferguson had developed in their days in the circus. Whitlock also performed banjo solos, which delighted the audiences. The troupe developed fantastical characters that allowed them to showcase the banjo as well. Dan Emmett frequently performed a song called "The Fine Old Color Gentleman," which depicted a "Tennessee Negro Sambo" from the backwoods, who was eleven feet tall, able to swallow "two small railroads wid a spoonful of ice cream," and constantly playing the banjo and singing—"He sung so long and sung so loud, he scared the pigs and goats."[50]

The first complete minstrel shows by the Virginia Minstrels, as performed in 1843, were an instant hit, quickly inspiring many imitators and "initiating what was to be the most popular of popular entertainments for the next forty years or more." Immediately other bands formed with a similar structure, instrumentation, and approach. They all consisted of white musicians who performed in blackface. One of the most influential subsequent minstrel troops was the Christy Minstrels, led by E. P. Christy. He had been inspired by music he heard in New Orleans as a young man. He managed a ropewalk where the performers were slaves, and became fascinated with their singing. He regularly visited Congo Square and listened to the music there, studying their "queer words and simple but expressive melodies." In Buffalo in the 1830s he began performing as a blackface entertainer, drawing on the singing styles of a man named Harrison, who sang in a local African-American church and whom he visited frequently. He founded the Christy Minstrels in the early 1840s and later claimed he—and not the Virginia Minstrels—had actually invented the form. He went so far as to get his claim to that effect endorsed by the New York Supreme Court. Though historians have ultimately sided with the Virginian Minstrels, it is clear that the Christy Minstrels played a central role in codifying the minstrel form by the mid-1840s. On stage Christy had a man with a tambourine on one side and another playing the bones on the other end, creating two "endmen" who were often referred to as "Tambo and Bones." They created a semicircle in which other musicians sat. At the center was "the Interlocutor," who served as master of ceremonies and often played the banjo. The Christy Minstrels garnered large and enthusiastic audiences in North America and beyond—E. P. Christy had done 2700 performances by the time he retired in 1856, though the company continued on without him after that.[51]

The minstrels built on the earlier acts of figures like T. D. Rice. Like him, these white musicians performed in blackface and developed various black stage characters. But they also offered something different and more structured than Rice's earlier performances, centered around the music. It was not so much "musical theater" as "theatrical music." The printed programs looked "like concert programs." At least twenty-nine different troupes performed in the United States between 1843 and 1847. Though the instrumentation varied, the troupes always had a banjo—which was "at the heart" of the ensembles. Some troupes even had two banjo players. All the minstrels had a tambourine player to accompany the banjo, and most had bones and fiddle players. Some had other kinds of percussion, as well as instruments like accordions or flutes.[52]

The meeting of the banjo and blackface was an epochal moment in the history of American and, indeed, global popular culture. By deploying the banjo on stage, the minstrels concretized the idea that they were channeling plantation music, serving as conduits and translators of the music of the enslaved. The instrument's sound and symbolism provided the perfect combination of sonic presence and romanticism, of content and form. And the minstrel show, in turn, brought and codified different strands of the banjo's history.

The banjo had been developed as a versatile instrument that could bring together diverse audiences; and for at least a hundred and fifty years, it had been creating solidarity through its sound within communities of the enslaved. But by the 1830s the banjo was also increasingly present in various kinds of literary texts as a symbol of plantation life, as a key prop in debates over the question of whether slaves were happy or not. It was, ultimately, in the meeting between these two realms—the symbolic and discursive construction of the instrument as a symbol of slave life, and its actual resonance as a source of music played by the enslaved—that the powerful and popular practice of blackface minstrelsy emerged. Minstrelsy depended on the social and symbolic meanings already carried by the banjo, but it also put them to new uses by bringing together a deeply rooted Afro-American performance tradition with an urgent need on the part of audiences to both confront and set aside the terrors of slavery itself. The form absorbed slavery and the forms of music it had produced and became, for a time, perhaps the most widespread and important way Americans thought about and experienced the central political and social question of their day. Minstrelsy became by far the most popular and profitable form of entertainment in nineteenth-century North America, spurring the construction of theaters along the frontier, and ultimately had a global reach stretching to Europe, Latin America, South Africa, and beyond.[53]

By the 1850s, thanks to the minstrel show, the banjo had become a deeply familiar sound on the American stage. In New Orleans the composer Louis Moreau Gottschalk, the son of two immigrants to the city, a father from England and a mother from Haiti, wrote a piano composition in honor of the banjo. The piece was part of a series in which Gottschalk sought to draw inspiration from Afro-American and Afro-Caribbean culture, which he had observed in New Orleans, notably at Congo Square. The direct inspiration for his piece is still a mystery, though one scholar has argued that Gottschalk most likely was attempting to capture the banjo playing of an African-American musician from New Orleans, making his composition "the most complete document we have of the nineteenth-century African-American banjo tradition." Called "The Banjo, Grotesque Fantasy" and subtitled "An American Sketch," the composition is an attempt to make a piano sound like a banjo, capturing a kind of sound that would have been made on the instrument through a skillful combination of percussive downstroke and picking. The enthusiastic and energetic flow of his composition "The Banjo" made it one of Gottschalk's best-loved compositions, one that influenced European composers, including Debussy. The illustration for the sheet music itself suggested powerfully the extent to which the banjo had taken over: there were banjos here and banjos there, enough to spell out the word banjo itself. And now, Gottschalk's composition suggested, it was other instruments that had to learn the music of this one-time newcomer, now established permanently on the American stage. In 1857 Gottschalk toured the Caribbean and played "The Banjo" to packed audiences in Cuba and St. Thomas. In 1859, he brought the song to Guadeloupe and Martinique, sounding out his piano composition on the islands where the priest Jean-Baptiste Labat had first noted the presence of the banza in the hands of slaves nearly two centuries earlier.[54]

Mark Twain captured the electric enthusiasm many felt for the banjo by the middle of the nineteenth century. In a response to Gottschalk's music, Twain ultimately pointed out that even if he was trying hard to make a piano sound like banjo, in the end there was truly no substitute for the humming, thumping instrument itself. "I like Gottschalk well enough," wrote Twain. "He probably gets as much out of the piano as there is in it. But the frozen fact is, that all that he does get out of it is 'tum, tum.' He gets 'tum, tum,' out of the instrument thicker and faster than my landlady's daughter, Mary Ann; but, after all, it simply amounts to 'tum, tum.'" While the piano might be fine for "love-sick girls," Twain went on, it just wouldn't do for him. "[G]ive me the banjo." "When you want genuine music—music that will come right home to you like a bad quarter, suffuse your system like strychnine whisky . . . ramify your whole constitution like the measles, and break out on your hide like the pin-feather pimples on a picked goose,—when you want all this, just smash your piano, and invoke the glory-beaming banjo!"[55]

In the years up to the Civil War, minstrelsy increasingly offered racist visions of African-Americans, and a corresponding apologia for plantation slavery. Proslavery writers offered exuberant depictions of happy, singing slaves, leaving U.S. abolitionists the unenviable task of "convincing the public that life under slavery was not like a minstrel show." An 1852 response to Harriet Beecher Stowe's *Uncle Tom's Cabin* described this happy scene on a plantation:

> There were several of the slaves who were tolerable musicians, and these having formed a band, played occasionally in the summer evenings in the lawn before the hall, for the amusement of the family. These were now ranged apart from the rest, near a sparkling fountain between the sycamore and the mansion, and even to the refined ears of the Colonel and his children, "discoursed most elegant music." The leader of the band was Jerry, who sat on top of a hogshead with his legs hanging over the side, doing great execution with his "fiddle and his bow." The others performed on banjoes, bones and other instruments, and were seated around their leader, some on the ground and some on rude benches brought from the cabins.[56]

"No matter where they may be or what they may be doing," wrote D. R. Hundley of the enslaved in 1860, "whether alone or in crowds, at work or at play, ploughing through the steaming maize in the sultry heats of June, or bared to the waist and with deft hand mowing down the yellow grain, or trudging homeward in the dusky twilight after a day's work is done—always and everywhere they are singing and happy, happy in being free from all mental cares or troubles, singing heartily and naturally as the birds sing." He praised this music, which he claimed no one could listen to "without being very pleasantly entertained." He recalled hearing "negro boatman" singing on a steamship heading up from Mobile and defied the reigning opera singers of the day to "produce, with the aid of many orchestras, a more soul-stirring melody than did those simple Africans then and there!" What Hundley found most "peculiar and striking" in the songs of the slaves were the "wild choruses and lullaloos, which their fathers must have brought with them from Africa." But he admitted that "even their tamest and most civilized efforts" were "surpassingly good." Still, he thought, the music's days were numbered: once properly introduced to the true freedom that came with conversion to Christianity, the enslaved "readily give up their banjos, their fiddles, their double-shuffles, and break-downs, and are eager to learn what is right and becoming."[57]

Once the Civil War began, the banjo traveled anew, this time in the hands of soldiers and sailors on both sides of the conflict. The ex-slave William Rose, interviewed in 1936 in Edisto Island, South Carolina, remembered going with his father into town near the end of the Civil War and watching a train full of Confederate soldiers heading from Charleston north into battle. They were, he recalls "all going down to die," and yet they played cards, laughed, and played music as they went. One of them, he recalls, played the fiddle, and another was picking a banjo. Another called out: "Boys, we going to eat our dinner in hell today." It was, Rose remembered, the "bravest" thing he had ever seen anyone do: laughing, and singing, "on their way to die."[58]

While some soldiers carried banjos alongside their weapons into battle, sailors on ships also played and listened to the instrument. In one 1861 picture of the gunboat *Mendota,* in the midst of the deck densely packed with sitting sailors, two musicians stare back at the camera. One of them is holding a banjo, while next to him is a drummer astride a drum, his two sticks at the ready. Several Union warships actually had fully formed minstrel troupes, made up of sailors who were either professional or aspiring amateur musicians. The *Wabash* was famous for its

Winslow Homer, *Defiance: Inviting a Shot Before Petersburg*, 1864.

Courtesy of the Detroit Institute of Arts. Founders Society purchase and Dexter M. Ferry Jr. Fund/ Bridgeman Images.

troupe, which sported two banjos, a guitar, fiddles, and other instruments and "whose good music and amusing songs helped to pass many a long evening."[59]

The curious way that minstrelsy haunted the Civil War is captured in a striking if opaque 1864 painting by Winslow Homer called *Defiance: Inviting a Shot before Petersburg*. Homer spent several weeks at Petersburg during the battle and made several sketches of the shattered landscape of tree stumps and churned earth. When he returned, he painted a work that centers on a Confederate soldier who, manifestly frustrated with the endless stalemate, is standing exposed on the earthworks taunting the distant Union troops. Around him are various other soldiers, taking cover. But below him sits a striking and somewhat surreal figure: a banjo player in uniform, strumming out a tune, looking up at the man with a kind of theatrical and sardonic grin. The musician, long ignored in discussions of the painting, is in fact the key to its interpretation. The banjo player is, in some sense, a minstrel: he in fact looks like he is wearing blackface. What is he doing sitting alongside a trench in Petersburg?[60]

The battle of Petersburg culminated in the Battle of the Crater. A regiment of Pennsylvania coalminers dug holes beneath the Confederate defenses and placed an enormous explosive charge there. As they worked, Confederates began hearing noises from the underground tunneling and sent listening shafts down into the ground to try and figure out what was going on. At times they heard music: during breaks, some of the soldiers tunneling played the banjo. When it was detonated, the charge created a massive crater, killing an entire southern regiment in the process; but when Union soldiers—including a regiment of black troops—charged into the crater, they found themselves trapped in the churning mud, and the battle became a fiasco that left more than six thousand dead. Homer's painting evoked the traumatic and vivid memory of that battle: viewers would have understood that the defiant soldier was literally standing on top of a powder keg that is ready to explode. But, as Homer was suggesting, the real "explosive charge" underneath the Confederacy was slavery itself, depicted here through the presence of the banjo-player, watching and waiting. He is "a ghost haunting the trench, a spectral embodiment of the underlying origins of the war."[61]

The banjo player's face is painted rather differently than the others in the painting, and than other black figures Homer painted in other works. It looks, in fact, like it is "blacked up," with painted lips, just as the face of a blackface minstrel would have been. This adds another curious layer to the painting. Minstrelsy was a well-known reference for soldiers fighting in the war: in 1861, a Union soldier described two "darkies" he saw in his barracks in Virginia by declaring that they "look exactly like our minstrels." If minstrelsy was itself a curious deferral and projection of the problem of slavery in American culture, Homer's statement here is even more complex: not just the fact of slavery, but the country's vexed incapacity to confront it directly, had led to the catastrophe of battles like Petersburg. Indeed the player's banjo parallels a gun held by a nearby sentry: the instrument is a kind of weapon, perhaps, more powerful than a gun. For the fate of the courageous—or perhaps just foolhardy—Confederate soldier is written in the painting. In the distance can be seen the puffs of sniper shots from the Union lines, bullets racing to kill the defiant soldier. "The banjoist essentially functions as a Greek chorus, providing the macabre accompaniment to the hero's downfall." Perhaps Homer—who himself played the banjo—sought in this painting to write a kind of song of the war by placing the blackface minstrel as a kind of apparition behind Confederate lines.[62]

Another Civil War-era painting depicts the banjo in a different light: as one of the few possessions being carried out of slavery by the newly freed who were seeking lives elsewhere. The 1864 work *Old Virginia Home* by Pittsburgh artist David Gilmour Blythe depicts a dark, clouded, apocalyptic landscape. Walking out onto the road from a broken-down house, a black man has a small bag of possessions over his shoulder and is carrying a banjo. Trailing behind him, on the ground, are broken chains, though his leg is still in a shackle linked to a part of the old chains. The painting is clearly a send-up of the image of the southern plantation as a space of peace and joy. Here, there is little but smoke and chains. But the future of the departing slave, who looks out at us with tired and worried eyes, is nothing if not uncertain. Still, the banjo is there, a precious possession—seemingly necessary for whatever journey lies ahead.[63]

6

Rings Like Silver,
Shines Like Gold

ON THE BANKS OF THE MISSISSIPPI, in the taverns that dotted a Cincinnati neighborhood known as Bucktown, the most popular song was an epic about the new era of freedom. Lafcadio Hearn, one of the keenest observers of popular culture in nineteenth-century America, heard the song in 1871. It was sung by the roustabouts, the mostly African-American men who worked the ports and boats of the Mississippi. Hearn described them as "a society of wanderers who have haunts but not homes," who found solace in music. A visitor to Bucktown could listen as "the sound of the wild banjo-thrumming floats out through the open doors of the levee dance houses." One of their favorite songs was called "Shiloh." It took twenty minutes to sing, as one man led with the verses and everyone else joined in for the chorus, "chanted by twenty or thirty voices of abysmal depth at the same time with a sound like the roar of twenty Chinese gongs struck with tremendous force and precision." The song was "accompanied with that wonderfully rapid slapping of thighs and hips known as 'patting Juba.'"[1]

Shiloh was one of the bloodiest battles of the Civil War and a critical Confederate defeat. The song recalled the battle and told of the desperate rebel soldiers in a prison camp in Columbus, Ohio. It celebrated a black roustabout character named "Limber Jim." And it named men who found their way from freedom to slavery in the midst of the chaos of the war: "John Morgan came to Danville and cut a might dash, / Las' time I saw him, he was under whip an' lash." For the roustabouts who sang along, the song was partly a reminder of how far they had come, an ode to freedom that was hard won and full of new obstacles and harsh realities.[2]

Bucktown, Cincinnati, was a site of refuge and a magnet for migration. The community was made up of "blacks and mulattoes from all parts of the States, but chiefly from Kentucky and Eastern Virginia, where most of them appear to have toiled on the plantations before Freedom." The memory of some residents of the town went further back than to the plantation: one recently deceased resident "was said to be a hundred and seventeen years old, and had been brought to the States from Africa by a slave-trader while a vigorous young woman, so that she remembered many interesting things—the tropical trees and the strange animals, the hive-shaped huts of her people, the roar of lions in the night, the customs of the tribe and some fragments of their wild tongue."[3]

The residents of Bucktown had brought music from the plantations of Kentucky and Virginia to the banks of the Mississippi, where they also created new songs like "Shiloh" and others that talked of "levee life in Cincinnati, of all the popular steamboats running on the 'Muddy Water,' and of the favorite roustabout haunts on the river bank and in Bucktown." Through song the roustabouts shared their experiences and also passed along information about the various places up and down the river where they might end up. Hearn was impressed with the capacious skills and wide-ranging influences musicians brought together when they performed. In an interesting turning of the tables, given that a number of blackface minstrels were of Irish background, several seemed to have specialized in a particular kind of imitation. One of the "negro singers," Hearn noted, "can mimic the Irish accent to a degree of perfection which an American, Englishman or German could not hope to acquire." Another, an African-American roustabout, sang to Hearn a "famous Irish ditty" with a perfect accent. This musician, Hearn noted, "could certainly make a reputation for Irish specialties in a minstrel troupe; his mimicry of Irish character is absolutely perfect, and he possesses a voice of great flexibility, depth and volume."[4]

One night, Hearn's wanderings brought him to a "well-conducted" establishment that catered to roustabouts. It cost ten cents to get in and had a local policeman on hand to contain any potential disorder. When the boats came in from New Orleans, he noted, the place was "over-flowing." The music was provided by a "well-dressed, neatly-built mu-latto" who "picked the banjo," another who played the fiddle "remarkably well and with great spirit," and Anna Nun, a "short, stout negress, illy dressed, with a rather good natured face and a bed shawl tied about her head" who "played the bass viol, and that with no inexperienced hand." The crowd included a prominent local African-American politi-cian, George Moore, who the previous year had been attacked by a mob at his home and killed a man in the process of defending himself. That night, though, he danced—and quite well, according to Hearn. Around him were people of many backgrounds, including a "lithe quadroon named Mary Brown, with auburn hair, gray eyes" and "very fair skin," and several white women. In Hearn's telling, though, all found solidarity in the music, which brought together a wide range of influences and types to bring the crowd an evanescent piece of heaven:

> The musicians struck up that weird, wild, lively air, known perhaps to many of our readers as "Devil's Dream," and in which "the musical ghost of a cat chasing the spectral ghost of a rat'" is represented by a succession of "miauls" and "squeaks" on the fiddle. The dancers danced a double quadrille, at first, silently and rapidly; but warming with the wild spirit of the music, leaped and shouted, swinging each other off the floor, and keeping time with a precision which shook the building in time to the music. . . . Then the music changed to an old Virginia reel, and the dancing . . . became wild; men patted juba and shouted; the negro women danced with the most fantastic grace, their bodies describing almost incredible curves forward and backward; limbs intertwined rapidly in a wrestle with each other and with the music; the room presented a tide of swaying bodies and tossing arms, and flying hair. . . . Once more the music changed—to some popular negro air, with the chorus—

"Don't get weary,
     I'm goin' home."
The musicians began to sing; the dancers joined in; and the
dance terminated with a roar of song, stamping feet, "patting
juba," shouting, laughing, reeling. Even the curious spectators
involuntarily kept time with their feet; it was the very drunkenness of music, the intoxication of dance. Amid such scenes
does the roustabout find his heaven; and this heaven is certainly
not to be despised.[5]

Bucktown was just one of many communities in the midst of major
transformations in the wake of the Civil War. With the agrarian life of
the South fundamentally transformed, the North industrializing, and settlers flowing into the Midwest in steady transformation, the banjo was
on the move, pulling up some of its roots and setting down new ones. It
traveled in the hands of African-American migrants like those who con-
gregated in Bucktown, as well as the minstrels who continued to perform "plantation songs" to the sound of the banjo. But it also found new
homes, in the upscale parlors of New York City and in the railroad tunnels and mountainsides of the Appalachians. The banjo, created in the
midst of exile and upheaval, spoke easily to the realities of a new era of
dispersal and motion, finding a place in a multiplicity of musical spaces and
musical forms. In time, it would be transformed as an object, more
and more mechanized both in the way it was built and the way it was sold
and deployed in sound. And it would find a new life in a kaleidoscope
of symbols, presented as the very expression and condensation of what
America had been, and was to be.

The sound of the banjo had made minstrelsy. But, in turn, minstrelsy
transformed the sound and shape of the banjo. As the instrument gained
ever-expanding audiences, it also gained more and more players. Professional musicians needed banjos, but so did increasing numbers of amateurs who wanted to play the songs they heard on stage. Banjo makers in
Baltimore, Philadelphia, and New York began to fulfill that need and in

the process experimented with new ways of constructing the instrument, resulting in the transformation of the structure and sound of the banjo.

Until the 1840s banjos were all made individually, a unique piece based on traditions and prototypes but constructed for a particular musician. That fact governed the sound of the instrument, which varied remarkably as a result of different types of construction. By the early nineteenth century, some people in North America and the Caribbean were trading the traditional gourd body and instead using rounded wooden hoops made for other purposes—for sifters or box covers, for instance—to make the resonators. One resident of Virginia recalled that in the early nineteenth century, banjos were made with a piece of maple or the "rim of a sugar box." A Michigan ex-slave interviewed in the 1880s recalled about his youth: "When we made a banjo we would first of all catch what we called a ground hog, known in the north as a woodchuck. After tanning its hide, it would be stretched over a piece of timber fashioned like a cheese box," he added. Nevertheless many, if not most, of the instruments were still made with gourd resonators. The first printed portrait of Joel Sweeney, in the sheet music of one of his songs published in 1840, seems to show him playing a banjo with a gourd resonator.[6]

Gourds have to be carefully grown, harvested, and dried; and they are fragile. Tacking the drumheads onto them is a delicate task. Changes in temperature and humidity can stretch or slacken a head, which puts tension on the tacks and can potentially rip the head or damage the resonator. Even on wooden frames, the tacking of head to body poses technical difficulties. These problems are made worse in colder and wetter climates, where the changes in weather could wreak havoc on drumskins stretched across resonators. This was one reason that, centuries earlier, European musical instruments had largely avoided the use of drumheads in favor of wooden instrument bodies. Preserved in African musical culture and maintained in the New World banjo, this form of construction had erupted into North American and European popular culture through minstrelsy. The result was a new level of demand for the instrument, as enthused audience members sought to learn to play the instrument they had seen on stage. In the 1840s a pioneering family of European instrument makers who had migrated to Baltimore found the key to fulfilling that demand, opening the way for an increasingly large-scale and standardized production of banjos.[7]

The family patriarch, Johann Friedrich Wilhelm Esprit Boucher, was born in 1790 in the Alsace region of France, but the family moved to Hanover, Germany, when he was a child. From there he migrated to the United States, carrying knowledge of instrument making with him. In Baltimore, he and his sons set up shop and gained a reputation for making excellent drums. Traditionally, drums were made with ropes holding the skins to the bodies of the instruments. But in 1837 a drum maker patented a new technology called the metal tensioning rod. Combined with a hoop made of wood or metal, it held the skin of a drum to its body tightly and firmly, distributing the tension equally and keeping it taut. The Boucher family used this technique in their drum manufacturing. Their business produced the instruments in a neighborhood in Baltimore that included a theater where minstrel acts regularly performed, and they likely got occasional and increasing requests for banjos. One day someone in their workshops had a revolutionary idea: to use the technology they had been using on their drums to make a new kind of banjo. One can almost imagine the moment when, perhaps looking at a banjo that had its drum head precariously held onto the round hoop with small tacks, one of the artisans looked from that to a nearby drum and said "Aha!" However it happened, it was a significant breakthrough. Stretching the skin across the rim with screws and brackets kept it much more taught, something that made the banjo easier to play in humid climates. It also made the instruments much more solid and easier to transport. Three banjos made in the style of those from 1845 through 1847, deposited in the Smithsonian in 1890, showcase the artistry of these instruments. In addition to the new method for attaching the skin, the necks were elegantly carved with a distinctive peg heads, usually in an "S" shape. Boucher banjos are today among the most treasured examples of the instrument among collectors.[8]

The Boucher music stores sold artisanal, handcrafted banjos throughout the nineteenth century, producing the instruments in batches. But their innovation opened the way for other businesses to start making banjos in a more industrial, largescale way. As more and more builders began producing banjos, some sought out the best wood for banjo necks, identifying particular trees—certain pear trees, the maple, and later tropical woods like mahogany and rosewood—as ideal for strength and sonority. They developed and patented various new banjo parts, many of them focused on improving the attachment of the skin to the resonator. Banjo builders sought not just to make the instruments more solid but also to improve the tone of the instrument. The increasingly industrial production of these instruments helped to standardize the construction, and instruments were produced in larger and larger numbers and at a lower price, putting the instrument in reach of many more potential players, spreading the banjo far and wide within American culture.[9]

The mass production of banjos was as much a cultural project as it was a commercial one. During the late nineteenth century, the banjo became known as "America's instrument," celebrated as an indigenous achievement, creating a sound more appropriate for the country's music than that of European instruments. When Walt Whitman imagined what an "American Opera" should sound like, he started with the instrument: "put three banjos (or more?) in the orchestra—and let them accompany (at times exclusively) the songs of the baritone or tenor." Yet in the racial context of the nineteenth century, those who wished to celebrate the instrument as "American" confronted a cultural conundrum. The banjo's popularity was based on its association with an African-American culture that was both disdained and fetishized. It was its very rootedness in the experience of slavery that made it particularly American rather than European. The reason it was seen as an instrument that could invigorate new forms of American music was because it was understood as an expression of "musical primitivism," a product of a black population made up of "emotional, not very rational, instinctively artistic souls" who lived "far from industrial life." The banjo's nineteenth-century boosters tried to find a way to absorb and channel the power of the instrument even as they distanced it, and themselves, from the people and culture that had offered it to them. Over the course of the second half of the nineteenth century, performers, critics, teachers, and banjo manufacturers all sought to find a way to make the banjo suitable for upper-class audiences, to "elevate" the banjo by bringing it "out of the sentimental shadows and into the bright light of official culture."[10]

At the center of this process were a series of figures—the Dobson Brothers, Frank Converse, and Samuel Swaim Stewart—who in different ways changed both the literal shape of the banjo and the contours of the cultural imagination that surrounded it. Their cultural work involved two interconnected strands of distortion: presenting the gourd banjo as nothing more than an inspiration or prototype for the "true" banjo as created by artisans starting in the 1840s, and portraying the musical styles and abilities of African-American players as essentially primitive. As these figures saw it, the banjo had always had potential, but it was only in the hands of white makers and players that it truly became what it was always meant to be.

One way to "elevate" the banjo was by showcasing the virtuosity of certain players through public competitions. In 1857, a "banjo tournament" was held in New York at the Old Chinese Assembly Rooms on Broadway. Twenty contestants competed in front of a crowd of three thousand people. Many players were there as representatives of their neighborhoods—one was from the Bowery, two from Brooklyn neighborhoods, another from an East Side uptown neighborhood called "the Hook"—and when they took the stage their supporters (sometimes several hundred strong) whooped and cheered. Each player had to offer five pieces: a waltz, schottische, polka, reel, and jig. The best-known banjoists in the competition performed last. The first of them was Picayune Butler—the white musician who had taken on the stage name of the legendary New Orleans banjoist. He was greeted enthusiastically, so much so that one observer "thought the roof would fall off." Unfortunately, however, Butler was "a little under the influence of liquor; so much so that he broke two strings during his trial" and gave an underwhelming performance. He lost out to Charles Plummer, who played "five tunes as a medley, running one tune into another . . . without stopping." Plummer received a "one hundred dollar prize banjo" and the title of "champion banjoist of America."[11]

By the late 1850s, with enthusiastic audiences attending minstrel shows and such banjo competitions, savvy musicians realized there was money to be made selling manuals on how to play the banjo to aspiring amateur musicians. The banjo began its movement from the stage to the page. During the 1840s minstrel troupes and individual composers had sold sheet music so that both other musicians and amateurs could learn to play and sing their songs. But the new banjo manuals did something different: they promised to teach someone who had never played an instrument how to master the banjo in easy steps. They offered tips on how to play the instrument, along with musical notation laying out the banjo accompaniment to popular songs. This was a significant transition in the way banjo playing was transmitted. Previously banjo players had always learned by ear, with playing styles and songs transmitted from one musician to the next. Musical notation communicates in a very different way and can't easily capture all the intricacies of playing, especially on an instrument like the banjo. There is much that isn't conveyed: precisely how hard strings are struck, the tapping of the drumhead, as well as various ways of stretching notes, not to mention rhythmic complexities. Although certain things were lost in translation to written music, the manuals also gave musicians an opportunity to shape banjo playing styles and to popularize new styles of playing. The first banjo manual, published under the name Phil Rice in 1858, collected minstrel songs and taught the down-stroke style favored in their playing. But two years later, James Buckley's book expanded to include European waltzes, schottisches, and marches that he had arranged for the banjo, helping to expand the repertoire of banjo players.[12]

The manuals enabled the banjo to travel faster and further, placing it in many new hands. By the 1860s America's cities were ringing with banjos. Writing a dispatch from New York City in 1866, one writer declared: "In 1844 there were not half a dozen banjos in this city, and they were only to be met with in grog-shops or bagnios [brothels]; today there are over 10,000 instruments in use, and the rich melody of its five strings reaches from the marble fronts of Fifth Avenue down to the slums of Baxter street. The instrument has become a universal favorite, and a banjo fever seems to possess the minds of even the most aristocratic and pretentious of Metropolitans." The new demand led to an "extensive commodification" of the instrument and the creation of a "veritable banjo culture" in which audiences for banjo music also wanted to play the songs in their own homes. To purchase and learn to play the banjo was a way of becoming, in a sense, one's own minstrel.[13]

One of the most influential voices shaping this emerging culture was a musician named Frank Converse, who published two popular and influential banjo manuals in 1865. He urged students to learn a picking, rather than down-stroke, style for playing the banjo: three or four fingers were to be used, picking upwards, while the thumb picked downwards. He also recommended ways to "soften" the sound of the banjo by avoiding touching the strings with the nails, as well as picking them close to the rim of the instrument rather than over the drumhead. His tutor was, in a sense, a manual for a sonic transformation: the banjo, as he saw it, needed to change from being loud, resonant, rhythmic to something more suitable for a different kind of tradition and cultural space.[14]

For Converse, this was part of a much larger project of "elevating" the banjo. Looking back decades later in a series of reminiscences about his life and career, he presented himself as a key player in the elevation of the banjo. "The first banjo I ever heard," wrote Converse, "was in the hands of a colored man—a bright mulatto—whose name I have forgotten." "He frequently played Elmira and the neighboring villages," Converse continued, "playing and singing and passing his hat for collections. His *repertoire* was not very extensive, but, with his comicalities, sufficed to gain him a living."

> I cannot say I learned anything from his execution, which, though amusing, was limited to the thumb and first finger, pulling or 'picking' the strings with both. He was quite conceited as to his abilities (pardonable in banjo players, I believe), and to impress his listeners with a due appreciation of them, he would announce that such a trifling circumstance as the banjo being out of tune caused him no inconvenience and so, with a seemingly careless fumbling of the pegs, he would disarrange the tuning—'fro de banjo out ' tune," he said—but merely pitching the second string a semitone higher. . . . His fingering was unique, requiring only the first finger of the left hand for stopping the strings—on the first string at the first fret and the second string at the second fret. With the right hand he used only the first finger and thumb.[15]

Years later, Converse wrote, he visited southern plantations and saw the same "manner of fingering," which he wrote was "characteristic of the early colored player." But such banjo players, he insisted, were "of rare occurrence," and the instrument they played was "of the rudest construction, often a divided gourd with a coon skin stretched over the large part for the drum." "With this for accompaniment he would improve his song as he went along," he added, "generally mentioning his massa or missues or some local incident." In these lines, Converse grudgingly acknowledged the fact that African-Americans were the first players of the instrument he loved. But he did so in a way that sought to contain and downplay their influence, claiming there weren't that many banjo players and presenting their playing as primitive and limited.[16]

Even as he assured his readers he had not "learned anything" from this player, whose name he didn't even remember, Converse offered up a portrait of what was in fact a complex and carefully cultivated style of playing. And he also admitted that hearing this man play was, in a sense, the most important event in his life. It was a moment of awakening and conversion. "There was *something* in the sound of that banjo—crudely manipulated though it was—that gave me a delight never before experienced, and my eagerness to possess one and play it dates from that time." Converse's father was a "super-conscientious Presbyterian" who had "imbibed the prevailing prejudice" about the banjo, so that the "instrument was tabooed in our home." He considered it "an instrument of but trifling consideration not susceptible to any improvement, and upon which labor and time would be foolishly thrown away." Converse persisted, secretly playing in the stable, his "only safe refuge for practice." He "devoted all his spare time" to studying the banjo and "applying to it theoretical musical principles, arranging a complete system of study bounded on correct musical rules acquired from his piano studies." With a few ill-advised interruptions—at one point he tried and failed to be a lawyer—he defined himself entirely through his playing of the banjo for the rest of his life. He sought to "elevate the position of his favorite instrument and its music" by seeking to convert "those musicians who, through ignorance of the capabilities of the instrument, have spoken against it." There were times when his missionary zeal just wasn't enough; he admitted that his efforts in an "Indian village" in Colorado met with failure: "they were quite indifferent to the banjo." But, elsewhere, Converse met with more success in working to redeem the banjo and gain in the respect he thought it deserved.[17]

Converse claimed to have modeled his own playing partly on that of the well-known minstrel Picayune Butler, whose drunkenness had gotten him a second place in New York in 1857. Butler, then "heralded as the greatest banjo player in the world," brought his musical troupe to the town of Elmira when Converse was a teenager. Converse watched Butler at his concert but also sat "unobserved below his window" listening to him practice. Unlike the playing of the "colored gentleman" whose name

Converse forgot, Butler played a style he admired and sought to imitate. "As he played with the thimble, his execution—unlike anything I had ever heard, powerful and brilliant—strongly impressed me, and in my enthusiasm I thought him the most favored mortal on earth." Converse got up the courage to introduce himself and garnered a few tips from Butler. Still, he ultimately considered Butler a foundation that had to be surpassed and left behind. "Butler's playing, while effective, was far from artistic, and his *repertoire* limited chiefly to jigs, reels, walkarounds and his comic songs." He wore blackface, along with a "patched, ill-fitting plantation get-up of old boots, exaggerated collar, slouch hat," and played his "plantation ditties" while "sitting with one leg thrown across the other."[18]

Converse was sensitive to the fact that many upper-class audiences disdained this kind of banjo playing. In fact his whole life as a musician was shadowed by a kind of nagging anxiety in the face of those who rejected the instrument because of its association with blackface minstrelsy. As he looked back at his long career, he lamented that "even at this day, despite the marvelous development it has shown in all that goes to make an instrument a *musical* instrument, there still exists a species with 'souls so dead' that they obstinately shut their ears to fact when the banjo is in question, preferring to cherish and hug the old prejudice." The fact that the banjo had been "singled out as the one 'black sheep'" among instruments was "well-nigh inexplicable," except for the fact of its origins: "the senseless reason that the instrument having first domiciled with the ignorant negroes on the plantation, it necessarily must have originated there and therefore, by inference, being of so humble an origin, could possess no intrinsic musical merit." He sympathized and understood this interpretation, given the low quality of the music played on the banjo on the plantation: "True enough, there were no players among the slaves capable of arousing its slumbering powers, and its destiny seemed fulfilled as an accompaniment to the darkey songs that told of the cotton fields, cane brakes, 'possum hunts, sweet tobacco posies, or 'Gwine to Alabama wid banjo on my knee,' etc." But that was, he suggested, only because it lay trapped in a social group incapable of realizing the instrument's true potential. What the banjo needed was to be embraced by its "white admirers in the North," who were the ones who ultimately awakened its "inherent beauties."[19]

In order to argue that it was whites who had awakened the slumbering possibilities of the instrument, Converse went to great lengths to minimize both its African and its African-American origins. For him the instrument played on the plantations wasn't *really* even a banjo, but rather "what may be called its prototype": "the gourd banjo." "History informs us," Converse wrote, that this instrument "was brought from Africa to America by the negro slaves in the days of the slave ship." But it was in fact a much more ancient instrument, one that "did not originate in Africa." With slightly nervous and convoluted prose, Converse found a way to skirt the African roots of the banjo by quickly moving to a much longer history.

> To trace its germ would extend research to pre-historic times—to the time when first was heard the musical twang of the bowstring; for instruments with characteristics essentially banjo—and so, doubtless, akin to it—are included among the earliest discoveries—a fact strengthening the belief that all our stringed instruments had one common ancestry; are derived from the same common root, or germ—inspiration, if you like—and the many modifications developing throughout its evolution consistently with the taste, needs and musical requirements of various peoples.[20]

Converse's brief history of stringed instruments was, of course, correct in principle. But it served here as a way of suggesting that although Africans brought the "prototype" of the instrument to the Americas, that was essentially just happenstance. Converse dulled and diffused the story of an African origin, deflecting its impact through a combination of absorption and forgetting. And he insisted that the instrument shouldn't be condemned to remaining in their hands, where its true musical potential would never be unleashed. In his manuals, he sought to create a distance from the African-American tradition by moving away from the rhythmic and louder "stroke-style" playing to what he considered to be a more delicate style of fingerpicking. Along with authors of other banjo manuals, he did manage to make fingerpicking styles increasingly common. In turn, composers took advantage of this, offering new and different pieces for the banjo that were seen as more sophisticated, often drawing on

European traditions. The result was that the banjo was increasingly welcomed into parlors of the middle and the upper classes, seen as an acceptable instrument for elite young men and women to play. These changes also meant that people began looking for something different in the construction of the banjo itself. The size and length of the neck, the distance between strings: all these things could affect how easy it was to pick the strings rather than stroke them. The rise of fingerpicking and the changing repertoire of music played on the banjo generated a period of "great technological experimentation and innovation" from 1860 to 1885. And the expansion of a wealthier base of customers encouraged the construction of more expensive and decorative instruments.[21]

At the center of this period of innovation was one family of five brothers: the Dobsons. An 1866 portrait of the family tells their story in a way that parallels Converse's reminiscences, insisting that they had helped to redeem and elevate the banjo through their work. The instrument, the writer claimed, was at first just an "offshoot of the brain of some nigrous savage in Africa," which was "brought to this country by kidnapped slaves." It had long "remained the peculiar property of the Southern negro," but thanks to minstrelsy "the peculiarity of the banjo and its singular richness in melody attracted the attention of the white man." Among them was Henry Dobson, who had frequently taken in minstrel shows at the Ethiopian Opera House and there "imbibed a passion for the banjo which pervaded his soul like the dream of a maniac." Later on, working at the Astor Hotel, he got some banjo lessons in the cloakroom from his African-American co-workers. He was infatuated, to the point that the banjo gave him insomnia: he "went to bed nights, and found it almost impossible to sleep, for the mellow notes of the band were continually ringing" in his ears. "All his thoughts and impulses" were "tinged with rich music" and all "his energies were bent toward the ownership of the instrument." "When I finally secured one," Henry himself explained, "the first touch of its strings thrilled me like the inspiration of a prophet." But he also had ambitions for the banjo. Like Converse, he felt a disdain for the "common negro jigs" and instead imagined the instrument finding a home in "the mystic realms of operatic music." He dreamed of a banjo repertoire "as varied as those of the most accomplished violinists and pianists." In time, he developed what the writer called a "classically educated banjo." "New chords were developed, and the peculiar bell tones of the harmonies were increased." Henry, in this account, had brought the banjo to its full potential. Thanks to him, the "richest banjo music in the world flows from its recesses."[22]

The love of banjo ran in the Dobson family. Henry's brother George became a well-known banjo instructor. One of George's female students didn't know how to read music, so he developed a "simplified method": a form of notation that had five lines, one for each string on the banjo, and two different kinds of symbols for different kinds of notes—those played with a finger on the left hand, and those played with an open string. He used this method, a kind of early version of what is now known as "tab," informally with students for years. In 1874 he presented the method to a broader audience in his *Simplified Method and Thorough School for the Banjo,* which largely replaced the earlier books by Rice, Buckley, and Converse. Learning to play music, George claimed, was a "little investment" that yielded "far more satisfactory returns than any other." For, "he or she who can perform up on any instrument need never be at a *loss for company:* a congenial friend is ever at hand." The banjo could gather friends around the performer, George hinted, but it could also itself become a true, loyal friend.[23]

George Dobson offered a more nuanced history of the instrument than did figures like Converse. "The early history of the banjo is wrapped in obscurity," George began, and the "commonly accepted" account was that "negro slaves, seeing and hearing their mistresses playing on the guitar, were seized by that emulative and imitative spirit characteristic of the race, and proceeded to make a guitar of their own out of a hollow gourd, with a coon-skin stretched across for a head." "This story is undoubtedly true," George went on, adding that some believe the name banjo came from *bandora,* which he called "a species of guitar." At the same time, however, George argued that it was necessary to go back further in time to find the "real, primitive origin of the instrument." Drawing on what seems to have been fairly extensive reading about the musical instruments of Africa, he wrote that the "Nubians" had an instrument called "the *kissar,* very much like the banjo" while "the negroes of Eastern Africa" had "the nana, a five-stringed instrument with head of wood and skin." He also mentioned West African instruments: "the *omlic* with eight strings, the *boulou* with ten strings, and in Senegambia the *bania,* which it is sometimes claimed was imported to the United

States by the negro slaves, and became the banjo." "Wherever the inspiration for its construction and development came from," George concluded, in America the instrument had clearly come from "southern negroes."[24]

For George Dobson, however, all that was, in a sense, only anecdotal history. The future of the banjo was to look very different. "From the rude contrivance which they put together," he effused, "the instrument has undergone a steady development and improvement." In its more developed form, "in its perfection and elegance, it is even superior to the guitar" and was capable of competing with the violin and piano. In his 1874 *Simplified Method,* George acknowledged the importance of what he called "the genuine banjo music made by the stroke," which he acknowledged was "characteristic of the instrument" and "much admired by all lovers of the banjo." But, following Converse's example, most of the songs in the second half of the *Simplified Method* were geared more toward a picking style, which George described as "the rich music of the guitar in soft, silver strains." George Dobson and other banjo entrepreneurs of his generation carefully navigated between different banjo traditions in a way that ultimately confirmed a hierarchy and a narrative of progress, with stroke style as "traditional," and the picking styles seen as more complex, more modern, and ultimately something to be aspired to by those seeking to impress others with the way they played the instrument. This, in turn, influenced the construction of banjos, notably in the increasing presence of frets, which were particularly important for those learning to play from instruction books.[25]

While his brother George focused on teaching, Henry Dobson spent much of his energy developing, and patenting, new techniques for banjo construction. By this time, Boucher's innovation of using drum technology to attach the skin to the body of the instrument had become standard. In the era of the Dobson brothers, many banjo makers seeking to improve the instrument looked to the guitar as a model as they modified the neck and pegs of the instrument. They put a lot of energy into changing the tone of the banjo, seeking to make it "more powerful and finer" in the words of one banjo maker. With the increasing popularity of fingerpicking styles as well as new venues for playing, such as parlors of private homes, many sought a tone that was sharper and cleaner. Several banjo makers found ways to get rid of protruding brackets, making the body of the banjo itself more streamlined and smoother, in part so that the banjo was less likely to get caught up in the costumes of performers as well as the dresses of Victorian women who were increasingly taking up the instrument. Henry developed and patented a closed-back banjo, with the intention of creating more resonance and projecting the sound more through the front of the instrument. This was, interestingly, a return of sorts to the original model, since resonators built of gourds are essentially enclosed by their very nature. Henry Dobson's closed-backed banjo became one of the most popular models on the market in the 1870s. Banjo makers continued to work on and improve the rim that held the drumskin down and attached it to the body of the instrument. Originally made of wood, these were increasingly made of metal, and their manufacture seen as a crucial part of defining the tone of the instrument. In time the Gibson Mastertone banjo featured a particularly sophisticated rim that used ball bearings. The instruments were often works of art, with beautiful carvings or pearl inlays on the necks. One 1873 banjo made by Henry Dobson featured a beautiful carving of a banjo on the neck of the instrument, nestled up against the metal rim surrounding the drumhead: a banjo within a banjo.[26]

Throughout the late nineteenth century, builders poured energy into innovations for banjo construction. There had been one patent application in 1859, another in 1862. In 1869 four were filed for new banjo constructions. Between 1880 and 1900, however, the trickle became a flood: 135 patent applications were filed. There were patents for banjos but also for any number of banjo parts: tailpieces, resonators, drumheads, leg rests, bells, bridges, and brackets. "Dozens of bizarre and ingenious designs for new methods of evenly tightening banjo heads were patented," and inventors developed "every conceivable variation of screw, nut, and bolt-operated brackets." There was a push for more brackets, since makers thought that a greater number would help distribute the force more evenly around the rim and therefore keep the drumhead tighter. As is so often the case, the proliferation of new technology created new problems: after all, each bracket had to be tightened one by one. So some banjo makers aimed for newfound simplicity, producing "wildly elaborate methods of tightening all the brackets at once by means of a single large screw." Driving all these new inventions was a desire for control over the ever-shifting, pesky drumhead that made the banjo a banjo. This could go to extremes: "Internal electric lights were added to many banjos in an at-tempt to keep the calfskin head uniformly tight and dry."[27]

Some banjo makers were a bit *too* inventive, and the history of banjo design has many developments that have ended up in the dustheap—probably for the best. The ever-present desire to make the banjo even more exciting than it might otherwise be led some to add bells and buzzers to the instruments to "enable the enterprising musician to liven up his performance." The new banjos were significantly heavier, so companies offered armrests and instrument stands, as well as finger guards to pro-tect the crucial members from getting gouged or torn by an inoppor-tunely placed piece of metal on the instrument. And, having made banjos brighter and brighter and louder and louder, instrument makers almost immediately offered countervailing cures: a variety of mutes that could be used to dampen the sound of the strings. Perhaps the most amazing accomplishment in banjo making in the nineteenth century was a unique piece, never to be replicated. It was built on a whaling ship in the 1850s, its body and neck carved entirely out of whalebone, its drumhead and strings made from the skin of a porpoise.[28]

All of these changes in banjo construction profoundly altered the sound of the instrument. They represented a significant encroachment of metal on an instrument that had long been made essentially of wood, skin, and gourd. The metallic brightness that is almost inevitably associ-ated with the banjo today was the result of these modifications, which transformed the mellow and rounded resonance of the older instrument into the more familiar bling and blang that we usually hear today. In time the change would come to seem eternal: it is difficult today for most people to imagine what the banjo actually sounded like for the first centuries of existence, before it changed from something fabricated al-most entirely from plants to something festooned with metal.

Along with the Dobsons, the most important banjo maker and booster for the instrument was Samuel Swaim Stewart. Stewart carried out what he called a "crusade" against the "ham," that is, the minstrel performers who used ham fat mixed with burnt cork to make their blackface. Stewart derided the "ham" as someone who learned to play the banjo by ear and who performed only the old minstrel songs, ig-noring all the other music that could be produced on the instrument. When some wrote to complain about Stewart's criticism of this music, he responded trenchantly that his attack against "hams" was "a purely humanitarian act"—or at least a banjo-itarian one. "We saw, long ago, that unless something was done to save the banjo from the 'ham,' that 'ham fever' would become contagious, and the rise of the banjo impeded for another generation."[29]

Stewart successfully brought together three intertwined missions. He built a banjo-manufacturing company that ultimately became the most successful and important in the United States. He performed himself and wrote updated banjo playing manuals, which he published and distributed himself. And, importantly, he became the major voice for and interpreter of the banjo and what it should mean in the United States. Through his newspaper *Stewart's Guitar and Banjo Journal,* which he published from 1884 to 1899, as well as through two books—*The Banjo Philosophically* from 1886 and *The Banjo! A Dissertation* from 1888— he codified the idea that the instrument had found its true fulfillment in the hands of white manufacturers and musicians. He claimed in *The Banjo Philosophically* that the banjo was "not of negro origin," but instead came from Spanish instruments and took its name from the lute-like bandore. Two years later, in *The Banjo!,* he had accepted the possibility of an African origin of the banjo, but added that if it was indeed the case that Africans had first developed the instrument that was just evidence of the fact that "truth has often come into the world through lowly channels."[30]

Stewart's influence on the place and vision of the instrument was profound. By the late nineteenth century, the banjo was broadly embraced as "America's instrument"—meaning that it had also become thoroughly appropriated as a "white" instrument. In 1883 the Georgia-born journalist and folklorist Joel Chandler Harris wrote an article denying that the banjo was even played that much by African-Americans in the South, suggesting that the whole idea of its origin on the plantations was a theatrical fantasy. In any minstrel performance, he noted, "an entire scene is devoted to the happy-go-lucky darkey with his banjo." The stage is cleared, the banjo player "disguised in burnt cork, is black, and sleek, and saucy" and "carries his banjo on his shoulder." The instrument, he added, is "inlaid with silver" and cost seventy-five dollars. As Harris noted sardonically, the banjo player would then make "various allusions that savor strongly of the plantations through which the back alleys of New York

City run" and play songs "just as they were played on the plantations that exist on the stage." For audiences throughout the United States, "this scene is real and representative, because it falls in with their idea of the plantation negro." One woman from Massachusetts had written to a newspaper that she would be "shocked to learn that the negroes of the South know nothing of the banjo. Somehow it has been a great comfort to me to associate them with that instrument." The only problem, Harris wrote, was that they didn't play it. Through all his years growing up in Georgia, he wrote, he had seen plenty of instruments played by "planta-tion negroes,"—fiddles, flutes, pipes, trumpets. "But I have never seen a banjo, or a tambourine, or a pair of bones in the hands of a plantation negro." Harris's essay incited various responses by writers who assured him that they *had* seen southern African-Americans playing the banjo. The debate, though, highlighted the ways in which minstrelsy had in-deed become its own world, a kind of plantation of the mind in which the banjo played a central role. As another commentator put it in 1884, "the negro minstrel is getting to be a law unto itself, and ceasing to be an imitator of the exact facts of plantation life."[31]

Such attempts to disaggregate the banjo and the plantation, to depict the minstrel stage as nothing more than an outworn phantasm, also pro-vided an opening for a new way of configuring and imagining the instru-ment. It was freeing, in a way, to think that the whole plantation origin story for the banjo was made up. If that was true, the banjo could be anything, in anyone's hands. You didn't need to blacken your face to play it. By the 1890s there were "banjo clubs" at all the Ivy League universi-ties and many other colleges and universities. Women began playing the banjo in increasing numbers on stage: Lotta Crabtree, known as "Little Lotta" or "Miss Lotta," got her beginnings performing banjo in Cali-fornia gold-mining camps before embarking on a successful career as a performer on the East Coast. Her example opened the way for many other female banjo players who played both solo and in bands. Many women also took up the banjo as amateurs, forming orchestras of their own: one of these, from the 1890s, included seven banjos out of ten stringed in-struments. In 1894 Mary Cassatt produced a pastel called *The Banjo Lesson,* showing a woman demonstrating to a girl how to play the banjo. A 1910 short story called "Banjo Nell," by James Hopper, described the sad fate of a woman who, after her missionary husband forbade her to play her beloved banjo, died of being "starved" of the "tinklings and sounds of mirth" of the instrument.[32]

In 1894 Rudyard Kipling wrote a poem called "The Song of the Banjo," in which the instrument has found its true home in the hands of a soldier of the British Empire. The poem's narrator is a banjo itself, which presents itself as the toughest of instruments. "You must leave a fiddle in the damp," the banjo crows, and you "couldn't raft an organ up the Nile, / And play it in an equatorial swamp." But the banjo marches everywhere: "*I* travel with the cooking-pots and pails," between the "coffee and the pork," offering a sound that can "spur the rearguard to a walk!" Kipling tried to make the banjo sound in his poem, offering up the *"pilly-winky-winky-winky-winky-popp!"* and the *"strumpty-tumpty"* and the *"tumpa-tumpa-tumpa-tumpa-tump!"* of the instrument. He recognized its complex lineage: "The grandam of my grandam was the Lyre," the banjo reminds us, allowing the instrument to the "wisdom of the centuries" even as it sings "the everlasting Wonder-song of Youth!" "I am Memory and Torment," the banjo claims. But Kipling most vividly evokes the instrument as an inspiration for imperial conquest. It plays "in the silence of the camp before the fight / When it's good to make your will and say your prayer." "I'm the prophet of the Utterly Absurd, / Of the Patently Impossible and Vain." The banjo teaches that what might seem unimaginable—the conquest of the globe by a small nation—was in fact within reach. "There was never voice before us till I led our lonely chorus, / I—the war drum of the White Man round the world!" And ultimately its vocation, in Kipling's imagination, is—like that of empire—a global one: "I draw the world together link by link." Kipling's poem is testament to the way in which, by the turn of the twentieth century, the banjo had become a potent and malleable symbol. It could be many things to many people: no longer a clear symbol of the plantation, in the right hands it could—in the ultimate irony—actually serve as the sonic accompaniment to the imperial conquest of Africa.[33]

By both building and selling banjos and changing the image of the instrument, figures like Henry Dobson and Stewart turned the banjo into a mass-produced instrument, sending it into all corners of the culture and landscape of North America and beyond. By the end of the nineteenth century, "the five-string banjo adorned Park Avenue mansions and Mississippi shotgun shacks." But while it sounded in the hands of minstrels

Mary Cassatt. *The Banjo Lesson,* 1893.
Brooklyn Museum, Bequest of Mary T. Cockcroft, Elizabeth Varian Cockcroft, and Elizabeth
Cockcroft Schettler.

on stage and amateurs in Victorian parlors, the banjo also remained a
deeply vernacular instrument, embedded in the music of varied rural
communities. The banjo was, increasingly, everywhere: it was relatively
easy to acquire, a familiar sound. It could accompany old songs and new
songs, voices singing in whatever intonation, providing melody and

rhythm. In this new phase of its life, it kept doing what it had originally been built to do on the plantations of the Caribbean and North America: create solidarity amidst landscapes of dispersal and movement. A brand new banjo, shipped from Stewart's factory, still could manage to sound old. It could still create the sound of a community. Despite all the attempts to erase the instrument's history, its origins at the center of the experience of slavery remained vital and alive. For it was that origin, its foundational ability to bring together the disparate and diverse cultures of Africa in the midst of the pressures of the plantation, that made it capable of finding new homes everywhere it went and creating a sense of home along the way.[34]

"I'm going back to the Swannanoa Tunnel / That's my home, baby, that's my home." The song "Swannanoa Tunnel"—recorded in the 1930s by the banjo player Bascom Lamar Lunsford—tells the story of an impressive, but deadly, feat of railroad engineering that connected the east of North Carolina to its mountain communities. Eighteen hundred feet long, the tunnel was the longest on a stretch between Old Fort and Asheville, North Carolina, built by five hundred convict laborers, many of them African-American, between 1887 and 1889. A hundred and twenty-five of them died as they hammered and blasted out the rock in the tunnel with an explosive paste concocted out of nitroglycerine, sawdust, and cornmeal. Almost two decades earlier, in 1871, a convict named John Henry had raced a steam drill in Virginia's Appalachian Mountains; and in time that story became a powerful and enduring myth, captured in song. By the time of the construction of the Swannanoa Tunnel, convicts themselves were likely recalling and singing his story. In turn, they left traces of their experience in song. "Swannanoa Tunnel" recalled the kind of accident that killed many workers over the years: the tunnel got "all caved in, baby, all caved in." The words served as memory and memorial: "When you hear that hoot owl squalling / Somebody dying, baby, someone's dying."[35]

Songs are an archive, but one made of fragments and the infinitely layered practice of absorption, repetition, and alteration. As Greil Marcus writes, they frequently bring together "verbal fragments" that are "drawn from a floating pool of thousands of disconnected verses, couplets," and "one-liners." By the end of the nineteenth century, with enough songs in circulation through various media—vernacular performance, but also the circulating minstrel shows, circuses, and other venues—"there were enough fragments abroad in the land to reach a kind of critical mass," bits of song "passing back and forth between blacks and whites as common coin, to generate more fragments, to sustained within the matrix of a single musical language an almost infinite repertory of performances." This kind of accumulation of song and memory was particularly powerful in contexts of social oppression and control, where as Scott Reynolds Nelson notes "coded language" was often used to speak of experiences of violence and suffering that were too dangerous to articulate openly. As such language circulated, it became "mangled and transformed, while growing stronger and richly metaphorical." Experiences, secreted away into the code of song "moved from mouth to ear again, for many who sang could read neither lyrics nor musical notes. People sang in groups, repeating lines for emphasis, to aid memory, and to recycle old stories for new purposes." And songs were everywhere, a form of re-membrance but also of analysis of the social world. People sang in churches but also "at work, in cotton fields and tobacco factories." "They sang to mules, cows and pigs to get their attention and tell them what to do. They sang at night, in crowded roadhouses between sips of applejack brandy, and they sang to put their children to sleep. Children sang as they walked, in high and warbling tones, to make their presence known to parents and neighbors." "Field hollers" rang out to call people home at the end of the day. "Song blended into regular talk and stretched into praise. It was omnipresent."[36]

The songs of the nineteenth century, such as "John Henry" and "Swannanoa Tunnel," weren't recorded until the twentieth century, often many decades after they first began to circulate. But in them we have a registry—often the only one—of the experiences of the poor, the mi-grant, the convict who sowed fields and built the new landscape of rail-roads and towns. And we also have an archive of their encounter with music itself. In later versions of "Swannanoa Tunnel"—sung by Roscoe Holcomb under the name "Swanno Mountain,"—there are lyrics cel-ebrating the instrument that had long accompanied the song. "Got sixteen brackets / on my banjo!," Holcomb rejoices in an inimitable high, piercing voice—one that sounds almost like a banjo. The song, a celebration of survival and return, here also becomes an ode to the new technologies that made the sound of string and skin spread out more loudly and powerfully than ever. Holcomb luminously captures the sound of the banjo: it "rings like silver, shines like gold!"[37]

During the second half of the nineteenth century, the banjo found a new home in the Appalachian Mountains. Its sound probably resonated in some of the tunnels that opened up the region to more industry and migration; and in time the banjo sounded in the mountaintops and hollows, the streets and taverns of junctions and towns, the prisons, and eventually on the radio that carried sound from and to the region. It became so at home in these regions that many people came to think that the banjo came from the mountains, that it was quintessentially the instrument of whites from the Appalachians. This was at once a curious erasure of the instrument's history and a curious confirmation of the power with which its original makers on the plantations of the New World had endowed it to be an instrument without borders, harboring a seemingly infinite sound.

How did the banjo get to the mountains? There were probably some banjos played by slaves in different parts of the region going back to the eighteenth century. But it seems to have spread widely in the region only in the late nineteenth century and early twentieth century, when many people were on the move there, including African-American migrants and laborers. The banjo was probably heard in labor and lumber camps as well as in rural towns and larger cities in the region. But it also circulated through the region through minstrelsy, as troupes traveled through these regions and popularized the instrument. As it sounded out in these various contexts, it put down roots in the region. All these processes, of course, were ultimately rooted one way or another in the playing of African-Americans, whether that came directly through railroad laborers and migrants or through the detour of minstrel playing itself: the mountain banjo is a black instrument, embraced and taken in by white musicians. By the early twentieth century it was firmly anchored in many mountain communities, integrated into musical life, and a cherished part of gatherings and dances. As Alan Lomax put it in 1947, the banjo "found its final home, after everyone else had grown tired of it, in the lonesome hollers of the Southern mountains." Mountain musicians "sat down with the contraption and worked on it until they had produced a kind of music that was neither African-American, nor minstrel style, nor a transcription of their old tunes, but a peculiar and wonderful mix of all of these."[38]

Though much of the spread of the banjo into the mountains was possible because of the industrial production of inexpensive banjos, many mountain players still made their own instruments. This allowed them to make fretless necks, preferred by most musicians there. When store-bought banjos were used, they were often modified by shaving off the frets or else by putting tin or Formica to make the necks smooth. "The banjo is home-made," Louise Rand Bascom explained in 1909, "and very cleverly fashioned too, with its drum head of cat's hide, its wooden parts of hickory (there are no frets)." In 1962 banjoist Edgar A. Ashley recalled that his first banjo was a "homemade banja. Killed a cat, tanned its hide, made the head, and he carved out the rest of it." The musician and banjo-maker Frank Proffitt recalled how he'd learn to make the instrument from his father, going into "the woods to get the timber for banjo-making." He would select the right tree "by its appearance and by sounding," by "hitting a tree with a hammer or axe broadsided to tell by the sound if it's straight grained." The boy watched him "shaping the wood for a banjo" and came to "love the smell of the fresh shavings as they gathered on the floor of our cabin." "When the strings was put on and the pegs turned and the musical notes began to fill the cabin, I looked upon my father as the greatest man on earth for creating such a wonderful thing out of a piece of wood, a greasy skin, and some strings."[39]

The "mountain style" of banjo playing often used the frailing or clawhammer technique, striking the strings with the back of the fingers and popping the high string with the thumb. But there were also various styles of picking, including dropping the thumb to hit strings, and two-fingered and three-fingered picking, which would ultimately become the basis for bluegrass banjo styles. Many musicians played notes with their left hands, hammering or pulling off the strings as they strummed or picked with the right, creating a rhythmic cascade of sound. All these styles coexisted, and there were many variations, with a premium placed on the individuality of each particular player. "Can you read music?" asks one joke common among mountain banjo players. "Not enough to hurt my playing." Banjo playing was learned by ear and eye, and particular and unique styles cultivated and appreciated. As a result there was a profusion of different kinds of tuning, often "open" forms that allowed the musician to play a chord by striking all the strings at once. Much of this music uses pentatonic scales that were part of the Anglo-American ballad tradition, creating a sound that is often "haunting and unfamiliar" to those who haven't heard this style before. The remarkable range of playing styles has made the archive of mountain banjo music a vast country of its own, a place to which contemporary banjo players return to find many mysterious tunes and tunings, and a well of ever-unfamiliar and sustaining sound.[40]

Like song lyrics, the melodies, lines, developments, and configurations that constitute banjo music are themselves part of a circulating set of fragments that can be called up, evoked, and reconfigured in seemingly infinite ways. We get a sense of this tradition in a 1929 recording by Clarence Ashley of the song "The Coo Coo Bird." Ashley, born in 1895 in Tennessee, played with minstrel troupes and medicine shows. When he recorded the song, writes Greil Marcus, he was "in his mid-thirties; he sounded seventeen, or one-hundred-and-seventeen, as if he died seventeen or one-hundred-and-seventeen years before." His performance of the song "made one thing clear: however old the singer was, he wasn't as old as the song." Ashley's singing "rises and falls, dips and wavers, playing off the rhythm his banjo makes like a tide eddying up to a bank again and again." The sound of the banjo in "The Coo Coo Bird" is clear, a clarion, beckoning but also inscrutable. "The banjo could be from another song or another world. The music seems to have been found in the middle of some greater song; it is inexorable. The opening and closing flourishes of the banjo seem false, because the figures in the music make no progress, go from no one place to any other; the sound was here before the singer started and it will be here when he's gone." And it is somehow the perfect accompaniment to a set of fragmentary lyrics that coalesce around a theme: "displacement, restlessness, homelessness." The "cadence of Clarence Ashley's banjo," writes Marcus, "is both counterpoint and contradiction to any law."[41]

Many other banjo players have interpreted this same song, often with different lyrics and a different sound. The cadence, intonation, and structure of the song stretch and refract in different ways in the hands of different musicians. What, ultimately, makes it the same banjo song at all? Through an analysis of a series of recordings of the song, David Garner found both wide variation and a few aspects of consistency, parts that might constitute the definition of "The Coo Coo Bird" as song, a particular phrase or two without which the song was not the song. And yet this kinship is tentative, a community stretched and delicate, a song always on the verge of spinning out into another one, with the same name or a different name, constituted out of fragments familiar but also estranged.[42]

As residents from the mountains left rural areas for cities of the South and other regions, this music—and the banjo itself—traveled along new routes. In the early twentieth century it was recorded and marketed as "mountain music" or "hillbilly music." One of the most important vehicles for this was Uncle Dave Macon, who became one of the main stars at the Grand Old Opry in Nashville. Born in 1870 in Warren County, Tennessee, Macon had grown up in a boardinghouse run by his parents, where musicians and performers frequently stayed. Macon started playing in vaudeville acts and traveling medicine shows as a teenager and absorbed a wide range of songs and styles. By the time he started playing at the Opry, he carried "an encyclopedic range of folk material" gathered not just from "entertainers but from railroaders, miners, and riverboatmen both black and white." "He brought, too, a panoply of banjo styles which contemporary folk banjoists are still struggling to absorb." Macon always wore a "double-breasted waistcoat" and a "black felt hat," and offered an "uninterrupted patter of song, story, satire, anecdote, laughter, and joke, seasoned with wry social and political commentary," along with his fast, percussive, bright banjo playing. In a 1924 song called "All I've Got is Gone / Hill Billie Blues," Macon sang: "I am a billy and I live in the hills." It was the first use of the term "hillbilly" in a song title. At the time, writers and folklorists increasingly presented Appalachia as a place of isolated white communities, arguing that their traditions provided a link back to earlier centuries of European migrants to the Americas. Appalachian music was conceived of, and marketed as, the ultimate expression of these deep European and American roots, with the African-American part of the story largely elided. This helped code the banjo as "white," despite the fact that the music of figures like Macon was deeply rooted in African-American tradition. When the blues musician John Jackson was interviewed and asked about Uncle Dave Macon, Jackson—having heard but never seen the musician—assumed he was black.[43]

What is striking about all this history, though, is the way that the sound of the instrument ultimately carries through and beyond such categories. The banjo has called to audiences and musicians, over and over again, called them to play and keep playing, to find a way to make the instrument sound out what they needed and wanted to hear. Musicians have brought all kinds of traditions to it but also their affinity for individual styles, tunings, and musical motion. In a recent recording of the song "Swannanoa Tunnel" by Joe Newberry, that ongoing rootedness is celebrated. In its last lines, the recording combines earlier verses by Lunsford and Holcomb to issue a warning to any of those—numerous as they are, notably among friends and family of banjo players—who think they can somehow get rid of the banjo, drown it out:

> This old banjo, rings like silver, shines like gold.
> Take this banjo, throw it in the river!
> It rings right on baby shines right on.[44]

A similar sense of the indestructability and ongoing resonance of the banjo comes to us in the form of a short African-American song called "The Other Side of Jordan," recorded in 1927 by Uncle Dave Macon:

> Rain forty days and rain forty nights,
> Rain forty days and rain forty nights,
> Rain forty days and rain forty nights,
> Johnny kept a-pickin' on the banjo.[45]

7

Black Banjo

In an 1889 drawing the banjo is leading the way. African-Americans are leaving behind slavery and the plantation in what the newspaper *The Freeman* called "The Great Southern Exodus." The image depicts what is driving them away: a white man whipping a black woman, a scene of a lynching, and a dog chasing an escaped convict. In the corner, with a caption entitled "In Dixie's Land," a black banjo player sits on a barrel playing for a group of dancing whites. Now the banjo is heading north. At the front of the giant but orderly crowd of black migrants making up the exodus is a man with a banjo, guiding them with song.[1]

Throughout the late nineteenth and early twentieth centuries, the banjo remained central to the musical life of African-American communities. Ex-slave Fanny Randolph remembered occasions when people got together in one of the log cabins, warmed by a "big log fire," and danced to the music of fiddle, banjo, and bones. When a man called the sets, "feets would fly!" And she remembered dances that took place when people gathered to help a fellow farmer shuck a harvest of corn. "When there was a big barn full of corn to be shucked," Henry Rodgers similarly remembered, "the neighbors gladly gathered in, shucked the corn for the owner, who had a fiddler and maybe someone to play the banjo.

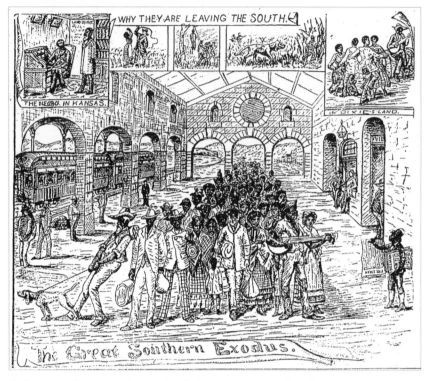

"The Great Southern Exodus," *The Freeman,* November 5, 1892.

The corn was shucked to gay old tunes and piled high in another barn."
When the work was done, the farmer provided supper for everyone, and
sometimes a dance was held in the cleared barn. Music helped with the
labor and accompanied the celebration when it was done. The instrument was also played in northern African-American communities. In
1889 the instrument sounded in a celebration of Emancipation Day that
took place in Jamaica, New York: "A band of vocalists with guitars and
banjos sang through the village in the afternoon, to the great delight of
all who heard them. Their voices harmonized finely and the effect was
excellent." The instrument's presence was a continuation of a long tradition: it was not far from there that, in 1736, banjos were played as part of
a Pinkster celebration, generating what was the first recorded appearance
of the instrument in North America.[2]

Late nineteenth-century engravings and paintings registered the ongoing presence of the banjo in African-American communities. An 1878 engraving called *Scene on the Mississippi* shows a group of African-American roustabouts resting among merchandise, while one plays the banjo and another dances. In the 1881 work *A Pastoral Visit,* by Richard Norris Brooke, a rural family listens to a visiting preacher, gathering around the table. Laid out next to the father, as if it had just been set down from playing when the visitor appeared, is a well-built but also clearly well-played banjo. A decade later the African-American painter Henry Ossawa Tanner produced one of the most powerful and enduring images of the banjo, and of generational connection and transmission, in his work the *Banjo Lesson.* Here the banjo is a clear reference point, a source of gathering and memory.[3]

Banjos also sounded out in African-American churches. In 1887 a letter from the town of Grenada, Mississippi, published in the New Orleans *Daily Picayune* described the ministry of a female African-American preacher known as Scinda, whose church of "High Priest-Worship" included "Singing, Dancing and Banjo Music." The church, on the outskirts of town, had a massive following of about eight hundred participants and included some local whites, though in a reversal of usual Jim Crow practice they were required to sit in the back of the church. Her services began at eight in the morning on Sundays and lasted all day. The writer of the letter described the interwoven music and preaching that drew such large crowds in this way:

> Long before we reached the church we could hear the picking of the banjo and the shuffling of feet. Alighting,
>
> SCINDA,
>
> arrayed in gorgeous red and yellow, came to the door to greet us and welcome us in. The church is a small structure made of pine logs. Around the walls hang her paraphernalia used in her marches through the country. In the center of the room stood a little table covered with a red cloth of grotesque figures of white sewed on it. This is where the members speak.

When we arrived a "soldier" was telling his inspirations of the day. He consumed about ten minutes, then they danced and sung and played the banjo and shouted. When dancing begins they all stand up and as many as can join hands until a circle is formed. They march around and around, singing their own chants, occasionally stopping and each one goes through a "shuffle" to the music of a banjo. This performance lasts about ten minutes, then another preaches, then a dance and so on until a few minutes before they break up for the day. Then every voice is hushed and a stillness pervades the house.

Rising slowly and deliberately from her seat Scinda, the priestess of this new, original and strange religion, proceeds to the appointed stand. Every one watches her with wide-eyed wonder and is eager to catch every syllable of her utterances.

Scinda's sermons touched on many topics—virtue, cleanliness, the prompt paying of debts—and they ended as they began, with "consider-able ceremony" that was "marked by a procession, single file, each one carrying a symbol marked by design, moving under the music of the fiddle and banjo. After rounds of marchings they assemble in solemn awe around their priestess Scinda." This particular church was part of larger matrix of evangelical movements in the late nineteenth-century South, many of which likely also used the banjo as part of the spiritual arsenal and holy sound.[4]

African-American banjo players continued to play in southern com-munities throughout the early twentieth century. A postcard from 1905 showed two musicians, one on the fiddle and one on the banjo. A cap-tion described the banjo player as "Billy Smith—former slave, had a whip scar on his back." The fiddle player was named Billy Russell, and the two "played for dances in the early 1900s" and were "Great old men." Such musicians had a crucial role not just in animating dances and gatherings but also in cultivating memory. One of the more stunning examples of how they did this is a song performed by a banjo player from northern Mississippi named Sid Hemphill. He was interviewed by Alan Lomax in 1942, and among the songs he played was one called "The Strayhorn Mob." It told the story of a lynching that had happened decades before. A lynch mob from the town of Strayhorn had demanded that an African-American prisoner be released from a jail in the town of Senatobia; and when the jailer refused, they killed him, broke into the prison, and took the prisoner back to their town and hung him. As the song notes, everyone was acquitted at a subsequent trial. Hemphill's song described every detail of the event, listing many members of the mob by name. It was, in fact, one of the white men involved in the lynching who had originally asked Hemphill to write the song. Yet Hemphill's song was more than an ode to its perpetrator. It served as "testimony and an accusation masked as a simple narrative" for African-Americans. For them, it "kept alive the memory of white terrorism." Hemphill himself kept and cultivated deep memory in the form of his musical practice. When Lomax met him, he sang the song "John Henry" but also put down his banjo and performed a remarkable version of "Devil's Dream" on a type of flute known as the quills, accompanied by a drum, channeling a deep tradition of fife-and-drum music kept alive in Mississippi, with roots that likely stretch back to Central Africa.[5]

The African-American string band music of Virginia, North Carolina, and other parts of the South has often been overlooked because very little of it was recorded commercially. Those who recorded and released string band music as "hillbilly" music in the early twentieth century presented it as the music of white rural communities and for the most part didn't record African-American string bands. At the same time, recording labels that presented African-American music, often under the term "race music," also excluded this music, focusing instead on newer styles they considered more attractive to black audiences. "This left black string bands in a double bind: They were banned from the hillbilly catalogues because they were black, and from the race catalogues because they played hillbilly music." Some groups, like the Mississippi Sheiks, found a compromise by recording blues songs while continuing to play string band music for black audiences, many of whom embraced this style of music they considered very much part of their roots.[6]

The commercial choices that excluded black string band music had enduring consequences, helping to obscure both the place of the banjo in African-American music and the place of black performance in shaping white "hillbilly" and later "bluegrass" styles. But Bill Monroe, who was born in 1911 and grew up in Rosine, Kentucky, in a small rural community, was influenced early on by an African-American blues musician named Arnold Schultz, whom he first heard play for a dance as part of a string band with guitar, banjo, and fiddle. Though he admitted he could never quite play like Schultz, he "tried to keep in mind a little of it—what I could salvage to use in my music." And African-American banjo players continued to offer music for dances throughout the South, and several of them—including Dink Roberts, Lucius Smith, and Sid Hemphill—were recorded by folklorists, their banjo playing preserved in the Library of Congress. In the 1960s and 1970s they offered a crucial link back to early musical styles, inspiring contemporary musicians like Taj Mahal in his embrace of the banjo. Starting in the 1970s the folklorist Cecelia Conway interviewed many of these players and documented their history, as well as releasing their music on Folkways Records. The tradition was ultimately sustained and revived when fiddle player Joe Thompson helped to mentor the Carolina Chocolate Drops, who in recent years have brought black string band music to rapt and eager audiences.[7]

The banjo left its traces on African-American music in another way, through its influence on early blues music. We can see that link most clearly in the story of Gus Cannon. Born in 1883 in the Mississippi Delta, the son of former slaves, Cannon learned to play fiddle, guitar, and piano as a young boy. When he was twelve, he built his own banjo with a guitar neck and a bread sifter as a body and apprenticed for two years with a man named Old Sum Russel, a hunter who lived on the banks of the Sunflower River and was an excellent banjo player. Cannon then found work performing in touring medicine shows in the region. These shows were an opportunity for various doctors and hucksters to sell their wares to rural people and frequently featured music and comic acts as a way to drum up business. They were a crucial site of employment for itinerant musicians, playing an important role in maintaining various performance traditions, including minstrel music and vaudeville, throughout the late nineteenth century. Under the employ of a doctor from Mississippi, Cannon had to blacken his face and paint his lips white, and recalled that the only way he managed to perform in those conditions was to drink a lot of alcohol beforehand. Drunk, he threw himself into playing the banjo, wandering around and selling soap and tonic to the crowd.[8]

After years on the medicine show circuit, Gus Cannon teamed up with the blues guitarist Blind Blake to record a few songs. He called himself "Banjo Joe," and soon formed his own band called the Cannon's Jug Stompers. The "jug bands" of this period got their name from the bass sound provided by blowing into a half-full jug, which sounded a bit like a tuba. Cannon recruited an old companion from the medicine shows, Elijah Avery, who played banjo and guitar, and the group recorded a series of songs in the late 1920s, often with several banjos. On some songs, including "Poor Boy, Long Ways from Home," Cannon used a bottle to slide up and down the banjo. To make the slide work, he placed dimes under the strings in order to give it the proper sustain. Though Cannon was able to use the banjo to record blues numbers, he was among the last musicians to do so. African-American musicians playing in this style turned instead to the guitar, whose sound better suited the vocal styles they were developing. The guitar has longer sustain than the banjo, meaning that when its strings are strummed the sound lasts longer, so it could better accompany slower singing. It also had a mellower, lower sound. The fact that the twentieth-century banjo was in some ways less well-suited for new vocal styles, however, was one of the curious and ironic consequences of the way the banjo had been transformed in the late nineteenth century. The higher-pitched, more metallic-sounding instrument made it less useful as an accompaniment. The older styles of banjos, notably those with gourds, would have offered a different tonality that may have in fact suited it better for the blues. But by the twentieth century, the guitar ultimately did better work, filling in the space between blues lyrics, offering bass notes that can almost beat like a drum. The influence of the banjo lived on even as the instrument was traded for the guitar, however, in the kinds of right-hand playing and open tuning that many blues musicians used. The use of the back of the fingers in a rhythmic pattern is a way to play clawhammer banjo style on a guitar.[9]

After 1930 Cannon for the most part stopped playing and found work in Memphis as a garbage collector. Then, in 1963, the Roof Top Singers did a version of one of his greatest and most exuberant songs, the 1929 "Walk Right In." It became a hit, and other musicians released versions throughout the world in the next years. Cannon came out of retirement, did an album of jug band music with the legendary Stax Records company in Memphis, and played banjo again until his death in 1979. Meanwhile, through the remakes of his song, listeners heard Cannon's invitation, the ultimate celebration of what music—and the banjo itself—were meant to do: to "walk right in, sit right down," and "let your mind roll on."[10]

*

"The real beginnings of the Negro in American theatre," the African-American composer James Weldon Johnson wrote in his 1930 *Black Manhattan,* "were made on the minstrel stage." In the wake of the Civil War, black musicians and actors found they had one option for getting access to the stage: putting on blackface and performing as minstrels. As Johnson noted, they "accepted almost wholly the performance pattern as it had been worked out and laid down by the white minstrels during the preceding twenty-five years." Still, once they were on stage, they "could not help bringing something fresh and original to the stage." If blackface minstrelsy was ultimately capacious enough to become a foundation for twentieth-century African-American performance, Johnson argued, it was because in a sense black musicians were actually, through a curious detour, reconnecting with their roots. "Negro minstrelsy, everyone ought to know, had its origin among the slaves of the old south. Every plantation had its talented band that could crack negro jokes, and sing and dance to the accompaniment of the banjo and bones. . . . When the wealthy plantation owner wished to amuse his guests, he needed only to call for his troupe of black minstrels." There was, Johnson wrote, "a record of at least one of these bands that became semi-professional and travelled around from plantation to plantation giving performances." Johnson emphasized the filiation with these "original plantation artists," seeking to present a kind of interrupted continuity from plantation performance to nineteenth-century African-American music and dance. Of course, the interruption of minstrelsy was more than that: it left black musicians in a very strange, and enduring, situation. The plantation performers, Johnson notes, had never thought of the "expedient" of blacking their faces, as the whites who appropriated their music for the stage would. But the African-American musicians who came to the stage in the wake of white minstrelsy inherited this new layer of practice. "Working through excruciating contradictions," as two recent scholars note, these musicians "began the long process of reestablishing the rights to their own creative identity."[11]

The story of what Yuval Taylor and Jake Austen have recently dubbed "black minstrelsy" is a complex and difficult one. It forces us to confront a curious fact: the history of black performance in the United States is fundamentally tied to the history of blackface performance. "Since emancipation, black performers have alternately embraced, exploited, subverted, and turned stereotypes inside out, quite often becoming tremendously successful with both black and white audiences in the process." This tradition created a foundation for the performance practices of the twentieth, and even twenty-first, centuries. "The black minstrel tradition is an umbilical cord that feeds contemporary performers both the genius and frustrations of their ancestors." As Taylor and Austen note, already in the 1840s the famed dancer William Henry Lane, known as "Master Juba," had toured with white minstrel troupes and was a "black man performing as a white man performing as a black man." In a sense, that is what many African-American performers chose to do in the late nineteenth century: they were blacks in blackface, drawing on the music and performance of whites in blackface, who themselves were channeling much older theatrical and vernacular cultures of masking and imitation. Black minstrelsy was one more stage in the vertiginous sedimentation of Atlantic performance cultures.[12]

The stakes and possibilities of this process were particularly high when it came to the instrument at the center of minstrelsy: the banjo. Blackface, after all, was a European tradition that had been deployed as part of the creation of minstrelsy. But the banjo was an African-American instrument, now thoroughly integrated into theatrical culture, and physically transformed through the work of the banjo manufacturers of the North. What did it mean, in the wake of this, to be an African-American banjo player?

Many, many African-American banjo players performed on stage in the second half of the nineteenth century. They performed in all kinds of venues and in all kinds of formats. Some were part of all-black troupes, others integrated into larger minstrel groups or circus performances. One of these banjo players, Ike Simond—whose career stretched through most of the late nineteenth century—wrote a remarkable book recounting his experiences and naming several hundred other black banjo players of his era. And yet this history of African-American banjo performance is strangely lacking from the common understanding of the history of the instrument. The gap in our sense of who played the banjo has allowed for the received idea that blackface minstrelsy represented a kind of break in the history of the instrument, a transition from black to white that has essentially never been reversed. The idea, writes Tony Thomas, is that "negative images of black banjo playing created by European American minstrelsy and racist propaganda led African Americans to abandon the banjo." But, as he notes, "no one can point to a single banjoist who gave up the banjo for this reason." Though African-American musicians did increasingly embrace the guitar rather than the banjo in the mid-twentieth century, the instrument never completely disappeared from these communities, and the transmission and lineage was never really broken.[13]

There were a few black minstrel performers before the Civil War, including a group called the Alabama Slave Minstrels who performed in Brooklyn in 1857, but these were short-lived experiments. In 1865, however, five black minstrel troupes were founded, including the very successful Georgia Minstrel Troupe. They advertised themselves by playing up the fact that they were all ex-slaves and "natural" black men. Theater owners and managers, as well as black musicians themselves, realized there was an opportunity in showcasing black musicians who many now considered more "authentic" than whites in blackface. In 1870 an African-American former slave from Baltimore, Charles Hicks, took a company made up entirely of black musicians on tour in Germany and Ireland. Another African-American musician, James Bohee, ended up staying in England and becoming the personal banjo instructor for the Prince of Wales. There were always conflicts over who would manage and profit from these troupes, with many black performers ending up under the control of white managers. There was, too, a constant tug-of-war over what vision of black life and black music was to be put on stage. It was then, as it is now, a never-ending discussion, subject to currents and crosscurrents of artistic and aesthetic experimentation and regimentation, market forces, and desire.[14]

In 1871 the first tour of the legendary Fisk Jubilee Singers, ex-slaves on a mission to raise money for Fisk University, brought African-American religious music to the stage for the first time. Their massive success in the United States, in Europe, and later in South Africa—where they toured in the 1890s—helped to reshape the contours and horizons of black musical performance. Many African-American minstrel troupes subsequently incorporated spirituals into their repertoire, and these songs offered a different way of transmitting and condensing the experience of the enslaved and of post-emancipation African-Americans in the United States. They brought elements of African-American folklore, including stories about animal characters such as Brer Rabbit, into the shows. When they performed classic plantation songs, they sometimes sought to shift their meaning, evoking bygone days of childhood and family and friends who had passed on, and avoiding the sentimental songs about masters and mistresses that were often featured in earlier minstrelsy. Whether these changes registered with most audiences is, of course, difficult to know, but it signaled an attempt on the part of performers to shift the terrain of performance and connect with African-American musical traditions in a different way. In the long term, the rise of black minstrelsy helped enable a small number of musicians to rise to prominence and fame and to lay the foundation for the continuing and expanding black presence in musical and theatrical performance in the early twentieth century.[15]

Some African-American musicians were able to craft wide-ranging and successful musical careers during this era. One of them was J. R. Matlock, who told his life story in 1877 while he was on tour in New Zealand. He explained that he had been born in 1839, one of 350 slaves on a cotton plantation in Tennessee. He recalled the whippings and auction block but also the music. On Saturday evenings there was "a weekly concert, if the overseer don't interfere." Musicians played fiddles and banjos, as well as tin cans, clappers, and jawbones made of a mule's jaw, performing "jubilee songs and plantation walk-rounds." Banjos were built with strings "made of horse-hair," and a frame made out of "cheese boxes." During the Civil War, Matlock traveled with his master and witnessed the battle of Shiloh. He escaped and defected to a regiment of Union soldiers from Illinois and in 1864 found his way to Chicago, where he found work as a waiter in a hotel. There, along with a "young drummer" from Missouri, he formed what he called a "zouave company" of blacks who played military music for Chicago audiences. In 1864 Charles Hicks arrived in Chicago "in search of black talent to form a minstrel troupe," and Matlock decided to join him, beginning a decades-long career as a musician who traveled throughout the United States and the world. Matlock's story suggests the layers of experience that went into the musical careers of the African-American musicians of the late nineteenth century. He had grown up hearing the music of fiddles and banjos on the plantation and experienced the war before arriving in Chicago, where he drew on new urban musical influences. The creative process here was a complex one, for sure, at the crossroads of heritage and expectation, of tradition and invention. It brought together the world of vernacular music with that of existing theater, representing not a simple evolution but rather one more cycle in the circulation of forms that had generated minstrelsy in the first place.[16]

The most celebrated African-American banjo player of the late nineteenth century was Horace Weston, who in Ike Simond's words "made every banjo player in the land lay chilly." Weston was the son of a Connecticut dancing teacher and musician named Jube Weston and played a wide variety of instruments. He began with the accordion, then moved on to violin, along with trombone and guitar, but finally settled on the banjo as his major instrument. He made his first banjo himself and began earning a living playing in the streets. In 1861 Weston tried to join the Union Army and was turned away—no black volunteers were accepted at the time; but he was able to join the Navy. He carried his banjo with him onto the ship, receiving "fifty cents per month from each sailor of the crew for playing for their amusement." He eventually was able to join the army as part of the famed Massachusetts Fifty-Fourth Volunteers. He was wounded several times and was discharged in 1863 and began playing in minstrel troupes, first Buckley's Minstrels and then the Georgia Colored Minstrels in the 1860s. In 1878 Weston performed in a production of *Uncle Tom's Cabin,* where his banjo playing was a major attraction: a full thirty minutes of the production were devoted to his solo banjo performance. His wife, Alice Weston, was also a banjo player and sometimes performed with him on stage. By 1884 Horace had become well-known enough that Samuel Swaim Stewart published a novel called *The Black Hercules; or, The Adventures of a Banjo Player* based on Weston's life. Weston boasted fourteen medals won in banjo competitions in Europe. When he died in 1890—in part because of the lingering effects of a wound suffered during the war—a New York newspaper declared him perhaps "the greatest banjoist the world has ever heard." He went into the ground in a "black walnut casket, decked with wreaths of flowers," and followed—we might imagine—by the sound of the banjo he had carried to new heights through his life of playing.[17]

Thanks to the brilliance of musicians like Weston, black minstrel troupes gained tremendous popularity. One of them, the Genuine Colored Minstrels, performed for six weeks in New York and drew 60,000 people to their shows, continuing the next year for a longer stretch and then going on a "triumphant tour" of England. In the 1880s, a "Colossal Colored Carnival" with more than a hundred performers traveled the country. There was a "minstrel festival" in Cincinnati in 1883 with two hundred performers: "twenty banjo players, twenty song and dance men, and sixteen vocalists." The black minstrels, writes Robert Toll, "traveled in small rag-tag groups and in companies of over one hundred in their own railroad cars. They played in small frontier settlements, in the largest cities, and in the greatest theaters. They entertained poor, backcountry farmers, black and white, and gave command performances for English royalty." Troupes and managers were always on the lookout for good banjo players: an 1891 advertisement in New York asked for "Colored (Black) Performers," and specified a desire for "Banjo Players who are Good Singers." Musicians toured far and wide for decades in the United States, including in many southern states. Several troupes also traveled abroad, to Europe but also in Australia, New Zealand, and Southeast Asia: Charles Hicks died in 1902 while on tour in Java. By 1890, according to the federal census, there were 1490 "Negro actors and showmen." In 1910 there were 3088. These numbers were probably low, failing to include those who worked part-time or had other jobs. In 1894 a promoter in New York published an advertisement saying he needed forty black minstrels. More than 2,000 contenders appeared at his office.[18]

Many black minstrels spent their winters in New Orleans, playing in the numerous concert halls. Memphis, too, was a "musical center," sending many locals on to fame elsewhere in the country. And the Mississippi and Ohio rivers provided both a route between different places and, on its steamboats, a regular source of employment for musicians. "All the large boats had a concert party on board," wrote Simond, and "in fact all the principal boats between St. Louis and New Orleans gave nightly entertainments." Another crossroads for musicians was Chicago, which in the 1880s had a massive minstrel show playing at the Grand Opera House. There were "over three hundred minstrel men in town at the same time," often congregating at another concert hall where there was a "nightly scene of revelry; it was singing, dancing, banjo playing" from the morning until "until late at night." Many African-American performers took their first banjo lessons there.[19]

Early minstrelsy got its energy and gained its following in part because of the transgression and novelty of white men transforming themselves, at least for a while, into black men. Though they had inherited the roles developed by white men in black face, in time some African-American performers sought to escape the constraints of this form. One banjo player, Sam Lucas, grew tired of wearing blackface, and "quit the minstrel stage." "He told me," Ike Simond wrote, "that he would never black his face again, and as I have met him in nearly every city of the United States since that time I don't think he ever has." Lucas went on to perform the role of Uncle Tom on both the stage and in film. In time, more and more African-American musicians would search for a way out of the traditions of blackface performance, seeking to use the stage to offer a different vision and a different aesthetic. In the early 1890s the manager William Foote sought to offer a more "refined and elevated" performance by African-Americans, setting aside "plantation melodies and peculiar dialect" and instead focusing on a more historical approach to the black experience. He created a troupe to go on a tour in Europe, advertising that he needed "Genuine Negro Talent." He added applicants "Must Be Unmistakable African Descent," and that he didn't want any who played the role of "Freak" or "Monstrosity." Instead, he was seeking performers who were "High Class."[20]

Still, throughout the 1880s and 1890s many African-American musicians found themselves locked into performances that offered the stock stereotypes of minstrelsy, which often contrasted "the happy, contented 'darky'" of the South with the "unruly, inept Northern Negro." The contrast was a meaningful one in the era of the Great Migration of African-Americans from the South to the North, and minstrelsy provided a theater through which the experiences and anxieties this migration had created were laid out and performed. The presence of black men on the minstrel stage, rather than undermining racial stereotypes, could often be used to confirm them. And although there were a number of racially integrated minstrel troupes, black and white performers usually performed separately on stage. The black musicians were often confined to playing older minstrel numbers and "dressed in the old-time style," according to one account. And black minstrels found themselves part of a larger swirl of exoticism: one troupe in Cleveland offered a show made up of "35 white minstrel stars, 15 male and female Japanese, 35 genuine colored minstrels," and for good measure "15 Moorish-Bedouin Arabs." Among the minstrel performances in the city was one called "The Feast of the Voudoos." Some of the flavor of these performances is captured in a short note from a New York newspaper from 1890: "Tom Williams is doing captivating work with his banjo. The Egyptian jugglers are doing well."[21]

By the mid-1890s several large productions offered a kind of "purification," and also perhaps an apotheosis, of black minstrelsy. A massive "theatrical extravaganza" called *Black America* was performed in 1895 in a Brooklyn park, advertised as "a Panorama of the Negro, from the Jungles of Africa to the Civilization of America." It was the brainchild of a free-born African-American minstrel named Billy McClain and was financed by the promoter of Buffalo Bill's Wild West show. He gathered together five hundred performers, including sixty-three vocal ensembles, and members of the famed African-American cavalry unit known as the "Buffalo Soldiers." One advertisement claimed audiences would experience the best entertainment on offer since ancient times: in the park would be "More Fun, Jollity, Humor and Character presented in Marvellously Massive Lyric Magnitude for the Millions than since the days of Cleopatra." Audiences could stroll through a reconstructed southern plantation, complete with transported cotton plants with blooming buds and log cabins to depict slave quarters. The performers didn't wear blackface, and they offered a varied repertoire of spirituals and showcased the "home life" and "folklore" of "Southern Colored People." On one level the show clearly sought to fulfill minstrel stereotypes, which deeply shaped the expectations of white audiences and critics. But it also insisted that the best interpreters of minstrel music were African-Americans; for unlike whites in blackface, they were "southerners whose act was no act at all." The advertisements assured visitors that they would see "Real Blacks from the Southern Plantation," and not "Northern negroes." In the next years other African-American performers would mount other large-scale productions that sought simultaneously to play to minstrel stereotypes and to carve new spaces of performance. In 1898 *A Trip to Coontown*, the first full-length black musical comedy, opened in New York. It was written by the Georgia-born musician Bob Cole, who was the son of former slaves. In the play Cole performed the role of a white man named Willie Wayside and, turning the tradition of blackface on its head, wore white makeup. Though attacked by some white critics, the play was a hit and toured to Chicago and other cities. Other similar musicals composed and performed by African-Americans followed, including the 1902 *In Dahomey*, which told the story of a group of African-Americans who return to Africa and become the rulers of the Kingdom of Dahomey. It had a successful run in New York before touring to the United Kingdom and throughout the United States for several years.[22]

We can see the complex cultural dynamics at work in this process in the life of the musician and composer named W. P. Dabney. Born near Richmond in 1865, he studied at Oberlin College. By the late 1880s he began learning to play the banjo during a sojourn in Newport, Rhode Island. Back home, he formed the Richmond Banjo and Guitar Club, which put on a local production of a play called *Uncle Tom's Cabin*. It was advertised as being the "first drama" produced by "colored people in Virginia" and a "faithful portrayal and accurate delineation of the most important epoch of Negro History." In its form, the production offered the spectrum of common music from plantation songs to religious music, along with string band dance songs. But for Dabney, this was clearly an opportunity to produce art by and for African-Americans, dwelling on their history collectively. The event included a presentation of one of his own compositions, played by the Richmond Banjo and Guitar Club, called "Phantasmagoria Waltz."[23]

Dabney was inspired, as other African-American composers and intellectuals were, by an essay about American music published in 1893 by the Czech composer Antonín Dvořák, who came to the United States in 1892 to head the National Conservatory of Music in New York. Dvořák had long insisted on the need for European composers to incorporate vernacular and folk traditions into their music. The "future music" of America, he argued, had to be "founded upon what are called the Negro melodies." "These are the folk songs of America, and your composers must turn to them," he announced. They had everything that was needed to create a "great and noble school of music." At the conservatory Dvořák trained an African-American student whose "compositions are based upon Negro melodies," and though the other students thought this was "not in good taste," Dvořák disagreed. In 1894, invited to do a concert at Madison Square Garden, he chose to showcase "Negro music," with all but one of his solo singers young African-American musicians. In 1895 W. P. Dabney came to meet Dvořák and at first tried to impress him by playing compositions by other musicians. Then he began playing a "little plantation melody of my own composition, known as 'Uncle Remus,' written in E minor." Immediately the Czech composer lit up and was inspired to go to his piano and begin composing. He invited Dabney to his house that night; and the Virginia musician went "carrying my banjo" and spent the evening with the Czech composer and his family "playing the many melodious minor airs for which the banjo is the instrument most conveniently adapted."[24]

African-American writers who grappled with the question of music and culture tended to judge the minstrel tradition harshly. In 1878 James Monroe Trotter published *Music and Some Highly Musical People,* which chronicled the history of African-American musicians, particularly those who performed classical music. Like the Abbé de Gregoire a century earlier, Trotter used their achievements in order to critique the racial order and the cultural stereotypes it produced. He criticized minstrel music and excluded the black musicians who performed it from his genealogy. In 1903, W. E. B. Du Bois published his famous thoughts on the centrality of African-American music to American music. Unlike Dvořák, who seemed relatively comfortable seeing minstrel music and its "plantation melodies" as an expression of African-American folk culture, Du Bois was deeply suspicious of this genre. He celebrated the contributions of the Fisk Jubilee Singers as a contrast to minstrelsy. And, like Dvořák, he emphasized the need for the cultivation and transmission of African-American music, which he also saw as the only true American music.[25]

These debates shaped the work of early twentieth-century African-American composers, who sought a way to create music that drew on folk roots but also could find a space at the center of American musical culture. One of the most important innovators in this regard was James Reese Europe, who was born in Mobile, Alabama, in 1881 to a father who was a former slave active in the Baptist Church and a mother who was the daughter of a leader of the Episcopal Church. Music was integral to their religious lives, and he learned to play piano as a child. When Europe was still a boy, the family migrated to Washington, DC, where he studied with the famous brass-band leader John Philip Sousa. He then made his way to New York, where he established himself as a musician and composer. In 1910 Europe led the formation of the Clef Club, an organization for African-American musicians whose goal was to lobby on behalf of black musicians, pushing for better wages and treatment as well as more access to venues. In order to raise money, and also to showcase the range of talent among them, the group organized a large symphony-sized concert made up entirely of black musicians.[26]

Europe's dream was to create an African-American orchestra that could perform on the most prestigious stages of the United States, as a way of gaining access to and respect from the highest and most lucrative levels of the cultural sphere. But he did not want to do so by playing traditional European classical music. Instead, he sought to develop an African-American orchestral sound. Europe believed that the popularity of ragtime—which he described as just "a fun name given to Negro rhythm by our Caucasian brother musicians many years ago"—proved there was a space for African-American music at the highest levels of cultural life. In New York in 1905, he was part of a group called the "Memphis Students"—although "none of its members was a student and none hailed from Memphis"—a twenty-one-member orchestra consisting of strummed instruments, including several banjos, that created a "tightly coordinated aggregate" that was powerfully rhythmic and syncopated.[27]

This kind of music was, in Europe's mind, a true expression of African-American culture. "You see, we colored people have our own music that is part of us," he explained in 1914. "It's us; it's the product of our souls; it's been created by the sufferings and miseries of our race." Rather than turning their backs on this, African-American musicians and composers should make their mission to adapt this music to a new context. Europe asserted that it was a mistake to cross racial lines in musical performance. "Our symphony orchestra never tries to play white folk's music. We should be foolish to attempt such a thing. We are no more fitted for that than a white orchestra is fitted to play our music."[28]

But what should an African-American orchestra sound like? For decades minstrelsy had defined what audiences understood black music to be. The challenge for Europe was to both draw on and escape this legacy, to conjure with it. He did so by taking on the instrument that had been central to the minstrel sound—the banjo—and deploying it in a new way. This was partly making a virtue out of necessity: given the structure of the music industry, in which black minstrelsy still dominated, there were many more African-Americans playing banjo and guitar than playing oboe or French horn. But for Europe the rhythm of the banjo, alongside other strummed instruments like guitars and mandolins, created a more African-American sound. As he explained in 1914, "although we have first violins, the place of the second violins is taken by the mandolins and banjos." The result was "that peculiar stead strumming accompaniment." Europe also took the bold move of putting ten pianos on stage and, in a subtly provocative cultural move, used not the grand pianos audiences were accustomed to but the uprights that black musicians tended to play in hotels and bars. The result was "a background of chords which are essentially typical of negro harmony."[29]

In 1912 Europe got a golden opportunity: he was asked to perform at Carnegie Hall with his symphony orchestra. The event was a benefit concert for a project called the Music School Settlement for Colored People, whose goal was to establish a free music school in Harlem. Europe put together a wide-ranging program that included "plantation songs," religious music, a banjo and guitar ensemble known under the pleasing name of the Versatile Entertainers Quintet, and larger orchestral numbers showcasing his signature hard-strumming rhythmic sound. By the day before the performance only a third of the tickets had been sold, mostly to African-Americans. Then an editorial appeared in the *Evening Journal* calling attention to the concert and declaring: "The Negroes have given us the only music of our own that is American—national, original and real." Suddenly the performance became a not-to-be-missed cultural event, and Carnegie Hall was packed the night of the concert. It was also a social watershed: for probably the first time, the crowd was about half black and half white, and the audience was mixed together. "Some of the leading white citizens sat in evening dress in seats next to some of our highly respectable colored citizens, who were also in evening clothes," one reviewer noted. There was, he went on, "no calamity," though he added that this was probably because both the whites and blacks in attendance "represented the best elements of their race."[30]

James Reese Europe and his Clef Club Orchestra, Ca. 1911. Photograph.
Eubie Blake Collection. Courtesy of the Maryland Historical Society.

The night began with Europe coming out on stage to conduct his 125-person Clef Club Orchestra, which launched into their anthem, the syncopated "Clef Club March." The orchestra had "sections of banjos, mandolins, guitars, strings, and percussion that entirely filled the stage," wrote one reviewer, creating "an absolutely distinctive sound, a 'tang' like the flavor of pineapple amid other fruits." Another reviewer described the orchestra's sound as "very imposing and seductively rhythmic," and noted his "surprise" at "the beautiful, soft sound of this strange conglomeration of unassorted instruments." The "Clef Club March," with its "biting attack and infectious rhythm," ended with the orchestra bursting into song. This brought the audience to its feet, and at the end of the piece the "applause became a tumult." By the end of the first piece of

music, those in attendance, according to one observer, had awoken to the fact that their city had just gained "something new in music."[31]

The success of the Carnegie Hall concert helped to propel Europe's career. He played again there in the following years and began to tour widely. The year 1913 was the fiftieth anniversary of the abolition of slavery, and African-American promoters organized major cultural events to celebrate. Europe's orchestra played in one of these in New York, which also featured a pageant on the history of black people written by W. E. B. Du Bois. They toured to other East Coast cities as part of these emancipation celebrations, garnering large audiences everywhere they went, offering concerts that included the large orchestra pieces as well as an occasional banjo solo. In the ensuing years, notably through collaboration with two white dancers, Vernon and Irene Castle, Europe's orchestra became one of the hottest acts of the time. When they traveled, he asked that seating at their concerts be racially integrated—a request granted everywhere except Richmond, Virginia—carrying the example of the Carnegie Hall concert to other venues. To the driving sound of the banjo, a new kind of theatrical life was being cultivated; and Europe's project of creating an African-American orchestra thrived—for a time.[32]

With the arrival of World War I, Europe became the leader of a celebrated military band. He died in 1919, but his example—notably his strategic use of the banjo as a core rhythm instrument—had an impact on some of the new bands that emerged in New Orleans in what would come to be seen as the birth of early jazz. Many street bands in the city—sometimes called "spasm bands"—used homemade stringed instruments, including "tin-bucket banjos with thread and fishing-line strings," as part of their instrumentation. The first instrument played by Louis Armstrong, in fact, was something similar: a "gitbox" made from a cigar box with four copper wires for strings. Some more established bands also included banjo players, such as the Big Four String Band, which featured Charles C. Henderson, who according to an 1908 newspaper had already "won great fame with his banjo" playing in New Orleans before he joined the band.[33]

But as the jazz banjoist Lawrence Marrero recalled, when he was growing up in New Orleans around 1910, most of the bands used guitars as their rhythm instrument. Then, around 1915—with possible thanks to the influence of Europe—a few musicians began switching to the banjo, including his brother John Marrero. Both Lawrence and his brother liked the banjo better: once they started playing it, they got more fans—"white and colored, and girls too." "When you playing jazz you make anything as long as you make it right," he explained. In that same year the sheet music for one of Jelly Roll Morton's first compositions, the "Jelly Roll Blues," featured a tuxedo-wearing banjo player on the cover. The two Marrero brothers would help develop a style of banjo playing that created the rhythmic core of early jazz.[34]

The most celebrated jazz banjo player to emerge from New Orleans was the African-American musician Johnny St. Cyr, whose story also illustrates how and why the banjo became so central to the music. St. Cyr was born in 1890, his father a musician who taught him to play flute and guitar. As a boy he apprenticed as a plasterer and started working at the age of fifteen; and for much of his musical career, he worked construction during the day and then played music at night. He played in small bands throughout his teen years and at nineteen was to play guitar in one of New Orleans's best groups, led by A. J. Piron. St. Cyr co-wrote one of Piron's hit songs, *Mama's Baby Boy*. Around 1917 Piron told him: "John, banjos are getting popular now. . . . You're pretty good at woodwork— suppose you get a regular banjo and make a guitar neck for yourself. You'd use the same fingering you use on the guitar neck." St. Cyr could have purchased a tenor banjo with four strings, which was easy to find on the market, but that would have required learning his chords and techniques anew. Instead, on Piron's suggestion and using his skills at carpentry, he created his very own "banjo guitar." St. Cyr bought a Stewart five-string banjo—"one of the best banjos made," he recalled—then removed the banjo neck and replaced it with one he handmade out of oak. "I was the first banjo player in New Orleans," St. Cyr claimed—stirring up the ghost of Picayune Butler and many other forebears—but then specified that he meant he was the "first banjo player to play in a dance orchestra in New Orleans."[35]

In 1918 St. Cyr was hired by a bandleader named Fate Marable to begin playing on a riverboat alongside a young Louis Armstrong. These boats offered patrons the chance to spend an evening cruising up the Mississippi, dining, and dancing. Banjo player Danny Barker claimed that the inspiration for having bands on riverboats had initially come from the roustabouts, the descendants of those described in 1871 by Lafcadio Hearn. Passengers on the upper decks sometimes heard the roustabouts singing and playing below and "they would come downstairs" to listen. That gave one boat owner the idea of hiring musicians to play for passengers. The boats served as a giant, floating "hook-up scene": "Most everyone came alone, but left with someone on their arm," one observer recalled. The dance floors were enormous—on one ship they could welcome up to three thousand people at a time—and were much longer than they were wide. Playing for such a crowd, the band had to be loud, creating a "coordinated attack that could reach as many dancers as possible." Without amplification, a guitar simply couldn't hold up as a rhythm instrument in this context. A banjo, however, could cut through more powerfully. To increase the sound of his banjo, St. Cyr crafted his own picks out of toothbrushes or combs, which gave him a "better grip" than on manufactured picks. He and other banjo players were what he described as "chord men," whose hard strumming drove the music and held the band together. On most songs the bass and bass drum players played "a solid two-beat rhythm," while the banjo and piano players, along with the snare drummer, played four-beat. For the last, "hot" chorus, everyone got together to play a four-beat rhythm. The music was electrifying, setting the massive crowds on the riverboats dancing and bringing in a steady and profitable business. Most nights on the riverboats, the bands played to all white audiences, but some boat owners offered special Monday night cruises for black customers. On these nights the passengers could remind themselves that "there was now, because there had always been, a black Mississippi." And the music of the riverboats moved onshore and shaped musical life in towns like St. Louis and Memphis, helping to lay the foundations for later generations of musical innovation and invention.[36]

The time on the riverboats consolidated St. Cyr's style; and throughout the 1920s he played with many of the best bands in New Orleans, including those of Louis Armstrong and Jelly Roll Morton. His playing also drove a series of key early jazz recordings. At the time recording technology was relatively basic, with bands recorded all together by one device. Some instruments were difficult to record in this context: drum sets were too loud, overpowering the other instruments, and guitars were too soft. The banjo turned out to be the perfect stringed instrument for a recording studio. It could hold its own as part of a larger band, and it also provided a strong rhythm in the absence of the drum sets used in live performances. St. Cyr's most famous recordings were made with Louis Armstrong's Hot Five and Hot Seven recordings in Chicago in 1925. Among these songs was one of his own compositions, "Oriental Strut." These recordings "crystallized a new idiom for jazz" and in time became legendary, founding documents in the history of the music. Though they are most remembered for Armstrong's "soaring solo style," the banjo playing of St. Cyr is central to these recordings. As one French jazz critic has noted, he made up "an entire rhythm section" that drove the music.[37]

The banjo played a pivotal role as a rhythm instrument in most of the major New Orleans jazz bands of the late teens and early twenties, including Edward "Kid" Ory's bands and the Original Tuxedo Jazz Band. These ensembles needed "a musician in the group who could serve as its nerve center, cueing the chord changes for the collective improvisations among the front line instruments and serving as a base for the close harmonies that make the great jazz band." The piano could serve this role, and did in some bands. But the banjo had a major advantage: its portability. Recalling the work of banjo player Johnny St. Cyr, the bandleader Kid Ory noted: "His banjo used to take the place of the piano in the real old days." It was, writes Al Rose, essentially an "outdoor piano" during jazz's early days, when the music "was played mainly for picnics, parades, funerals and lawn parties." Starting in the late nineteenth century, residents of New Orleans gathered for Sunday picnics on the banks of Lake Pontchartrain, continuing the tradition of the weekly public dances at the Place Congo. The best bands in New Orleans vied for attention among the Sunday picnickers. Because the banjo was perfect for such outdoor concerts, it became a key instrument for all the bands of the era. "It could beat the rhythm. It was loud. It could handle the chording—and there *is* something the crowd loves about watching those flying fingers."[38]

It could be hard work: as banjo player George Guesnon joked in an interview, if he was to be born again he would be a trumpet player, because they "get to rest." Banjo players, including Johnny St. Cyr, occasionally fell half-asleep on stage while continuing to play. Banjoist Johnny Dave, who like St. Cyr worked construction during the days, once put down his banjo on the floor during a break. When the band started up again, he immediately woke up and started strumming the rhythm—but his banjo was still on the floor in front of him.[39]

The banjo connected generations of New Orleans musicians. Danny Barker was born in 1909 and came of age in the midst of the burst of early jazz in the city. He later described growing up amidst all the musical sounds of New Orleans—the calls from street vendors, including his mother, who sold food to the workers along the river; the singing of a guitar player named Blind Tom, who gathered crowds a few hundred strong and sang a twenty-minute "Ballad of the Titanic"; and the music at banquets and picnics. One evening, Barker was on the banks of the Mississippi when he heard Fate Marable's band start to play on one of the riverboats, before it set out on the river. Barker started with drums, then switched to clarinet, but ultimately found his calling when an aunt bought a banjo–ukulele and, after trying to play for a bit, left it around the house. Barker didn't know how to tune it, but a neighbor did and came by every evening to tune the instrument for him. Barker created a band called the "Boozan Kings," with a washboard player, kazoo, and tambourine, and his banjo-ukulele as the lead. They played in local bars; and when he was fourteen, he got a lucky break: the banjo player for Kid Rena's band was too drunk to play. They asked Barker if he could play a traditional banjo, and though he said no they insisted he take to the stage, tuning the banjo in the ukulele style. He played well and "was like a hero." His uncle soon got him his own banjo from Chicago, and he began a rich career playing in the city, going on to record with jazz greats including Louis Armstrong, Jelly Roll Morton, and later Cab Calloway and Sidney Bechet.[40]

Though Barker switched to the guitar relatively early in his career, he continued to play the banjo occasionally for the rest of his life. Along with banjo player George Guesnon, Barker played and recorded songs in Creole, preserving a critical part of New Orleans's linguistic and musical culture in the process. In time Barker became famous not just as a musician but as one of the great raconteurs of the history of jazz, creating an archive that recorded the history of many New Orleans musicians who never made recordings and therefore might otherwise have been forgotten. He emphasized the influence of what he called "Spanish" styles, including those coming from Cuban music, on the history of jazz, describing how the banjo offered a mix of "African and Spanish" instrumentation. He recalled the banjo player Willie Santiago, of Cuban background, whose hands were as flexible as "poplar leaves." Another of Barker's favorite banjo players was a man named Saint-Thomas, who played in one of the town's parade orchestras and could carry the entire rhythm for a band as they moved through the streets.[41]

The banjo was incorporated into most of the great jazz ensembles of the period. One of Duke Ellington's early bands, the Washingtonians, was created and first led by banjoist Elmer Snowden. After Ellington took over in 1925, he hired banjo player Fred Guy, who stayed with the band for the next two decades. In 1930 they performed in London with a backdrop decorated with huge pictures of banjo players. In the same year Danny Barker witnessed the ongoing passion for the banjo in a jazz club in New York City called the Rhythm Club. "What I saw and heard I will never forget," he later recalled. It was a "wild cutting contest" among dozens of musicians. Around the piano were three of the top banjo players in the city. Each of them played choruses, but the crowd insisted that another musician, a man named Seminole, show them how it was done. Seminole picked up one of the banjos; but because he was left-handed, he flipped it around and "started wailing on the banjo playing it upside down, that is playing everything backwards." He'd taught himself to play everything this way and silenced the other banjo players, who were deeply impressed by his solos and after that just accompanied him playing rhythm.[42]

In time technological changes gradually undermined the banjo's place in jazz recording and performance. In 1927 Western Electric developed an electric microphone that could capture individual instruments. In 1934 guitar makers developed louder guitars with larger bodies, and then in 1937 the electric guitar was invented. The banjo's capacity to carry and cut through the music of brass and drums was no longer an advantage. The electric guitar essentially spelled the demise of the tenor banjo in jazz as well as in other popular ensemble music. Banjo sales plummeted, to the point that during World War II residents offered up their unused banjos to local foundries so they could be melted down and turned into weaponry. How many banjos, one author has wondered, did it take to build a tank? The cycle of boom and bust, of course, was a boon to some: the banjoist Earl Scruggs, who would define the bluegrass style of the 1940s, recalled that in the late 1930s, pawnshops in the Carolinas were literally filled with some of the most valued instruments made in the previous decades—beautiful Gibson Mastertone and Fairbanks Whyte Ladie banjos—going cheap.[43]

The bebop jazz music of the 1940s didn't use banjo, in part because of the prominence given the cymbal in the percussive landscape of the music. In terms of timbre, cymbals and banjos have a common energy, and putting them together is a kind of "musical redundancy." Leaving aside the banjo was also a very visible and audible way to make a break with past jazz traditions and strike out in a new direction. A few African-American banjo players continued to showcase the instrument in their work, notably Elmer Snowden, who had started playing in the early twentieth century in Washington and Baltimore and in 1960 released a record called "Harlem Banjo." But the instrument was increasingly performed in venues structured by nostalgia, like Preservation Hall in New Orleans. The fossilization of banjo playing in New Orleans meant that, in time, many people forgot the energy and dynamism the instrument had brought to the birth of jazz. By the early 1960s the brilliant banjoist Johnny St. Cyr could only find work playing on a riverboat called the *Mark Twain*—at Disneyland. When he was interviewed in 1958, Lawrence Marrero admitted that he had not played the instrument in a long time: "I haven't touched my banjo in God knows how long. Stroking those chords was nice." When he died in 1959, he was described as the last of the "real archaic jazzmen." Still, he had hopes the banjo would be picked up by another generation. In a 1953 letter to a young, aspiring banjo player named Bill, Marrero wrote: "Just keep on your banjo. . . . Keep up the good work . . . don't be afraid or scared of anyone just play like hell."[44]

The banjo, born of global crossings, also became a global instrument. Minstrel troupes in the nineteenth century had already brought the instrument to many parts of the world. The ragtime and jazz music of the early twentieth century, combined with the production and distribution of increasingly inexpensive banjos of all kinds, helped to spread the instrument into new musical realms. It was during this period that the banjo was most likely incorporated into Irish music, in time becoming a standard instrument in many bands. It found its way into almost every corner of Western Europe, played side-by-side with accordions in France, Germany, and Scandinavia. In 1902 the "Troupe Fallone," which toured in Belgium and other parts of Europe, featured a young girl playing the banjo. One of those who fell in love with the instrument during this period was Django Reinhardt. Born in Belgium in 1910 and raised in France, Reinhardt was of Romani ethnicity and as a young boy got hold of a guitar-banjo and fell head over heels: he used to sleep with the instrument. By the age of twelve, he was performing in banjo competitions. He eventually switched to the guitar, becoming one of the most celebrated European jazz musicians of the twentieth centuries. The passion for the instrument continued in France: a 1930 advertisement for a banjo method published in Paris asked a series of questions and answers meant to reassure potential banjo players that they really could do it: "Are you black?" "No." "Is it necessary to be black to play the banjo?" "No." "Do you know how to play music?" "No matter." "Can you learn to play the banjo in three months?" "Yes!" In 1936 some workers on strike in Paris formed a band almost worthy of James Reese Europe, composed of a violin, a saxophone, an accordion, and five banjos! They performed for a large crowd of workers gathered in the courtyard of their factory.[45]

The popularity of banjos in France led to a kind of homecoming for the instrument, when a group of Martinican musicians led by Alexandre Stellio arrived in Paris in 1929. Drawing on traditions of music from the French Antilles and Guiana, they had played for social dances and marriages, as well as accompanying silent movies, in their home island for nearly a decade. They used an instrumentation of drums, cello, violin, trumpet, and clarinet. The group had heard ragtime records and sought to bring some of their styles into their music. In Paris they encountered a rich culture of "black transnational music," including that performed by African-American jazz musicians as well as performers from Cuba and Haiti. In this context, they expanded their repertoire of sounds, and of instruments, adding a banjo. The instrument would become standard in the music that came to be known as beguine, providing a strong rhythm as it had in early jazz music. Stellio recorded 130 songs in the next decade. Throughout the 1930s he was the leading figure in a wave of music that was extremely popular in Paris dance clubs, particularly the Bal Nègre, which drew crowds of upwards of five hundred people night after night. When bands returned to the Caribbean, they often included a banjo. It is likely that some rural residents on the island were still familiar with the instrument first observed by Labat and later by Lafcadio Hearn and perhaps had maintained traditions of making homemade banjos. But it was ultimately the circulating form of beguine that brought the sounds of the instrument back into popular music in the Antilles. It also traveled to other parts of the French empire: an undated photograph from the Indian Ocean island of Réunion, probably taken in the early twentieth century, shows a band called "La jeunesse ouvriere de Bagatelle"—"The young workers of Bagatelle"—playing drums, accordion, and banjo outside a house alongside what looks like a cane field.[46]

Something similar happened in Jamaica with a music known as mento. Rooted in various forms of rural music and dance and influenced by calypso music, the style emerged in the 1940s and became especially popular in the 1950s. It, too, featured a banjo as a central rhythm instrument. As in New Orleans, the instrument was useful because mento bands often played outdoors in rural areas, and the instrument's sound could carry. Although the musicians usually acquired their instruments from the United States and were influenced by jazz and ragtime sounds, in Jamaica, as in the French Antilles, there was likely some memory and link back to earlier banjo traditions. Indeed, in a curious echo of the situation in the United States, mento in time became seen as consummately "rural" music and also a form that was particularly showcased in tourist settings. That was also true in the Bahamas, where musicians like Blind Blake and Nathaniel Saunders made careers playing local music on the banjo for North American visitors at resorts. But mento banjo had a long-lasting influence: several of the early guitarists who developed the styles that were a foundation for reggae music had previously played the banjo. On the electric guitar they often muffled the strings to create a sharp percussive sound not unlike that of the banjo and used the instrument as the rhythmic foundation for the music.[47]

In Jamaica and other parts of the Caribbean, some individuals continued to make their own instruments, including banjos. In 1934 a journalist in Kingston saw a man and his wife come on board a tram. The man was carrying an instrument made of "a long bamboo fixed into the half of a gourd, across which a skin was stretched. A rough wooden screw at the top of the cane served to tighten or slacken the single wire." He "thrummed" it and sang in a "high-pitched voice," stamping his feet on the floor of the car, and eventually stood up and danced as he finished his song. The journalist was pleased to see this "troubadour" in an age of "canned music," and added that Jamaica could "boast a pretty long catalogue" of native musical instruments, including the "banjar," but that the skill of making most of these was fast fading as musicians preferred store-bought instruments. In fact, though, such traditions of making instruments have never vanished. Working in Kingston in the mid-1950s, anthropologist Sidney Mintz met a man named Percy Barrett, who lived in Sturge Town, a hilltop community founded when slavery was abolished in 1838. He made a body for the banjo out of plaster and took brass pieces cut from a scale used for weighing vegetables to make frets. Ethnomusicologist Kenneth Bilby has interviewed and photographed musicians throughout the Caribbean, many of whom continue to make and play their own banjos.[48]

The banjo had other kinds of homecomings as well. In South Africa the visits of minstrels to Cape Town in the mid-nineteenth century, then of the Fisk Jubilee Singers, and later of African-American troops performing "Coon Songs" all left a deep mark on the culture. These visits contributed to the development of a remarkable street carnival that brings together elements of North American theatrical culture with Islamic festivals to produce an explosion of sound and theater known as the "Coon Carnival" on the first and second of January each year. A swirling and slightly surreal repurposing of minstrel styles and tropes—many parade in the ill-fitting suits and hats and painted faces and lips that were a central part of the minstrel get-up—the "Coon Carnival" is a kind of living museum of the curious sedimentation of performance cultures that came together in the United States in the nineteenth century. The festival begins with small ensembles playing guitar, mandolin, violin, and banjo and singing old minstrel tunes, which are then joined by layers of other migrant music—Portuguese-Indonesian songs, Malaysian choir music—all pulled into a kind of never-ending global minstrel repertoire.[49]

Elsewhere in Africa the banjo became part of the main instrumentation of colonial-era dance bands in Central and East Africa, including a series recorded in the early 1950s. These included the Dar-es-Salaam Jazz Band, who played a style of music known as "Swahili rumba" and used a tenor banjo as a rhythm instrument. In Nairobi, Kenya, the Lake Victoria Band showcased a banjo and sang in the Dholuo language. And Chippy's Dance Band, which was influenced by the dance music coming from South Africa, had two banjos, playing quickstep and singing a tune in English called "Love Is a Merry-Go-Round," and another in the Shona language called Ndinokuziwa. Another of their songs was based on the sounds of the Shona mbira, more commonly known as the thumb piano. In the 1950s these regions were places of tremendous migration set in motion by colonial exploitation, sites of artistic creativity in which bands had to speak to people on the move. And so it was fitting that they found an ally in the banjo in the process bringing the instrument back home to Africa, taking advantage of its long-rooted capacity to bring people together through its sound.[50]

Perhaps the most remarkable homecoming for the banjo has been in North Africa, where starting in the 1940s the instrument was incorporated into a range of musical styles, notably the celebratory chaabi music performed at weddings in Algeria and Morocco. The instrument, according to one theory, arrived in the hands of U.S. soldiers during World War II. The Algerian musician Dahmane El Harrachi, considered the "Father of the Algerian banjo," has recorded many albums and performed for decades on the instrument. And the Orchestra El Gusto performs with a variety of Arabic lutes but also a row of banjo players, and their performances include banjo solos. It was in North Africa—in Marrakech—too, that in the late 1920s Claude McKay wrote his ode to the instrument, *Banjo*. He would later be the first American to write about Gnawa music, recognizing the filiation between the lutes played in this ritual music in North Africa and the banjo carried in the hands of his character. In these new journeys that are also returns, the layers of the banjo's history come together. After a journey hundreds of years long, from the Arabic lutes to West and Central African instruments, to the Caribbean and North American slaves who made a new instrument, to the blackface minstrels and the black minstrels and jazz musicians who followed them, the sound of the banjo, that sound of strings humming over skin, returned in new form to North Africa.[51]

8

Sounding America

"I WOULD LIKE TO BUY A BIG BANJO and play in the very little jazz band up here that has just been started," a teenage Pete Seeger wrote to his mother in 1932. He had been borrowing a banjo from the music teacher at his boarding school, but it had become "awful awkward to keep borrowing it." Pete was learning fast: "It's not half so hard to play one as I thought and I've already learned about ten chords last week. I'm having lots of fun." Perhaps missing his banjo a bit, Pete's teacher told him it would be easy enough for them to drive over to a pawnshop in Hartford and pick one up for a few dollars. "Will you let me get one?" he asked his mother. "Please?"[1]

So it was that Pete Seeger got his banjo, a four-string tenor of the kind that had been played in many jazz bands in the 1920s. But several years later, he switched to a five-string banjo made by the Stewart banjo company. He'd bought it in a pawn shop—for five dollars. He took it on a trip across the country, playing it in bars and homes and camps until the day he was jumping off a freight train and smashed the instrument. When Seeger got back to New York, he paid ten dollars for a fine replacement—a Fairbanks Whyte Laydie banjo. That one lasted him nearly a decade. But in the meantime banjos were becoming more popular, in part because of Seeger's influence. In 1949 he left it in an unlocked car in New York, and someone stole it. When he headed back to the pawnshop to get a new banjo, he discovered "how expensive banjos were getting—they had gone up to several hundred dollars apiece!"[2]

Once upon a time, people had made their own banjos rather than getting them cheap in pawnshops. Seeger opted to tap into that venerable tradition. He got a "pot"—the skin-covered resonator—direct and "at cost" from the "nice man" who ran the Vega banjo company. And then he got a nice long piece of lignum vitae, a hardwood long cherished by carpenters for its solidity and heft. The tree is indigenous to the Caribbean and may well have been used centuries earlier by those who built the earliest banjos in Martinique, Jamaica, and Haiti. Seeger got a guitar-maker in New York to "rough out" the neck from the piece of wood, and then he took a rasp and "rounded it off." He never needed to varnish the wood, since lignum vitae "takes a natural shine and you don't need to." He then brought it back to the guitar maker, who added frets. The result was a banjo with a much longer neck than usual at the time. Seeger kept playing the same instrument for the rest of his life.[3]

"Pete Seeger," writes Robert Cantwell, "looks like, and in a sense *is,* his banjo." The instrument sings out the "anomalies of anomalies in his anomalous personality." The particular banjo he had built for himself was "an oddly elongated variety of its nineteenth-century original, with a tuning peg fixed halfway up a neck to which three extra frets had been added." This "permitted him to play more keys" and "exposed the conspiracy of elongation, legs, arms, and banjo neck, in which man and instrument were passionately involved." The collusion, confluence, and conflagration of banjo and man, of instrument and singer, was the result of an encounter between an individual and a powerful, if in some ways hidden, accumulation of cultural symbols. There was, at the time, something a bit mysterious about the banjo: it was an "enigma," the "instrument that history had left behind." In picking it up, Seeger was carrying out an act of "cultural scavengery," bringing to the foreground an instrument that had become somewhat unfamiliar to many audiences. As such, playing the banjo was a kind of rebel act, a search for independence from the reigning musical landscape. But the banjo also offered to Seeger a deep well of meanings and symbols, the result of its long and complicated history. It brought together many strands of American history, and it enabled him to craft a character as a performer who "spun the fibers of diverse cultural traditions into a continuous thread."[4]

Pete Seeger saved the banjo. Or maybe it was the banjo that saved him. The transformation of a musicologist's son, educated at boarding school and Harvard, into an icon of American roots and rootedness would have been impossible without the instrument. When he picked up the banjo, he drew on its on strength, and symbolism, and made it his own. It was as much an act of creative invention as it was a journey into tradition. It was, too, an act of brilliance, one that somehow ignited many of the latent possibilities of the banjo, setting the instrument on a new set of journeys, into a new set of hands. The banjo enabled Seeger to channel and condense a sense of American music and American protest all at once, creating new solidarities through the instrument. As such, Seeger made the instrument live again its original purpose and promise as something that produced a sound that could allow people to sing out against oppression and imagine new worlds. In this sense Seeger completed a circle begun long ago on the plantations of the Americas by enslaved people seeking solace, community, and the promise of something harmonious.

Pete Seeger's life was, from the first, intertwined with one of the great cultural projects of the early twentieth century: the study and recording of American vernacular music. At the center of this movement was his father, Charles Seeger, and a family friend named Alan Lomax. Both of these men believed that collecting and preserving American music was ultimately a way of changing America. It was a mission that no one fulfilled more dynamically than Pete Seeger.

The Seegers were descendants of a German immigrant who arrived in the United States in 1787, having become "obsessed with America after reading a copy of the U.S. Constitution that had been peddled on the streets." Charles was born in Mexico City, where his father was working as a businessman, and made his way to Harvard, where he got a degree in music and began work as a conductor and composer. While conducting in Europe, he met Pete Seeger's mother, Constance de Clyver Edson, a violinist who had grown up in France and Tunisia. The two soon moved to Berkeley, where Charles became the chair of the music department, expanding its curriculum and offering the first course in musicology in the United States. In Berkeley's anthropology department, he found 1,200 wax cylinder recordings of Native American songs. Listening to them spurred his interest in non-European music, and he began to argue against the dominant idea in his field that only European classical music was worthy of scholarly study.[5]

Charles Seeger also began to speak out politically. He visited ranches in Northern California and was shocked by the condition of migrant laborers. He also spoke out against U.S. involvement in World War I after his brother Alan, who had volunteered for the French Foreign Legion, died in combat. His activism angered the Berkeley administration, and, under pressure, he resigned his academic position. The family moved to New York, where in 1919 Pete Seeger was born. The one-time professor now embarked on a new project. He devoted a year to building a wooden trailer with a canvas top and a portable stage. The plan was for the family to "travel around bringing music to rural Americans."[6]

Near Pinehurst, North Carolina, in 1921, though, Charles Seeger had a realization. As Pete Seeger told it, the family visited the farmhouse of a family called the McKenzies to play them "the good music, Bach and Beethoven." "The McKenzies were very polite. They said, 'Oh, that's very nice. We play a little music too.' They took down banjos and fiddles off the wall and fiddled up a storm." Years later, Charles told his son Pete that the stay with the McKenzie family had made him realize, for the first time, "that people had a lot of good music in them. They didn't need my good music as much as I thought." Pete laughed when he told that story, which encapsulated the twist in consciousness that defined his entire musical career. Years later, in 1995, after a concert he played in Chapel Hill, Pete met a great granddaughter from the McKenzie family. She told Seeger: "My mother never stopped talking about that family from New York that spent the winter with them."[7]

Charles Seeger's "grand scheme of taking classical music to the masses" was a strain on his family as well as on his rickety trailer, which collapsed in Richmond. By 1929 Charles and Constance's marriage had collapsed as well. Soon afterwards he met Ruth Crawford, the first woman to receive a Guggenheim in musical composition. The two were married in 1932, and among their children was Pete's half brother, Mike Seeger, who alongside his brother would become one of the great collectors and interpreters of banjo music of the late twentieth century.[8]

Charles and Ruth Seeger were part of a group of composers who aspired to write music that would help spur political change. He helped animate a composer's collective whose goal was to introduce classical music to workers and write pieces "that would reflect proletarian interests." They believed that "music for revolution should be musically revolutionary" and composed songs meant to challenge listeners' habits and expectations. It turned out, though, that few people actually wanted to listen to them—particularly not the workers to whom the music was supposed to be geared. Over time, the Seegers concluded that this project was ultimately too "rarified" in a context where workers were struggling for daily survival. "Let's face it. The workers don't seem to like our music," Pete recalled his father saying. "Let's learn the vernacular. If we want to create new music, let's start with the music that people already know." This represented a departure, as many leftist thinkers had considered vernacular and rural music "hopelessly reactionary." But the Seegers threw themselves into this new project with gusto.[9]

Pete Seeger grew up quite literally surrounded by the project of recovering, documenting, and channeling American vernacular music. All around him, in his childhood home, were recordings and a bewildering array of musical instruments. "I remember my mother left musical instruments all around the house," including "a marimba, and a squeezebox, and a penny whistle." When he was eight years old, Seeger recalled, "she gives me a ukulele and I've been into fretted instruments ever since." His mother allowed him to buy his first banjo from a pawnshop when he was at boarding school. But Pete wasn't satisfied, and soon asked if he might be able to get a "good banjo with a nice tone and everything?" "I'd like to a lot," he added, "and honestly I think that it would be worth it because I'm awfully interested in the banjo and I'd like to learn how to play it really well."[10]

In the summer of 1936, after he finished high school, Pete Seeger traveled south with his father to attend the Folk Song and Dance Festival in Asheville, North Carolina. The festival was created in 1928 by the musician Bascom Lamar Lunsford with the goal of bringing visitors to Asheville and celebrating and promoting Appalachian culture. Lunsford was a celebrated banjo player; among his recorded songs was the 1927 "I Wish I Was a Mole in the Ground," whose words alight upon rolling, captivating banjo melody. When Pete Seeger heard Lunsford play in Asheville in 1936, he "fell in love with the old-fashioned five-string banjo, rippling out a rhythm to one fascinating song after another. I liked the rhythms. I liked the melodies, time-tested by generations of singers. I liked the words." The songs, sung in a "strident vocal tone" had "all the meat of life in them." "They sang of heroes, outlaws, murderers, fools." "Above all, they seemed frank, straightforward, honest." Pete left behind his four-stringed tenor banjo for the five-stringed instrument. He went home to his father's house, which was full of Library of Congress recordings of southern banjo music. He borrowed a banjo, put the recordings on the turntable and slowed them down with his finger so he could pick out each note and try to play what he heard. "Hours and hours he tinkered," Alan Lomax recalled, "trying to figure out by ear what those southern banjo aces were playing." In the next years Seeger made pilgrimages to meet great banjo players, including the Kentuckian Rufus Crisp. "It is a fine thing to watch his finger fly" and "let the strings ring out," Seeger wrote.[11]

After two years at Harvard—where he was particularly put off by a sociology professor who announced to students "You can't change the world"—Pete dropped out and moved to New York. In April 1939 he gave his first public concert, presenting "a group of authentic banjo ballads" for a square dance group. He met folklorists who had been collecting "folk songs with teeth," written by "Irish miners and railroad workers, Negro cotton farmers from the deep south" and white "backwoodsmen." He began "learning songs of Kentucky miners, Wisconsin lumberjacks, and Texas farmers," and performing them. That summer he joined a group called the Vagabond Puppeteers, who traveled through rural New York presenting songs and skits for milk farmers who were on strike against the Milk Trust, which set prices for their products. Audiences loved Pete's banjo playing, and he transformed the ballad song "Pretty Polly"—a haunting song about the murder of a young girl—into "Mister Farmer," a cautionary tale about a dairy farmer who was "seduced and cheated by the big-money boys." The Puppeteers didn't make much money of their own: they netted a grand total of $13.34 in profit for the whole summer. But Pete had found a vocation as a banjo picker whose songs could warm and encourage political protest.[12]

That fall Alan Lomax invited Pete to come down to Washington to work as his assistant, going through piles of records discarded by Columbia Records and other labels to "set aside the schmaltz, and pick out the best." Thanks to Lomax, Seeger gained access to a seemingly inexhaustible archive of music. Among them were recordings by Uncle Dave Macon, who fascinated Seeger with his intricate, driving banjo playing and a song he sang about an 1892 rebellion among coalminers. Lomax had collected a series of protest songs and gave them to Seeger and Woody Guthrie, who transcribed them and eventually published them as a book. Lomax encouraged Seeger to continue studying his adopted instrument. "He just *looked* like a banjo," Lomax later recalled.[13]

One day in New York, Lomax called Seeger and invited him to meet someone and told him to bring his banjo. They went to the apartment of the legendary African-American singer Huddie William Ledbetter, known as Lead Belly. The encounter was a humorous clash of styles: Seeger was dressed down, "trying my best to shed my Harvard upbringing, scorning to waste money on clothes other than blue jeans," he recalled. "But Lead Belly had on a clean shirt and starched collar, well-pressed suit, and shined shoes." Seeger was taken by Lead Belly's playing: "his genius was not so much in the notes he played as in the notes he didn't play." He was inspired to take up the guitar along with the banjo, modeling his style on that of the blues musician.[14]

He stumbled along the way. In 1940, at an early performance alongside Lead Belly and other leading folksingers of the day, Seeger froze up on stage. "I didn't know how to play the banjo, I was playing it the wrong way, and my fingers froze up on me. Tried to do it too fast. Forgot words. I got polite applause for trying, and retired in confusion." But another of the performers that night was the singer Woody Guthrie. Seeger recalled how this "curly headed guy with a cowboy hat shoved on the back of his head" sang and told stories "as though he didn't much care if the audience was listening or not." At one point he cleaned his fingernails with his guitar pick. But the audience was rapt. As Seeger recalled: "One song after another was a revelation to this audience of New York intellectuals." Guthrie took the young banjo player under his wing. "I could find the right notes to accompany him anytime," Seeger remembered, and "didn't try anything too fancy."[15]

Guthrie invited Seeger to join him on a trip out to Oklahoma to visit his family. They made a curious pair, an "intellectual from New England" alongside a "self-made intellectual" from Oklahoma. "He was determined not to let himself be changed," Seeger later wrote about the journey. "I was eager *to* change." For him Guthrie's genius was rooted in his understanding of a basic truth: "Any damn fool can get complicated, but it takes a genius to attain simplicity." Guthrie was a voracious observer and reader. "I'll never forget the week he discovered Rabelais and read through the two-inch-thick volume in a couple of days. During the following weeks I could see him experimenting with some of the techniques of style that Rabelais used, such as paragraphs full of images, adjective after adjective getting more fantastic." On the road together, Seeger and Guthrie wrote a few songs, including "66 Highway Blues" and "Union Maid," with its resounding chorus: "Oh, you can't scare me, I'm sticking to the Union. . . . I'm sticking to the Union 'til the day I die." When Guthrie arrived to see his family, Pete continued on his own, fortified with advice from his mentor. "Pete, if you go into a bar, sling your banjo on your back but don't play it right away," Guthrie told him. "Buy a nickel beer" and "sip it slow as you can." "Sooner or later, somebody's gonna say, 'Kid, can you play that thing?' Now don't be too eager. Say 'Maybe a little,' and keep on sipping your beer." Eventually, someone would say "Kid, I got a quarter for you if you pick us a tune." That was the moment to "swing it around" and "play your best tune." Seeger made enough money to travel that way and honed his skills as a performer. He also heard new songs. In a camp of evicted sharecroppers in Missouri, he heard "beautiful" music in their "little church." "I began there to really work on my banjo."[16]

He returned to New York soon after and teamed up with the singer Lee Hayes in December 1940. "I know some songs, and you know the banjo," Hayes said. Along with another musician, they formed a group called the Almanac Singers. The handwritten poster for one of their early concerts described them as "Rhythmic, rarin' banjo balladeers" singing "Hot labor & defense songs!" "Free—All Welcome!" The group at times added other musicians, including Woody Guthrie and a man named Arthur Stern, who brought "a big booming voice," and a "sharp sense of humor," along with "a strong sense of dialectical materialism." All the members of the Almanac Singers had sympathies with the Communist Party. Seeger had been a member of the Young Communist League at Harvard and in New York and now joined the Communist Party itself. "We had weekly sessions with a nice young man who tried to guide us in learning a little more about dialectical materialism," he recalled, "but none of us were really that enthusiastic about becoming great Marxist scholars." They "trusted the Communists to know generally the right thing we should be pushing for," and all read the party newspaper, *The Daily Worker.* "It was one of the best newspapers in the world. It had a great sports section." The *Daily Worker* published positive stories about the group, including one that announced "America Is in Their Songs." Theodore Dreiser extolled their work, proclaiming "If there were six more teams like you, we could save America."[17]

The Communist Party had long defined itself as anti-fascist and supported the Republicans in Spain, but in 1939 Stalin signed a nonaggression pact with Hitler. The Communist Party line, therefore, was that war with Hitler was "an imperialistic, capitalistic struggle that ignored the interests of the working class." The Almanac Singers wrote antiwar songs, attacking Franklin Delano Roosevelt for pushing through the draft. Eleanor Roosevelt offered a restrained response, seeing the song as clever "but in poor taste," while Franklin himself apparently asked an advisor "Can't we forbid this?" A Harvard Professor described the Almanac Singers as "Poison in Our System" and their songs as "strictly subversive and illegal." When Hitler attacked the Soviet Union in July 1941, the party line shifted. The group heard the news while playing at a gathering, and Guthrie noted: "Well, I guess we won't be singing any more peace songs." "The Almanac Singers flipped without skipping a beat," and quickly produced a series of songs about supporting the Allies against the Nazis and encouraging unions to sign a wartime "no-strike" pledge. They went on CBS radio and sang one of these songs, "Round and Round on Hitler's Grave." They were still seen as a menace by some, however: one newspaper ran an article with the headline "Commie Folksingers Try to Infiltrate Radio" the day after their CBS appearance. It was the last time the group appeared on a network radio show.[18]

They continued to write and play strong prolabor songs, including one written called "Talking Union" that was essentially a singing manual on how to start a union. Sitting on the roof of the group's loft with his banjo, Seeger wrote the final, rousing verses: "If you don't let Red-baiting break you up," and "if you don't let race hatred break you up," Seeger proclaimed, "You'll win." The song was an instant hit, and the CIO sponsored the group on a national tour of unions. The William Morris Agency approached the Almanac Singers to offer them representation and get them more shows, including one at the upscale Rainbow Room in Rockefeller Center. The manager thought they could use the band, but "of course we'll have to put all the men in overalls, and we can put the girls in sun bonnets." Woody Guthrie was not taken with the idea, and the group immediately improvised a song that joked that at the Rainbow Room, they stirred the salad "with Standard Oil." Not surprisingly, they did not get the gig. "I've forgotten whether Woody urinated on the balcony or not," Seeger remembered, "but I know he swiped some of the silverware; and a couple of weeks later when our friend from William Morris was visiting us, he ruefully saw this silverware on our table as we served him dinner." The agency gave up on them, both for their "radical reputation" and "Woody's unconventional ways in hotels."[19]

The group mainly performed at political events at local parties. They sometimes held "rent parties" to raise money for their loft in Union Square. On a trip to Seattle, they learned a new term used there for such fundraising parties: "hootenanny." The group adopted the term, and in time it would become a fixture of the folk music scene to describe any informal, participatory musical gathering. The music of the Almanacs was an opening, and an invitation, helping to lay the groundwork for the folk revival that would take shape a decade later. Out of the cultural crossroads that was Greenwich Village at the time, musicians from "different places" had come together, as Seeger later wrote, "to work out a new form—somewhat new. Somewhat old and somewhat new." The group's "antiestablishment" and "anticommercial" outlook, which saw the music industry itself as an extension of the corrupt capitalist system, would shape the ethos of the folk revival as well.[20]

The Almanac Singers also brought Seeger together with his future wife, Toshi Ohta. She was the daughter of a Japanese father and an American mother who had met in Germany, and grew up in New York. In early 1942 she volunteered to catalog the Almanac Singers. Her mother insisted that she couldn't walk across Washington Square by herself at night, so Seeger walked her home when the work was done, and "pretty soon we were going steady," he recalled. He was drafted a few weeks later, and she said "I'll wait for you." They were married in Greenwich Village while he was on furlough in 1943. She would work as a filmmaker, activist, folklorist, and producer in the coming decades, often in collaboration with Pete. In 1949 the couple borrowed money from friends and family and bought a plot of land along the Hudson River, in Beacon, New York. They built a house there, where they lived for the rest of their lives.[21]

When Seeger was drafted in 1942, he went to war with his banjo. During his early days in the service, which consisted mostly of "long waiting," he played for other soldiers. "My banjo was very popular, and in fact once the boys took up a collection for me, some 5 bucks." He later entertained troops on the ship that took him to Hawai'i and once there was recruited to perform for troops. In Oahu, he played the banjo in a role of the "perennially dissolute Mountaineer" in one popular skit. In Saipan, he played for groups of children and learned songs from the local population. The war confirmed his sense that music was his vocation: "I have got one helluva dissipation and that is music and I can get quite drunk on it, too and lost in it—I hope you are a patient wife," he wrote to Toshi in 1945. Years later he recalled joyously a night of music among soldiers when he was studying aircraft mechanics at Keesler Field, Mississippi, in 1943. Seeger was "sitting with a banjo on the steps of the barracks, picking a few tunes to myself, when a small cluster gathered." A man stepped forward and asked Seeger if he would bring the banjo over to the barracks. "I got a mandolin, and there's a buddy of mine plays a good fiddle." Once at the barracks, it turned out there were a few guitar players too. They all started "playing up a storm." Just then the sergeant shouted that it was time for lights out. "Hell, we're just getting warmed up," the soldiers responded—so they "adjourned to the latrine." The sound quality was perfect: "The echoing walls made us sound so great, we didn't want it to ever stop." Soon there were "twenty, then thirty, and finally almost forty people in it, standing in the shower stalls, sitting on sinks and toilet seats." Seeger never saw the other musicians again, but "if anyone ever asks me where was it I made some of the best music I ever made in my life, I'm liable to reply: 'In a latrine.'"[22]

When Pete returned home he was, as the *New Yorker* later put it, "an enormous young ex-G.I. who looks like a telescope, also sings, accompanying—or rather, encouraging—himself on a banjo." Seeger was reunited with Woody Guthrie, who had also served during the war, in Europe and North Africa. Both men had learned and written songs along the way. Seeger, Guthrie recalled, played "louder, faster, better than ever," singing "songs of satire, wit, anger, protest, hope and longings of the GIs that he had played with and sang with out in the Pacific." "By now that right hand on the banjo had become a steel stallion that could gallop out any kind of rhythm," remembered Alan Lomax. Guthrie and Seeger decided to create an organization called People's Songs in order to offer music for workers. As Guthrie put it, the "bosses" had long "paid artists to play their complacent crap." The only way to offer music supporting rather than sapping resistance was "to all get together in one big song-writers and song singers union, and we will call our union by the name of People's Songs. And if we all stick together, all hell and melted tear-gasses can't stop us, nor atoms hold us back." "We envisioned," Seeger later wrote, "a singing labor movement spearheading a nationwide folk-song revival."[23]

People's Songs was in some ways an adapted version of what Pete's father, Charles Seeger, had attempted decades earlier with his Compos-er's Collective, and it faltered in similar ways. As Seeger himself admitted, many union leaders "could not see any connections between music and pork chops." Perhaps more importantly, by 1947 and 1948 the Cold War politics in the United States was creating new strains and splits within the labor movement, which was increasingly wary of associations with the Communist Party and therefore with figures like Seeger. The result was partly that the labor union cut itself off from its own history: the classic union song "Which Side Are You On," Seeger opined, was "known in Greenwich Village but not in a single miners union local." By 1949, People's Songs closed its doors, unable to raise the funds necessary "to pay printers and landlords." And yet, as Seeger also noted brightly looking back on the experience, the organization had ended up having unintended consequences. The "banishment" of singers from the union circuit meant that they began playing concerts in schools and colleges. And the kids they played to remembered the songs, which "were good songs, as any fool could plainly see," and began to play them themselves, looking to publications like the People's Songs bulletins or the magazine *Sing Out!,* which Seeger helped publish starting in 1950, for lyrics.[24]

Seeger's second group, the Weavers, brought many of these songs to the stage. The group was in some ways a continuation of the Almanac Singers, featuring Lee Hays alongside Seeger and two other musicians. They drew on a broad repertoire, including songs collected during the People's Songs project and traditional tunes, including "Michael, Row the Boat Ashore," from the Georgia Sea Islands. The Weavers wrote and recorded "If I Had a Hammer." Though its political overtones made some nervous at the time, it ultimately became a familiar classic of the folk revival. The Weavers also recorded a song by Lead Belly, "Goodnight, Irene," which became a massive hit, selling two million copies. By the early 1950s the group was extremely popular and making good money from their record sales and performances. Their success helped to open up a space in the commercial music industry for folk music. The Weavers became "the most imitated group in the business," according to *Time,* creating a model that would later be followed in the 1960s by popular groups like the Kingston Trio. Pete Seeger was the center of the Weavers, "the fire, the flames leaping from his driving banjo, his passion welding the group."[25]

In the liner notes for a 1950 solo recording by Pete Seeger, Alan Lomax captured the transformation being wrought by the musician. Seeger was the sound of "the banjo rippling and stinging in perfect time, beginning to gallop, rolling into a tearing run on the home-stretches of song and then thundering into a finale of Spanish *rasgados* just as if a herd of wild horses had suddenly milled, bunched and stopped, trembling." In Seeger's playing of the instrument, Lomax saw the whole musical history of the Americas condensed: "What happened across three hundred years to Anglo-Scots melodies tropically stimulated by contact with African music in the new land of America has happened to Yankee Peter Seeger across 15 years of contact with southern singing and banjo-playing."[26]

In 1952 Harry Smith released his *Anthology of American Folk Music,* which was a kind of sonic version of the People's Songs project. Made up of rare commercial recordings from the 1920s and 1930s, it gathered and codified a curious collection and made it an offering to enter into what Greil Marcus calls an "imaginary home and a real exile." It became "the founding document of the American folk revival." The Smith anthology provided a rich archive to which generations of musicians have returned, seeking inspiration, finding complexity and confusion, and dreaming that they could channel long-lost recordings and make them live in the present. The depth and mystery of some of these songs is, in a sense, what enabled a profusion of never-ending, and never fully real-ized, returns in the form of the folk revival. In the playing of banjo players like Clarence Ashley and Bascom Lamar Lunsford included in the anthology, new converts to the instrument found inspiration, a horizon of possibility.[27]

"I saw Pete carry the five string banjo back from the dead," Woody Guthrie wrote in 1953. He had been there when "Pete went over his first Blue Ridge smelling in after banjo folks." But now he saw before him "our champion all-around oldtime five-string banjo picker." Though Guthrie admitted there were "a few champs" like Uncle Dave Macon, Bascom Lunsford, and Earl Scruggs who could "outplay Pete on some special tricky tune or two," he argued that Seeger "pulls away out ahead of them all, like Joe Louis does, on the long, hard allnite drags." He now heard "every kind of dialect of a voice" in his singing, in his "Calypso and Spanish and West Indian and Korean songs to march along by or to lay down to take a little nap by, to jump up by and to work by in every land for the better world sees yonder coming. All Union. All Free. All Singing." In the sound of his banjo, he carried "all of our fighting hearts."[28]

For decades, Seeger would sound the instrument in the largest concert halls and in the streets, in kindergarten classes and colleges, and on records that carried music into homes. He would take the banjo on many new journeys: in India he got a demonstration of sitar technique from the legendary Imrat Khan, then returned the favor by teaching the Indian musician how to play "Sourwood Mountain" on the banjo. And Seeger gave many new players their start with his instruction manual, *How to Play the 5-String Banjo*. It was first published in 1948 and would go through many editions, teaching a new generation to play and embrace the instrument. As Alan Lomax noted, the modestly titled book was in fact "a brilliant analysis (and the first one) of our most significant instrumental style." At first it circulated among a small group: it had only sold 100 copies by 1951. But by 1963 it sold 20,000 in one year, and in the same year the magazine Seeger helped edit, *Sing Out!*—which featured many banjo songs and articles on playing the instrument—reached a circulation of 25,000 a year. The banjo's old, eternal sound would never quite be the same again.[29]

Seeger believed deeply in the power of music, and song, to change the world. He realized early on, writes biographer Alec Wilkinson, that songs were "a way of binding people to a cause," because they could "make someone feel powerful when he isn't by any measure except his determination." "A piece of writing might be read once or twice," but "a song is sung over and over." Seeger's mission, then, was to be "an implement for delivering song." He always tried, and usually succeeded, in getting audiences to participate rather than sitting and listening as was done in the "European fine arts tradition," which he joked should be "ruled to be cruel and unusual punishment." A 1964 reviewer described how he would introduce a "strange song" to an audience by saying "You all know this one," in the process making it seem somehow true. "His inevitable 'Sing it with me'," was "not a command, but an invitation to share in his joy." His performances were "one of the phenomenal spectacles of our time." As British music critic Sidney Carter put it: "When he sings, you feel, in a sense, that he is singing part of *you*." "His performances have changed lives," wrote Robert Cantwell, because "unlike the great mass of performers who have secured their personal privacy behind a façade of public masks, Seeger makes in performance, I believe innocently and unconsciously, a most intimate revelation." In revealing himself, he opened up his audience's hearts and spirits, gathering them into a kind of communion.[30]

Seeger wrote extensively about music and politics, reflecting on what the social role of a singer should be. In these writings, he spoke of channeling a vast and powerful tradition of music that was much larger than him, or any of us. He described the "funny feeling" he sometimes got after someone applauded him for "some little banjo piece." It was "embarrassing" to have so many people listen to him rather than listening to the recordings of the great banjo players he was seeking to emulate and learn from. He looked forward to someone putting out an LP of "nothing but the singing and banjo picking of the late Uncle Dave Macon" so people could delve directly into the music of one of his models. At the same time, however, there was something valuable about performing the role of "intermediary." He could "introduce music to audiences to whom the straight stuff would seem too raw, crude, or unintelligible." And he could also offer "a broader picture of folk music than any true folk musician could," since they might be "a genius at his or her own kind of music—but that one kind is liable to be all he knows." Still, hearing him should just be the beginning: his audience should "go on and hear it done by people who have been raised on it since they were knee high, who have it in their bones, whose music blends in with their lives, the way music always ought to."[31]

Seeger celebrated ongoing creativity as being at the heart of tradition. "We are all in the process of building up new traditions out of
many old ones, and as folks change, folk music will. But we will do a
better job of building up new traditions when we take time to learn the
best of the old." As he wrote in 1960, debates about what constituted
true "folk" music versus "pop" music could easily lead to dangerous
dichotomies, not unlike those that "fascist racists have in defining the
difference between colored and white races." He quoted the blues singer
Big Bill Broonzy, who when asked if something he'd sang was a "folk
song" replied: "It must be. I never heard horses sing it." The only solution in confronting those bent on creating divisions and categories within
music was to "confound the enemy" through an open and generous approach to music. "A song is ever moving and changing. A folk song in a
book is like a picture of a bird in midflight, printed in a bird book. The
bird was moving before the picture was taken, and continued flying afterwards," and "no one is so foolish as to think that the picture *is* the
bird." Folk songs had been changing for generations and would continue
to change "for many generations more, we trust." To briefly capture it
in a moment in time, sound it out, and pass it on was the mission of the
performer.[32]

What Seeger passed on to many audiences, with enduring consequences, was the sound of—and love for—the banjo. It was that sound
that allowed his songs to take flight. The instrument traveled with him
everywhere—and he went a lot of places. As one critic wrote in 1954,
his banjo had been in concerts "heard in every one of the 48 states and
all over Canada." Many who saw him perform decided, right then and
there, that they had to learn to play the instrument. For Roger Abrahams,
who would go on to become one of the great folklorists of his generation,
hearing Seeger play at Swarthmore in 1953 was an awakening. Seeing
that concert with a friend, Abrahams later recalled, "we realized that
this was what we wanted to do for the rest of our lives." The first step
was obvious: they both immediately "went out to buy banjos." Robert
Cantwell had a similarly transformative experience encountering Seeger.
He first heard his songs at a summer camp thanks to a counselor who
played the Weavers songs over the public address system. Cantwell heard
"a kind of neighborliness, which I never forgot." When he got to the
University of Michigan, "all my friends had guitars or banjos."

I had a beautiful long-necked banjo, the 'Pete Seeger' model, with a smiling white face, white as table linen, a whiskery surface, and a set of shining steel strings that crossed it like the Golden Gate Bridge, and I played it constantly. I had a sweetheart too, who gave me a Pete Seeger album for my birthday, and we let one of his lonesome banjo tunes carry us out over the yellow hinterlands beyond the bower of tender new caresses where we lay. At last Pete Seeger came to Chicago's Orchestra Hall, and spread wide his arms as we sang to him, and it changed me. It was thirty years ago, and I have not changed back.[33]

"All of us who participate in the folk-music revival are, in varying degrees of kinship, Pete's children," wrote one reviewer in 1964. "It was he who first put a banjo in our lap and told us, 'Here, this thing is simple— just go ahead and play it. You'll sound great!' And such was his conviction, we did as we were told; and his conviction became our own: by God, we did sound good!"[34]

Replicated throughout the country, these individual conversion experiences were common enough that they created a new banjo boom that one journalist diagnosed as a sickness. "Rash of Banjo Fever Breaks Out in the U.S.," a 1955 article from *Billboard* announced. "Record Hits Start Epidemic," the subtitle read, "TV carries 'Bug'; Instrument Shortage a Problem." The alarming tone almost could be something straight out of Ishmael Reed's 1972 novel *Mumbo Jumbo,* a brilliant parody of the ways African and African-American music and dance have periodically been seen as a threat to the body politic. Reporting from a byline in New York, Bill Simon described the scene:

The banjo is back, by jingo! An instrument long regarded as a relic of the ragtime and flapper eras, minstrel shows and even Civil War days, the banjo is disappearing fast from hock shop windows and showing en masse on phonograph records and on TV.

Kids on campuses are catching the fever, and as the supply of used instruments is dwindling, manufacturers have resumed production of new banjos, including a wide variety of new models.[35]

The article laid out various causes for the sudden epidemic and attendant panic. "Seven years ago every instrument maker was out of the banjo business," the author noted. But then came a series of recordings: Art Mooney's big band used the banjo in their hit recording of "Four Leaf Clover," and there was a revival of New Orleans style jazz. But it was starting in 1954 and 1955 that the banjo "flowered profusely." Musicians penned songs celebrating the banjo, including the Ames Brothers' "The Man With the Banjo," and a recording by Sammy Kaye that declared "The Banjo's Back in Town." But the most important driver for the new boom was the "banjo stylings of Pete Seeger." Ted McCarthy, owner of the Gibson instrument company and director of the National Association of Musical Merchandise Manufacturers, offered the requisite statistics: banjo sales increased by a modest 27 percent between 1953 and 1954, but during the first three months of 1955—with a series of new banjo recordings on the market and Seeger an increasingly popular presence among young audiences—sales were already up a hundred a fifty percent from the first three months of the year before. Gibson, as well as Vega and other companies, were rushing to put out new banjo models to sate the throngs of young players.[36]

Those who picked up the banjo during these years found themselves at a crossroads of a cultural movement that was experienced as deeply, personally, transformative. Carrying the instrument became a way of connecting not just with a sound but with a kind of cultural movement, one that pointed ahead even as it promised to connect with the past. Because of its many different appearances in and disappearances from different popular music forms in America, the banjo called up a range of references and symbols. But because many who encountered it in the 1950s were unfamiliar with and cut off from its earlier history, the banjo itself was a kind of revelation, but from which many different things could be projected. The "strange lanky fellow ambling up Fourth Avenue with a banjo on his back" might look as if he was heading off to combat, with his instrument like a "soldier's carbine." Rather than being a reassuring sign of belonging to a particular, structured, musical tradition—the way a musician with a violin or trumpet might have been—the banjo was untethered, an invitation to new meaning. But what was clear was that it was in some sense deeply, obdurately American. It had always been here, even if you had never seen it. And it sounded like a place you wanted to go home to.[37]

*

The folk revival of the 1950s and 1960s was about simultaneously connecting with and reinventing tradition, about finding new energy and community by seeking a connection to a deep and enticing past. It pivoted around the banjo because the instrument had long done, and in fact had been made to do, just that: sounding like something very old even as it was being constantly reinvented. The instrument played a similar role in another musical form that emerged during the same period, intertwined with other forms but ultimately distinct in its journey: bluegrass.

The recognized founder of bluegrass was a man named Bill Monroe, who was born in 1911 and grew up in Rosine, Kentucky, in a small rural community. As a child he took in the music played by a local group, the Foster String Band, who as he later recalled "played breakdowns, dance music and a few waltzes and little Hawaiian music." He was fascinated by an African-American man who hauled freight into the community on a mule, "whistling the blues" as he went, and by the playing of the blues guitarist and string band musician Arnold Schultz. He first started playing himself as he journeyed with his uncle Pen Vandiver, who traveled the countryside bartering and trading household goods and playing fiddle for dances in rural homes. As a teenager Monroe—like many other young men from the region—left home looking for work and ended up in East Chicago, Illinois, where he stacked gasoline barrels off and on freight trains for Sinclair Oil. He and his brothers played house parties for extra money and were recruited to play on a series of tours sponsored by a Chicago radio station. In their early years the Monroe brothers were marketed as players of "hillbilly music." A writer in 1925 described the musicians who played this style as coming "from the mountain regions of our southern states, with a collection of old-time melodies, some of which have never been written down but have been passed on from fiddler to fiddler through the generations."[38]

The Monroe brothers had a fast, striking sound driven by Bill's virtuoso mandolin playing. They moved to Raleigh, North Carolina, and released a song called "What Would You Give in Exchange for Your Soul?" that became a hit on southern radio stations. The group disbanded by the late 1930s, but a few years later Bill formed his own band. He decided it needed an additional instrument to supplement the mandolin, fiddle, and guitar. "What I wanted was the sound of the banjo, because I'd heard it back in Kentucky." He recruited a banjo player named David Akeman, who went by the stage name "Stringbean." Akeman was rooted in the tradition of minstrel and vaudeville banjo playing: he told jokes and acted out skits in between songs and, like other white performers, sometimes performed in blackface. In 1945 Stringbean left Monroe's band, and a year later Monroe found a replacement banjo player: Earl Scruggs.[39]

Scruggs had grown up in the Piedmont region of North Carolina and grew up listening to the music of Charlie Poole, whose band the North Carolina Ramblers had become popular in the state starting in 1918. Their style was centered on three-finger banjo picking, in which the thumb, index finger, and middle finger picked the strings rapidly. Poole's banjo playing was rooted in the nineteenth-century finger-picking styles championed by Dobson and Stewart; but unlike the earlier classical and parlor picking styles, which used the flesh of the fingers in order to create a softer sound, Poole picked with his fingernails, creating a brighter and stronger sound. He played in a "raggy, percussive style" with a prominent upbeat that "echoed the rhythmic pulse of the older mountain clawhammer and frailing styles." He often played high up the neck with "tight, stiff chords" that accentuated the music. He was also heavily influenced by ragtime music, notably the banjo playing of a musician named Fred Van Eps, who had been famous for playing the "banjo rag" in vaudeville acts in the South. After Poole's death other bands maintained the style spread by the North Carolina Ramblers. Among them was the popular Jenkin's String Band, fronted by the banjo player Snuffy Jenkins, who played with a fast, bright three-fingered picking style.[40]

Scruggs brought this style to Monroe's group, transforming their music in the process. Whereas Stringbean sometimes had difficulty keeping up with the fast tempo set by Monroe's galloping mandolin playing, not so with Scruggs. He played banjo fast and bright. As he traveled with Monroe's band, he wowed audiences who were not familiar with the Carolina picking style. As he later recalled, in Nashville "no one had heard the three-finger style before. People would gather around me like I was a freak almost." But he was preternaturally talented and "could play the melody on the banjo in a way never before heard." His banjo playing soon became a hallmark of the band. Monroe introduced him on stage as "Earl Scruggs and his fancy banjo," and frequently his solos "brought down the house." A 1947 review of Monroe's band described Scruggs as "the boy from North Carolina, who makes the banjo talk." The *New York Times* saw Earl Scruggs as a musician "who bears about the same relationship to the five-string banjo that Paganini does to the violin."[41]

Scruggs's "pyrotechnic three-finger banjo" style was a central part of what set Monroe's band apart: speed and pitch. Scruggs, like Charlie Poole and Snuffy Jenkins, played with his fingernails and in time began to use metal finger picks, shaped like spoons attached to the ends of the fingers, to create an even stronger and brighter sound. This added one more layer to the steady increase in metal surrounding the banjo that had begun in the mid-nineteenth century, bringing the transformation from the mellow gourd and minstrel instruments to the modern metallic sound to its extreme. This tone was similar to that of the banjo in jazz and ragtime, with its hard-strumming styles. And in fact the connection goes deeper than that. Scruggs's famous three-fingered roll, "with its groups of three and one of two, is identical to the basic ragtime phrase" made most popular by the pianist Scott Joplin—whose father was a banjo player. Bluegrass banjo playing was tied to the African-American tradition in multiple ways, both through the long tradition of clawhammer styles rooted in the rural south and through the more recent innovations of jazz and ragtime. Though this fact has often been hidden by the way it has been marketed, bluegrass is very much rooted in African and Afro-Atlantic musical traditions, both through the presence of the banjo and through the larger structures of its music.[42]

Bill Monroe's legendary band with Earl Scruggs and guitarist Lester Flatt was called the Blue Grass Boys, taking its name from the nickname for his home state of Kentucky. But the term "bluegrass" itself became attached to the music firmly only in the mid to late 1950s as a result of the links and connections with the folk revival. By the early 1950s the music was increasingly popular among urban audiences, notably in Washington, DC. For many of those involved in the folk revival, especially fans of Pete Seeger, bluegrass was attractive because it showed them that "the five-string banjo was alive and well" in a thriving form of music connected to southern folk traditions. Earl Scruggs's playing impressed and attracted many other musicians. "We would gather at my brother Pete's house," Pete's brother Mike Seeger later recalled, "and try to figure out what Earl Scruggs was doing. We'd share what we were able to figure out. One person might get very, very close to Earl during one of his appearances and then try to learn that way. Then that information would be shared with at the next get-together." In New York, the banjo players who gathered in Washington Square Park traded tips on how to play Scruggs's style. In 1955, when Pete published a new edition of his five-string banjo instruction manual, he included a new short chapter on "Scruggs-style banjo." And in 1957 Mike Seeger produced an LP for Folkways records called *American Banjo Scruggs Style,* and the liner notes included the first use of the term "bluegrass" to describe a style of music.[43]

Two years later Mike Seeger produced another Folkways LP called Mountain Music Bluegrass Style, which offered the first detailed description of the style. "Instrumentally," Seeger wrote, "bluegrass music is a direct outgrowth of traditional hill music styles, its two most distinctive features being that it has no electrified instruments and that it uses a five string banjo for lead or background in all songs." It came out of the "old corn-shucking party banjo and fiddle music," Seeger went on, as well as ballads and religious music of the southern mountains. It took "its classic and most competent form" in the years after World War II, especially with Monroe's band. As for the songs, they were most often about "unsuccessful love" but also covered "home, mother, catastrophes, religion, and almost anything under the sun." Seeger's LP helped to spread the word about bluegrass music among folk revivalists, and bluegrass bands were invited to festivals and colleges. The concerts at colleges and in urban settings sometimes fell flat with audiences used to the left-wing politics and styles of the folk revival. The references to religion and the comedy routines, as well as the styles of dress, were a bit of a reach for many college kids. But the "fast instrumentals" on the banjo, which had been enthusiastically embraced by the folk revival, cut through the differences, bringing audiences together as it so often had before.[44]

The early entanglements of folk and bluegrass would, in time, be obscured by the condensation of new symbols and marketing around the music. This was a continuation of a longer process through which a set of assumptions about race and music ultimately contributed to what Karl Hagstrom Miller calls "segregating sound." Those who marketed music, and often those who studied it as well, claimed and cemented a sharp distinction between the music of blacks and whites, a distinction that was used to promote and characterize each to mass audiences. This represented a radical erasure of the truth of the music, which had constantly crossed social and racial boundaries, to the point where distinguishing between what is "white" and what is "black" in American music is essentially impossible. Like other racial fictions, however, the distinctions have had an enduring interpretive and cultural impact to this day. They are one reason that many came to see the banjo as a "white" instrument during the mid to late twentieth century—a remarkable, almost surreal, act of historical silencing.[45]

One result of this has been the way in which bluegrass, despite its origins, has come to be associated with negative images of a backwards, rural white south. By the 1970s the most famous popular representation of the banjo was in the 1972 movie *Deliverance* about a canoe trip by Atlanta businessmen into the Georgia wilderness gone horribly wrong. In the film there is a moment of convivial interaction between one guitar-playing businessman and a porch-bound rural banjo-playing boy with an odd look and funny teeth. But, in the broader plot of the film, the instrument registers as a symbol for a backward, primitive, and frightening white southern culture. In a 2012 review of an album by the Dixie Chicks, the comedian Kid Mero humorously expressed the consequence of such associations: "Here's a secret you may not know," he explained, unless you are either "in the music industry or a minority": "Banjos (banjoes?) make everything sound racist." "If you played a Martin Luther King Jr. speech and had a banjo playing in the background," he went on, it would make him sound like "Rush Limbaugh at a Klan rally."[46]

Bluegrass has remained a strongly anchored music, thriving in festival circuits, influencing more popular forms of country music. And it has persistently called people to the banjo, many of them embarking on a never-ending quest to play almost—or at least just a little bit—like Earl Scruggs. It is a curious artifact of late twentieth-century U.S. culture, with its enduring racial and cultural fault lines, that the image surrounding the music—sometimes cultivated by practitioners themselves—is so often unhinged from the Afro-Atlantic roots of both its style and its most visible and symbolic instrument. But whatever divisions have been articulated through and projected onto the music, it has also centrally served to preserve and raise up an instrument whose history streaks through the music.

Earl Scruggs's performances and recordings have inspired countless banjo players. Growing up in Orange County, California, a teenager named Steve Martin heard Scruggs's rendition of "Foggy Mountain Breakdown" and decided to learn to play the banjo. "I had taught myself by slowing down banjo records on my turntable and picking out the songs not by note," Martin later recalled. "The only place to practice without agonizing everyone in the house was in my car, parked on the street with windows rolled up, even in the middle of August." The banjo turned out to be the perfect prop as he developed a persona as a comedian at the Knott's Berry Farm amusement park, performing "hillbilly" routines that combined jokes with musical numbers. In the process Martin tapped into a long tradition stretching back to the nineteenth century: he was, in a way, a late minstrel. The banjo became a fundamental part of his comedic persona, featuring on his posters, accompanying his often surreal and hilarious songs. Martin ultimately became a comedian who deconstructed comedy, an incomparable persona who simultaneously captured and upended theatrical traditions. The banjo has never left his side, and he ranks today as one of the great bluegrass musicians in the country.[47]

The past decades have seen many new innovators rooted in bluegrass, including the brilliant banjoists Bill Keith, Tony Trischka, and Bela Fleck, who would create an explosion of banjo music that drew on the bright electric styles of bluegrass but also took it in new directions, even back to Africa once again. And it says something about the banjo that during many decades it sounded out in parallel musical forms that are often seen as expressions of totally different political and regional affiliations—but still somehow always sounding just like America, whatever America might mean.

*

"What is your profession or occupation?" Frank Tavenner asked Pete Seeger in 1955, at a hearing of the House Un-American Activities Committee (HUAC). "Well, I have worked at many things," Seeger replied, "and my main profession is as a student of American folklore, and I make my living as a banjo picker—sort of damning in some people's opinion." Seeger was dressed in a tweed jacket, plaid shirt, and a yellow tie; and his wife, Toshi, sat in the audience holding his banjo at the ready. Throughout the hearing Seeger tried to get the committee to listen to a few of his songs. They wouldn't, even though it was his songs—and the places he had sung them—for which he was on trial.[48]

Seeger had made a choice before arriving that day: to invoke the First Amendment and defend his right to free speech. It was a risky approach. Several other musicians who had been called before the committee, including folk singers Burl Ives and Josh White, had answered the committee's questions and escaped indictment. Some had invoked the Fifth Amendment, which gave them the right to refuse self-incrimination but in the process suggested that they were in fact guilty of something. Others, including Pete's father Charles, had appeared and challenged the committee in various ways by refusing to answer certain questions. But when a group of Hollywood writers and directors had done so in 1947, they had ended up in jail for contempt of Congress. Still, Seeger felt that this was the only option he could pursue. "I want to get up there," he told his attorney, "and attack these guys for what they are, the worst of America."[49]

By then Seeger had been feeling the effects of political repression for several years. In 1949 he had performed at a concert in Peekskill, New York, organized to raise money for the Communist Party's civil rights activism. Twenty-five thousand attended, and Seeger played a few songs on his banjo before the main act, Paul Robeson, took to the stage. Just outside the concert, however, a small group of demonstrators linked to the Ku Klux Klan shouted at the crowd, calling them "nigger-lovers." The police were in cahoots with the protestors and forced the departing cars down a single narrow road, which was flanked by protestors who threw rocks at the passing cars. All the windows of Seeger's car were smashed, and Toshi and his three-year-old son, Danny, were covered in shards of glass by the time they escaped the two-mile gauntlet. The next year, a pamphlet called *Red Channels,* which purported to identify the Communist influence on the U.S. media, singled out Pete Seeger. By 1951 the Weavers found themselves blacklisted and increasingly found their radio appearances and concerts cancelled. By late 1952 the group had disbanded.[50]

Unable to perform in established performance venues, Seeger turned to churches and other gathering places to share his songs. In concerts to college audiences, he would remind the young that protest and hope for a better world were alive and well as long as they could sing along with him. He always made time to play at political rallies, particularly those of the Civil Rights Movement. In 1953 in St. Louis he joined a gathering of the local Negro Labor Council, which was leading a campaign against racial discrimination in hiring at the local Sears. The group had its own chorus, and Seeger taught them and the crowd a South African chant called "Baleka." He then joined the protestors as they went out to picket Sears: "a single tall, skinny white man with a long-necked banjo leading the pickets in a complex African chant, interspersed with rhythmic phrases in English about Sears bigotry." For many audiences the banjo sounded out freedom. Seeger's performances often brought his audiences to tears.[51]

Seeger remained defiant when called before HUAC in 1955. The committee's approach was to present Seeger with documentation showing he had performed at events sponsored by or linked to the Communist Party and to ask him to confirm that he was indeed there. They began by reading an advertisement in the *Daily Worker* saying he had performed in 1947 at the "Allerton Section housewarming," and asked Seeger whether this was a "section of the Communist Party." He replied: "Sir, I refuse to answer that question, whether it was a quote from the *New York Times* or the *Vegetarian Journal*." When pressed, he announced: "I am not going to answer any questions as to my association, my philosophical or religious beliefs, or how I voted in any election, or any of these private affairs. I think these are very improper questions for any American to be asked, especially under such compulsion as this." When asked about whether he had "lent his talent" at another event, a 1948 May Day Rally, he again refused to answer the question. He had "never done anything conspiratorial" and resented the implication that because his opinions differed from those of the committee that he was "any less of any American than anybody else. I love my country very deeply, sir." "Why don't you make a contribution toward preserving its institutions?" he was asked. "I feel that my whole life is a contribution."[52]

Seeger never answered a specific question about whether he'd sung a particular song at any particular event. He gladly confirmed that he had sung certain songs in his life as a performer but declined "to say who has ever listened to them, who has written them, or other people who have sung them." One of the songs the committee pressed him about was "Wasn't That a Time," which he had co-written with Lee Hayes and performed with the Weavers. It celebrated the long history of resistance to tyranny, from Valley Forge to Gettysburg, recalling the heroism of those who stood fast in difficult times. The chorus went:

> Wasn't that a time, wasn't that a time,
> A time to try the soul of man,
> Wasn't that a terrible time?

Then the verses of the song turned from past to present:

> And now again the madmen come,
> And should our vic'try fail?
> There is no vic'try in a land
> Where free men go to jail.
>
> Isn't this a time!
> Isn't this a time!
> A time to try the soul of man,
> Isn't this a terrible time?

When asked whether he had sung this song at a recent Fourth of July event, Seeger again demurred. "I have sung that song. I am not going to go into where I have sung it. I have sung it in many places." He then offered to sing it for the committee: "I can sing it. I don't know how well I can do it without my banjo." When the committee refused his invitation, he told them: "I am sorry you are not interested in the song. It is a good song." As the committee pressed him, Seeger finally exclaimed: "I have sung for Americans of every political persuasion, and I am proud that I never refuse to sing to an audience, no matter what religion or color of their skin, or situation in life. I have sung in hobo jungles, and I have sung for the Rockefellers," he added. "I am proud of the fact that my songs seem to cut across and find perhaps a unifying thing, basic humanity, and that is why I would love to tell you about these songs, because I feel that you would agree with me more, sir." He added a personal plea: one of the members of the committee was from Western Virginia, and Seeger told him: "I know many songs from your home county, Carbon, and Monroe, and I hitchhiked through there and stayed in the homes of miners."[53]

Seeger went home that day, but in 1957 he was indicted for contempt of Congress. Whenever he left New York, he was required to send a telegram to the government saying where he was going and how he was traveling there. But it took the government until 1961 to bring the case to trial. Before going into court, Seeger organized a press conference where he sang three songs to the assembled journalists, including "Wasn't That a Time," accompanying his singing with his banjo. The journalists applauded after his final song, and he read a statement from poet Carl Sandburg, who declared that Seeger should "be a free man, roving the American landscape, singing for the audiences who love him, Republican, Democrat, and independents." But in a courtroom packed with five hundred spectators, Seeger was found guilty. At his sentencing hearing, he noted that HUAC had not allowed him to sing "Wasn't That a Time." Since it was "apropos of this trial," he asked the judge for "permission to sing it here before I close?" "You may not," replied the judge—who had in fact once heard Seeger sing, at a Weavers concert. "Well, perhaps you will hear it some other time," Seeger concluded. "A good song can only do good, and I am proud of the songs I have sung."[54]

In 1962 Seeger's sentence was overturned on a technicality. By then, the influence of HUAC was waning. Still, throughout the 1960s, as many other folk singers hit the pop charts and were invited to play on television and radio, Seeger wasn't. In solidarity, some singers refused to appear on shows until Seeger was allowed. In 1963 he, Toshi and their three children took a trip around the world to study vernacular music in different contexts, learning songs that he would perform in the coming years. They visited thirty countries, and at one point in India Seeger performed to sixty thousand people at an outdoor concert. But back home Seeger's musical life continued to center around smaller concerts at colleges and schools. His recordings circulated among fans, animating the folk revival. In time that probably made his singing and banjo playing all the more powerful, for it became a kind of tectonic cultural force, suppressed and often somewhat invisible, but inciting long-term transformations in ways of seeing and hearing nonetheless.

One of Seeger's most enduring contributions to the Civil Rights Movement was helping to turn "We Shall Overcome" into a foundational anthem. It was an old spiritual, one sung by the Fisk Jubilee Singers. In Alabama in 1909 a miner's union that brought together African-American and white workers adopted it, and "that good old song was sung at every meeting." And in 1946 workers, mostly African-American women, on strike at a Charleston, South Carolina tobacco factory sang the song on the picket line. They sang it "very, very slowly . . . so that the harmony could develop, with high and low voices." Some of the strikers visited the Highlander Folk School in Tennessee and taught the song to the music director there, who taught it to Pete Seeger. It was published in 1948 in the newsletter of People's Songs and in the 1950s began to circulate in union and protest circles. Seeger "gave it a banjo accompaniment" and changed the "Will" to "Shall." In 1956 he sang the song at a gathering at Highlander School, to a crowd that included Martin Luther King Jr. and Ralph Abernathy, who had just led the Montgomery Bus Boycott. Traveling the next day, in the back seat of a car, King said "'We Shall Overcome'—that song really sticks with you, doesn't it?"[55]

In 1960 another musician sang the song at the founding convention of the Student Nonviolent Coordinating Committee and started the tradition of "everyone crossing arms in front of them" and grasping hands with each other, "swaying slowly from side to side." Seeger recorded the song at a 1963 concert at Carnegie Hall, and the album sold half a million copies. His manager warned him: "Pete, if you don't copyright this song, some Hollywood character will. He'll put new lyrics in like 'Baby, let's you and me overcome tonight.'" Along with two others Seeger copyrighted an arrangement of the song but set it up so that all royalties would go to a "We Shall Overcome Fund" chaired by singer and activist Bernice Johnson Reagon and used to support "black music in the South." It became the soundtrack to protest throughout the 1960s and circulated globally as well: in 1994 Seeger was visiting a village outside Calcutta and a man and his daughter sang it to him in Bengali.[56]

By the late 1960s Seeger had become an icon of the counterculture. In 1967—still banned from network television—he began filming his own show, called Rainbow Quest, for public television. Toshi produced the

James Kavillines, "Pete Seeger at the Yorktown Heights High School," 1967.
Library of Congress.

thirty-nine episodes of the show, while Pete invited musical guests. Johnny Cash came on the show stoned but played a great set—and didn't ask for a penny for the appearance. The Stanley Brothers came on and played bluegrass, and the great Kentucky banjo player Roscoe Holcomb, dressed "in a suit and hat, like an undertaker," was featured in another show.[57]

In 1967 Seeger also wrote a powerful song criticizing the Vietnam War. He saw a photograph of U.S. soldiers fording a river in the newspaper, and the phrase "Waist Deep in the Big Muddy" came to him. The song is set in Louisiana in 1942 and tells the cautionary tale of a captain who insists his recalcitrant soldiers must cross a deep river, and he ultimately drowns in the water. "It was an allegory," Seeger later explained, "and a very obvious one." The blindly stubborn captain was Lyndon Johnson, the soldiers in the song all those being told to wade into a muddy conflict. Seeger sang the song on tour, including in Moscow. In September of 1967 he was, finally, invited to play on network television, on the Smothers Brothers Comedy Hour. He played his much-beloved hit "Wimoweh," based on a South African song, and then "Waist Deep in the Big Muddy." But before the segment was aired, the producers had cut out the segment where he played that song. Seeger exposed what had happened in the *New York Times,* noting that the airwaves were being "censored for ideas as well as for sex." He was invited back by the network in February of 1968, and this time performed the song to an audience of seven million people.[58]

It was for this appearance that Seeger decorated his banjo with a circle of words, along with a peace sign. What he wrote was an homage to his mentor Woody Guthrie, who during World War II had written on his guitar: "This Machine Kills Fascists." The slogan actually came from workers in munitions factories who had written this on the machines they used to make weapons for the war. Seeger's version in 1968 was: "This Machine Surrounds Hate and Forces It to Surrender." But it encapsulated what he hoped his banjo had done and would continue to do: offer music that could confront a violent world and put something else in its place. The banjo bore out its stated truth one day at a concert near Seeger's home in Beacon, New York. After he played, a man walked up to him and shook his hand. "Mr. Seeger," he announced, "I think I should tell you, I came here this afternoon to kill you." A Vietnam vet, the man was enraged by Seeger's stance against the war. But he had first listened to him playing his banjo, and began to sing with the rest of the audience, and suddenly his hatred faded away. "I feel cleansed," he told Seeger before walking away.[59]

In 1956 Seeger had written a letter to Woody Guthrie, who at the time was suffering from the Huntington's disease that eventually took his life. "Do you know why you don't get more letters from me? I feel you're here all the time. Singing your songs, and whanging away on mandolins and guitars like I first heard you do. Same way everywhere I go." Seeger had visited camps during that summer to play "where kids holler out in that nice open way kids do, not covering up or trying to make their voices sound pretty"; they were all singing Woody's song: "This land is yourrr land, this . . ." "In a way, we are all your children, Woody. You may have thought you only had eight kids, but you ended up having several hundred thousand, there's several million or billion not even born yet."[60]

In a sense the same could be said of Seeger. Those like HUAC who tried to silence him ultimately made a great strategic blunder. They kept him off the radio and television, but instead he crisscrossed the country and sang at smaller concerts, at camps and elementary schools, at colleges and protests. A generation of music teachers taught his songs to the next generation, who then did the same. When Seeger died in 2014, one of the many whose lives were touched by him remembered, as a child, attending a Jewish camp just over the hill from Seeger's house in Beacon, New York. "He would climb over Mt. Beacon with his banjo in tow just to sing to the campers." They had to cut across his farm to get to town, and whenever he was home and saw them coming, "he rushed out to greet and sing to us. One day it began to rain so he rushed us into his barn and entertained us there." Later, when this camper went on voter registration drives in the South during the Civil Rights movement, she recalled how "Mr. Seeger was always around, strumming his banjo and singing his songs." She and her husband were married, she recalled, "on September 10, 1967, the day Pete Seeger was finally allowed to appear on television. I don't remember which was more important to me; our marriage or that Mr. Seeger would be on TV."[61]

One of Seeger's most important and moving appearances came six years before his death, when he performed on the mall the day before President Obama's 2008 inauguration. His appearance came at the end of a long concert that had seen an incredible pastiche of musicians parade by, from Beyonce to Garth Brooks to Renée Fleming to U2. Seeger took to the stage just after a speech by the soon-to-be president. He was wearing jeans, a flannel shirt, and a floppy wool cap and was flanked by his grandson Tao Rodríguez-Seeger and by Bruce Springsteen; and Spring-

Donna Lou Morgan, Pete Seeger sings "This Land Is Your Land," 2009.
(Wikimedia Commons).

steen introduced him as "the father of American folk music," and said he
would sing "perhaps the greatest song ever written about our home."
"You sing it with us—we'll give you the words," Seeger announced. And
then he picked out the first notes of "This Land Is Your Land" on his
banjo. The notes rang out, stretched out across the mall, clear, infinite,

across the Tidal Basin all the way out to the Washington Monument, where I was standing.

The freezing crowd was pretty young, with lots of people in their twenties and thirties; but it was Seeger's banjo, rather than anything that had come before, that for the first time set everyone, unanimously, bopping and singing along. We were his children, there, back in elementary school with our hippie music teachers. It turned out we needed Seeger to feed us the words, for there were a few verses most of us had never learned in the expurgated versions we had been taught: the more radical verses Woody Guthrie had written, describing his people waiting in soup lines and at the Relief Office, and pointing out that if a sign said "No Trespassing" on one side, well "On the other side, it didn't say nothing. . . . This land belongs to you and me!"

Seeger knew precisely what he was doing singing these trenchantly political verses on the steps of the Lincoln Memorial that day. He smiled as he called out those verses, for Woody and for us. And he did so in a spot layered with a history of dreams—the African-American opera singer Marian Anderson's 1939 concert on the Mall, after Constitution Hall refused to have her sing because she was black, Martin Luther King's 1963 "I Have a Dream Speech," the protests against the Vietnam War—and played an instrument with an even deeper history. Right there, calling all of us to join together in community to sing a different future, the always-wandering banjo was right at home.

Epilogue

TODAY, THE BANJO IS ON THE MOVE. You can hear it backing up Ani DiFranco or Taylor Swift and find it at the center of the music of Mumford and Sons and Old Crow Medicine Show. You can catch a sold-out concert and hear Bela Fleck or Tony Trischka play jaw-dropping solos on the instrument and Abigail Washburn sing a traditional Chinese tune accompanied by her banjo. You can hear it chunking along with old jazz standards at Preservation Hall in New Orleans, but you'll hear it on the streets there too. Each year, across the country, hundreds gather in various "banjo camps" to learn to play and share songs, finding themselves in a world where every single person is walking around with a banjo. And of course you can hear the banjo at summertime bluegrass concerts and a thousand old-time jams from Chapel Hill homes to Brooklyn pubs. In the south of France, a yearly festival brings together banjo obsessives from throughout the country and beyond. You can hear the instrument in Japan, in North Africa, and on the street in Jacmel, Haiti. The banjo can seem like it is everywhere, and in a way it is: in flight, sounding out unhesitant in places you expect it and places you don't.

The banjos that are seen and heard today are mostly the complex metallic contraptions inherited from the great explosion of banjo manufacturing of the late nineteenth century. After more than a century of mass production of the banjo, our country is quite literally littered with them. There are beautiful banjos, collected and cared for by lovers of the instrument, catalogued and exhibited, their necks inlaid with gorgeous pearl, their tuning mechanisms and tone rims and brackets testament to the devotion and genius of generations of instrument makers. And there are plenty of cheap banjos, too, in attics and pawnshops, buzzing and bent, but sometimes just as good for knocking out a tune and singing along.

But we are also living in a time where all the layers of the banjo's history are coming alive again. The Carolina Chocolate Drops have successfully transformed a relatively obscure brand of string band music back into a beloved and popular sound, and banjo players who have been part of this group—Dom Flemons, Rhiannon Giddens, and Leyla McCalla—keep the instrument humming in their solo careers. We can now buy beautifully made banjos in the style of Boucher or other banjo makers of the minstrel age, with large pots and less metal and fretless necks. Other banjo makers are going back further: they grow gourds and, when it is time to harvest them, dry them and cut them carefully. They delicately attach skins to them with tacks or chords, reliving the arduous and careful artistry of those who, centuries ago, first built the instruments. They look to images like *The Old Plantation* or Sloane's engravings, or to the Haitian banza in Paris, and find themselves inspired to bring back that old sound, the mellow hum of plant and wood. In the process they make sure that every generation of the banjo is not just remembered but resurrected.

Where will the instrument journey from here? How will its accumulated history sound out? That part of the story is as yet unwritten: it is the musicians to come who will keep it living, twisting, and spiraling through our cultural and sonic landscape. But wherever and whenever they pick up the instrument, whatever song they choose to play, they will be inheriting something from those musical ancestors who first invented the instrument on the plantations of the Caribbean and North America. They will feel the hum of an instrument that was created to cross cultural boundaries and create new solidarities. They will hold on to an object that has been reinvented over and over again but made generation after generation feel like they were connecting to deep wells of tradition. In its richness and flexibility as both sound and symbol, the banjo has been a tremendous, inexhaustible gift. Whenever we listen to that sound of strings humming over skin, we should remember to say a word of thanks to those who, in the midst of unimaginably dark conditions, created this source of illumination, solidarity, and unending wonder.

Notes

INTRODUCTION

1 Claude McKay, *Banjo* (New York: Harper and Brothers, 1929), 6.

2 McKay, *Banjo,* 11–12.

3 Fernando Ortiz, *Cuban Counterpoint, Tobacco and Sugar* (Durham: Duke University Press, 1995), 97–103.

4 Filippo Buonanni, *Antique Musical Instruments and Their Players: 152 Plates from Bonanni's 18th Century "Gabinetto Armonico,"* ed. Frank Harrison and Joan Rimmer (New York: Dover Publications, 1964); one of the founding works of the field, published in 1861, is Adolphe Le Doulcet Pontécoulant, *Organographie* (Amsterdam: F. Knuf, 1972).

5 André Schaeffner, *Origine des instruments de musique: Introduction ethnologique à l'histoire de la musique instrumentale* (Paris: Mouton, 1968), 185; for one illustrative example of early twentieth-century organology, see Henri Bouasse, *Instruments à vent,* 2 vols. (Paris: Delagrave, 1929).

6 Schaeffner, *Origine,* 185–186; André Schaeffner, *Les Kissi: Une Société noire et ses instruments de musique,* Collection l'Homme (Paris: Hermann et Cie, 1951).

7 Johannes Fabian, *Time and the Other: How Anthropology Makes Its Object* (New York: Columbia University Press, 2002).

8 Stephen Blum, "European Musical Terminology and the Music of Africa," in *Comparative Musicology and Anthropology of Music: Essays on the History of Ethnomusicology,* ed. Bruno Nettl and Philip Bohlman (Chicago: University of Chicago Press, 1991), 13.

9 Gerhard Kubik, *Theory of African Music* (Chicago: University of Chicago Press, 2010), 2:5–6; Blum, "Musical Terminology," 19, 29 n. 11; for one classic work

on African music that offers a very different way of thinking about these issues, see Paul F. Berliner, *The Soul of Mbira: Music and Traditions of the Shona People of Zimbabwe* (Chicago: University of Chicago Press, 1978).

10 Schaeffner, *Origine,* 185–186.

11 Cecelia Conway, *African Banjo Echoes in Appalachia: A Study of Folk Traditions* (Knoxville: University of Tennessee Press, 1995); Philip F. Gura and James F. Bollman, *America's Instrument: The Banjo in the Nineteenth Century* (Chapel Hill: University of North Carolina Press, 1999); for a wide-ranging exhibit on the banjo that produced an excellent catalogue, Leo G. Mazow, ed., *Picturing the Banjo* (University Park: Pennsylvania State University Press, 2005). Much of this work has been shared at conferences, including the yearly Banjo Collectors Gatherings and the two Black Banjo Gatherings organized by Cecelia Conway at Appalachian State University, as well as in various online fora and email lists, notably the Black Banjo group animated by Tony Thomas. Of particular note in this process has been the tireless work of Shlomo Pestcoe, most of whose findings have been generously shared via Facebook; the contributions of Ulf Jagfors and Pete Ross; and the digital archive brought together by Greg Adams in the Banjo Sightings database. Adams was also one of the curators of the 2014 exhibit Making Music: The Banjo in Baltimore and Beyond.

12 Elijah Wald, *How the Beatles Destroyed Rock 'n' Roll: An Alternative History of American Popular Music* (Oxford: Oxford University Press, 2009), 20.

13 On the challenges surrounding reconstructing and analyzing the early history of black music, see Ronald Michael Radano, *Lying up a Nation: Race and Black Music* (Chicago: University of Chicago Press, 2003), 5. An important and influential work on this topic is Peter Van Der Merwe, *Origins of the Popular Style: The Antecedents of Twentieth-Century Popular Music* (Oxford: Clarendon Press, 1989). I find inspiration for my specific approach here in a series of historically rich reflections on African and Afro-Atlantic music, particularly Tal Tamari, *Les Castes de l'Afrique occidentale: Artisans et musiciens endogames* (Nanterre: Société d'ethnologie, 1997); Eric S. Charry, *Mande Music: Traditional and Modern Music of the Maninka and Mandinka of Western Africa* (Chicago: University of Chicago Press, 2000); Robert Farris Thompson, *Tango: The Art History of Love* (New York: Pantheon Books, 2005); Ned Sublette, *Cuba and Its Music: From the First Drums to the Mambo* (Chicago: Chicago Review Press, 2004).

14 Dena J. Epstein, *Sinful Tunes and Spirituals: Black Folk Music to the Civil War* (Urbana: University of Illinois Press, 2003 [1977]), xx–xxi; Orlando Patterson, *The Sociology of Slavery: An Analysis of the Origins, Development, and Structure of Negro Slave Society in Jamaica* (Rutherford, NJ: Farleigh Dickenson University Press, 1969).

15 Epstein, *Sinful Tunes*; Christopher J. Smith, *The Creolization of American Culture: William Sidney Mount and the Roots of Blackface Minstrelsy* (Urbana: University of Illinois Press, 2013).

16 W. E. B. Du Bois, *Writings* (New York: Library of America, 1986), 536.

17 Du Bois, *Writings,* 538–539.

18 Paul Gilroy, *The Black Atlantic: Modernity and Double Consciousness* (Cambridge, MA: Harvard University Press, 1993), 89–91.

19 This formulation about the redundancy of the term "Black Atlantic" was inspired by a conversation with historian Julius Scott in the context of our discussion of the title of an edited collection we produced together: Laurent Dubois and Julius Sherrard Scott, eds., *Origins of the Black Atlantic* (New York: Routledge, 2010). My approach here has been deeply influenced by the reflections on the analysis of black music in Gilroy, *The Black Atlantic,* notably pp. 100–101; and Radano, *Lying up a Nation,* xii–xiv.

20 Joseph Miller, closing comments at The Black Atlantic and the Biographical Turn conference, National Humanities Center, February 25, 2011.

21 André Schaeffner, *Variations Sur La Musique* (Paris: Fayard, 1998), 48–49; Wald, *How the Beatles Destroyed Rock 'n' Roll,* 6, 21–22.

1. SOUNDING AFRICA

1 Pierpont Morgan Library, Saint Beatus, Presbyter of Liebana, d. 798, *Commentary on the Apocalypse,* 940, MS M.644, vol. II, fol. 174 verso. Spain, perhaps in Taibara, ca. 940–945.

2 I've drawn here on the definitions provided in Marie-Thérèse Brincard, ed., *Sounding Forms: African Musical Instruments* (New York: American Federation of Arts, 1989), 196–197.

3 My approach is inspired by Ned Sublette's magisterial study of Cuban music, which shows how the long history of interactions in Iberia helped lay the foundation for a new round of interactions in the Caribbean. Ned Sublette, *Cuba and Its Music: From the First Drums to the Mambo* (Chicago: Chicago Review Press, 2004).

4 Klaus P. Wachsmann, "A 'ShipLike' String Instrument from West Africa," *Ethnos* 38 (1973): 43–56.

5 Douglas Alton Smith, *A History of the Lute from Antiquity to the Renaissance* (Lexington, MA: Lute Society of America, 2002), 1.

6 Smith, *Lute,* 3–4.

7 Athanassios Vergados, *The Homeric Hymn to Hermes: Introduction, Text and Commentary* (Berlin: De Gruyter, 2013), 103; on Greek turtle-shell lyres in images and archaeological remains, see Helen Roberts, "Reconstructing the Greek Tortoise-Shell Lyre," *World Archaeology* 12, no. 3 (February 1, 1981): 303–312.

8 I am indebted to James Millward, who generously shared with me his recent research on the earliest depictions of lutes. Some, but not all, of this material is presented in James A. Millward, *The Silk Road: A Very Short Introduction* (Oxford: Oxford University Press, 2013), 91–93. A fuller version was presented by James Millward, "Silk road journeys of the Eurasian lute," talk at Natural History Museum of Los Angeles County, 30 January 2014. The British Museum piece, a Cylinder Seal from Uruk, is BM 141632; the second piece mentioned is from the Iraq Museum, IM 46588; and the piece from Susa is Musée Guimet Sb 6579.

9 Smith, *Lute,* 7–8; Eric Charry, "Plucked Lutes in West Africa: An Historical Overview," *The Galpin Society Journal* 49 (1996): 3; Sue Carole DeVale, "African Harps: Construction, Decoration, and Sound," in *Sounding Forms: African Musical Instruments,* ed. Marie-Thérèse Brincard (New York: American Federation of Arts, 1989), 54.

10 John Gardner Wilkinson, *The Manners and Customs of the Ancient Egyptians,* ed. Samuel Birch (New York: Scribner and Welford, 1878), 480–484 and Plate XI; Hans Hickmann, *Catalogue général des antiquités égyptiennes du Musée du Caire: Instruments de musique* (Cairo: Imprimerie de l'Institut français d'archéologie orientale, 1949), 159–163 and Plates XCVII to CII; Hans Hickmann, *Musicologie pharaonique; études sur l'évolution de l'art musical dans l'Égypte ancienne* (Kehl: Heitz, 1956).

11 Smith, *Lute,* 8–9.

12 Sublette, *Cuba and Its Music,* 12–14; Veit Erlmann, *Music and the Islamic Reform in the Early Sokoto Empire* (Stuttgart: Steiner Verlag Wiesbaden GmbH, 1986), 10–11.

13 Sublette, *Cuba and Its Music,* 14–15; Smith, *Lute,* 16.

14 Sublette, *Cuba and Its Music,* 16.

15 Christian Poché, *La Musique Arabo-Andalouse* (Arles: Actes sud, 1995), 35–39.

16 Smith, *Lute,* 17.

17 Poché, *Musique Arabo-Andalouse,* 17–18, 38, 99.

18 Smith, *Lute,* 19–20.

19 Smith, *Lute,* 3–4.

20 I am indebted to Pete Ross, a maker of banjos (including gourd banjos), for this insight on the impact of climate on the construction of the instrument, and to David Garner for pointing out that this problem would have been less serious for drums than for chordophones.

21 DeVale, "African Harps."

22 Joseph Cuoq, *Recueil des sources arabes concernant l'Afrique occidentale du VIIIe au XVIe siécle (Bilād Al-Sūdān)* (Paris: Editions du CNRS, 1985), 272–273, 305; J. F. P. Hopkins and Nehemia Levtzion, *Corpus of Early Arabic Sources for West African History* (Cambridge: Cambridge University Press, 1981), 252–253, 266–267, 291; C. Defrémery and B. R. Sanguinetti, trans., *Voyages* (Paris: Imprimerie Nationale, 1922), 406; Ibn Battuta, *Travels in Asia and Africa, 1325–1354,* trans. H. A. R. Gibb (London: G. Routledge, 1929), 326; Veit Erlmann, "Some Sources on Music in Western Sudan from 1300–1700," *African Music* 5, no. 3 (January 1, 1973): 34–39, 37. Al-'Umari lived in Damascus and Cairo in the first half of the fourteenth century and gathered his information on Mali from Egyptian officials who had visited there and from former residents in the kingdom.

23 Erlmann, "Some Sources," 37; H. R. Palmer, "The Kano Chronicle," *The Journal of the Royal Anthropological Institute of Great Britain and Ireland* 38 (January 1, 1908): 90, doi:10.2307/2843130.

24 Charles Hercules Read, *Antiquities from the City of Benin and from Other Parts of West Africa in the British Museum* (New York: Hacker Art Books, 1973); Philip J. C. Dark and Matthew Hill, "Musical Instruments on Benin Plaques," in *Essays on Music and History in Africa,* ed. Klaus P. Wachsmann (Evanston: Northwestern University Press, 1971), 65–78; for the Akan sculpture see Brincard, *Sounding Forms,* 189.

25 Charry, "Plucked Lutes," 3; Eric S. Charry, *Mande Music: Traditional and Modern Music of the Maninka and Mandinka of Western Africa* (Chicago: University of Chicago Press, 2000); for a detailed study of griot practice see Sory Camara, *Gens de la parole: Essai sur la condition et le role des griots dans la société Malinke* (Paris: Kharthala, 1992).

26 Djibril Tamsir Niane, *Sundiata: An Epic of Old Mali* (London: Longmans, 1965), 39–41, 63, 75, 78.

27 Tal Tamari, *Les Castes de l'Afrique occidentale: Artisans et musiciens endogames* (Nanterre: Société d'ethnologie, 1997), chap. 3, esp. 118, 124–126.

28 Niane, *Sundiata,* 39–41; Tamari, *Les Castes,* 151–152; J. H. Kwabena Nketia, "The Aesthetic Dimensions of African Musical Instruments," in *Sounding Forms: African Musical Instruments,* ed. Marie-Thérèse Brincard (New York: American Federation of Arts, 1989), 21; the most detailed and careful study of these instruments in West Africa has been done by Eric Charry. See Charry, "Plucked Lutes," 3; and Charry, *Mande Music.*

29 Erlmann, "Some Sources," 35; Charry, *Mande Music,* Appendix A provides an excellent compendium of both early Islamic and European sources relating to Mande music; and Tamari's *Les Castes* offers a detailed bibliography of sources as well as a useful appendix explaining the interpretive issues surrounding each.

30 Alvise Cà da Mosto, *The Voyages of Cadamosto and Other Documents on Western Africa in the Second Half of the Fifteenth Century,* ed. Gerald Roe Crone (London: Printed for the Hakluyt Society, 1937), 51; Valentim Fernandes, *Description de la côte occidentale d'Afrique,* ed. Théodore Monod, Avelino Teixera, and Raymond Mauny (Bissau: Centro de Estudos da Guiné Portuguesa, 1951), 9–11; Charry, *Mande Music,* 358–359.

31 Pieter de Marees, *Description and Historical Account of the Gold Kingdom of Guinea (1602)* (Oxford: British Academy by Oxford University, 1987), 171; Richard Jobson, *The Golden Trade: Or, A Discovery of the River Gambra, and the Golden Trade of the Aethiopians* (London: Nicholas Okes, 1623), 105–108; excerpts from Jobson are reproduced in Eileen Southern, ed., *Readings in Black American Music,* 2nd ed. (New York: W. W. Norton, 1983), 1–3; and Charry, *Mande Music,* 360–361.

32 Jobson, *Golden Trade,* 105–106; Charry, *Mande Music,* 360–361.

33 A translation of key excerpts is provided in Charry, *Mande Music,* 364–365; Michel Jajolet de La Courbe, *Premier voyage du sieur de la Courbe fait a la coste d'Afrique en 1685,* ed. Prosper Cultru (Paris: E. Champion, 1913), 43, 172.

34 Jacques-Joseph Le Maire, *Voyage of the Sieur Le Maire to the Canary Islands, Cape-Verd, Senegal and Gamby* (London: F. Mills and W. Turner, 1696), 82–84; a modern translation of these selections from the French is presented in Charry, *Mande Music,* 364–365. A 1705 account by the Dutch voyager Willem Bosman describes a similar instrument, which he declares is "the best they have": "a hollow piece of Wood of two hands breadth long, and one broad; from the hinder part of this a Stick comes cross to the fore-part, and upon the Instrument are five or six extended Strings: So that it bears some sort of Similitude to a small Harp . . . and affords by much the most agreeable Sound of any they have here." Charry, *Mande Music,* 365–366; Willem Bosman, *A New and Accurate Description of the Coast of Guinea, Divided into the Gold, the Slave, and the Ivory Coasts* (New York: Barnes & Noble, 1967), 139–140.

35 Duarte Lopes, *A Report of the Kingdom of the Congo and of the Surrounding Countries, Drawn out of the Writings and Discourses of Duarte Lopez, by Filippo Pigafetta, in Rome, 1591,* trans. Margarite Hutchinson (New York: Negro Universities Press, 1969).

36 Pierre Avity, *Description Generale de l'Afrique, Seconde Partie Du Monde* (Paris: Chez Claude Sonnius, 1637), 445; André Schaeffner, *Variations Sur La Musique* (Paris: Fayard, 1998), 87, 93–94.

37 Cavazzi's images are reproduced and analyzed in Ezio Bassani, "Un Cappuccino nell'Africa Nera Del Seicento: I Disegni Dei Manoscritti Araldi Del Padre Giovanni Antonio Cavazzi Da Montecuccolo," *Quaderno Poro* 4 (1987); John Thornton has done a translation of the work, available online: Giovanni

Antonio Cavazzi, *Missione Evangelica,* trans. John K. Thornton (http://www.bu
.edu/afam/faculty/john-thornton/cavazzi-missione-evangelica-2/, n.d.). The
image is available at http://hitchcock.itc.virginia.edu/SlaveTrade/collection
/large/Bassani-19.JPG at www.slaveryimages.org, compiled by Jerome Handler
and Michael Tuite, and sponsored by the Virginia Foundation for the Humanities and the University of Virginia Library.

38 Erlmann, *Sokoto Empire,* 10–11.

39 Erlmann, *Sokoto Empire,* 10–11, 38–39; For a detailed examination of the
problems surrounding the use of the term "molo" in writings about the banjo,
see Ken A. Gourlay, "Letters to the Editor," *Ethnomusicology* 20, no. 2 (May
1976): 327–332; Gourlay, "Letters to the Editor."

40 Mungo Park, *Travels in the Interior Districts of Africa: Performed Under . . . the
African Association, in the Years 1795, 1796, and 1797* (London: W. Bulmer and
Co., 1799), 278–279; the full excerpt is reproduced in Southern, *Readings in Black
American Music,* 4–7.

41 Olaudah Equiano, *The Interesting Narrative of the Life of Olaudah Equiano,*
ed. Robert J. Allison (Boston: Bedford Books, 2007), 46.

42 Hugh Clapperton, *Journal of a Second Expedition into the Interior of Africa, from
the Bight of Benin to Soccatoo; to Which Is Added the Journal of Richard Lander from
Kano to the Sea-Coast, Partly by a More Eastern Route* (London: F. Cass, 1966),
103, 129–131; Dixon Denham et al., *Narrative of Travels and Discoveries in Northern
and Central Africa, in the Years 1822, 1823, and 1824,* 2nd ed. (London: John
Murray, 1826), 208; image between pages 106 and 107.

43 DeVale, "African Harps," 53; Jean-Sébastien Laurenty, *Les Cordophones du
Congo belge et du Ruanda-Urundi* (Tervuren: Annales du Musee Royale du Congo
Belge, 1960).

44 Stephen Chauvet, *Musique Nègre* (Paris: Sociéte d'Editions Géographiques,
Maritimes et Coloniales, 1929), 106–113.

45 DeVale, "African Harps," 58–59.

46 Anthony V. King and David Ames, *Glossary of Hausa Music and Its Social
Contexts* (Evanston: Northwestern University Press, 1971), 40–47. See also
David W. Ames, "Igbo and Hausa Musicians: A Comparative Examination,"
Ethnomusicology 17, no. 2 (May 1, 1973): 256.

47 Henry George Farmer, *Studies in Oriental Musical Instruments* (Road Town,
British Virgin Islands: Longwood Press, 1978), 40; Philip D. Schuyler, "Music
and Meaning Among the Gnawa Religious Brotherhood of Morocco," *The
World of Music* 23, no. 1 (1981): 5.

48 DeVale, "African Harps," 53–54; Nketia, "Aesthetic Dimensions," 25.

49 DeVale, "African Harps," 59.

50 DeVale, "African Harps," 57 and p. 181 of the same volume for the sculpture; Nketia, "Aesthetic Dimensions," 25.

51 Greg C. Adams and Shlomo Pestcoe, "The Jola Akonting: Reconnecting the Banjo to Its West African Roots," *Sing Out!* 51, no. 1 (Spring 2007): 43–51.

52 Brincard, *Sounding Forms,* 92; Wachsmann, "A 'Ship-Like' Instrument."

2. THE FIRST AFRICAN INSTRUMENT

1 Derek Walcott, *Omeros* (New York: Farrar, Straus and Giroux, 1990), 133, 148.

2 Walcott, *Omeros,* 149–151.

3 Sidney Wilfred Mintz and Richard Price, *The Birth of African-American Culture: An Anthropological Perspective* (Boston: Beacon Press, 1992); Kamau Brathwaite, *The Development of Creole Society in Jamaica, 1770–1820* (Kingston: Ian Randle, 2005); Édouard Glissant, *Caribbean Discourse: Selected Essays,* trans. J. Michael Dash (Charlottesville: University Press of Virginia, 1989).

4 Sidney W. Mintz, *Three Ancient Colonies: Caribbean Themes and Variations* (Cambridge, MA: Harvard University Press, 2010), 198.

5 On the meaning of "Africa" in the context of eighteenth-century North America, see James Sidbury, *Becoming African in America: Race and Nation in the Early Black Atlantic* (Oxford: Oxford University Press, 2007).

6 Jean-Baptiste Labat, *Nouveau voyages aux isles de l'Amerique: Contenant l'histoire naturelle de ces pays, l'origine, les mœurs, la religion & le gouvernement . . . Nouv. ed. augm. considérablement,* vol. 4 (Paris, 1742), 463.

7 Labat, *Nouveaux voyages,* 4:463, 465–466.

8 Labat, *Nouveaux voyages,* 4:466–470.

9 Labat, *Nouveaux voyages,* 4:463, 467–470.

10 Labat, *Nouveaux voyages,* 4:461–462.

11 Labat, *Nouveaux voyages,* 4:463–464.

12 Labat, *Nouveaux voyages,* 4:468–469. Labat's description of the instrument was incorporated into various later texts. Thomas Jefferys, for instance, in his 1760 history of the French colonies of the Americas, described two of the musical instruments of the slaves in the Caribbean colonies as "a sort of drum, being a piece of hollow wood covered with sheepskin, and a kind of guitar, made of a calabash." Thomas Jefferys, *The Natural and Civil History of the French Dominions in North and South America* (London, 1760).

13 Richard Cullen Rath, *How Early America Sounded* (Ithaca: Cornell University Press, 2003), 78–79, 84.

14 John Taylor, *Jamaica in 1687: The Taylor Manuscript at the National Library of Jamaica,* ed. David Buisseret (Kingston, Jamaica: University of West Indies Press, 2008), 269.

15 Taylor, *Jamaica in 1687,* xi–xv; Pratik Chakrabarti, "Sloane's Travels: A Colonial History of Gentlemanly Science," in *From Books to Bezoars: Sir Hans Sloane and His Collections,* ed. Alison Walker, Arthur MacGregor, and Michael Hunter (London: The British Library, 2012), 74.

16 Richard S. Dunn, *Sugar and Slaves; the Rise of the Planter Class in the English West Indies, 1624–1713* (Chapel Hill: University of North Carolina Press, 1972); on the early history of Jamaica and its Maroons, see Kenneth M. Bilby, *True-Born Maroons* (Gainesville: University Press of Florida, 2005); Vincent Brown, *The Reaper's Garden: Death and Power in the World of Atlantic Slavery* (Cambridge, MA: Harvard University Press, 2008).

17 Taylor, *Jamaica in 1687,* 271. On the early development of Afro-Atlantic religion, see Mintz and Price, *The Birth of African-American Culture;* Karen McCarthy Brown, *Mama Lola: A Vodou Priestess in Brooklyn* (Berkeley: University of California Press, 1991).

18 Hans Sloane, *A Voyage to the Islands Madera, Barbados, Nieves, S. Christophers and Jamaica,* vol. 1 (London: B. M., 1707), xlviii.

19 Mark Purcell, " 'Settled in the North of Ireland' Or, Where Did Sloane Come From?" in *From Books to Bezoars: Sir Hans Sloane and His Collections,* ed. Alison Walker, Arthur MacGregor, and Michael Hunter (London: The British Library, 2012), 25–27; Michael Hunter, "Introduction," in *From Books to Bezoars,* 1.

20 Hunter, "Introduction," 1, 3, 7; Chakrabarti, "Sloane's Travels," 72–73; James Delbourgo, "Collecting Hans Sloane," in *From Books to Bezoars,* 14.

21 Delbourgo, "Collecting Hans Sloane," 10–11, 18.

22 Sloane, *Voyage,* 1: Preface; Delbourgo, "Collecting Hans Sloane," 17; Chakrabarti, "Sloane's Travels," 78–79.

23 Delbourgo, "Collecting Hans Sloane," 17; Hunter, "Introduction," 7.

24 Rath, *How Early America Sounded,* 69–70, 201 n. 44. Rath offers an "imaginative reconstruction" of the scene, placing it on the edge of a Jamaica plantation. On music and theater in Saint-Domingue, see Bernard Camier and Laurent Dubois, "Voltaire et Zaïre, Ou Le Théâtre Des Lumières Dans L'aire Atlantique Française," *Revue D'histoire Moderne et Contemporaine* 54, no. 4 (2007): 39–69; Jean Fouchard, *Plaisirs de Saint-Domingue* (Port-au-Prince: Impr. de l'État, 1955).

25 Rath, *How Early America Sounded*, 72.

26 Rath, *How Early America Sounded*, 72–73; on the cultural and demographic landscape of Jamaica, see Brown, *The Reaper's Garden;* for an example of a slave conspiracy in which Akan leaders play a key role, see David Barry Gaspar, *Bondmen & Rebels: A Study of Master-Slave Relations in Antigua, with Implications for Colonial British America* (Baltimore: Johns Hopkins University Press, 1985).

27 Rath, *How Early America Sounded*, 79–81.

28 Hans Sloan, *A Voyage to the Islands*, 1:xlviii–xlix.

29 Shlomo Pestcoe, "Banjo Beginnings: The Afro-Creole 'Strum-Strumps' of Jamaica, 1687–1689," Facebook (May 23, 2013), https://www.facebook .com/notes/banjo-roots-banjo-beginnings/banjo-beginnings-the-afro -creole-strum-strumps-of-jamaica-1687–89/596163280402853 offers the most detailed examination of the history of these instruments. I am grateful to him, and also indebted to James Delbourgo, who in personal correspondence helped me enormously both in understanding the details surrounding these instruments and their representations and with the interpretation I lay out here.

30 The Kickius sketch is BL, Add. MS 5234, fol. 75, and is reproduced in Delbourgo, "Collecting Hans Sloane," 13; Henry George Farmer, "Early References to Music in the Western Sūdān," *Journal of the Royal Asiatic Society of Great Britain and Ireland,* no. 4 (October 1, 1939): Plate XI, p. 579.

31 Pestcoe, "Banjo Beginnings."

32 Rath, *How Early America Sounded,* 80; Pestcoe, "Banjo Beginnings." On Taino aesthetics and Haitian Vodou, see Milo Rigaud, *Vèvè: Diagrammes Rituels Du Voudou,* Trilingual ed., French-English-Spanish (New York: French and European Publications, 1974); Maya Deren, *Divine Horsemen: The Living Gods of Haiti,* Myth and Man (New York: Documentext, 1959).

33 Sally Price, "When Is a Calabash Not a Calabash?," *New West Indian Guide/ Nieuwe West-Indische Gids* 56, no. 1/2 (1982): 69–82; on the complexities of interpreting the history of Taino music, see Donald Thompson, "The 'Cronistas de Indias' Revisited: Historical Reports, Archeological Evidence, and Literary and Artistic Traces of Indigenous Music and Dance in the Greater Antilles at the Time of the 'Conquista,'" *Latin American Music Review / Revista de Música Latinoamericana* 14, no. 2 (October 1, 1993): 181–201, doi:10.2307/780174.

34 The Kickius sketch is BL, Add. MS 5234, fol. 75, and is reproduced in Delbourgo, "Collecting Hans Sloane," 13. The presence of what might well be an African instrument led one early analyst of this image, the leading musicologist George Farmer, to describe it as an illustration of "Musical Instruments of the

Western Sudan" in a 1938 publication, and as one of the earliest visual depictions of African musical instruments. Though this was an error, it was an understandable one, since the instruments were, in a sense, African—but of an Atlantic variety. See Farmer, "Early References to Music in the Western Sūdān," Plate XI, p. 579.

35 I explore the symbolism of the cross in more detail in Chapter 3. Robert Farris Thompson, *Flash of the Spirit: African and Afro-American Art and Philosophy* (New York: Random House, 1983); Wyatt MacGaffey, *Religion and Society in Central Africa: The BaKongo of Lower Zaire* (Chicago: University of Chicago Press, 1986), 116–120.

36 The reconstructions of the music piece are available via Richard Rath, "African Music in Seventeenth Century Jamaica," http://way.net/waymusic/?p =13 (consulted July 24, 2014).

37 For a collection of essays reflecting on circulation in the Atlantic world, see Laurent Dubois and Julius Sherrard Scott, eds., *Origins of the Black Atlantic* (New York: Routledge, 2010); the classic, foundational study of the circulation of news and information among Afro-American communities is Julius S. Scott, "The Common Wind: Currents of Afro-American Communication in the Era of the Haitian Revolution" (Ph.D., Duke University, 1986).

38 The Spy, "Letter," *New York Weekly Journal,* March 7, 1736.

39 Shane White and Graham White, *The Sounds of Slavery: Discovering African American History through Songs, Sermons, and Speech* (Boston: Beacon Press, 2005), 8–9; Eileen Southern, ed., *Readings in Black American Music,* 2nd ed. (New York: W. W. Norton, 1983), 41–47.

40 White and White, *Sounds of Slavery,* 8; James Fenimore Cooper, *Satanstoe* (Lincoln: University of Nebraska Press, 1962), 60.

41 The Spy, "Letter"; White and White, *Sounds of Slavery,* 8.

42 The Spy, "Letter."

43 Orville Platt, "Negro Governors," in *Papers of the New Haven Colony Historical Society* 6 (1900): 323–324. Platt does not cite the source of this account, though it was clearly written after the American Revolution (since it explains that this tradition ended after 1776), so it is not an eyewitness account. For a detailed history of election day celebrations, see Joseph Reidy, "Negro Election Day and Black Community Life in New England, 1750–1860," *Marxist Perspectives* 1, no. 3 (Fall 1978): 102–117; see also Sam Kinser, *Carnival, American Style: Mardi Gras at New Orleans and Mobile* (Chicago: University of Chicago Press, 1990), 334–335, n. 74; Dale Cockrell, *Demons of Disorder: Early Blackface Minstrels and Their World* (Cambridge: Cambridge University Press, 1997), 37–38.

44 Walter Johnson, *River of Dark Dreams: Slavery and Empire in the Cotton Kingdom* (Cambridge, MA: Harvard University Press, 2013), 224; on the complexities of using runaway advertisements as a historical source, see David Waldstreicher, "Reading the Runaways: Self-Fashioning, Print Culture, and Confidence in Slavery in the Eighteenth-Century Mid-Atlantic," *The William and Mary Quarterly,* Third Series, 56, no. 2 (April 1, 1999): 243–272.

45 Southern, *Readings in Black American Music,* 34–35.

46 Philip F. Gura and James F. Bollman, *America's Instrument: The Banjo in the Nineteenth Century* (Chapel Hill: University of North Carolina Press, 1999), 13–14; "Eighteenth Century Slaves as Advertised by Their Masters," *The Journal of Negro History* 1, no. 2 (1916): 163–216, 210.

47 Philip Vickers Fithian, *Journal and Letters of Philip Vickers Fithian, 1773–1774: A Plantation Tutor of the Old Dominion,* ed. Hunter Dickinson Farish, New Edition (Williamsburg, VA: Colonial Williamsburg, Inc., 1957), 62; Cecelia Conway, *African Banjo Echoes in Appalachia: A Study of Folk Traditions* (Knoxville: University of Tennessee Press, 1995), 64.

48 John Oldmixon, *British Empire in America, Containing the History of the Discovery, Settlement, Progress and Present States of All the British Colonies on the Continent and Islands of America* (London: J. Brotherton, 1708), 2:135; Johann David Schoepf, *Travels in the Confederation, 1783–1784.,* trans. Alfred J. Morrison (Philadelphia: W. J. Campbell, 1911), 2:261–262; James Barclay, *The Voyages and Travels of James Barclay* (Privately Printed, 1777), 26; Jean Benjamin de Laborde, *Essai sur la musique ancienne et moderne* 1 (Paris, 1780), 291.

49 Douglas Chambers, *Murder at Montpelier: Igbo Africans in Virginia* (Jackson: University of Mississippi Press, 2005), 180.

50 Trudi Martinus-Guda and Hillary de Bruin, *Drie Eeuwen Banya: de geschiedenis van een Surinaamse slavendans / Bruin, Hillary de.* (Paramaribo: Ministerie van Onderwijs en Volksontwikkeling (Minov) / Directoraat Cultuur, 2005), 39ff.

51 Martinus-Guda and de Bruin, *Drie eeuwen Banya,* 39ff.

52 Martinus-Guda and de Bruin, *Drie eeuwen Banya,* 39ff. The classic study of the early history of the Maroons of Suriname is Richard Price, *First-Time: The Historical Vision of an Afro-American People* (Baltimore: Johns Hopkins University Press, 1983); see also Richard Price, ed., *Maroon Societies: Rebel Slave Communities in the Americas,* 3rd ed. (Baltimore: Johns Hopkins University Press, 1996).

53 John Gabriel Stedman, *Narrative of a Five Years Expedition against the Revolted Negroes of Surinam; Transcribed for the First Time from the Original 1790 Manuscript,* ed. Richard Price and Sally Price (New York: IUniverse, Inc., 2010), xv, xxi, xxiv, lxii.

54 Stedman, *Narrative,* xiv.

55 Stedman, *Narrative,* 292.

56 Stedman, *Narrative,* 537.

57 Stedman, *Narrative,* 538.

58 Stedman, *Narrative,* 538–540; Paul F. Berliner, *The Soul of Mbira: Music and Traditions of the Shona People of Zimbabwe* (Chicago: University of Chicago Press, 1978), 17.

59 Stedman, *Narrative,* 540; on the discovery of the piece and the broader context of Stedman's collection, see Richard Price and Sally Price, "John Gabriel Stedman's Collection of 18th Century Artifacts from Suriname," *Nieuwe West-Indische Gids* 53 (1979): quote p. 138. An in-depth discussion of the artifact itself, carried out via a group email discussion in 2007 between Ulf Jagfors, Shlomo Pestcoe, and Richard Price highlighted the curious construction of the instrument in which the strings are set in grooves, thus making them difficult to play.

60 Stedman, *Narrative,* 538. I am indebted to Kenneth Bilby for this interpretation of the issue of the name, which he laid out to me during a conversation in New Orleans in April 2013.

61 "No. 26," Jun. 28, 1828, Reports of Protectors of Slaves, Berbice, Colonial Office 116/144, National Archives, Kew, UK. Randy Browne, who shared this source with me, makes rich use of such documents in his dissertation: Randy Browne, "Surviving Slavery: Politics, Power, and Authority in the British Caribbean, 1807–1834" (University of North Carolina at Chapel Hill, 2012).

62 John Matthews, *A Voyage to the River Sierre-Leone* (London: B. White and Son, 1788), 105–106; Eric S. Charry, *Mande Music: Traditional and Modern Music of the Maninka and Mandinka of Western Africa* (Chicago: University of Chicago Press, 2000), 368–369. A. M. Falconbridge, *Narrative of Two Voyages to the River Sierra Leone During the Years 1791–1792–1793* (Liverpool: Liverpool University Press, 2000), 47; Thomas Winterbottom, *An Account of the Native Africans in the Neighbourhood of Sierra Leone,* vol. 1 (London: Frank Cass, 1803), 113.

63 John Davis, *Travels of Four Years and a Half in the United States of America; During 1798, 1799, 1800, 1801, and 1802* (London: R. Edwards, 1803), 1–2.

64 Davis, *Travels,* 378–381.

65 Samuel Mordecai, *Richmond in by-Gone Days Being Reminiscences of an Old Citizen* (Richmond, VA: G. M. West, 1856), 180, 310.

66 Kenneth Bilby, "Africa's Creole Drum: The Gumbe as Vector and Signifier of Trans-African Creolization," in *Creolization as Cultural Creativity,* ed. Robert Baron and Ana C. Cara (Jackson: University of Mississippi Press, 2011), 137.

67 Bilby, "Africa's Creole Drum," 137–138.

68 Bilby, "Africa's Creole Drum," 140, 147.

69 Bilby, "Africa's Creole Drum," 138–139, 147–149.

70 Bilby, "Africa's Creole Drum," 150–151.

71 *Antigua and the Antiguans: A Full Account of the Colony and Its Inhabitants,* vol. 2 (London: Saunders and Otley, 1844), 107; Lafcadio Hearn, *Two Years in the West Indies* (New Yorker: Harper, 1923), 145.

3. THREE LEAVES

1 Benjamin Henry Boneval Latrobe, *Impressions Respecting New Orleans, Diary and Sketches, 1818–1820* (New York: Columbia University Press, 1951), 49–50. The Latrobe manuscript is reprinted in full in Latrobe, *Impressions.* The original is held by the Maryland Historical Society.

2 Latrobe, *Impressions,* 49–50.

3 Latrobe, *Impressions,* 49–51.

4 Jerah Johnson, "New Orleans's Congo Square: An Urban Setting for Early Afro-American Culture Formation," *Louisiana History: The Journal of the Louisiana Historical Association* 32, no. 2 (April 1, 1991): 142; Gary A. Donaldson, "A Window on Slave Culture: Dances at Congo Square in New Orleans, 1800–1962," *The Journal of Negro History* 69, no. 2 (1984): 64.

5 Johnson, "New Orleans's Congo Square," 119–120; Ned Sublette, *The World That Made New Orleans: From Spanish Silver to Congo Square* (Chicago: Lawrence Hill Books, 2008), 283.

6 The image here, from the original manuscript at the Maryland Historical Society, is available at http://www.mdhs.org/digitalimage/stringed-instruments-february-21–1819 (consulted March 8, 2014).

7 Victor Schoelcher, *Colonies Étrangères et Haiti: Résultats de L'emancipation Anglaise,* vol. 2 (Paris: Pagnerre, 1843); on Schoelcher's visit to Haiti and the broader political context of the time, see Laurent Dubois, *Haiti: The Aftershocks of History* (New York: Metropolitan Books, 2012), esp. chap 3.

8 Florence Gétreau, "Gustave Chouquet, Léon Pillaut, et l'unique catalogue du Musée Instrumental du Conservatoire de Musique de Paris," in *Le Musée du Conservatoire de Musique* (Geneva: Editions Minkoff, 1993), 5–6.

9 Gustave Chouquet, *Le Musée du Conservatoire de Musique* (Geneva: Editions Minkoff, 1993), ix–x.

10 Florence Gétreau, *Aux origines du musée de la musique: Les collections instrumentales du Conservatoire de Paris: 1793–1993* (Paris: Klincksieck, 1996), 135, 205–206, 234, 417.

11 Chouquet, *Le Musée du Conservatoire de Musique,* xii.

12 Chouquet, *Le Musée du Conservatoire de Musique,* 222.

13 I met with Bruguière in Paris in June of 2006, and this and the following paragraphs are based on our conversations. The museum description of the instrument, along with several photos, is here: http://mediatheque.cite-musique .fr/masc/play.asp?ID=0157295 (consulted July 30, 2014).

14 My discussion of the banza here and throughout this chapter are informed by conversations and correspondence with Pete Ross and Ulf Jagfors, who was also kind enough to share with me his unpublished article about the instrument, which describes its construction and the story of how it was found: Ulf Jagfors, "A Banza from Haiti," 2005.

15 Thomas Granger, "The Sugar-Cane: A Poem," in Thomas Krise, ed., *Caribbeana: An Anthology of English Literature of the West Indies, 1657–1777* (Chicago: University of Chicago Press), 257.

16 William Beckford, *A Descriptive Account of the Island of Jamaica* (London: T. and J. Egerton, 1790), 1:387–388; on Beckford's life, see Kamau Brathwaite, *The Development of Creole Society in Jamaica, 1770–1820* (Kingston: Ian Randle, 2005), 131.

17 Beckford, *Jamaica,* 1:388–390.

18 *A Short Journey in the West Indies, in Which Are Interspersed, Curious Anecdotes and Characters* (London: Published by the Author, 1790), 1:88–90.

19 Thomas Clarkson, *An Essay on the Slavery and Commerce of the Human Species, Particularly the African* (London: J. Phillips, 1788), 147, 150–151.

20 Clarkson, *An Essay on Slavery,* 151–152.

21 Gilbert Francklyn, *An Answer to the Rev Mr. Clarkson's Essay on the Slavery and Commerce of the Human Species, Particularly the African, in a Series of Letters from a Gentleman in Jamaica to His Friend in London* (London: Logographic Press, 1789), 206–207.

22 Lida Tunstell Rodman, ed., "Journal of a Tour to North Carolina by William Attmore," *The James Sprunt Historical Publications of the North Carolina Historical Society* 14, no. 1 (1916): 43; J. F. D. Smyth, *A Tour in the United States of America,* vol. 1 (Dublin: G. Perrin, 1784), 46.

23 Thomas Fairfax, *Journey from Virginia to Salem Massachusetts, 1799* (London, 1936), 2.

24 Thomas Ashe, *Travels in America, Performed in 1806, For the Purpose of Exploring the Rivers Alleghany, Monongahela, Ohio, and Mississippi* (London: John Abraham, Clement's Lane, 1808), 1:233–235.

25 Robert Coates, *The Outlaw Years: The History of the Land Pirates of the Natchez Trace* (New York: The Macaulay Company, 1930), 27.

26 James Kirke Paulding, *Letters From the South* (New York: Harper & Brothers, 1835), 1:96–98.

27 William Dickson, *Letters on Slavery* (London: J. Phillips, 1784), 73–74.

28 Thomas Jefferson, *Notes on the State of Virginia: With Related Documents,* ed. David Waldstreicher (Boston: Bedford/St. Martins, 2002), 177.

29 John Luffman, *A Brief Account of the Island of Antigua* (London: T. Cadell, 1789), 135–137; Charles MacPherson, *Memoirs of the Life and Travels of the Late Charles MacPherson, Esq in Asia, Africa and America* (Edinburgh: Arch. Constable, 1800), 186.

30 Bryan Edwards, *The History, Civil and Commercial, of the British Colonies in the West Indies* (London: John Stockdale, 1807), 2:102–103.

31 Robert Renny, *A History of Jamaica* (London: J. Cawthorn, 1807), 167–168.

32 Renny, *A History of Jamaica,* 168.

33 R. R. Madden, *A Twelvemonth's Residence in the West Indies during the Transition from Slavery to Apprenticeship* (Westport, CT: Negro Universities Press, 1835), 2:9–10.

34 George Pinckard, *Notes on the West Indies, Including Observations Relative to the Creoles and Slaves of the Western Colonies, and the Indians of South America,* vol. 1 (London: Messrs. Baldwin, Cradock and Joy, 1816), 127–130.

35 Frederick Bayley, *Four Years Residence in the West Indies, During the Years 1826, 7, 8, and 9, by the Son of a Military Officer,* vol. 3 (London: William Kidd, 1833), 437.

36 Sylvester Hovey, *Letters from the West Indies: Relating Especially to the Danish Island St. Croix and to the British Islands Antigua, Barbadoes and Jamaica* (New York: Gould and Newman, 1838), 36.

37 On the place of masking and parody in Caribbean culture, see Richard D. E. Burton, *Afro-Creole: Power, Opposition, and Play in the Caribbean* (Ithaca: Cornell University Press, 1997).

38 Robert C. Smith, "Liberty Displaying the Arts and Sciences: A Philadelphia Allegory by Samuel Jennings," *Winterthur Portfolio* 2 (January 1, 1965): 85–105, 87–89. For a wide-ranging study of depictions of African-American music and musicians from the eighteenth through the early twentieth century, see Eileen Southern and Josephine Wright, *Images: Iconography of Music in African-American Culture, 1770s–1920s* (New York: Garland Publishing, 2000).

39 Smith, "Liberty," 85, 92, 96–99; David Hackett Fischer, *Liberty and Freedom: A Visual History of America's Founding Ideas* (Oxford: Oxford University Press, 2005), 234–235; Southern and Wright, *Images,* 20–22.

40 Smith, "Liberty," 99–100.

41 Smith, "Liberty," 101.

42 Susan P. Shames, *The Old Plantation: The Artist Revealed* (Williamsburg, VA: Colonial Williamsburg Foundation, 2010), 10–11, 18, 36–40, 43–47; Southern and Wright, *Images,* 17–20.

43 Shames, *The Old Plantation,* 26–27; on the complex dynamics of sexuality in master-slave relations, see Joan Dayan, *Haiti, History, and the Gods* (Berkeley: University of California Press, 1995); Trevor G. Burnard, *Mastery, Tyranny, and Desire: Thomas Thistlewood and His Slaves in the Anglo-Jamaican World* (Chapel Hill: University of North Carolina Press, 2004).

44 Shames, *The Old Plantation,* 11, 56–60.

45 Shames, *The Old Plantation,* 12.

46 Shames, *The Old Plantation,* 12; Robert Farris Thompson, *Flash of the Spirit: African and Afro-American Art and Philosophy* (New York: Random House, 1983).

47 Thompson, *Flash of the Spirit;* Wyatt MacGaffey, *Religion and Society in Central Africa: The BaKongo of Lower Zaire* (Chicago: University of Chicago Press, 1986), 116–120; James Denbow, "Heart and Soul: Glimpses of Ideology and Cosmology in the Iconography of Tombstones from the Loango Coast of Central Africa," *The Journal of American Folklore* 112, no. 445 (July 1, 1999): 407–408.

48 Shames, *The Old Plantation,* 12; Maria Franklin, "Early Black Spirituality and the Cultural Strategy of Protective Symbolism; Evidence from Art and Archaeology," in *African Impact on the Material Culture of the Americas: A Conference Presented by Diggs Gallery at Winston-Salem State University* (Winston-Salem, NC: Museum of Early Southern Decorative Arts, 1998), 8.

49 The painting is in the collection of the Mint Museum of Art in Charlotte, North Carolina. Tests on pigment from the painting, curator Jonathan Stuhlman of the Mint Museum wrote to me in a 2009 email, found traces of titanium dioxide, a product produced only after 1919.

50 Franklin, "Early Black Spirituality," 8–10.

51 Franklin, "Early Black Spirituality," 8–10; Leo G. Mazow, "From Sonic to Social: Noise, Quiet, and Nineteenth-Century American Banjo Imagery," in *Picturing the Banjo,* ed. Leo G. Mazow (University Park: Pennsylvania State University Press, 2005), 95–113, 109–111.

52 Franklin, "Early Black Spirituality," 7, 10.

53 Franklin, "Early Black Spirituality," 10.

54 The entire archive of runaway advertisements from this newspaper has been digitized by a group at Sherbrooke University in Canada. For this advertisement, from *Affiches Américaines,* 14 December 1772, see http://www.marronnage.info/fr/lire.php?type=annonce&id=3464.

55 L'annonce, publié dans les *Affiches Américaines* le 15 Decembre 1784, est en ligne ici: http://www.marronnage.info/fr/lire.php?type=annonce&id=7199.

56 Ada Ferrer, *Freedom's Mirror: Cuba and Haiti in the Age of Revolution* (Cambridge: Cambridge University Press, 2014), 165–166.

57 Henri Grégoire, *De la littérature de Nègres, ou Recherches sur leurs facultés intellectuelles, leurs qualités morales et leur littérature* (Paris: Maradan, 1808), 184.

58 Fr. Richard de Tussac, *Cri des Colons contre un ouvrage de M. L'Eveque et Senateur Gregoire* (Paris: Les Marchands de Nouveautes, 1810), 292.

59 M. L. E. Moreau de Saint-Méry, *Description topographique, physique, civile, politique et historique de la partie francaise de l'isle Saint-Domingue,* vol. 1 (Philadelphia: Chez l'Auteur, 1797), 44.

60 Saint-Méry, *Description,* 1:51–52.

61 Claude Dauphin, *Histoire Du Style Musical d'Haïti* (Montréal: Mémoire d'Encrier, 2014), 117.

62 Michel Etienne Descourtilz, *Flore pittoresque et médicale des Antilles,* vol. 5 (Paris: Imprimerie de J. Tastu, 1833), 85–86.

63 Gaspard-Théodore Mollien, *Histoire et mœurs d'Haïti: De Christophe Colomb á la révolte des esclaves,* ed. François Arzalier, vol. 1 (Paris: Le Serpent de Mer, 2001), 84.

64 I spoke to Ti-Coca about the song before a concert he gave in Petionville, Haiti, on May 22, 2015. On Vodou song see Max G. Beauvoir, *Le Grand Receuil Sacré, Ou Répertoire Des Chansons Du Vodou Haïtien* (Port-au-Prince: Edisyon Près Nasyonal d'Ayiti, 2008); Benjamin Hebblethwaite, *Vodou Songs in Haitian Creole and English* (Philadelphia: Temple University Press, 2012).

65 The image "Sick Slaves," published by Thomas McClean, Hay Market, London, in 1822, is in the Musée Acquitaine de Bordeaux, Collection Chatillon, 2003.4.313.

66 An image and description of the instrument is available through the online catalogue of MIMO, Musical Instrument Museums Online, here: http://www .mimo-international.com/MIMO/doc/IFD/SPK_BERLIN_DE_EM_OBJID _169626/banjo (consulted July 30, 2014). I am indebted to Shlomo Pestcoe, who shared his discovery of this instrument in the database soon after it went online in a group email to banjo researchers dated June 4, 2014, as well as sharing information provided to him by Richard Price about the instrument.

67 My discussion of the use of the banjo in trobado music draws on conversations I had with Ti-Coca and Richard Hector before and after a concert they gave on May 22 in Petionville, Haiti. In his 1960 ethnography of Haiti, Harold Courlander noted that the term banza, once used to describe a "stringed in-

strument resembling a banjo," had by the twentieth century come to be "applied to the homemade fiddle which is used to accompany the minuet and other old dances of European origins." He also noted that he had seen a "children's instrument" in the mountains, constructed of "half of a calabash shell, across the opening of which have been stretched a number of chords." See Harold Courlander, *The Drum and the Hoe: Life and Lore of the Haitian People* (Berkeley: University of California Press, 1960), 202.

68 Mimi Barthélémy, *Le mariage d'une puce* (Montréal: Editions Québec / Amérique, 1991), 25–32.

69 Barthélémy, *Le mariage d'une puce,* 25–32.

4. THE SOUND OF FREEDOM

1 George William Featherstonhaugh, *Excursion Through the Slave States: From Washington on the Potomac, to the Frontier of Mexico; with Sketches of Popular Manners and Geological Notices* (New York: Harper and Brothers, 1844), 36–37; I draw here on the illuminating reading of this text in Saidiya V. Hartman, *Scenes of Subjection: Terror, Slavery, and Self-Making in Nineteenth-Century America* (New York: Oxford University Press, 1997), 32–33.

2 For a detailed analysis and portrait of this slave trade, see Walter Johnson, *Soul by Soul: Life Inside the Antebellum Slave Market* (Cambridge, MA: Harvard University Press, 1999); Walter Johnson, *River of Dark Dreams: Slavery and Empire in the Cotton Kingdom* (Cambridge, MA: Harvard University Press, 2013).

3 Featherstonhaugh, *Excursion,* 37; Johnson, *River of Dark Dreams,* 218, notes that, as slaves were brought further from home, they were eventually allowed to walk "unfettered."

4 Alexander Mackay, *The Western World; Or, Travels in the United States in 1846–47,* 2nd ed. (New York: Negro Universities Press, 1968), 2:132–133.

5 George P. Rawick, *The American Slave: A Composite Autobiography* (Westport, CT: Greenwood, 1972), vol. 3, South Carolina Narratives Parts 1 & 2, Part 2, 279–281, and Parts 3 & 4, Part 3, 202–204 and 273.

6 Orlando Kay Armstrong, *Old Massa's People: The Old Slaves Tell Their Story,* 1st ed. (Indianapolis: Bobbs-Merrill, 1931), 261–262; this account is discussed in Mark Knowles, *Tap Roots: The Early History of Tap Dancing* (Jefferson, NC: McFarland & Co., 2002), 41; on Armstrong's work, see Sterling A. Brown, "Negro Character as Seen by White Authors," *The Journal of Negro Education* 2, no. 2 (April 1933): 186; and John W. Blassingame, *Slave Testimony: Two Centuries of Letters, Speeches, Interviews, and Autobiographies* (Baton Rouge: Louisiana State University Press, 1977), lxi.

7 Lynn Abbott and Doug Seroff, *Out of Sight: The Rise of African American Popular Music, 1889–1895,* American Made Music Series (Jackson: University Press of Mississippi, 2002), 242.

8 Hartman, *Scenes of Subjection,* 8, 32.

9 William W. Austin, *"Susanna," "Jeanie," and "The Old Folks at Home": The Songs of Stephen C. Foster From His Time to Ours,* 2nd ed. (Urbana: University of Illinois Press, 1987), xvi–xvii, 6–7, 238–239; Morrison Foster, *My Brother Stephen* (Indianapolis, 1932), 49–50.

10 Austin, *Songs of Stephen C. Foster,* 6–7.

11 Josiah Henson, *Father Henson's Story of His Own Life* (Boston: P. Jewett and Company, 1858), 1–7; Howard L. Sacks and Judith Rose Sacks, *Way up North in Dixie: A Black Family's Claim to the Confederate Anthem* (Washington: Smithsonian Institution Press, 1993), 31.

12 Emmett D. Preston, "The Fugitive Slave Acts in Ohio," *The Journal of Negro History* 28, no. 4 (October 1, 1943): 433, 438.

13 Preston, "The Fugitive Slave Acts in Ohio," 441–456.

14 Solomon Northrop, *Twelve Years a Slave* (New York: Penguin, 2013), 7.

15 Northrop, *Twelve Years a Slave,* 142–143.

16 Northrop, *Twelve Years a Slave,* 143, 189; the first three accounts of Junkanoo from Jamaica are excerpted in Roger D. Abrahams and John F. Szwed, eds., *After Africa: Extracts from British Travel Accounts and Journals of the Seventeenth, Eighteenth, and Nineteenth Centuries Concerning the Slaves, Their Manners, and Customs in the British West Indies* (New Haven: Yale University Press, 1983), 234, 241, and 249; for the full version of Lewis's account see Matthew Lewis, *Journal of a West India Proprietor, Kept During a Residence in the Island of Jamaica,* ed. Judith Terry (London: Oxford University Press, 1999), 36; Dale Cockrell, *Demons of Disorder: Early Blackface Minstrels and Their World* (Cambridge: Cambridge University Press, 1997), 40; for Phillippo's comments, in a book published in 1843, see James Phillippo, *Jamaica: Its Past and Present State* (London: Dawsons of Pall Mall, 1969), 243.

17 Elizabeth Fenn, "'A Perfect Equality Seemed to Reign': Slave Society and Jonkonnu," *North Carolina Historical Review* 65 (April 1988): 128–129; Cockrell, *Demons of Disorder,* 39–40. The most detailed study of the tradition of Junkanoo in Jamaica is Judith Bettleheim, "The Afro-Jamaican Jonkonnu Festival: Playing the Forces and Operating the Cloth" (Yale University, 1979); on the possible Ewe etymology, see Frederic Cassidy, "'Hipsaw' and 'John Canoe,'" *American Speech* 41 (1966): 45–51, pp. 50–51; for a broader study of the place of public performance traditions in the Caribbean, see Richard D. E. Burton, *Afro-Creole: Power, Opposition, and Play in the Caribbean* (Ithaca: Cornell University Press, 1997).

18 Lewis, *Journal of a West India Proprietor,* 36; Peter P. Reed, *Rogue Performances: Staging the Underclasses in Early American Theatre Culture* (New York: Palgrave Macmillan, 2009), 118.

19 Abrahams and Szwed, *After Africa,* 235, 248–249; Cockrell, *Demons of Disorder,* 41; Maria Nugent, *Lady Nugent's Journal of Her Residence in Jamaica from 1801 to 1805,* ed. Philip Wright (Kingston, Jamaica: Institute of Jamaica, 1966), 219.

20 Fenn, "Perfect Equality," 132–136.

21 Harriet A. Jacobs, *Incidents in the Life of a Slave Girl: Written by Herself* (Boston, 1861), 179–180.

22 William B. Smith, "The Persimmon Tree and the Beer Dance," in *The Negro and His Folklore in Nineteenth-Century Periodicals,* ed. Bruce Jackson (Austin: Published for the American Folklore Society by the University of Texas Press, 1969), 3–5.

23 William B. Smith, "Persimmon Tree," 5.

24 William B. Smith, "Persimmon Tree," 7–8.

25 John Finch, *Travels in the United States of America and Canada* (London: Longman, 1833), 238.

26 Bob Carlin, *The Birth of the Banjo: Joel Walker Sweeney and Early Minstrelsy* (Jefferson, NC: McFarland, 2007), 4; John Kennedy, *Swallow Barn, or a Sojourn in the Old Dominion,* vol. 1 (Philadelphia: Carey and Lea, 1832), 101–103.

27 Martin Robison Delany, *Blake; Or, The Huts of America, a Novel,* ed. Floyd J. Miller (Boston: Beacon Press, 1970), 251–252; for a rich reading of the novel, see Robert S. Levine, *Martin Delany, Frederick Douglass, and the Politics of Representative Identity* (Chapel Hill: University of North Carolina Press, 1997), chap. 5.

28 Delany, *Blake,* 251–252.

29 Johnson, *River of Dark Dreams,* 229, 232–234.

30 Robert B. Winans, "Black Instrumental Music Traditions in the Ex-Slave Narratives," *Black Music Research Journal* 10, no. 1 (Spring 1990): 43–53. On the value of the WPA narratives, and the complexities of using them as sources, see Mia Bay, *The White Image in the Black Mind: African-American Ideas about White People, 1830–1925* (New York: Oxford University Press, 2000), 114–116.

31 Rawick, *American Slave,* vol. 3, South Carolina Narratives Parts 3 & 4, Part 3, p. 7. Rawick, *American Slave,* vol. 12, Georgia Narratives Parts 1 & 2, Part 2, p. 52–53. Thomas E. Barden, Charles L. Perdue, and Robert K. Phillips, eds., *Weevils in the Wheat: Interviews with Virginia Ex-Slaves* (Charlottesville: University Press of Virginia, 1992), 326.

32 Rawick, *American Slave,* vol. 17, Florida Narratives, p. 244. Rawick, *American Slave,* vol. 7, Georgia Narratives Parts 1 & 2, Part 1, p. 197. George P.

Rawick, ed., *American Slave: A Composite Autobiography, Supplement Series 2* (Westport, CT: Greenwood Press, 1979), vol. 1, 88–89, 115.

33 Barden, Perdue, and Phillips, *Weevils in the Wheat*, 141.

34 Barden, Perdue, and Phillips, *Weevils in the Wheat*, 82.

35 Rawick, *American Slave*, vol. 7, Oklahoma and Mississippi Narratives, p. 272; Barden, Perdue, and Phillips, *Weevils in the Wheat*, 297–299.

36 For the James Davis narrative, see Rawick, *American Slave*, Vol. 8, Arkansas Narratives Parts 1 & 2, Part 2, p. 109–111. Other descriptions of the use of grape vines against patrols are in Ophelia Settle Egypt, *Unwritten History of Slavery, Autobiographical Account of Negro Ex-Slaves*, Social Science Source Documents, No. 1 (Nashville, TN: Social Science Institute, Fisk University, 1945), 78; Barden, Perdue, and Phillips, *Weevils in the Wheat*, 290; Hartman, *Scenes of Subjection*, 68.

37 Barden, Perdue, and Phillips, *Weevils in the Wheat*, 326; Rawick, *American Slave*, vol. 10, Arkansas Narratives Parts 5 & 6, Part 6, p. 366–367; Part 5, pp. 25–26, 268, Part 6, pp. 366–367.

38 Barden, Perdue, and Phillips, *Weevils in the Wheat*, 316.

39 Rawick, *American Slave*, vol. 8, Arkansas Narratives Parts 1 & 2, Part 1, p. 295; Part 2, p. 114.

40 Rawick, *The American Slave*, vol. 10, Arkansas Narratives Parts 5 & 6, Part 6 p. 28. Rawick, *The American Slave*, vol. 8, Arkansas Narratives Parts 1 & 2, Part 1 p. 64–65.

41 Rawick, *The American Slave*, vol. 8, Arkansas Narratives Parts 1 & 2, Part 2, p. 81. Georgia Writers' Project, *Drums and Shadows: Survival Studies Among the Georgia Coastal Negroes* (Athens: University of Georgia Press, 1940), 148, 186–187. Eighty-nine-year-old Soloman Lambert of Holly Grove, Arkansas also remembered how slaves had made their own fiddles and banjos; see Rawick, *The American Slave*, vol. 9, Arkansas Narratives Parts 3 & 4, Part 4 p. 230.

42 Rawick, *The American Slave*, vol. 12, Georgia Narratives Parts 1 & 2, Part 1 p. 81, 181, 190.

43 Rawick, *The American Slave*, vol. 12, Georgia Narratives Parts 1 & 2, Part 1 pp. 151, 161–167, 170; Part 2, pp. 6, 216, 248.

44 Rawick, *The American Slave*, vol. 10, Parts 5 & 6, Part 6, p. 143–144.

45 John Davis, "Johnson's Negro Life at the South and Urban Slavery in Washington, D.C.," *The Art Bulletin* 80, no. 1 (March 1998): 67–92.

46 Davis, "Johnson's Negro Life at the South," 75–78.

47 Davis, "Johnson's Negro Life at the South," 79.

48 Davis, "Johnson's Negro Life at the South," 79.

49 David Crockett, *Sketches and Eccentricities of Col. David Crockett of West Tennessee,* ed. David Manning White (New York: J. & J. Harper, 1833), 38–41.

50 Carlin, *Birth of the Banjo,* 3–5; "Old Titus—The Original Banjo Man," *Richmond Dispatch,* April 21, 1852.

51 Douglas R. Egerton, *Gabriel's Rebellion: The Virginia Slave Conspiracies of 1800 and 1802* (Chapel Hill: University of North Carolina Press, 1993); James Sidbury, *Ploughshares into Swords: Race, Rebellion, and Identity in Gabriel's Virginia, 1730–1810* (New York: Cambridge University Press, 1997).

52 Robert C. Toll, *Blacking Up: Minstrel Show in Nineteenth-Century America* (London, Oxford, and New York: Oxford University Press, 1974), 83–84; Firth, Pond and Co., "Uncle Gabriel" (New York, 1848), Microfilm M 3106 M1.A12V vol 29 Case Class, Library of Congress, Music Division, Music Copyright Deposits, http://www.loc.gov/item/sm1848.441700/.

53 C. Holt Jr., "Uncle Gabriel" (New York, 1848), Microfilm M 3106 M1. A12V vol 29 Case Class, Library of Congress, Music Division, Music Copyright Deposits, http://www.loc.gov/item/sm1848.441750/.

54 The letter is reprinted in Rosa Faulkner Yancey, *Lynchburg and Its Neighbors* (Richmond, VA: J. W. Fergusson & Sons, 1935), 218–221; Carlin, *Birth of the Banjo,* 127.

55 Carlin, *Birth of the Banjo,* 5.

56 Carlin, *Birth of the Banjo,* 5.

57 Carlin, *Birth of the Banjo,* 20–21.

58 Yancey, *Lynchburg and Its Neighbors,* 218–220.

59 Carlin, *Birth of the Banjo,* 1–2.

60 Cecelia Conway, *African Banjo Echoes in Appalachia: A Study of Folk Traditions* (Knoxville: University of Tennessee Press, 1995) chap.2, esp. 85–87; Robert Winans, "The Folk, the Stage, and the Five-String Banjo in the Nineteenth Century," *Journal of American Folklore* 89, no. 354 (1976): 407–437 p. 417–418; Toll, *Blacking Up,* 46; Hans Nathan, *Dan Emmett and the Rise of Early Negro Minstrelsy,* 1st ed. (Norman: University of Oklahoma Press, 1962), chap. 13.

61 On later versions of the song "Run, Nigger, Run," see John A. Lomax and Alan Lomax, *American Ballads and Folk Songs* (New York: Macmillan, 1934), 228–231. Two recorded versions of the song, one by Rufus Crisp of Kentucky recorded in 1946 (AFS 8547), and another by Thaddeus C. Willingham of Gulfport, Mississippi, recorded in 1939 (AFS 3115), are in the American Folklife

Collection of the Library of Congress. Eric Lott, *Love and Theft: Blackface Minstrelsy and the American Working Class* (New York: Oxford University Press, 1995); Karen Linn, *That Half-Barbaric Twang: The Banjo in American Popular Culture* (Urbana: University of Illinois Press, 1991), 42, 66. For a recent example of the deployment of the term "minstrel" in debates about popular culture, see the responses to Miley Cyrus's VMA performance, which some critics described as a contemporary "minstrel show": Jody Rosen, "Rosen: The 2013 VMAs Were Dominated by Miley's Minstrel Show," *Vulture,* August 26, 2013, http://www .vulture.com/2013/08/jody-rosen-miley-cyrus-vmas-minstrel.html.

5. THE BANJO MEETS BLACKFACE

1 Kim F. Hall, *Things of Darkness: Economies of Race and Gender in Early Modern England* (Ithaca, NY: Cornell University Press, 1995), 131; Virginia Mason Vaughan, *Performing Blackness on English Stages, 1500–1800* (Cambridge: Cambridge University Press, 2005), 65–66.

2 Vaughan, *Performing Blackness,* 67–69.

3 Hall, *Things of Darkness,* 6–7.

4 Vaughan, *Performing Blackness,* 35, 38, 43, 48, 57.

5 Vaughan, *Performing Blackness,* 75, 81–82.

6 Vaughan, *Performing Blackness,* chap. 9.

7 Peter P. Reed, *Rogue Performances: Staging the Underclasses in Early American Theater Culture* (New York: Palgrave Macmillan, 2009), 110; Dale Cockrell, *Demons of Disorder: Early Blackface Minstrels and Their World* (Cambridge: Cambridge University Press, 1997), 32–34; Edward Palmer Thompson, *Whigs and Hunters: The Origin of the Black Act* (New York: Pantheon Books, 1975).

8 Hans Nathan, "Negro Impersonation in Eighteenth Century England," *Notes* 2, no. 4 (September 1, 1945): 252–253; W. T. Lhamon Jr., ed., *Jump Jim Crow: Lost Plays, Lyrics, and Street Prose of the First Atlantic Popular Culture* (Cambridge, MA: Harvard University Press, 2003), 34–35.

9 Nathan, "Impersonation," 251; Hans Nathan, *Dan Emmett and the Rise of Early Negro Minstrelsy,* 1st ed. (Norman: University of Oklahoma Press, 1962), 25–28.

10 Cockrell, *Demons of Disorder,* 15–19; Reed, *Rogue Performances,* 109–111.

11 Bernard Camier and Laurent Dubois, "Voltaire et Zaïre, Ou Le Théâtre Des Lumières Dans L'aire Atlantique Française," *Revue D'histoire Moderne et Contemporaine* 54, no. 4 (2007): 39–69; Jean Fouchard, *Le théâtre à Saint-Domingue* (Port-au-Prince: H. Deschamps, 1988), 281, 297–298. For an annotated transcription of the play in the original Creole, see Bernard Camier and Marie-Christine

Hazael-Massieux, "Jeannot et Thérèse un opéra-comique en créole au milieu du XVIIIIème siecle," *Revue de la société haïtienne d'Histoire et de Géographie,* 215 (2003): 135–166.

12 On Lise and her more famous sister Minette see Fouchard, *Théâtre,* 310, 322–323, 341. The novelist Marie Vieux Chauvet drew on Fouchard's work in producing a historical novel about these two sisters: Marie Vieux Chauvet, *La Danse Sur Le Volcan* (Paris: Plon, 1957). For the descriptions of blackface performance, see *Affiches Américaines,* Port-au-Prince, October 30, 1781; Le Cap, January 28, 1784; Le Cap, May 4, 1785; Le Cap, February 9, 1788.

13 Camier and Dubois, "Voltaire et Zaïre"; Fouchard, *Théâtre,* 67, 72, 180–181, 192; Jean Fouchard, *Plaisirs de Saint-Domingue* (Port-au-Prince: Impr. de l'État, 1955), 133; M. L. E. Moreau de Saint-Méry, *Description Topographique, Physique, Civile, Politique et Historique de La Partie Française de L'isle Saint Domingue,* Nouv. éd (Paris: Société de l'histoire des colonies françaises et Librairie Larose, 2004), 1:358–362, 2:986–987, 1100. *Affiches Américaines,* Le Cap, September 1, 1784; *Moniteur de la Louisiane,* December 20, 1809; on audiences in North America, see Cockrell, *Demons of Disorder,* 17.

14 Ned Sublette, *The World That Made New Orleans: From Spanish Silver to Congo Square* (Chicago: Lawrence Hill Books, 2008). On the Louisiana performance of the play, see *Moniteur de la Louisiane,* March 18, 1807 and March 21, 1807.

15 Reed, *Rogue Performances,* 101–109; for a contemporary novel about Jack, see William Earle, *Obi, Or, The History of Three-Fingered Jack,* ed. Srinivas Aravamudan (Peterborough, Ontario: Broadview Press, 2005).

16 Reed, *Rogue Performances,* 121–122; James O'Rourke, "The Revision of Obi; Or, Three-Finger'd Jack and the Jacobin Repudiation of Sentimentality," *Nineteenth-Century Contexts* 28, no. 4 (December 1, 2006): 285–303, p. 288. On Brown's theater, see Marvin Edward McAllister, *White People Do Not Know How to Behave at Entertainments Designed for Ladies & Gentlemen of Colour: William Brown's African & American Theater* (Chapel Hill: University of North Carolina Press, 2003).

17 Reed, *Rogue Performances,* 115, 122.

18 W. T. Lhamon Jr., *Raising Cain: Blackface Performance from Jim Crow to Hip Hop* (Cambridge, MA: Harvard University Press, 1998), 22–24; Joseph Roach, *Cities of the Dead* (New York: Columbia University Press, 1996).

19 Christopher J. Smith, *The Creolization of American Culture: William Sidney Mount and the Roots of Blackface Minstrelsy* (Urbana: University of Illinois Press, 2013), 6, 18, 25–28, 33.

20 Reed, *Rogue Performances,* 127, 130–131, 133.

21 Reed, *Rogue Performances,* 129–130.

22 Reed, *Rogue Performances,* 145; Henry A. Kmen, "Old Corn Meal: A Forgotten Urban Negro Folksinger," *The Journal of American Folklore* 75, no. 295 (March 1962): 29–31; T. Allston Brown and Charles Day, "Black Musicians and Early Ethiopian Minstrelsy," *The Black Perspective in Music* 3, no. 1 (April 1, 1975): 78.

23 Kmen, "Old Corn Meal," 29–32; Reed, *Rogue Performances,* 145.

24 Brown and Day, "Black Musicians," 78.

25 Phil Rice, *Phil Rice's Method for the Banjo: With or Without a Master* (Boston: Oliver Ditson & Co., 1858), 32–33; Philip F. Gura and James F. Bollman, *America's Instrument: The Banjo in the Nineteenth Century* (Chapel Hill: University of North Carolina Press, 1999), 268 n. 70; Frank Converse, *A History of the Banjo: Frank Converse's Banjo Reminiscences,* ed. Paul Heller (Lexington, Kentucky, 2011), 17–18. Tony Thomas has done extensive research on the original Picayune Butler as well as the later musician who took his name; see, for instance, his discussion at the Minstrel Banjo website, "Hard Truths About Picayune Butler," October 26, 2013, at http://minstrelbanjo.ning.com/forum/topics/the-hard-truths-about-picayune-butler, and at the Banjology website at https://sites.duke.edu/banjology/the-banjo-in-new-orleans/picayune-butler/.

26 Rice, *Method,* 33.

27 Théodore Pavie, *Souvenirs Atlantiques; Voyage aux Etats-Unis et au Canada,* 2 vols. (Paris, 1833), 2:319–320.

28 Joseph Holt Ingraham, *The South-West by a Yankee,* vol. 1 (New York: Harper, 1835), 162; James R. Creecy, *Scenes in the South, and Other Miscellaneous Pieces* (Washington: T. McGill, 1860), 19–23.

29 Sam Kinser, *Carnival, American Style: Mardi Gras at New Orleans and Mobile* (Chicago: University of Chicago Press, 1990), 21; Roach, *Cities of the Dead,* chaps. 5 and 6.

30 Alcée Fortier, "Bits of Louisiana Folk-Lore," *Transactions and Proceedings of the Modern Language Association of America* 3 (January 1, 1887): 161–162 offers the original song as published by Cable, translated into more accurate Creole. Maud Cuney-Hare, *Six Creole Folk-Songs: With Original Creole and Translated English Text* (New York: Carl Fischer, 1921), 7–10.

31 Brown and Day, "Black Musicians," 78; the article was originally published in Charles H. Day, *Fun in Black, Or, Sketches of Minstrel Life* (New York: R. M. De Witt, 1874); Kmen, "Old Corn Meal," 32.

32 Lhamon Jr., *Jump Jim Crow,* 36–40.

33 Lhamon Jr., *Raising Cain,* 58; Lhamon Jr., *Jump Jim Crow,* vii, 1, 71.

34 Lhamon Jr., *Jump Jim Crow,* 3–4.

35 Lhamon Jr., *Jump Jim Crow*, vii–x, 4–5, 8, 11, 37, 65.

36 Lhamon Jr., *Jump Jim Crow*, 27, 101, 263.

37 Lhamon Jr., *Jump Jim Crow*, 75–82, 88–89.

38 Carlin, *Birth of the Banjo*, 22–24; Cockrell, *Demons of Disorder*, 80, 148.

39 Cockrell, *Demons of Disorder*, 80, 148.

40 Cockrell, *Demons of Disorder*, 148.

41 Rosa Faulkner Yancey, *Lynchburg and Its Neighbors* (Richmond, VA: J. W. Fergusson & sons, 1935), 220–221; Gura and Bollman, *America's Instrument*, 48–49, 161.

42 Cockrell, *Demons of Disorder*, 148; Nathan, *Dan Emmett*, 109–110; Howard L. Sacks and Judith Rose Sacks, *Way up North in Dixie: A Black Family's Claim to the Confederate Anthem* (Washington: Smithsonian Institution Press, 1993), 84; Carlin, *Birth of the Banjo*, 58.

43 Nathan, *Dan Emmett*, 110–113; Lowell Schreyer, *The Banjo Entertainers: Roots to Ragtime, a Banjo History* (Mankato, MN: Minnesota Heritage Publishing, 2007), 21–25.

44 Nathan, *Dan Emmett*, 113–114.

45 Nathan, *Dan Emmett*, 71, 114–115; Robert C. Toll, *Blacking Up: Minstrel Show in Nineteenth-Century America* (London, Oxford, and New York: Oxford University Press, 1974), 45–46; Carlin, *Birth of the Banjo*, 56, 58.

46 Nathan, *Dan Emmett*, 116–117; Cockrell, *Demons of Disorder*, 151.

47 Nathan, *Dan Emmett*, 118–120; Thomas Riis, "Crossing Boundaries: Black Musicians Who Defied Musical Genres," in *Beyond Blackface: African Americans and the Creation of American Popular Culture, 1890–1930* (Chapel Hill: University of North Carolina Press, 2011), 153.

48 Cockrell, *Demons of Disorder*, 151–152.

49 Robert B. Winans, "Early Minstrel Show Music, 1843–1852," in *Inside the Minstrel Mask: Readings in Nineteenth-Century Blackface Minstrelsy*, ed. Annemarie Bean, James Vernon Hatch, and Brooks McNamara (Hanover, NH: Wesleyan University Press, 1996), 142.

50 Nathan, *Dan Emmett*, 116, 123–134; Winans, "Early Minstrel Show Music," 142.

51 Toll, *Blacking Up*, 46–47; Nathan, *Dan Emmett*, 143–145; Russell B. Nye, *The Unembarrassed Muse: The Popular Arts in America* (New York: Dial Press, 1970), 163–164.

52 Winans, "Early Minstrel Show Music," 141–142.

53 Minstrelsy remains an inescapable reference point in contemporary debates about race and appropriation, music and performance, and braided construction of whiteness and blackness. The scholarship on minstrelsy has taken various twists and turns, some of it celebratory and some condemning, all of it fascinated but also often befuddled by the layers of contradictory meaning packed within the form. The pioneering work of Nathan, *Dan Emmett;* and Toll, *Blacking Up* in the 1960s and 1970s was followed by a burst of rich scholarship in the 1990s; the generative contribution of Eric Lott, *Love and Theft: Blackface Minstrelsy and the American Working Class* (New York: Oxford University Press, 1995) has remained a touchstone; each of the following works make their own critical and unique contribution to the discussion: Cockrell, *Demons of Disorder;* Lhamon Jr., *Raising Cain;* William J. Mahar, *Behind the Burnt Cork Mask: Early Blackface Minstrelsy and Antebellum American Popular Culture* (Urbana: University of Illinois Press, 1999); an excellent collection of the major contributions from a range of perspectives is Annemarie Bean, James Vernon Hatch, and Brooks McNamara, eds., *Inside the Minstrel Mask: Readings in Nineteenth Century Blackface Minstrelsy* (Hanover, NH: Wesleyan University Press, 1996).

54 Paul Ely Smith, "Gottschalk's 'The Banjo,' Op. 15, and the Banjo in the Nineteenth Century," *Current Musicology* 50 (1992): 47–61 quote p. 57; Nicolas Bardinet, *Une histoire du banjo* (Paris: Outre Mesure, 2003), 61; on Gottschalk's life and musical career see S. Frederick Starr, *BamBoula: The Life and Time of Louis Moreau Gottschalk* (New York and Oxford: Oxford University Press, 1995); Louis Moreau Gottschalk, *Notes of a Pianist: The Chronicles of a New Orleans Music Legend,* ed. Jeanne Behrend, new ed. (Princeton: Princeton University Press, 2006), xxxv, 9, 13, 23.

55 Mark Twain, "Enthusiastic Eloquence," *San Francisco Dramatic Chronicle,* June 23, 1865.

56 George F. Rehin, "The Darker Image: American Negro Minstrelsy through the Historian's Lens," *Journal of American Studies* 9, no. 3 (December 1, 1975): 369; Nye, *The Unembarrassed Muse,* 167; Robert Criswell, *"Uncle Tom's Cabin" Contrasted with Buckingham Hall, the Planter's Home, Or, A Fair View of Both Sides of the Slavery Question* (New York: D. Fanshaw, 1852), 113–114.

57 Daniel Robinson Hundley, *Social Relations in Our Southern States* (New York: Henry B. Price, 1860), 344–349.

58 Rawick, *American Slave,* vol. 3, South Carolina Narratives Parts 3 and 4, Part 3, pp. 48–50.

59 Francis Trevelyan Miller, *The Photographic History of the Civil War,* vol. 6: The Navies (New York: The Review of Reviews Co., 1911), 278, 281.

60 Peter H. Wood and Karen C. C. Dalton, *Winslow Homer's Images of Blacks: The Civil War and Reconstruction Years* (Austin: Menil Collection, 1988), 48–49.

61 Wood and Dalton, *Winslow Homer's Images of Blacks,* 49–50; John Davis, "A Change of Key: The Banjo During Civil War and Reconstruction," in *Picturing the Banjo,* ed. Leo G. Mazow (University Park: Pennsylvania State University Press, 2005), 55–56.

62 Davis, "Change of Key," 55–56; on the Union soldier see Nathan, *Dan Emmett,* 97.

63 Davis, "Change of Key," 58.

6. RINGS LIKE SILVER, SHINES LIKE GOLD

1 Lafcadio Hearn, *Lafcadio Hearn's America: Ethnographic Sketches and Editorials,* ed. Simon J. Bronner (Lexington: University Press of Kentucky, 2002), 37, 40, 44.

2 Hearn, *Lafcadio Hearn's America,* 44–45.

3 Hearn, *Lafcadio Hearn's America,* 38, 82.

4 Hearn, *Lafcadio Hearn's America,* 38, 47.

5 Hearn, *Lafcadio Hearn's America,* 48–49.

6 Bob Carlin, *The Birth of the Banjo: Joel Walker Sweeney and Early Minstrelsy* (Jefferson, NC: McFarland, 2007), 116, 130; Isaac D. Williams and William Ferguson Goldie, *Sunshine and Shadow of Slave Life: Reminiscences* (New York: AMS Press, 1975), 62.

7 Thomas Adler, "The Physical Development of the Banjo," *New York Folklore Quarterly* 28, no. 3 (September 1972): 192–193.

8 Philip F. Gura and James F. Bollman, *America's Instrument: The Banjo in the Nineteenth Century* (Chapel Hill: University of North Carolina Press, 1999), 55–64; Adler, "Physical Development," 193; Carlin, *Birth of the Banjo,* 135–136; Nicolas Bardinet, *Une histoire du banjo* (Paris: Outre Mesure, 2003), 68–69.

9 Bardinet, *Une histoire du banjo,* 65–69.

10 Gura and Bollman, *America's Instrument,* 76; Karen Linn, *That Half-Barbaric Twang: The Banjo in American Popular Culture* (Urbana: University of Illinois Press, 1991), 8–9.

11 Linn, *Half-Barbaric Twang,* 3.

12 Gura and Bollman, *America's Instrument,* 81–82; Phil Rice, *Phil Rice's Method for the Banjo: With or Without a Master* (Boston: Oliver Ditson & Co., 1858); James Buckley, *Buckley's New Banjo Book* (Boston: Oliver Ditson & Co., 1860). The issue of what is gained and lost in various forms of musical notation has stirred much debate in musicology and ethnomusicology; my own thoughts on this

were shaped through a course taken with Paul Berliner at Duke University; for reflections on this problem, see Paul F. Berliner, *The Soul of Mbira: Music and Traditions of the Shona People of Zimbabwe* (Chicago: University of Chicago Press, 1978).

13 The 1866 dispatch was published in the *Boston Daily Evening Voice,* signed under the name "Ziska," and is reprinted in Philip Foner and Pete Seeger, eds., "Dobson Banjo: A BNL Reprint," *Banjo Newsletter* 4, no. 7 (May 1977): 20–21; Gura and Bollman, *America's Instrument,* 76, 78, 134–135.

14 Gura and Bollman, *America's Instrument,* 85–87; Frank B. Converse, *Frank B. Converse's Banjo Instructor, without a Master: Containing a Choice Collection of Banjo Solos, Jigs, Songs, Reels, Walk Arounds, Etc., Progressively Arranged and Plainly Explained, Enabling the Learner to Become a Proficient Banjoist without the Aid of a Teacher* (New York: Dick and Fitzgerald, 1865); Frank B. Converse, *Frank B. Converse's New and Complete Method for the Banjo with or without a Master* (New York: S. T. Gordon, 1865).

15 Frank Converse, *A History of the Banjo: Frank Converse's Banjo Reminiscences,* ed. Paul Heller (Lexington, Kentucky, 2011), 16–17.

16 Converse, *Reminiscences,* 16–17.

17 Converse, *Reminiscences,* 6–8, 11.

18 Converse, *Reminiscences,* 17–20.

19 Converse, *Reminiscences,* 15–16.

20 Converse, *Reminiscences,* 14–15.

21 Gura and Bollman, *America's Instrument,* 88.

22 Foner and Seeger, "Dobson Banjo"; Gura and Bollman, *America's Instrument,* 109–110; p. 275 n. 36.

23 Gura and Bollman, *America's Instrument,* 116, 119; Rice, *Method.*

24 Gura and Bollman, *America's Instrument,* 12; George C. Dobson, *Complete Instructor for the Banjo* (Boston: White, Smith & Co., 1880), 4.

25 Dobson, *Complete Instructor for the Banjo,* 4; Gura and Bollman, *America's Instrument,* 174; Adler, "Physical Development," 199.

26 Gura and Bollman, *America's Instrument,* 89–90, 92, 110–113, Plate 2–9; Adler, "Physical Development"; Bardinet, *Une histoire du banjo,* 69.

27 Adler, "Physical Development," 192–193.

28 Adler, "Physical Development," 192–194; Bardinet, *Une histoire du banjo,* 68–69.

29 Linn, *Half-Barbaric Twang,* 9.

30 Gura and Bollman, *America's Instrument,* 151, 160–161; Samuel Swaim Stewart, *The Banjo Philosophically: Its Construction, Its Capabilities, Its Evolution, Its Place as a Musical Instrument, Its Possibilities and Its Future* (Philadelphia: S.S. Stewart, 1886); Samuel Swaim Stewart, *The Banjo! A Dissertation* (Philadelphia: S.S. Stewart, 1888); Samuel Swaim Stewart, *The Complete American Banjo School* (Philadelphia: S.S. Stewart, 1887); Samuel Swaim Stewart, *An Exposition of the Harmonic Tones Used in Banjo Playing and Their Philosophy* (Philadelphia: S.S. Stewart, 1887). The entire run of Stewart's *Guitar and Banjo Journal* has been digitized and made available by the University of Rochester Library: http://hdl .handle.net/1802/2586.

31 Joel Chandler Harris, "Plantation Music," in *The Negro and His Folklore in Nineteenth-Century Periodicals,* ed. Bruce Jackson (Austin: Published for the American Folklore Society by the University of Texas Press, 1969), 178–179; Bruce Jackson, ed., "Banjo and Bones," in *The Negro and His Folklore in Nineteenth-Century Periodicals* (Austin: Published for the American Folklore Society by the University of Texas Press, 1969), 183.

32 Linn, *Half-Barbaric Twang,* 33–34; Lowell H. Schreyer, *The Banjo Entertainers: Roots to Ragtime, a Banjo History* (Mankato, MN: Minnesota Heritage Pub, 2007), 133–134; Bardinet, *Une histoire du banjo,* 96; Sarah Burns, "Whiteface: Art, Women, and the Banjo in Late-Nineteenth-Century America," in *Picturing the Banjo,* ed. Leo G. Mazow (University Park: Pennsylvania State University Press, 2005), 71–90.

33 Linn, *Half-Barbaric Twang,* 34–35; Rudyard Kipling, *A Choice of Kipling's Verse,* ed. T. S. Eliot (Garden City: Doubleday, 1962), 55–59; the poem was originally published as Rudyard Kipling, "The Song of the Banjo," *The New Review,* June 1895.

34 Tony Thomas, "Why African Americans Put the Banjo Down," in *Hidden in the Mix: The African American Presence in Country Music,* ed. Diane Pecknold (Durham: Duke University Press, 2013), 143–170, p. 148.

35 Scott Reynolds Nelson, *Steel Drivin' Man: John Henry, the Untold Story of an American Legend* (New York: Oxford University Press, 2006), 103–105; Fred Fussell and Steve Kruger, *Blue Ridge Music Trails of North Carolina: A Guide to Music Sites, Artists, and Traditions of the Mountains and Foothills* (Chapel Hill: University of North Carolina Press, 2013), 144–145.

36 Greil Marcus, *The Old, Weird America: The World of Bob Dylan's Basement Tapes* (New York: Picador, 2011), 112–113; Nelson, *Steel Drivin' Man,* 95–96.

37 Roscoe Holcomb, "Swanno Mountain," was recorded in New York City 1964 and is available on *Roscoe Holcomb: An Untamed Sense of Control* (Smithsonian Folkways Records, 2003). He explained he had learned it at a lumber camp in Hazard, North Carolina. In the version sung by Lunsford it is not a banjo but the

hammer that rings out: "This old hammer rings like silver, / Shines like gold, shines like gold / Take this hammer, throw it in the river, / It rings right on, baby shines right on." Fussell and Kruger, *Blue Ridge Music Trails of North Carolina,* 145.

38 Gene Bluestein, "America's Folk Instrument: Notes on the Five-String Banjo," *Western Folklore* 23, no. 4 (October 1964): 243, 246; John A. (John Avery) Lomax et al., *Folk Song U.S.A.: The 111 Best American Ballads* (New York: New American Library, 1966), 78; Jay Bailey, "Historical Origin and Stylistic Developments of the Five-String Banjo," *The Journal of American Folklore* 85, no. 335 (1972): 62–63; William Tallmadge, "The Folk Banjo and Clawhammer Performance Practice in the Upper South: A Study of Origins," in *The Appalachian Experience: Proceedings of the Sixth Annual Appalachian Studies Conference* (Boone, NC: Appalachian Consortium Press, 1983), 174–175; Robert Winans, "The Folk, the Stage, and the Five-String Banjo in the Nineteenth Century," *Journal of American Folklore* 89, no. 354 (1976): 407–437.

39 Cherrill P. Heaton, "The 5-String Banjo in North Carolina," *Southern Folklore Quarterly* 35, no. 1 (March 1971): 65–68.

40 Bailey, "Historical Origin," 62–63; Heaton, "The 5-String Banjo in North Carolina," 68–69.

41 Marcus, *The Old, Weird America,* 112–114, 121.

42 David Garner's transcriptions and analysis of different versions of "The Coo Coo Bird" are available at sites.duke.edu/banjology.

43 Robert Cantwell, *Bluegrass Breakdown: The Making of the Old Southern Sound* (Urbana: University of Illinois Press, 1984), 78–79; Archie Green, *Torching the Fink Books and Other Essays on Vernacular Culture* (Chapel Hill: University of North Carolina Press, 2001), 8–46, esp. 26; Karl Hagstrom Miller, *Segregating Sound: Inventing Folk and Pop Music in the Age of Jim Crow* (Durham: Duke University Press, 2010), 102–103; Elijah Wald, *Escaping the Delta: Robert Johnson and the Invention of the Blues* (New York: Amistad, 2004), 49.

44 Joe Newberry's version is on *Two Hands* (5-String Productions, 2005).

45 Thomas Washington Talley, *Thomas W. Talley's Negro Folk Rhymes,* ed. Charles K. Wolfe (Knoxville: University of Tennessee Press, 1991), 193–194.

7. BLACK BANJO

1 Lynn Abbott and Doug Seroff, *Out of Sight: The Rise of African American Popular Music, 1889–1895,* American Made Music Series (Jackson: University Press of Mississippi, 2002), 52.

2 George P. Rawick, *The American Slave: A Composite Autobiography* (Westport, CT: Greenwood Publishing Group, Inc., 1972), Volume 13, Georgia Narratives Parts 3 & 4, Part 1, p. 124, 196, 224. Abbott and Seroff, *Out of Sight,* 56. On the earlier Pinkster celebration, see Chapter 2.

3 David M. Lubin, *Picturing a Nation: Art and Social Change in Nineteenth-Century America* (New Haven: Yale University Press, 1994), 140; On the context surrounding Tanner's composition of this painting, see Naurice Frank Woods, "Henry Ossawa Tanner's Negotiation of Race and Art: Challenging 'The Unknown Tanner,'" *Journal of Black Studies* 42, no. 6 (September 1, 2011): 894–896.

4 Jas. S. Evans, "A New Religion in Mississippi," *The Daily Picayune,* September 18, 1887 no. 237, p. 12; Randy J. Sparks, *On Jordan's Stormy Banks: Evangelicalism in Mississippi, 1773–1876* (Athens: University of Georgia Press, 1994), 197.

5 For the postcard, see Philip F. Gura and James F. Bollman, *America's Instrument: The Banjo in the Nineteenth Century* (Chapel Hill: University of North Carolina Press, 1999), 154; Karl Hagstrom Miller, *Segregating Sound: Inventing Folk and Pop Music in the Age of Jim Crow* (Durham: Duke University Press, 2010), 81; John F. Szwed, *Alan Lomax: The Man Who Recorded the World* (New York: Viking Penguin, 2010), 318. The recordings by Lomax of Sid Hemphill playing "John Henry" and "Devil's Dream" are available on *Black Appalachia: String Bands, Songsters and Hoedowns* (Rounder Records, 1999); "Strayhorn Mob" was released on *Rock Me, Shake Me: Field Recordings Vol 15, Mississippi 1941–1942* (Document Records, 2002). On fife-and-drum music, see the profile of Otha Turner in Steve Winick, "Tossing Out the Fish: In Memoriam—Othar Turner," *Dirty Linen,* August 2003.

6 Elijah Wald, *Escaping the Delta: Robert Johnson and the Invention of the Blues* (New York: Amistad, 2004), 52; Cecelia Conway, *African Banjo Echoes in Appalachia: A Study of Folk Traditions* (Knoxville: University of Tennessee Press, 1995).

7 Thomas Goldsmith, ed., *Bluegrass Reader* (Urbana: University of Illinois Press, 2004), 36–42; Conway, *African Banjo Echoes.*

8 Nicolas Bardinet, *Une histoire du banjo* (Paris: Outre Mesure, 2003), 197–198; on the banjo in Medicine shows, see Brooks McNamara, *Step Right Up* (Jackson: University Press of Mississippi, 1995), esp. chap. 9.

9 Bardinet, *Une histoire du banjo,* 198–199; I have sought here to synthesize the careful analysis of the move from banjo to guitar offered in Tony Thomas, "Why African Americans Put the Banjo Down," in *Hidden in the Mix: The African American Presence in Country Music,* ed. Diane Pecknold (Durham: Duke University Press, 2013), 155–161.

10 Bardinet, *Une histoire du banjo,* 199.

11 James Weldon Johnson, *Black Manhattan* (New York: Da Capo Press, 1991), 87–89; on the broader debates about the place of music in African-American history and culture during the Harlem Renaissance, see Paul Allen Anderson, *Deep River: Music and Memory in Harlem Renaissance Thought* (Durham: Duke University Press, 2001); Abbott and Seroff, *Out of Sight,* 60.

12 Yuval Taylor and Jake Austen, *Darkest America: Black Minstrelsy from Slavery to Hip-Hop* (New York: W. W. Norton, 2012), 3, 21.

13 Abbott and Seroff, *Out of Sight;* Lynn Abbott and Doug Seroff, *Ragged but Right: Black Traveling Shows, "Coon Songs," and the Dark Pathway to Blues and Jazz* (Jackson: University Press of Mississippi, 2007); Ike Simond, *Old Slack's Reminiscence and Pocket History of the Colored Profession from 1865 to 1891* (Bowling Green: Popular Press, 1974); Thomas, "Why African Americans Put the Banjo Down," 143–144.

14 See Robert Toll, "Introduction," and Francis Lee Utley and Robert Toll, "Major Dates in Black Minstrelsy," in Simond, *Old Slack's Reminiscence,* xx, 43, 45; on Hicks see Abbott and Seroff, *Out of Sight,* 60–61; Johnson, *Black Manhattan,* 89.

15 Toll, "Introduction" to Simond, *Old Slack's Reminiscence,* xxv, xxvii. The Fisk Jubilee Singers have been the subject of excellent work beginning with J. B. T. Marsh, *The Story of the Jubilee Singers; with Their Songs* (Boston: Houghton Mifflin, 1881); on their tour in South Africa, see Veit Erlmann, *African Stars: Studies in Black South African Performance* (Chicago: University of Chicago Press, 1991), chap 2.

16 Abbott and Seroff, *Out of Sight,* 61–62.

17 Simond, *Old Slack's Reminiscence,* 24, 11; Johnson, *Black Manhattan,* 92–93; Gura and Bollman, *America's Instrument,* 153; Karen Linn, *That Half-Barbaric Twang: The Banjo in American Popular Culture* (Urbana: University of Illinois Press, 1991), 45–46; Abbott and Seroff, *Out of Sight,* 95–97.

18 Frances Lee Utley and Robert Toll, "Preface," and Robert Toll, "Introduction," in Simond, *Old Slack's Reminiscence,* viii–x, xvii, xxiii see also Simond's own reflections, esp. p. 18; Abbott and Seroff, *Out of Sight,* 193.

19 Simond, *Old Slack's Reminiscence,* 5–6, 10–11.

20 Simond, *Old Slack's Reminiscence,* 9 and 36 n. 13; Abbott and Seroff, *Out of Sight,* 148–149.

21 Toll, "Introduction" to Simond, *Old Slack's Reminiscence,* xxiii–xxiv; Taylor and Austen, *Darkest America,* 63–64; Abbott and Seroff, *Out of Sight,* 110–112.

22 Miller, *Segregating Sound,* 98–101, 129–130; Taylor and Austen, *Darkest America,* 64–65; Abbott and Seroff, *Ragged but Right,* 69–70, 81–87; Francis Lee Utley and Robert Toll, "Major Dates in Black Minstrelsy," in Simond, *Old Slack's Reminiscence,* 49–50.

23 Abbott and Seroff, *Out of Sight,* 251–252.

24 Abbott and Seroff, *Out of Sight,* 254, 273–274; Miller, *Segregating Sound,* 109–110.

25 Miller, *Segregating Sound,* 112–117; W. E. B. Du Bois, *The Souls of Black Folk* (New York: Library of America, 1990); for a deep and sustained analysis of Du Bois's interpretation of music, see Anderson, *Deep River* chap. 1.

26 Reid Badger, *A Life in Ragtime: A Biography of James Reese Europe* (New York: Oxford University Press, 1995), 10–16, 20, 54.

27 Badger, *A Life in Ragtime,* 29–31.

28 Badger, *A Life in Ragtime,* 29–31, 51, 96; Linn, *Half-Barbaric Twang,* 91.

29 Badger, *A Life in Ragtime,* 54, 68, 95–96.

30 Badger, *A Life in Ragtime,* 61, 65–67.

31 Badger, *A Life in Ragtime,* 66–67.

32 Badger, *A Life in Ragtime,* 74–76, 86.

33 Nathan Huggins evokes the impact of Europe's military band in Nathan Irvin Huggins, *Harlem Renaissance,* updated ed. (New York: Oxford University Press, 2007), 55–56; Charles Hersch, *Subversive Sounds: Race and the Birth of Jazz in New Orleans* (Chicago: University of Chicago Press, 2007), 16; Thomas David Brothers, *Louis Armstrong's New Orleans* (New York: W. W. Norton, 2006), 101; Lawrence Gushee, "The Nineteenth-Century Origins of Jazz," *Black Music Research Journal* 22 (2002): 65–66. The history of early jazz—and the place of New Orleans within it—has been the subject of a great deal of excellent work and also much debate. For an excellent analysis of the ways in which New Orleans has figured in jazz scholarship, see Bruce Boyd Raeburn, *New Orleans Style and the Writing of American Jazz History* (Ann Arbor: University of Michigan Press, 2009).

34 Lawrence Marrero interviews, April 10, 1958 and January 2, 1959, Hogan Jazz Archive, Tulane University; George Guesnon interview, June 10, 1960, Hogan Jazz Archive; on the Jelly Roll Morton cover, see Bardinet, *Une histoire du banjo,* 128–129.

35 Johnny St. Cyr interview, August 27, 1958, pp. 1–2, Hogan Jazz Archive. Bardinet, *Une histoire du banjo,* 137; Brothers, *Louis Armstrong's New Orleans,* 229.

36 Brothers, *Louis Armstrong's New Orleans,* 251–254; William Howland Kenney, *Jazz on the River* (Chicago: University of Chicago Press, 2005), 46–47, 51, 57–58; Hersch, *Subversive Sounds,* 20. Johnny St. Cyr interview, August 27, 1958, pp. 4, 15, Hogan Jazz Archive.

37 Brothers, *Louis Armstrong's New Orleans,* 276; Bardinet, *Une histoire du banjo,* 137, 157.

38 Al Rose and Edmond Souchon, *New Orleans Jazz: A Family Album* (Baton Rouge: Louisiana State University Press, 1984), 16; Al Rose, "Emmanuel Sayles: Playing Plectrum Banjo in Jazz Band," *Pickin'* 1, no. 6 (July 1979): 35–37; Brothers, *Louis Armstrong's New Orleans,* 222–223; for detailed studies of New Orleans groups in which the banjo played an important role, see Sally Newhart, *The Original Tuxedo Jazz Band: More than a Century of a New Orleans Icon* (Charleston, SC: History Press, 2013); John McCusker, *Creole Trombone: Kid Ory and the Early Years of Jazz* (Jackson: University Press of Mississippi, 2012).

39 George Guesnon interview, June 10, 1960, Hogan Jazz Archive; Bardinet, *Une histoire du banjo,* 158–159.

40 Danny Barker interview, June 18, 1959 and June 30, 1959, Hogan Jazz Archive. Rose and Souchon, *New Orleans Jazz,* 9, 51; Sidney Bechet, *Treat It Gentle: An Autobiography* (Cambridge: Da Capo Press, 2002), 187.

41 Bardinet, *Une histoire du banjo,* 160–162; Danny Barker, *A Life in Jazz,* ed. Alyn Shipton (New York: Oxford University Press, 1986); on the influence of Cuban music in New Orleans, see Ned Sublette, *The World That Made New Orleans: From Spanish Silver to Congo Square* (Chicago: Lawrence Hill Books, 2008), esp. chap. 11.

42 Bardinet, *Une histoire du banjo,* 165, 169–170; Barker, *A Life in Jazz,* 113–114.

43 Bardinet, *Une histoire du banjo,* 152–153.

44 Bardinet, *Une histoire du banjo,* 166, 180. Lawrence Marrero interviews, April 10, 1958 and January 2, 1959, Hogan Jazz Archive.

45 Bardinet, *Une histoire du banjo,* 144, 149, 179; for photographs of banjos in various European bands, as well as in the 1936 strike, see the photographic insert in Francois Billard and Didier Roussin, *Histoires de L'accordéon* (Castelnau-le-Lez: [Paris]: Climats-I.N.A., 1991), 184 ff; several of these photographs are from the private collection of Robert Santiago.

46 Brent Hayes Edwards, *The Practice of Diaspora: Literature, Translation, and the Rise of Black Internationalism* (Cambridge, MA: Harvard University Press, 2003), 172–173; Jean Pierre Meunier and Brigitte Léardée, *La Biguine de*

l'oncle Ben's: Ernest Léardée raconte (Paris: Editions caribéennes, 1989), 101, 111, 115, 119, and for photos of bands 144, 177, 186; on music and dance in late nineteenth-century Antilles, see Jacqueline Rosemain, *La Danse aux Antilles: Des rythmes sacrés au Zouk* (Paris: L'Harmattan, 1990), chap. 6; for the image from Réunion see Billard and Roussin, *Histoires de L'accordéon,* photographic insert pp. 184 ff.

47 On the history of mento, see Daniel Tannehill Neely, " 'Mento, Jamaica's Original Music': Development, Tourism and the Nationalist Frame" (PhD. diss, New York University, 2007). The information on the link between the banjo and reggae comes from conversations with Kenneth Bilby, who interviewed a number of musicians involved in the early days of reggae during his fieldwork in Jamaica.

48 Richard Roe, "A Jamaican Troubadour," *Daily Gleaner,* April 14, 1934. My thanks to Joy Lumsden for sharing this source with me. The banjo from Kingston is now held in the Museum of History, Anthropology and Art at the University of Puerto Rico, Rio Pedras. I gathered details about the banjo in the museum in Puerto Rico from Sidney Mintz during an interview at Duke University on April, 2012. My thanks to Kenneth Bilby for sharing his images of banjo players from the Caribbean region with me.

49 On the phenomenon of "coon songs," see James H. Dormon, "Shaping the Popular Image of Post-Reconstruction American Blacks: The 'Coon Song' Phenomenon of the Gilded Age," *American Quarterly* 40, no. 4 (December 1, 1988): 450–471; and Abbott and Seroff, *Ragged but Right;* on the "Coon Carnival" see Denis Martin, *Coon Carnival: New Year in Cape Town, Past to Present* (Cape Town: David Philip Publishers, 1999); and Denis-Constant Martin, "Le métissage en musique: Un mouvement perpétuel (Amérique du Nord et Afrique du Sud)," *Cahiers de musiques traditionnelles* 13 (January 1, 2000): 11–13; on U.S. nineteenth-century music in South Africa, see Dale Cockrell, "Of Gospel Hymns, Minstrel Shows, and Jubilee Singers: Toward Some Black South African Musics," *American Music* 5, no. 4 (Winter 1987): 417–432, doi:10.2307/3051450; Erlmann, *African Stars,* chap 1.

50 For the banjo music from East and Central Africa, see the album Colonial Dance Bands: Kenya, Tanganyika, Portuguese East Africa, Northern Rhodesia, Belgian Congo, 1950 & 1952 (International Library of African Music, South Africa), 2006.

51 I am indebted to Hisham Aidi for all these details about the banjo in North Africa. On the recent circulation and political meaning of North African music, see Hisham Aidi, *Rebel Music: Race, Empire, and the New Muslim Youth Culture* (New York: Pantheon Books, 2014). The 2011 documentary film *El Gusto* explores the history of the banjo in chaabi music.

8. SOUNDING AMERICA

1 Pete Seeger, *Pete Seeger: In His Own Words,* ed. Rob Rosenthal and Sam Rosenthal (Boulder, CO: Paradigm Publishers, 2012), 8–9.

2 Ken Perlman, "Pete Seeger: Father of the 5-String Banjo Revival," *Banjo Newsletter* 27, no. 11 (September 2000): 16–23, p. 17.

3 Perlman, "Pete Seeger: Father of the 5-String Banjo Revival," 17.

4 Robert Cantwell, *When We Were Good: The Folk Revival* (Cambridge, MA: Harvard University Press, 1996), 241–245.

5 Allan M. Winkler, *"To Everything There Is a Season": Pete Seeger and the Power of Song* (Oxford: Oxford University Press, 2009), 4–5; Bill C. Malone, *Music From the True Vine: Mike Seeger's Life & Musical Journey* (Chapel Hill: University of North Carolina Press, 2011), 12–13.

6 Malone, *True Vine,* 13–14; Winkler, *Seeger,* 5.

7 Ronald D. Cohen and James Capaldi, eds., *The Pete Seeger Reader* (Oxford: Oxford University Press, 2014), 46.

8 Malone, *True Vine,* 14–15.

9 Malone, *True Vine,* 15–20.

10 Cohen and Capaldi, *Seeger Reader,* 49; Winkler, *Seeger,* 2–3; Cantwell, *When We Were Good,* 249; Malone, *True Vine,* 12–13; Seeger, *In His Own Words,* 8–9.

11 Robert Cantwell, "Smith's Memory Theater: The Folkways Anthology of American Folk Music," *New England Review (1990-)* 13, no. 3/4 (April 1, 1991): 26; John F. Szwed, *Alan Lomax: The Man Who Recorded the World* (New York: Viking Penguin, 2010), 118–119; Winkler, *Seeger,* 8–9; Alec Wilkinson, *The Protest Singer: An Intimate Portrait of Pete Seeger* (New York: Alfred A. Knopf, 2009), 50–51; Lunsford had a very particular vision of what constituted "Appalachian" music, and African-American performers were excluded from the festival. He was politically conservative, and when in 1953 Folkways records released an album of Lunsford tunes recorded for the Library of Congress and he saw that the leftist Pete Seeger had written the notes he "almost choked on his coffee." Cohen and Capaldi, *Seeger Reader,* 55, 64–65, 114.

12 Winkler, *Seeger,* 9, 15–16; Cohen and Capaldi, *Seeger Reader,* 58–61; Seeger, *In His Own Words,* 11–13.

13 Wilkinson, *The Protest Singer,* 50, 59; Szwed, *Alan Lomax,* 144–145; Seeger, *In His Own Words,* 13; Cohen and Capaldi, *Seeger Reader,* 49, 65.

14 Winkler, *Seeger,* 15–16.

15 Seeger, *In His Own Words,* 13–14; Winkler, *Seeger,* 18–19.

16 Winkler, *Seeger,* 21–24; Seeger, *In His Own Words,* 49; Cohen and Capaldi, *Seeger Reader,* 114.

17 Winkler, *Seeger,* 17, 28; Seeger, *In His Own Words,* 25–26; Cohen and Capaldi, *Seeger Reader,* 69.

18 Winkler, *Seeger,* 28–31; Seeger, *In His Own Words,* 23.

19 Winkler, *Seeger,* 30–31; Seeger, *In His Own Words,* 23–25.

20 Seeger, *In His Own Words,* 21, 27.

21 Winkler, *Seeger,* 33–34, 52.

22 Seeger, *In His Own Words,* 29, 31, 33, 37.

23 Cohen and Capaldi, *Seeger Reader,* 81–82, 84, 114.

24 Seeger, *In His Own Words,* 39–40.

25 Winkler, *Seeger,* 56–63; Cohen and Capaldi, *Seeger Reader,* 17–19.

26 Cohen and Capaldi, *Seeger Reader,* 113.

27 Greil Marcus, *The Old, Weird America: The World of Bob Dylan's Basement Tapes* (New York: Picador, 2011), 85, 89, 94, 120–121; Marcus's reading of the anthology draws deeply from Cantwell, "Smith's Memory Theater."

28 Cohen and Capaldi, *Seeger Reader,* 111–112.

29 Cohen and Capaldi, *Seeger Reader,* 34, 95, 114; Pete Seeger, *How to Play the 5-String Banjo,* 3rd ed. (Beacon, New York, 2002); Seeger, *In His Own Words,* 75.

30 Wilkinson, *Protest Singer,* 12–13; Cohen and Capaldi, *Seeger Reader,* 5, 13, 177; Cantwell, *When We Were Good,* 241–242.

31 Seeger, *In His Own Words,* 41–42.

32 Seeger, *In His Own Words,* 41–42, 67–69.

33 Cantwell, *When We Were Good,* 243; Cohen and Capaldi, *Seeger Reader,* 26.

34 Cohen and Capaldi, *Seeger Reader,* 177.

35 Bill Simon, "Rash of Banjo Fever Breaks Out in U.S." *Billboard,* June 25, 1955, in Southern Folklife Collection, Subject Files, Folder 32, No. 7. Ishmael Reed, *Mumbo Jumbo* (Garden City, NY: Doubleday, 1972).

36 Simon, "Rash of Banjo Fever."

37 Cantwell, *When We Were Good,* 244–245.

38 Thomas Goldsmith, ed., *The Bluegrass Reader* (Urbana: University of Illinois Press, 2004), 36–42; Neil V. Rosenberg, *Bluegrass: A History*, Music in American Life (Urbana: University of Illinois Press, 2005), 34, 56–58; on the phenomenon of "hillbilly music," see Archie Green, *Torching the Fink Books and Other Essays on Vernacular Culture* (Chapel Hill: University of North Carolina Press, 2001), 8–46.

39 Rosenberg, *Bluegrass,* 56–58.

40 Rosenberg, *Bluegrass,* 32–34; Robert Cantwell, *Bluegrass Breakdown: The Making of the Old Southern Sound* (Urbana: University of Illinois Press, 1984), 53–54, 102–104.

41 Rosenberg, *Bluegrass,* 70–77, 152.

42 Cantwell, *Bluegrass Breakdown,* 102–105.

43 Goldsmith, *Bluegrass Reader,* 97–99; Rosenberg, *Bluegrass,* 147–148.

44 Goldsmith, *Bluegrass Reader,* 101–103; Rosenberg, *Bluegrass,* 158.

45 Karl Hagstrom Miller, *Segregating Sound: Inventing Folk and Pop Music in the Age of Jim Crow* (Durham: Duke University Press, 2010).

46 The Kid Mero, "The Dixie Chicks Greatest Hits Reminds Me That Banjos Are Always Racist," *Noisey,* December 4, 2012, http://noisey.vice.com /blog/the-dixie-chicks-greatest-hits-reminds-me-that-banjos-are-always -racist.

47 Steve Martin, *Born Standing Up* (New York: Scribner, 2007), 53, 62, 83.

48 Wilkinson, *Protest Singer,* 75–76, 125.

49 Wilkinson, *Protest Singer,* 73–75; Winkler, *Seeger,* 76–78.

50 Winkler, *Seeger,* 54–55, 62, 66–69.

51 Cohen and Capaldi, *Seeger Reader,* 26.

52 Wilkinson, *Protest Singer,* 127–130.

53 Wilkinson, *Protest Singer,* 79, 132–137, 147.

54 Winkler, *Seeger,* 83–86.

55 Seeger, *In His Own Words,* 116–117.

56 Seeger, *In His Own Words,* 117; Wilkinson, *Protest Singer,* 89–90.

57 Wilkinson, *Protest Singer,* 95–97.

58 Wilkinson, *Protest Singer,* 97–101.

59 Wilkinson, *Protest Singer,* 101–102.

60 Seeger, *In His Own Words,* 52–53.

61 These memories were shared with me via email on February 1, 2014, by Jane Jordan of Boynton Beach, Florida, in response to an homage to Seeger I wrote that was published in the South Florida newspaper the *Sun-Sentinel*. I use them here with her permission. For my piece, published on January 30, 2014, see http://articles.sun-sentinel.com/2014–01–30/news/fl-opinion2-pete-seeger -remember-20140130_1_banjo-pete-seeger-lincoln-memorial.

Acknowledgments

This book began one day in Lansing, Michigan, when, enraptured by the sounds of Taj Mahal's banjo playing on his song "Colored Aristocracy," I drove over from my home in East Lansing to nearby Elderly Music. That store is as close to a church for guitars and banjos as you'll come by, and though my intent was just to buy a few CDs, I soon ended up on the way home with a beautiful Mike Ramsey banjo in the back of my car. The child of Belgian immigrants to the United States, I remember feeling vividly that—many years after having been naturalized formally as a citizen—I had, in that moment, finally become fully American.

That was about a decade ago. Since then, I've embarked on a spiral of journeys (both physical and imaginary) that have led me to Haiti and Senegal, Paris and Brussels, to ancient Egypt and Muslim Iberia, out and about in New Orleans, and through the alleys of Washington, DC. Along the way, as one does on such a journey, I depended on the generosity of strangers who became friends and wandered my way down plenty of winding paths that led me back where I started. The story laid out in the preceding pages is what it is thanks to those who, at a few key moments, gave me energizing and luminous suggestions that brightened the way forward.

This book was possible only because of the work of a collective of people, bigger than you might think, as obsessed as I am—or, actually, to be honest, in a lot of cases even more obsessed than I am—with the banjo and its history. They wander and lurk in various places, notably the yearly Banjo Collectors Gathering, but also in the many banjo camps and workshops that dot the land in summertime, creating the terrifying spectacle of literally hundreds of people carrying around the instrument, sending an endless hum and buzz into the heavens for days on end.

I was drawn into this world by the endlessly energetic Tony Thomas, with his Black Banjo discussion group, and Cece Conway, who organized the first Black Banjo Gathering at Appalachian State University in 2005. It was an event memorable and even epochal on many levels, for out of it came the Carolina Chocolate Drops (best thing to ever emerge from an academic conference, I'd hazard). It was also there, during a presentation about a Haitian banza that had been unearthed in France a few years earlier, that I decided that I should write this book. Whether that was a good or a bad thing, you'll need to decide for yourself; but ultimately what followed was driven by the sense that as a historian of the Caribbean, and particularly Haiti, I might have something to add to the already rich conversation that was underway about the instrument.

In Boone I also met several people who became constant interlocutors as I worked on this project, particularly Greg Adams (creator of the Banjo Sightings database) and the banjo maker Pete Ross, with whom I pleasingly shared the fact that we'd gone from DC punk kids to banjo-loving adults, a transition that actually makes perfect sense when you think about it. I didn't know it in 2005, but within a few years I'd end up making North Carolina my home, moving to Duke University, which happily happens to be not far from the University of North Carolina at Chapel Hill—a fact that, besides nourishing a bit of a basketball rivalry, meant that I lived in a place where some of the greatest scholars of American musical history sauntered about. My conversations with Phil Gura, Bob Cantwell, and Bill Ferris over the years were inspiring and shaped my thoughts here.

I was an ok banjo player by the time I left Michigan, I suppose—thanks in part to my enjoyable attendance at the Midwest Banjo Camp, run by Ken Perlman, held in the project-like dorms at Michigan State University, where I taught. I had the privilege there to take workshops with Mike Seeger, whose grace and brilliance and deep knowledge of the instrument were awe-inspiring, and whose demonstrations and teachings elate me still. When I got to North Carolina, of course, I became a much worse banjo player in comparison, because this is the kind of place where people say "I play a little, sure," and then bring you to tears with a haunting mountain tune or set their banjos on fire with a blue-grass tune as if it were nothing. As Taj Mahal himself announced when he played here one night at the Durham baseball stadium, North Carolina is one of the few places where people clap—rather than running away—when you pull out a banjo. It has been the perfect place to write this book.

I was lucky enough to get generous support for my work from a few different sources. Shortly after arriving here in North Carolina, I received a fellowship at the National Humanities Center and a Guggenheim Fellowship to support the project. And a few years later I received a multiyear Mellon New Directions Fellowship, which gave me the chance to go back to school, studying musicology and ethnomusicology. Classes with David Garcia at UNC and Louise Meintjes and Paul Berliner here at Duke were mind-expanding—and, in the case of Paul's class, during which we learned to play the mbira, thumb strengthening too—and Anthony Lewis was patient (if bemused) while I floundered through his music theory class, holding back the infinitely more advanced first-year students as I tried to understand time signatures and such.

But the teaching assistant for that class, David Garner, a brilliant composer and music theorist himself, also happened to have a weakness for the banjo. We began a collaboration that has shaped my work here, working to create a website called "Banjology" and spending many an hour listening to recordings, playing songs, and discussing the question of how, precisely, one should account for a banjo tune in musical transcription. Mary Caton Lingold, another brilliant Duke doctoral student studying early American and Atlantic music, worked with us on the site, and her insights have shaped this book as well. And years before that, my graduate student Julia Gaffield gathered together my already scattered bibliographical materials, teaching me that you can actually put references in a nifty software program on your computer, rather than rooting around your office looking for a book or a photocopy every time.

New Orleans, that ultimate crossroads between the Caribbean and North America, has been central to this book's journey. Bruce Raeburn guided me generously in my research at the Hogan Jazz Archive at Tulane—perhaps the only, or at least one of the few, archives that has a piano in it—giving me a complete list of every banjo player he knew of in the city on the day I arrived. Other friends and colleagues at Tulane, Emily

Clark and Randy Sparks, hosted me with their trademark unparalleled hospitality. These connections enabled me to organize an event, supported by the Mellon New Directions Fellowship, in collaboration with Joel Dinerstein, director of the Center for the Study of the Gulf South at Tulane, in April 2013. Planned to coincide with a conference on the links between Senegal and Louisiana, the event revolved around an encounter between the Senegalese group Demma Dia—five brothers, fishermen all, who play the ngoni—and the New Orleans banjo players Don Vappie and Carl LeBlanc. They took to the stage with no common language but music, played for each other, and then began to play together, creating a moment of communion that culminated in audience members—including Mardi Gras Indian Queen Cherise Harrison-Nelson—taking to their feet, and then to the stage. I've thought back often to that magic, evanescent moment, which as historian Lawrence Powell told me that day was a moment of "restorative history." I'm deeply grateful for all those who made that event, a reminder of all the many crossroads that have come before and are still to come, possible. The event also included a workshop and panel with Greg Adams, Kenneth Bilby, Jean Hebrard, Sarah Le Menestrel, Bruce Raeburn, Matt Sakakeeny, Ned Sublette, and Tal Tamari. Their insights during those events and our days in New Orleans profoundly shaped this book, helping me to gather the strands and pull them together into the argument here.

Many scholars generously shared sources and works in progress with me as I was researching this book. My Caribbeanist historian friends Vincent Brown, Randy Browne, and Ada Ferrer, having heard probably too much about the banjo from me, responded kindly by telling me when they came across one during their research. My work on Hans Sloane brought me in touch with James Delbourgo, who shared pieces from a forthcoming book and helped me untangle and contextualize the first image of the New World banjo.

I have presented parts of this work in many different venues and to many different audiences, and learned a lot from the questions and comments I got. These included the first Black Banjo Gathering, the Banjo Collectors Gathering, the Departments of History at the University of South Carolina and Florida International University, the University of Memphis, the Triangle Early American History Workshop—invited by Kathleen Duval, and which featured a long and entertaining argument between Jack Greene and Peter Wood—and the Chicago Humanities Festival, where I got probably the best introduction I'll ever get in my life, when Lieutenant-Governor Sheila Simon performed a banjo song specially composed for the occasion. It was one of many times when I experienced what is, ultimately, the main argument of this book: banjos have an amazing capacity to bring people together, in laughter and song.

What would we scattered, verbose, and often overstretched academics do without the amazing editors who somehow manage to get us to finish our projects against all odds? Joyce Seltzer of Harvard University Press, who edited my second book on the Haitian Revolution, lit up when I told her about this project; and she has been endlessly patient as it took more and more time, interrupted by various other projects, the ups and downs of life, and the fact that it turns out to be fascinatingly complex to write about music (as I guess I should have known before starting). She was fundamental in shaping the final project, telling me "that's not it!" when it wasn't, and then saying "this is it!" when it was. Also at Harvard Press, Brian Distelberg provided invaluable help shepherding the book to publication. And it was my agent, Wendy Strothman, who got the project to the right place in the beginning and has been calmly encouraging all along the way.

My family has been endlessly encouraging and supportive of this process, listening attentively when I describe one more super-cool tidbit I'd discovered about the banjo and putting up with—and at times even enjoying—many sudden bursts of banjo playing at odd hours. My wife, Katharine, always in the midst of weaving and writing her own stories, has constantly helped me see how to understand and tell this one. And my son, Anton—who knows that it actually crossed my mind to call him "Banjo Dubois" at one point before he was born—has grown up with a banjo on the wall and its hum surrounding his many steps. He has always been a reminder of what I hope this book ultimately offers: that to be human is ultimately to find, even in the midst of great difficulty, a way to sing out and move forward.

Index

organology p 6
chordophone
Ziryab
creolization
soundways p. 63
Twoubado - Ti Coca Haitian music p 135
      "Twa Fey"
coffle   p 139
"weevils in the wheat"   p 158
frolic / hoedown
Boucher banjo maker
Frank Converse
Gus Cannon / Blind Blake
Alexandre Stellio — beguine
mento — Jamaican music
"vernacular" music